P9-CRM-360

## Praise for Howard Blum's
### Investigative Milestone
# GANGLAND

"An exciting tale, full of brave words and heroic deeds and dashing men and sexy women . . . In its detail, *GANGLAND* convinces. . . . Fascinating . . ."
—Tom McNamee, *Chicago Sun Times*

"A blockbuster, this suspenseful and superbly written exposé written by former *New York Times* reporter Blum will surely hit the headlines. Blum chronicles the struggle . . . to build a flawless case against Gambino Family boss John Gotti by the FBI's C-16 squad, a latter-day incarnation of Eliot Ness's Untouchables."
—*Publishers Weekly*

"As easy to read as a crime novel—and the real-life denouement is easily as satisfying as that in any fictional police thriller. . . . *GANGLAND* offers amazing portraits of the inner circles of Gotti's underworld, and of the agents who worked the case, and a detailed reconstruction of how the FBI used one of the most sophisticated electronic surveillance operations in bureau history. . . . Blum's . . . tightly written narrative makes for a page-turning story of a classic struggle."
—Bill Wallace, *San Francisco Chronicle*

"The best Mafia book in quite a few years . . . Blum delivers . . . excitement and tension."
—Thomas Gaughan, *Booklist*

"Mr. Blum himself has clearly done a job of investigative digging. . . . An absorbing report on how a special unit of the Federal Bureau of Investigation eventually gathered enough evidence to convict John Gotti, the seemingly indestructible crime boss. . . . The story Blum tells is important."

—Christopher Lehmann-Haupt, *The New York Times*

"*GANGLAND* reads like a police thriller. . . . Chalk one up for the good guys."

—Bill Leyden, *Florida Times-Union*

"Fascinating . . . Blum has indeed written a book with a new Gotti angle. . . . He is a first-rate reporter."

—Steve Weinberg, *St. Louis Post-Dispatch*

"John Gotti . . . is the subject of Blum's intensively researched, hypnotically absorbing true-crime report. There have been other excellent books on Gotti, but none written with Blum's flair for drama. . . . Diligent research reveals itself in unusual details about Gotti's character. . . ."

—*Kirkus Reviews*

"A solid, readable . . . gripping tale . . . Blum's a talented writer who knows how to milk a scene for its dramatic potential."

—Ray Locker, *Tampa Tribune-Times*

"*GANGLAND* completes the job begun by Nicholas Pileggi in *Wiseguy*. . . . Blum has made good use of the transcripts of the wiretaps his FBI heroes planted in the Ravenite Social Club in Little Italy. He provides vivid shards of the daily digest of high crimes and low humor. . . . Blum handles his material like a good screenwriter. . . ."

—Bill McKibben, *New York Daily News*

"Chilling . . . Rich in detail, *GANGLAND* offers a blow-by-blow account of the FBI's effort. . . ."

—Ann Zivotsky, *Blade Citizen-Preview* (CA)

"The riveting behind-the-scenes account of the risks taken and the battles lost and won in the all-out effort that finally landed Gotti in jail. *GANGLAND* is an action-packed page turner, a real-life detective thriller. . . .While this true-life saga may rival the best in detective fiction, it also exemplifies the best in investigative reporting, documenting in detail the real inside story that was never covered in the national press. . . . Intensively researched and expertly written, *GANGLAND* is one unforgettable scene after another."

—*The Florida Newspaper*

**Books by Howard Blum**

NONFICTION

Wanted! The Search for Nazis in America
I Pledge Allegiance . . . The Story of the Walker Spy Family
Out There
Gangland: How the FBI Broke the Mob

FICTION

Wishful Thinking

For orders other than by individual consumers, Pocket Books grants a discount on the purchase of 10 or more copies of single titles for special markets or premium use. For further details, please write to the Vice-President of Special Markets, Pocket Books, 1633 Broadway, New York, NY 10019-6785, 8th Floor.

For information on how individual consumers can place orders, please write to Mail Order Department, Simon & Schuster Inc., 200 Old Tappan Road, Old Tappan, NJ 07675.

# GANGLAND

## HOW THE FBI BROKE THE MOB

## HOWARD BLUM

**POCKET BOOKS**

New York   London   Toronto   Sydney   Tokyo   Singapore

The sale of this book without its cover is unauthorized. If you purchased
this book without a cover, you should be aware that it was reported to
the publisher as "unsold and destroyed." Neither the author nor the
publisher has received payment for the sale of this "stripped book."

POCKET BOOKS, a division of Simon & Schuster Inc.
1230 Avenue of the Americas, New York, NY 10020

Copyright © 1993 by Howard Blum

All rights reserved, including the right to reproduce
this book or portions thereof in any form whatsoever.
For information address Simon & Schuster Inc.,
1230 Avenue of the Americas, New York, NY 10020

ISBN: 0-671-90015-3

First Pocket Books printing August 1995

10  9  8  7  6  5  4  3

POCKET and colophon are registered trademarks of
Simon & Schuster Inc.

Cover photo by UPI/Bettmann

Printed in the U.S.A.

# A Note to the Reader

This book could not have been written without the unprecedented help I received from the FBI. I was granted official access to everyone who played a role in building the Bureau's case against John Gotti. I interviewed officials in Washington and New York, members of the Special Projects Group in Quantico, Virginia, and agents from the C-16 squad who did the actual street work which culminated in Gotti's indictment and conviction. I met with members of the team who broke into the Ravenite Social Club in the middle of the night and planted the bugs. I spent time with the technicians who designed one-of-a-kind electronic devices used in the case. I spoke to the agents involved in turning Sammy "the Bull" Gravano, as well as the men who debriefed him and even boxed with him. I interviewed at length the men who, over a number of years, hunted for Gotti's spy in law enforcement. And I had an opportunity to question several of the agents who recruited confidential informants from the Mob's own camp. Some talked with me on the record. Others demanded anonymity. But in the course of all these interviews—many of which began while I was writing about the investigation for *The New York Times Magazine* and continued over many months—I was able to piece together the inside story of how the FBI made its case against John Gotti.

I also met with state and federal prosecutors, New

York City police officials, and defense attorneys. And I reviewed thousands of pages of trial and audio surveillance transcripts, as well as volumes of previously confidential police and FBI reports filed during the Gotti investigation.

Further, this book could not have been written without the cooperation of a few members of the Gambino crime family who, for whatever reason, also allowed themselves to be interviewed. Their story, too, is told in these pages.

A more extensive list of my sources and a detailed, chapter-by-chapter attribution for every quotation and incident I record is included in a final Author's Note.

*This book is for my gang: Jenny, Harold Anthony, and Anna.*

*With love.*

Revenge is a dish best eaten cold.

—An old Sicilian proverb

# I

## The Mole File

# 1

FROM THE APARTMENT WINDOW FIVE FLOORS ABOVE SOHO Billiards, Scott Behar had a perfect sight line. He sat on a steel folding chair that was cushioned with a blue and orange "Let's Go Mets" pillow. The chair had been placed right next to the window, and when he parted the white vertical blinds just a crack, he could look straight down Mulberry Street.

Staring through binoculars, he could see past the Korean market on the corner with its tiers of bright flowers crowding the sidewalk even on this drab winter afternoon, past the tall late-Gothic spire of the Catholic church, and past the storefront coffeehouse where each day the same intense young couple came to hold hands at the round table by the window. He focused on the steel door of a red-brick-faced tenement that was nearly three blocks away.

For the past nine months Behar had been part of the FBI team assigned to keep track of who entered the two narrow, dark rooms on the ground floor of 247 Mulberry Street. It was the Ravenite Social Club and, despite its run-down appearance, it was the headquarters of the richest and most powerful Mafia clan in America, the Gambino Family.

Surveillance was tedious work. He had clocked in at 3:47 that afternoon, the 17th of January, 1990, and soon it would be getting dark. The binoculars were already not much help. There was a tripod-mounted video camera fitted with a high-performance nitrogen-filled lens and a 25-mm intensifier tube; it could see in the dark for up to half a mile. He moved the camera to the window and, as was his routine, opened a Cel-Ray tonic, and waited.

Just before 5:00, they started arriving. They came in Cadillacs and Lincolns mostly. The big cars were soon double-parked along both sides of Mulberry Street. It would be, he realized, a busy evening. Five new members were being inducted into the Family tonight. They would become partners in an organization that ran businesses throughout the city worth hundreds of millions of dollars, a diversified portfolio that included trucking, cement, construction, garbage collection, manufacturing, pornography, loan sharking, and narcotics. Each of the five "made men" would be set for life. And all they had to do in return was obey without hesitation every order, no matter what it required, that was passed on from the head of the Family—John Gotti.

Like Scott Behar, John Gotti was also focusing his attention that afternoon, but on an object more closely at hand. The Boss of the Gambino crime family was sitting in a wood-paneled courtroom about a mile downtown from the Observation Post, very intently reading a frayed paperback edition of Friedrich Nietzsche's *Thus Spake Zarathustra*. In fact, so total was Gotti's absorption in the German philosopher's words that he seemed oblivious to the trial proceeding around him; and to the possibility that if he was convicted of the state assault charge he would be sentenced to a minimum of twenty-five years in prison.

"I'll give you three to one I beat this rap," Gotti, always quick with a sound-bite, had taunted the crowd of reporters who flocked to the trial's opening day. By this afternoon, less than three weeks into the case, there were many reporters who no doubt wished they had taken a piece of that action. The state was offering persuasive evidence to prove that Gotti had ordered the shooting of a troublesome union official. There was even a tape recording of Gotti, wild with indignant rage, ordering the attack. "Bust him up! Put a rocket in his pocket!" he had yelled; and when the tape was played in the courtroom, each word loud and precise and powerful, many of the jurors had seemed to cringe.

But John Gotti showed no concern as the trial moved forward. America's most notorious gangster, the Godfather who had appeared on the cover of *Time,* sat in the courtroom in his two-thousand-dollar DeLisi suit, his silver hair perfect; and with the gold-colored frames of a pair of bifocals pushed low on his long nose, he read Nietzsche.

He also, a clue to his steady mood, guarded a large and very valuable secret: He had an edge. The verdict was as good as guaranteed.

When the trial adjourned for the day, things began to pick up at the Ravenite. Behar had already shot a lot of footage, and he would very shortly need to insert a new tape. Yet as he was nearing the tail end of the first reel, at 6:24—the precise time duly noted on the surveillance log—the camera caught "Joe Butch" Corrao, lean and elegant, a silver-haired Mafia prince, entering the club. Walking behind him, but rushing forward awkwardly at the last moment to grab the front door, was a bear of a man, George Helbig. Even through the camera lens he looked big and fat and mean.

The pair did not stay long. After only six minutes inside the club, the two men left. Helbig again held the door, but Salvatore Gravano, the Gambino Family's underboss, now led the way. He was five-foot-six in his high-heeled boots, but he had been shooting three thousand dollars a week of Deca-Durabolin into his body for so long that he had beefed up to 175 pounds and had forearms nearly the size of beer kegs. That was one reason why people on the street called him "Sammy Bull." The other was that he killed people.

As soon as the three men began to walk up Mulberry,

Behar reached for the Motorola walkie-talkie on the windowsill. "This is co-op," he announced over the encrypted frequency. "Number three is out and walking north toward Prince with two friends."

The message was received by a female agent sitting in a tan Pontiac parked farther downtown on Lafayette Street. After so many evenings of waiting, it took her by surprise. It was the middle of a New York winter; she had never expected any of the boys to go for a "walk-talk" outside the club. Unless, she realized, it was very important.

"Roger," she acknowledged, and started the car's engine. The Pontiac turned left on Spring Street and then onto Mulberry. She drove up the narrow street with only her left hand on the wheel. In her right hand was a black plastic box about the size and weight of a television remote control. A silver-colored antenna probe extended almost a foot from the middle of the device. Deep Street—as the Bureau's Special Projects Group had christened their creation last fall—was ready to go operational for the first time.

At just about that moment, across the East River in another borough of the sprawling city, in a boxy office building along a stretch of Queens Boulevard still decked out with twinkling Christmas decorations, Bruce Mouw sat at his desk on the sixth floor trying to make up his mind. He could either call the stewardess he had been seeing and risk one more bitter fight about why he didn't want to get married, or he could go home alone and hope there was a Knicks game on cable. When the red phone rang, the head of the FBI's Gambino squad, the C-16 team, quickly learned there would be no time for making any small choices tonight.

It was the Observation Post above the billiard parlor calling to report that the curb-side listening device would soon be activated. The news filled Mouw with some anticipation: If the Technical crew had managed to devise a strategy for eavesdropping on the Gambino Family's conversations outside the Ravenite, when the mob least expected any electronic surveillance, the recordings could prove very interesting. The Techies had pulled off some amazing feats over the years to bring the investigation this far. Perhaps, he considered with some tactical detachment, his team would get a fresh lead worth exploring tonight. But after he was told that Gravano was accompanied by the unlikely pair of Joe Butch Corrao and George Helbig, whatever calmness he still managed to convey on the phone was all disguise.

The surveillance agent, however, went on unaware. Dutifully, he began to recite the long list of wiseguys who had shown up at the Ravenite that evening, while all the time, Mouw would later confide to one of his fellow squad members, his heart was racing "like someone trying to score from first on a shallow drive to right field."

For the past three years, Bruce Mouw had lived with one large and controlling ambition—to bring down John Gotti. What goaded him, what had pushed him to the brink of obsession, was not simply Gotti's position as Boss of Bosses. Or even the fawning publicity this murderer and thief had managed to attract. After all the adventures of his life, after all his years in the Bureau, he understood a system where both cops and robbers had a combative place.

What gnawed at him, and energized his anger, was *how* Gotti had managed to triumph so totally over his adversaries. Gotti, the master strategist, was always one jump ahead of the good guys. His invincibility had become the stuff of legend. "The Teflon Don," the tabloids called him. Over the past three years, city and federal prosecutors had confidently hauled Gotti into the courtroom. Yet at the conclusion of both cases, there were Gotti and his crew of feisty lawyers, their hands held high in victory like Olympic champions, posing for the television cameras. And today's image, Gotti smirking through his latest trial, a book coolly in hand, was just as indelible and infuriating. It left Mouw rattled.

Mouw was convinced that nobody was that smart. Or that lucky. The Don couldn't be playing fair. Someone had to be feeding him information that was allowing him to get away—quite literally—with murder. Gotti, Mouw had increasingly come to suspect, had a well-placed mole in law enforcement.

His suspicion, however, was nothing but a hunch. The "facts" that held this flimsy thesis together—a hint from an informant, an oblique reference caught on a wiretap—were, he knew, legally inadmissible. Worse, they were ultimately unconvincing even to others in the Bureau. One Washington deskman in the criminal division, in fact, had snidely worried about Mouw's "embattled imagination." "Maybe the man should take a vacation," he had advised with theatrical concern. And, catching just a sniff of the provocative trail Mouw was following, the Queens District Attorney's office had suggested (off the record, naturally) to the press that the FBI was a sore loser. Gotti was simply too shrewd for the Bureau.

In time, Mouw learned to keep his suspicions to himself. Still, he continued to gather clues. And in the past year he had started to notice a coincidence that occurred with a tantalizing regularity: Each time a hint of the mole's handiwork surfaced, the same two Gambino Family henchmen would also just have come out from the shadows. Like magic, the incongruous duo of a capo and a gofer, Corrao and Helbig, would appear in tandem at the Ravenite.

So when the agent in the Observation Post asked Mouw if he should telephone him at home to report on the results of the curbside device, Mouw put on his terse commander's voice and said he would wait at his desk. Call him as soon as the operation was complete. He hung up the phone without a good-bye and, guarding his secret, without mentioning what was at stake.

For the next hour, Bruce Mouw, a fieldman at heart, sat impatiently at his desk, smoking his pipe and waiting for the red phone to ring. On the wall across from him was a chart he had painstakingly put together over the last decade. It was a series of photographs, mug shots and surveillance pictures of members of the Gambino Family. The photographs had been arranged in a pyramid of sorts. At its peak was a jowly and hostile John Gotti, the Don caught in the unflattering glare of a police photographer's flashbulb. Mouw stared at the photograph of his nemesis; and while so many large and small thoughts swirled by as he waited, one, he would always insist, kept recurring: Gotti's luck couldn't last forever.

## 2

Or could it?

The technical challenge of eavesdropping on the Mob's walk-talks, Mouw had glumly realized five months earlier, was a particularly complicated one. Still Mouw, who had learned a bit about motivation in four years at Annapolis, took a giant step away from his normally soft-spoken reserve and had taunted the Techies: "When I was an engineering officer on a nuclear sub, we'd be able to hunker down right under the polar ice cap and send a radio message halfway across the world to Command at Norfolk. Now don't tell me you can't figure out a way to get a clandestine transmission out of Little Italy."

The head of the New York Tech unit, Jim Kallstrom, an ex-Marine infantry officer and still very gung ho, bit immediately at the bait. "We'll find a way," he promised. His assistant, John Kravec, the man who *actually* had to solve the problem, was a more crusty type. After the session with Mouw, people heard him muttering for weeks. "You'd think," Kravec would snarl at anyone who would listen, "six months of sitting in a goddamn submarine under the

goddamn ocean would've taught that man some patience."
But all the time, Kravec, who was also a bit of a genius, was
busy trying to get the job done.

Kravec began to take long walks down Mulberry Street. In
his mind's eye he carefully noted all the parking meters,
street lamps, and traffic lights: the usual "sweet spots" where
over the years he had hid an outdoor microphone or two.
None of the tried-and-true tricks, he decided, would pass
muster for this operation. At last, when he had come close to
thinking his way through it, he hopped a ride on a Bureau
Cessna down to Quantico, Virginia. He had a plan, but he
needed help.

The Bureau's Engineering Research Facility was a low-
slung, modernistic building tucked into a remote and very
leafy corner of the Quantico Marine Base. The name was a
bit of bureaucratic cover. People who worked there simply
called it "the Q Building," after James Bond's fictive
technical magician. The Special Projects crew on the second
floor, though, prided themselves on being the real thing.

Kravec met with the SP group in a sparkling lab. One wall
of glass windows faced a shaved lawn that stretched to a
thick forest. Another looked out toward an atrium glowing
with diffused sunlight. I'm a long way from Mulberry Street,
Kravec thought to himself. But he shoved this momentary
misgiving aside and swiftly sketched out the operational
challenge Mouw had given him. Then, backtracking, he
enumerated all of what he termed "the worry spots."

First, he said, the microphone or maybe even *microphones* had to be strong enough to pick up conversations
from up and down the block since you never knew what
direction the bad guys would take in strolling. Naturally,
they also had to be small enough so that no one would spot
them. More troublesome, though, was that the mikes would
somehow have to be planted outside on a city street always
bustling with activity. If you could sneak by the people
coming in and out of the grocery, or the bakery where they
made cakes all night, or the church with its busy schedule of
masses, you still had to worry about the tenements lining

both sides of the block. There was a small army of babushkaed grandmothers housed in each one, and they seemed to spend most of their waking hours at their windows on the lookout for anyone who wasn't a *paisan*.

Then, Kravec went on, there were all the normal technical headaches that came with working in New York. If you used a battery-powered radio transmitter, it would have to be a particularly strong one since the electronic frequencies in the city were jammed with hundreds of thousands of signals. And even then, the receiving base, or "plant," would have to be fairly close by. You could, instead, go hard wire; that is, hook the mikes up to an existing electrical system, say a street lamp or a telephone pole, and piggyback a free ride on this current. That would make receiving the signal relatively simple. However, it also meant that you would have to do all this extensive wiring more or less out in the open on a busy street. And to complicate matters further, since these were outdoor mikes, they had to be sophisticated enough to pick up whispered conversations while screening out honking horns, howling ambulances, and rushing fire engines.

Naturally enough, there was, Kravec concluded, one final rub. As in all electronic surveillance cases, federal law mandated minimization. The mikes could not remain "hot." You had to be able to switch the mikes on and off in an instant since it was illegal to monitor anyone walking down Mulberry Street other than the court-sanctioned targets. Moreover, the monitoring agents also had to shut down the tape if the conversation strayed into matters that were extraneous (and here, the agents' interpretation was generally quite broad) to the criminal investigation.

"So," demanded Kravec of his audience, "what would you suggest?" Even in the best of times he affected a world-weary mood, but that morning he outdid himself. He sounded and looked positively morose. Yet this, too, was part of his act. He waited a moment or two, but certainly not much longer. Before any of the Special Projects whiz kids could beat him to it, he solved his own riddle. "A car," he announced quite proudly. "Actually, a number of cars."

The solution was ingenious. His plan, in broad strokes,

was to outfit a small fleet of cars with a number of miniature directional microphones. All the difficult and time-consuming wiring could be done off-site. Then early each morning, assuming the very believable cover of a frazzled New Yorker looking for a valid alternate-side-of-the-street parking space, an agent would park as close as he could to 247 Mulberry Street. The empty vehicle, a four-wheeled recording and transmitting studio, would stay in place all day. Who would notice? Later that night, after the Ravenite had shut down, the car would be driven back to headquarters and the day's tapes retrieved. As for minimalization, that was simple, too: The car mikes would be activated by remote control whenever the Observation Post spotted the targets taking to the street for a conversation.

"Can you whip me up something like that?" Kravec asked.

It took some time, but the Special Projects crew delivered. They outfitted a few cars confiscated by the Drug Enforcement Agency with a number of highly sensitive black-colored microphones about the size and length of a number two pencil. The mikes were hidden in wheel wells, bumpers, and hubcaps. Two thin wires ran from each mike and snaked underneath the car's chassis and up through a small hole that had been drilled into the trunk. Inside the trunk, the wires were connected to a standard Bureau battery-powered transmitter package and a Nagra tape recorder; the agents in the apartment three blocks away could listen in while the recorder kept a permanent record. The remote control device was a bit trickier. They had experimented with a unit that could be run from the Observation Post, but it was always a dicey business to send radio signals any distance in a city with so much airwave traffic. In the end, they decided not to risk it. An agent would simply have to be on call to walk or drive by and surreptitiously aim the remote at the transmitter in the car's trunk.

Best of all, the lab crew added one refinement that Kravec had not even requested: Many of the cars were wired for video. The box of tissues that had been placed on the shelf next to the rear window of the silver Buick Riviera, for example, was more than just a careful touch of domestic cover. Inside the box was a miniature video camera that was connected to a VCR in the trunk.

After a successful test run in the streets of Washington near the Hoover Building, the cars were ready to be shipped to the headquarters garage beneath 26 Federal Plaza in downtown Manhattan. On the day the motorcade left Quantico, the lab boys toasted their creations. It was in this heady rush of accomplishment (and perhaps fueled by a celebratory beer or two) that one wag came up with the name for the project that was to stick—Deep Street.

At 6:30 on the evening of January 17, 1990, Deep Street, once merely a small tactical glimmer in Bruce Mouw's operational eye, was about to be thrown into the long-running battle against John Gotti. Only now, a jumpy Mouw was convinced as he sat in his distant office waiting for a report from the field, its success was vital.

Everything went as planned. A videotape made from the fifth-floor apartment recorded the drama as it began to unfold. There was Gravano, the Family's second-in-command, his legs anchored to the sidewalk as if set in cement, looking up with joyless eyes at Corrao. Corrao was doing nearly all the talking, his long arms swinging about expansively. From time to time, Helbig, a sleepy expression on his face, leaned into the circle to offer a few words. And behind them, parked a yard or two south on Mulberry, was a silver Buick Riviera.

The camera remained focused on the trio locked in conversation. It did not record the tan Pontiac moving along with traffic up the block. Or the split second it took for the agent at the wheel of the Pontiac to aim a small black box toward the Riviera's trunk. But the moment she did, the mikes hidden in the car went "hot," the Nagra in the trunk started rolling, and a speaker in the apartment simultaneously began to broadcast.

What came through was mostly a long, irritating hum. Now and then a stray word filtered through the noise. One

14

agent thought he heard the word "bug." But another was convinced Corrao had said "book." It was anyone's guess.

As this squeaky hum filled the apartment, one of the exasperated agents took a long look down Mulberry Street and in an instant realized what had gone wrong. It was a worry spot Kravec had never anticipated. Wiseguys don't care where they park their cars; pulling onto the sidewalk was, after all, a small crime in their scheme of things. On that evening, with so many of the twenty-one Gambino captains showing up to witness the ceremony that would induct five new members into the Brotherhood, the narrow street was jammed with vehicles. A haphazard row of parked cars, a small mountain of metal, was wedged on the sidewalk separating the Buick Riviera from the trio of targets. The Quantico outdoor microphones had not been designed to listen through walls of steel.

It was just bad luck, Mouw was told when the Observation Post reported in. There would be other, less crowded nights on Mulberry Street, and other walk-talks. Deep Street would, the agent assured his boss, eventually deliver. But this was small consolation to Bruce Mouw. In the three years since he had received the orders from Washington to bring down Gotti, he had never before felt so defeated. For if he and the Bureau, despite all the technology, all the manpower, all the resourcefulness, were always going to get only *this* close, then maybe the enemy he was up against was truly invincible.

**3**

JOHN GOTTI'S MOOD, MEANWHILE, WAS ALSO SINKING. THE DON, ignorant of the victory luck had just helped him score against the Feds, was caught up in his own despairing evening. Gotti's temper, always mercurial, had started turning when his *consigliere,* Frank Locascio, a diffident, almost elderly sort, began to fret about his role in that night's induction ceremony. "Is it all right if I ask them, 'Is there any reason why you shouldn't be a member?' " he had suggested hesitantly to his Don. Locascio had never conducted a "make" before and he wanted to be sure he played his part correctly.

Locascio's stage fright irritated and depressed Gotti. It was unseemly and, more telling, weak. "I ain't got time for games," he barked. And the more Locascio tried to stutter his way toward an explanation, the more Gotti's anger was provoked. It grew and grew, and then exploded:

"It's not a toy. I'm not in the mood for the toys, or games, or kidding, no time. I'm not in the mood for clans. I'm not in the mood for gangs, I'm not in the mood for none a that

16

stuff there. And this is gonna be a 'Cosa Nostra' till I die. Be it an hour from now, be it tonight or a hundred years from now when I'm in jail. It's gonna be a 'Cosa Nostra'!"

His speech, part tantrum and part an ardent plea for his Family's future, went on without interruption. No one dared to speak. When at last he was done, without a moment's pause he turned to Gravano and said it was time to get on with the rest of the evening's business.

"All right," Gotti ordered, his voice suddenly surprisingly weary. "This 'Grim Reaper,' where is he, this fuckin' bum?"

Quickly, George Helbig and Joe Butch Corrao were brought before their Don.

"What's up, brother G?" Gotti asked. It was his *goombah* voice, and it was all contrivance. "Good news?"

The Grim Reaper, George Helbig, was like an excited schoolboy who couldn't wait to show his teacher what he knew. His answer rushed out: "I brought you bad news."


Hours later, the ceremony began. Johnny Rizzo, Richie, Fat Dom, Tommy Cacciopoli, and Fat Tony Pronto stood at attention.

"Would you kill if I asked you to?" demanded Gotti.

"Yes," said Johnny Rizzo.

"Yes," said Richie.

"Yes," said Fat Dom.

"Yes," said Tommy Cacciopoli.

"Yes," said Fat Tony Pronto.

In front of the candidates was a long table. On the table were a revolver and a knife with a blade that ended in a sharp point. The weapons had been arranged to form a cross. A picture of a saint covered this crucifix.

"This is the gun you live by, and this is the knife you die by," Locascio intoned.

Each man repeated the *consigliere's* words.

"Give me your trigger finger," said Locascio.

He pricked each extended finger with the point of the knife. Then he wiped the knife on the picture of the saint. The face of the saint became streaked with blood.

A match was lit and the saint was set on fire. As it burned, Locascio warned, "If you should betray La Cosa Nostra, your soul will burn like this saint."

Everyone in the room began to chant, "Now you are born over. You are a new man." The saint had been reduced to dark ashes.

Each man went up to his Don and gave him a solemn kiss on one cheek, then the other. Gotti returned the embrace. At that instant, they became part of the tradition, power, and prosperity of the Gambino Family. They had pledged to serve forever.

Yet, it was a future whose prospects were under siege. For even as the ceremony proceeded, Bruce Mouw, now home in the small cottage he rented just a stone's throw from Oyster Bay, received a phone call. It was Carol Kaczmarek, one of the agents assigned to monitor and transcribe the conversations that were recorded nearly every night inside 247 Mulberry Street.

"Bruce," she blurted out immediately when her boss picked up the phone, "we got lucky tonight."

The Grim Reaper's "bad news" had been recorded. A microphone that had been planted three months earlier by John Kravec had picked up the entire report. The mike was hidden in the body of a VCR that was on a chrome-colored TV trolley. It was powered by the room's A/C current and then fed to the New York Telephone cables that stretched across the alley behind the Ravenite. From the alleyway, the transmission, through a series of well-placed cable splices, made its way to a Revox tape recorder sitting on a desk in a cubicle on the twenty-eighth floor of 26 Federal Plaza. This time every worry spot had been anticipated. Each word came in loud and clear.

Before dawn on the morning after that busy night of January 17, Mouw, anxious and unable to sleep, hurried to his empty office on Queens Boulevard. From the safe across from his desk, he retrieved a copy of the tape Kaczmarek had deposited some time around midnight. He threaded the

tape through the spools of the Nagra, put on his headphones, lit up his pipe, and for the next hour listened
intently. When he was done, he felt like a scientist who, after
years of futile experiments, has finally made a great discovery. Yet there were no shouts of "Eureka!" In fact, his mood
quickly turned. He began to consider the difficulty of what
lay ahead.

Suddenly daunted, he reached for the phone and made a
rapid series of calls. "I got something you should hear," he
announced, his voice soft and private as, one after another,
he pulled the agents of the C-16 team from sleep.

Shortly after eight on that bright winter's morning, they
assembled in his office. They were the key players on his
squad; "the inner circle," they called themselves. Leaning
against the closed door, as if standing guard to keep out the
floor full of agents and clerks on the other side, was George
Gabriel. He was long and wiry, a handsome Greek with jet
black curly hair and a thick bartender's mustache. He was
easily the youngest in the room; and his complicated
relationship with Mouw could skid between protégé, younger brother, and junior agent all in the course of one
conversation. Sitting opposite Mouw, making himself at
home as he arranged his cup of black coffee and buttered
bagel on his boss's desk, was Andy Kurins. He was short and
sly and up for anything. He and Mouw had been working
together since the beginning, a decade now, and over the
years they had built a partnership based on friendship,
respect, and a lot of late nights. And by the window,
blocking out the view of the Alexander's sign in the distance, were the Twins. Matty Tricorico and Frank Spero
didn't look alike. One was tall, the other short. One had
hair, the other didn't. But they had worked together as a
team for so long, they were so inseparable, that they might
just as well have been joined at the hip.

Mouw began without preamble. He had already advanced
the tape to the crucial moment, and now he turned the
switch. From the speakers, John Gotti's tired, put-upon
voice filled the room: "All right. This 'Grim Reaper,' where
is he, this fuckin' bum?"

As the tape continued to play, the agents heard Helbig's news. There were two ongoing bugs being run by the State Organized Crime Task Force aimed at Sammy Bull Gravano: one in the trailer on Sixty-fourth Street in Brooklyn which served as an office for his construction company, and another in Tali's, the Brooklyn bar where he met with his crew each Tuesday night. No one interrupted as the tape played on, but every agent in the room knew the information was correct. And that it was secret—a crucial, closely held secret. It was valuable intelligence betrayed by a highly placed traitor: a report from the mob's mole.

When it was over, Kurins was the first to speak. "The monster has reared its ugly head again," he said. "You were right all along. Johnny Boy's got his mole, all right. A damn good one."

"The smoking gun," Mouw agreed.

He went to the tall filing cabinet to the right of his desk, spun the combination lock, and removed a manila folder. Across its front was typed, "Gotti—Leaks from Unknown Subjects." It was at least three inches thick, and most of the papers inside were not the usual Bureau 302s, but notes in Mouw's careful and precise handwriting. It was a record of all the clues he had collected over the years that had provoked his suspicions, and then, in time, shaped his theory. The inner circle called it "the Mole File."

"Not that we're home free," Gabriel warned from the back of the room. Everyone in the room understood what he meant, but Gabriel, who liked to nail every inconsistency, felt he needed to make things clear. He pointed out that nowhere on the tape was there any mention of the traitor's name, what agency he worked for, how powerful his job was, or even why he served Gotti.

Mouw was quick to agree. "We might never ID him. But now at least we know for sure what we're up against. That we're not paranoid."

"Small comfort," Kurins interjected.

But Mouw ignored the barb and went straight into outlining the battle plan. Since they did not know whom to trust, since the traitor could be working for the prosecutors, or the police, or the state, or even the Bureau, they would trust no one. They would not even tell the Organized Crime Task Force that their bugs had been blown; the risk was too great that this information would make its way back to the mole and send him scurrying. The discovery would remain within this room. It would belong only to these five men of the C-16 squad. Unearthing the mole would be their private, perhaps impossible quest.

If they failed, John Gotti, their smirking adversary for so long, might remain forever beyond their reach.

It was only later that one of the squad added a small footnote to the thick record of events that filled the official history of that long night of January 17, 1990. After the induction ceremony, according to one of the team's usually reliable vest-pocket sources, John Gotti was driven in his black Mercedes to Régine's discotheque uptown on Park Avenue. It was there that, as planned, he caught up with the tall, pouty blonde who had just obtained a well-chronicled divorce from one of New York's most visible celebrities. Gotti had been seeing her every Wednesday for the past few months. As was their habit, they wound up at a friend of a friend's jewel-box apartment on Beekman Place. Every Wednesday night the apartment was empty, the key was with the doorman, and the two of them could share the view of the lights outlining the Queensboro Bridge as they reflected off the mirror on the bedroom ceiling.

Only this evening the divorcee wanted to talk first. Yes, she said, she was grateful for the gifts, the gold bracelet, the diamond pendant necklace. But it wasn't enough. One night a week wasn't enough. So she gave the Don an ultimatum: Either he leave his wife and move in with her, or get out of her life.

Gotti got up and walked out without a word. He was too proud to try to persuade her, and too powerful to argue. He could only do what his sense of honor required.

Minutes later there was a knock on the apartment door. She was certain John had come back; if he told her a story, however contrived, she was ready to welcome him.

Only it was Iggy Alogna, Gotti's driver. "Gimme," he ordered.

At first she was confused, but then he pointed to the bracelet and the necklace.

"John said to tell you 'Fair is fair,'" Iggy said in a flat voice that gave her chills. She quickly stripped off the jewels.

In the small hours of that morning, John Gotti sat in the back of his Mercedes, finally returning to his home in Howard Beach. His ex-mistress's jewels were stuffed like buried treasure in his pocket. Still, he must have felt pretty good, the way things were going. He was the Boss of Bosses and nobody—not the FBI agents following him around, not the D.A. playing his tapes, not the state with its microphones, and certainly not some whining blonde—was able to touch him.

# II

## Taking It to the Streets

# 4

THEY CALLED THEMSELVES THE SUN LUCK MAFIA, BUT THERE WAS nothing criminal, or even very organized, about their association. For that matter, there was little that was Oriental in their philosophy or their demeanor. The name was simply an attempt at irony, a bit of insiders' put-on. They were just drinking buddies, a clique of youngish, hard-edged FBI agents who got together after work to unwind.

The Bureau's all-out drive against organized crime may have had its historical roots in such well-publicized events as the revelatory testimony of Mafia-informant Joseph Valachi before the Senate in 1963, or in the 1968 Safe Streets Act that granted greater electronic surveillance powers to law enforcement agencies, or in the Organized Crime Control Act of 1970 which provided funds for a thousand new agents to fight La Cosa Nostra. But a good case could also be made that these boozy sessions in the early seventies around the horseshoe-shaped bar of the Sun Luck Chinese Restaurant played no less significant a role.

Night after night, the agents, new to the Bureau and to New York, would trek over from headquarters just a block away to the nearly pitch-dark front room of the Sun Luck at Sixty-eighth and Third. Charlie, the bow-tied barman, had a generous hand; you could scavenge a greasy dinner from the Happy Hour chafing dishes; and, a greater comfort, there would always be a crowd of comrades with nothing better to do than to shoot the breeze for hours. Mostly, they talked about the war.

Vietnam was still very much with them. They were the guys who had gone off to fight, volunteered even, because they believed it was their patriotic duty. And they were the guys who had wound up in the thick of it. Jim Kallstrom, for one, had signed up for the Marines straight out of the University of Massachusetts ROTC program and spent a tour on the front lines as a forward observer for the First Battalion gunners. It was a time when I Corps first lieutenants had a three-week life expectancy, but Kallstrom managed to survive and win his captain's bars. Jules Bonavolonta, another regular at the horseshoe bar, came out a captain too, only he was army, a Special Forces Green Beret. Jim Moody, after finishing up at the University of Oklahoma, had done two tours as a gunner on a helicopter gunship based in Da Nang. And their experiences, while exceptional, were not unique. There were fifty men in Moody's training class at Quantico in 1970; forty-five had served in Nam.

They were all survivors, but they had also paid a price. No one came out the same. In the cavelike front room of the Sun Luck, comforted by alcohol and fraternity, they would relive it. They would share the danger, and the risks taken, and the deaths. They would try to make some sense out of it all. And yet at closing time, night after night, they would still find themselves struggling with its inconclusiveness: that so many sacrifices, so freely given, had accomplished so little. It still stung.

"So when we joined the Bureau," Kallstrom said, looking back on those resolute days shaped by introspective nights at the Sun Luck, "a lot of us Young Turks still found ourselves chomping to get involved in another war. We were patriots. We wanted to serve our country. Only this time we wanted it to be a conflict where things would be clearly defined. Good and evil. Friend and foe. A fight we could believe in. That's why so many of us Vietnam vets signed on for Organized Crime. The war against the mob was our second chance—a war we would fight until it was truly over. This time the politicians wouldn't betray us, or tie our hands behind our backs. It would be a war we could throw ourselves into until only one side was left standing—them or us."

Over the next rush of years, the Young Turks of the Sun Luck Mafia put in their time. They shadowed wiseguys through the streets of Little Italy and shuffled papers through the twisting corridors of the Hoover Building in Washington. As the 1980s dawned, they were, at last, moving up in the ranks. They were now the bosses. And with those first grasps of power, they went on the attack. It was Jules Bonavolonta, on his way to becoming head of the New York office's Organized Crime and Narcotics division, who stumbled onto the strategic base from which the Sun Luck Mafia's new war against the Mob could be launched. He made his great discovery while sitting around an oval conference table in, of all places, a law school classroom.

It was June 1980, a warm, fresh spring day on the bucolic campus of Cornell University in upstate New York. Nevertheless, the mood in one classroom seemed to be turning perilously stormy. Or at least that's what many of the prosecutors and police officials attending the seminar on organized crime felt as Robert Blakey, a Notre Dame law school professor, went on with his lecture. He was, by all accounts, a man caught up in a full-scale passion. Paying no heed to the grim-faced FBI agents at the other end of the table, he insisted that the Bureau's war on the Mob was a waste of the taxpayers' money. The FBI, he announced to a room that had become ominously quiet, was going about things entirely the wrong way.

A more effective strategy, he contended, was to "zap the Mob, not mobsters." The FBI's current practice of targeting individuals, of sending out squads to combat specific crimes, was doomed to fail. It could take years to build a case against even, say, a low-level loan shark or gambler. And what would all those Bureau man-hours and taxpayer dollars have accomplished? There would simply be another soldier running a dice game or collecting the vig on the streets the next day. After all, Blakey pointed out with irrefutable logic, that was the structural essence of La Cosa Nostra; it was an ongoing criminal organization.

Therefore, he said as he launched into the heart of his argument, it was necessary to attack the *entire* organization. The battle, he said with genuine conviction, should be directed against the Families. Wiseguys were a dime a dozen. The FBI gambling and loan sharking squads were, regardless of how many cases they made, simply doing piecework. But destroy the structure and the Mafia will come tumbling down.

And best of all, Blakey went on, an instinctive showman building to his dazzling finale, the legal sledgehammer to deliver these mortal blows already existed. The Racketeer-Influenced and Corrupt Organizations Act had been federal law for a decade. RICO—as prosecutors called it—had been used to build successful cases against mob-infiltrated labor unions and businesses. These same "criminal enterprise" and "pattern of racketeering" statutes, Blakey explained, could be directed against the membership of an organized crime family. With RICO, the FBI could focus its resources on taking out an entire family, not just a few soldiers. There was only one catch: *You had to be smart enough to know how to use it.*

When he was done, all eyes in the room seemed to focus on Jules Bonavolonta. He was a short, compact man with a temper that was already famous in the Bureau. The book on Jules was that you never, ever wanted to get on his bad side. He had been a Green Beret, and he still took no prisoners. There was also a lot of talk about his stare: how he could get straight in your face, nose to nose, all his energy coiled, and those two gun-metal gray eyes of his would just burn through you. But that afternoon, Bonavolonta would say years later, "my eyes just flashed with the beauty of it all. As soon as Blakey finished, I jumped up and said, 'You're absolutely right! Now tell us how to do it.'"

Bonavolonta and his fellow FBI supervisor James Kossler spent the next three days huddled with Blakey at Cornell. By the time they left, they were convinced that the Bureau had to begin a complete overhaul. Persuading the U.S. Attorney's offices and the ruling hierarchy of the Bureau was another matter. But the agents knew they had to try. It was not long after that meeting at Cornell that Professor Blakey was invited by an anxious Bonavolonta to give a similar presentation at the FBI's new headquarters in lower Manhattan, at 26 Federal Plaza.

Blakey again was all caustic fire and brimstone. The mood was very tense. One assistant U.S. Attorney was particularly offended, and he, a veteran trial lawyer well accustomed to counterpunching, led the debate. Professor Blakey had most outrageously misinterpreted both the letter and spirit of the RICO statutes, he charged. RICO was not at all applicable to cases solely involving organized crime families.

Blakey shot back that the law's "criminal enterprise" and "pattern of racketeering" provisions had, indeed, been written with the prosecution of entire mob families in mind.

"Oh," needled the prosecutor, "I sincerely doubt that. Besides, how would you know?"

The professor's response was terse. "I wrote it," Blakey said with a sweet smile.

After that, whatever reluctance still lingered in the room seemed to evaporate. A decision was soon made. A new strategy was set in motion. The war against the Mob would be led by FBI teams that targeted specific crime families. And RICO would be the weapon of choice.

Then there was electronic surveillance. Since 1968 when Congress had passed the Safe Streets Act, the Bureau had the authority to place, after obtaining a court's approval, a bug on a mobster's telephone or a microphone in his house. But few in the Bureau saw the potential of those weapons either. In fact, Jim Kallstrom felt that his career in Organized Crime had come to an abrupt dead end when he was ordered to fill a vacancy on the New York office's Technical Squad. In those days, the Tech Squad mostly bugged the phones of Soviet diplomats or hid a mike in the bedroom of an Iron Curtain cultural attaché with the hope of getting something juicy. More often than not, the operations were failures; the technology was very primitive and the transmissions picked up nothing but static. Kallstrom doubted that as the fourth man on the Tech Squad's four-man roster he would be able to contribute much. He could barely run a tape recorder.

But Kallstrom underestimated his ability to learn, and to lead. In 1976, to his complete surprise, he was made head of the New York Tech Squad. And now that he was running things, he poured his heart into giving the squad, to use the phrase that became his maxim, "a real capability." "If you're going to get stuck doing something, you might as well do it right," a sergeant had lectured him at Parris Island and he had never found any fault with that boot camp logic. From the instant he took over, he began suddenly to have big plans for the Techies.

First off, he lobbied Washington for research and development funds. In his easygoing, backslapping way, he charmed and begged until he received the large appropriation he had demanded. He spent it quickly and extravagantly; and then, undaunted, he went back asking for more—and got that too. He insisted that his team's equipment be state-of-the-art. If what was needed didn't exist, he would find the technicians to make it. "Call me Q," he joked, but he was growing into the role. He commissioned some amazing pieces of technology: transmitters stuffed into martini olives, attaché cases that were miniature recording studios, wall clocks that held television cameras.

As success followed success, he persuaded the Bureau to assign additional agents to his team. And as soon as these new recruits were trained, he demanded more. He formed special surveillance squads and outfitted them with night-vision devices and encrypted walkie-talkies. He recruited tough-guy squads from the Bureau's "Quarter-Inch Club"; each agent could place three shots within a circle less than half an inch in diameter at two hundred yards. They would stand guard as his teams entered enemy territory to plant their devices. He persuaded dozens of civilian engineers and technicians to trade higher pay for what he buoyantly described as "the most exciting job in the world—and it's legal too." Within a decade, he had created—and commanded—a powerful empire. The New York Technical Squad had at least 350 men, and an annual budget of about $20 million.

And, most satisfying to Kallstrom's focused way of looking at things, "I gave them one hell of a stake to drive into the Mafia's heart."

But it was Jim Moody, more than anyone else in the Bureau, who understood how to mount the attack. He helped shape—the genesis of the *initial* inspiration, whether it was his or Jim Kossler's, was long ago buried deep in the bureaucratic mud—a new set of tactics for the Bureau's organized crime teams. Instead of striking out at the mob from the fortress headquarters at 26 Federal Plaza, the new plan was to infiltrate their home turf. Squads of organized crime agents would be set up near the neighborhoods where the wiseguys lived, in the boroughs beyond the bright lights of Manhattan where the mob soldiers retreated after a hard day's night of crime. "The idea was for us to sort of hunker down and establish beachheads in the midst of enemy territory," Moody, still very much a country boy even after twenty years in New York and Washington, explains in his slow-talking, down-home way. And, further testimony to the newfound faith in RICO, these five new squads would each have one specific target: an organized crime family.

So, as the 1980s began, the legacy of those late-night sessions at the Sun Luck had begun to be felt. The alumni had accomplished nothing less than a total reorientation of the FBI's attack on the Mob. It was becoming a war that could be won.

The battle plan was precise. A decade later, Jim Moody, now the chief of the Bureau's Organized Crime section, would sit in his large office in Washington and all at once seem to transform himself into a young officer leading his troops into the eye of the storm as, barking out the cadence, he recalled the total strategy: *"One:* We would take the attack into the streets. We would identify the enemy and put him in our sights. *Two:* We would bring it into his homes. We would hit him with electronic surveillance where he least expected it. *And three:* We would bite off his head. We'd use RICO to wipe out the leaders of each Family."

All that remained then, back in 1980, was to find someone to spearhead this new drive against the Mafia. The Bureau needed an agent to go into the newly opened office on Queens Boulevard and head its Gambino Family squad. This agent would lead a team whose mission would be the total destruction of the richest, most powerful, and most violent crime organization in America.

The Bureau chose a tall, gangly, rather scholarly-looking man. He smoked a pipe and wore button-down shirts with rep ties; a forelock of prematurely silver hair fell over his broad forehead. He had been born on a farm in the northwest corner of Iowa, and then went off to Annapolis. His mother was a librarian, and in another life he would have been a history teacher. He seemed, by demeanor and experience, to be colossally ill-suited for the task. The only thing was, Bruce Mouw was determined to get the job done.

# 5

FOR MOUW, THE SUMMONS TO HEAD THE GAMBINO SQUAD WAS two strokes of luck in one unanticipated swoop. It was his escape. And better still, his return.

Three years earlier, he had been plucked from Organized Crime in New York and assigned to headquarters in Washington. He was given a cubicle miles, it seemed, from the nearest window and a job description that was correspondingly bleak. A computer in personnel had recalled that the navy had trained him to be an electrical engineer; and so Mouw, suddenly promoted at the precocious age of thirty-one to supervisor, was brought in to observe the legions of construction workers who were putting the finishing touches on the block-long structure that was to be the Bureau's new headquarters. After three watchful years, Mouw still wasn't certain if he was expected to inspect the Hoover Building's complex electrical circuits to check if there was enough juice, say, to allow for TV cameras in the director's office at the same moment the exhaust fans in the crime labs might be going full blast. Or if he was simply to be a lurking taskmaster whose very presence was intended to discourage any sly civilian engineer from even thinking about cutting corners. All Mouw knew for sure was that he had to get out. He wanted back in the action.

A thoughtful, even introspective man, Mouw, if asked, would have acknowledged that this desire to be in the stormy middle of things was no sudden yearning. In fact, his life had been measured out in such conscious leaps. He had made the first at fourteen. "The great escape," he still called it, and without the least bit of irony.

It was just after his father suffered his final stroke and died, and the family had been forced to move into town. Life on the farm had become a bit hardscrabble, but once they were in Orange City, four kids and a young widow and a pile of debts, things became downright rocky. Bruce decided the time had come to go off on his own and, to his surprise, he did just that. He was a tall, comically skinny high school sophomore with a rigid crew cut, but he found a job as a night clerk at the Village Hotel. He started work when school let out each afternoon, and in return for his six-hour nightly shift, he was given meals and a cell-like room of his own.

It was a solitary life. He couldn't join any of the teams, and there was no hanging out after school with the other kids. Instead, he spent a lot of time reading. Behind the front desk in the empty lobby or in his small room, he would always have a book in hand. Night after night, as soon as he polished off his homework, he devoured books about the sea. He had never seen an ocean, never been on a ship, or for that matter, even a rowboat, but his devotion was consuming. He read biographies of naval heroes, all of C. S. Forester, even Melville. Each night, lying on his bed in a small hotel in a small town, he shipped out to an imagined world filled with great men living out great adventures. And he knew that was what he wanted.

He was also convinced it was his destiny. Like nearly everyone in that northwest corner of Iowa, Mouw was raised as a member of the Dutch Reformed Church. Since childhood, he had been inculcated with the virtues of hard work, devotion, material success, and an overwhelming sense of predestination. *That which is imagined, will, for the elect, be made real.* And for a teenager, straining to bust out from a town where life, day in and day out, was simply more of the same, these words became more than mere dogma. He needed to believe. He achingly wanted something else.

Mouw's unwavering faith, he was convinced, was affirmed (even rewarded!) when against all odds he was accepted into Annapolis. He had calculated that on grades alone he no doubt had a fair shot. His test scores, too, would help; the Orange City high school principal had called his mom to report that his I.Q. score was "so high we just couldn't believe it." But when he began to fill out the Naval Academy application, the naiveté of his ambitions suddenly struck him. He was, he suddenly realized, "a nobody from nowhere." He felt overpowered. Yet, in the end, he refused to allow himself to accept that fate had anything less momentous in store for him.

Even after the competition for the appointment had been winnowed down to just Mouw and another boy, and that boy's father was an Academy grad as well as a personal friend of Congressman Charles Hoeven, Mouw continued to hang adamantly on to his hopes. More impressive, when the other boy was chosen, he still did not panic. Nor, when this unlucky boy failed the navy's physical and Mouw, the runner-up, was all at once the winner, did he gloat. Even when his appointment was announced at graduation and the entire senior class of Maurice–Orange City High rose to their feet and gave him a standing ovation, Mouw allowed himself only a small glow of triumph. To his mind, from the moment he had moved out of his mother's home, it had always been inevitable. He was simply taking another leap toward the great adventure he was certain would be his life.

Nevertheless, when that summer, just seventeen, he began at Annapolis, Mouw could not help feeling "scared to death." "I was scared because everything was so new, but most of all I was scared that I would fail and would have to return to Orange City." A look in the mirror undoubtedly did little to bolster his sagging confidence. At six-three and a bony 152 pounds, he seemed in his resplendent midshipman's dress uniform more suitable for duty as a scarecrow in an Iowa cornfield. Still, he threw himself into the Academy and all its demands, and by graduation the rewards of this experience were apparent. The unsmiling face staring out from his yearbook photograph is a man's: fuller, certainly, but also confident and determined. As one of his classmates shrewdly—and prophetically—wrote in the brief paragraph that accompanied his photograph, "Bruce's ability to recognize a goal and work to reach it will insure his success in whatever field he chooses."

He chose submarines. Or perhaps it would be more accurate to say he was selected ("anointed" some veterans would contend was the truly appropriate verb) by Admiral Hyman Rickover himself to be part of the new, nuclear navy. After a year of training, the now pipe-smoking, rock-solid 210-pound Mouw shipped out on the *U.S.S. Lapon,* a nuclear fast attack sub. The skipper was the legendary Whitey Mack, and for the young lieutenant, j.g., the next four years were filled with a rush of adventures even more heart-in-your-mouth thrilling than those he had read about as a boy in his hotel room in Orange City.

It was the height of the Vietnam War, but attack boats always operated on a wartime footing. On mission after mission, the *Lapon* snuck up on Russian subs armed with enough thermonuclear warheads to destroy an American city; and then, rigged for ultra-quiet, she followed the enemy boomer for months at a time, always keeping the Russian boat dead in the sights of her Mark 48 torpedoes, the two nuclear boats sprinting and drifting four hundred feet undersea, often through miles of uncharted ocean depths. The chase would continue until the Soviet boomer maneuvered onto an undetected course, or one of the boats, tearing through the deep at nearly thirty knots, plunged head-on into a whale, or an iceberg, or the knife-edged ridge of an underwater mountain.

For long stretches during these tense cat-and-mouse chases, Mouw was the *Lapon*'s navigator. But after four years, breathing the antiseptic "test tube air" on a nuclear boat began to get to him. More troubling, Mouw also realized he would be stuck on submarines for the rest of his navy career; Rickover's protégés were too uniquely skilled to be considered for surface assignments. He had served on dozens of high-risk missions, even one that had earned the crew a Presidential citation (and would remain tightly and mysteriously classified to this day), and now he was convinced the time had come to find newer and, he was confident, larger challenges. In September 1970, he resigned his commission.

Within a month, he was certain he had made a tremendous mistake. Civilian life had nothing to offer a man of his romantic ambitions. Mouw shuffled out of job interviews with Xerox or Western Electric after hearing how he, to use his caustic shorthand, "could be earning $x$ dollars for turning out $y$ number of widgets," and felt positively morose. Things were not working as he had always been sure they would. And then in the midst of this bleak period, out of the blue came one more proof of his predestination. It was a call from the Sioux City, Iowa, resident agent of the Federal Bureau of Investigation.

"Your service record popped up on my desk," the agent said, "and I was wondering, you being a patriot and all, if you might miss the action?"

Bruce Mouw, after driving cross-country in his signal yellow Corvette, reported to the FBI Academy at Quantico, Virginia, on August 16, 1971. The next great adventure of his life was about to begin.

Straight out of the FBI Academy, he was, to his dismay, sent to New York City. Yet he rented an apartment with a terrace not much bigger than a Ping-Pong table in a white brick high-rise on the East Side, stopped in every now and then at the Sun Luck but mostly spent his evenings at a preposterously crowded place on Second Avenue that attracted a convivial singles crowd, still managed to get up early enough each morning for a jog around the reservoir in Central Park before reporting to work, and generally had the time of his life. He was assigned to an Organized Crime squad, and, one more complete surprise, he discovered he loved that too.

The thing about OC work, he realized, was that in its best moments it really wasn't all that different from being on a hunter sub. Sure, you might not be tailing the enemy pell-mell across the ocean depths. But you could find yourself in some pretty deep water when you went out on your own in the streets of New York in hot pursuit of a couple of wiseguys. And then, just like on the *Lapon,* you had better find the skill, and the luck, and the guts to get the job done. Or you would be in big trouble.

Mouw's always inquisitive mind could not help but be nothing less than, as he later put it, "fascinated" with the Mafia. "Here we are living in twentieth-century America," he would exclaim, after two decades on the job, his wonder still as wide as an Iowa schoolboy's, "and somehow this group of unskilled Italians managed to preserve a secret criminal society powerful enough to control labor unions, businesses, and even politicians. It's mind-boggling."

Yet there was also a fierce moral component to his initial fascination and, in time, to his commitment. A small experience during his first days in New York was unsettling, and instructive. A Bay Ridge loan shark had sent a couple of guys to talk with one of his customers who was behind on his payments. They talked, and when the customer still couldn't or wouldn't come up with the money, they started swinging a pair of Louisville sluggers. They aimed first for his knees, and then, taking turns, worked their way up his body. They were swinging for the fences with each blow. When they were done, the man lay crumpled on the sidewalk and they walked off. It was four o'clock in the afternoon on a busy Brooklyn street.

Mouw saw the crime scene photographs and glanced at the medical report with its long catalogue of broken bones and internal injuries, but his anger really started to boil when he talked to people in the neighborhood: "I'd ask them, 'Did you see who did it? Can you identify the guys?' and they'd look at me, fear screaming in their eyes, and say, 'I saw nothing. I don't want to get involved.' Or I'd go knock on a door, show them my FBI credentials, and they'd tell me to get lost. In Iowa, you tell people that you're a cop, that you're working for the government, and they'll invite you into their home and give you a beer. Here, they're afraid to talk. And that wasn't right. People living with that kind of fear in America today really upset me. I could never forget it."

And so Mouw, a born fieldman, driven by both a sense of duty and the thrill of the hunt, threw himself into the war on organized crime. Then the Bureau, in its pragmatic wisdom, sent him off to Washington to supervise electricians. Three years later, he couldn't wait to leave.

The call back to New York to head the Gambino squad was his big opportunity, and he was ready for it. He felt exactly as he had when he left Orange City, certain he was going off to make his mark in the world.

# 6

FIFTEEN MEN GOING AGAINST THREE THOUSAND.

From the start, Mouw hadn't liked the odds. He had done the math a day or so before reporting for the first time to the office on Queens Boulevard, and it had worked out like this. They were giving him the Gambino squad, or, in Bureau-speak, the C-16 team. That meant he would have the same as any other FBI criminal squad—15 agents—if, of course, he was lucky enough to get a full roster. The Gambinos included, beginning at the top of the pyramid, the Family's Administration: an all-powerful boss, the underboss who was second in command, and the *consigliere* who served as counsel to the head of the Family. Then there were the captains. The Gambinos had about 20 of these capos, and each ran his own crew. You had to figure that in each crew, or *decina*, as he had also heard them called, there were at least 10 or perhaps 15 soldiers. And these were just the made men, the wiseguys who had been formally inducted into the Family. For every soldier there were maybe a dozen or more associates hanging out with a crew, and each one of them was eager to do whatever it took to get made. So when Mouw added it all up, on one side of the ledger were his 15 agents, and on the other were the three thousand or so members of the Gambino Family his squad was supposed to put behind bars.

No doubt about it, the mathematics were pretty grim. But it didn't take him long after assuming his new command on that first morning in June 1980, an appropriately sullen, slate-gray day when the entire city was being drenched with a furious rain, to realize that numbers were the least of his problems. Or that the odds of his having any success were stacked a lot steeper against him than he could have previously imagined.

Straight off, he quite routinely discovered, there was the matter of the intelligence files—there weren't any. Headquarters had dutifully sent over *one* infuriatingly slim intell file—known as a "92" in FBI parlance—impressively titled "Gambino Family Hierarchy." But even its meager crumbs were useless. The information was ancient history, at least a decade old. For all Mouw knew, the few Family members it identified were now reduced to intimidating their fellow nursing home patients, or equally likely, long dead. A further sore point, whatever photographs were included in the folder were only more folly; "unsub. #1 conferring with unsub. #2" was a typically informative caption.

The first priority, then, Mouw decided in the busy days following his arrival in Queens, was to build an intelligence base. Before he could mount or even plan an attack, he had to go through the long and tedious process of identifying the enemy. Who were the Gambino Family leaders? What businesses were they involved in? Where did they live, hang out? Which were the most active crews? All these background questions had to be answered before he could go on an operational footing.

Yet in those first weeks as he began, however tentatively, to send his squad out into the streets on surveillance assignments, he found whatever hopes he had undermined by another discovery—the sorry state of his troops. Personnel had assigned to his command, with only a few exceptions, either agents who were totally unsuitable for OC work or those who were quite possibly the dregs of the entire Bureau. And the more he thought about it, the more he was certain it was the latter.

There were, and this he understood without a qualm, agents who preferred serving on what the Bureau called "reaction squads." Jumping into action whenever, say, a kidnapping or a bank robbery was reported was more to their liking than the slower duty of keeping track of wiseguys day after day. A couple of the younger men on his team felt that way, and he expedited their transfers with his sincere best wishes. But what set him off, what left him raging and exasperated, was the laziness, ineptitude, and woeful incompetence of many of the agents brought in to man his squad. He knew he couldn't count on them, and worst of all, that scared him.

What a crew they were! There was the slow-drawling, fat-necked hulk from Mississippi who took such an eternity to mutter a perfunctory "How y'all doin' today?" that the prospects of his making street-corner chitchat with a wiseguy from Bay Ridge were too ludicrous to consider. Then there was the agent who after two years working in New York could not even begin to figure out how to get to Staten Island. And there was the rail-thin female agent, a woman of deep religious convictions, who was brought to tears after she was assigned to accompany two wiseguys for fingerprinting and they, catching on to her devout prissiness, spent hours tormenting her by trading the dirtiest, foulest, and crudest jokes and observations they could come up with. But the most baffling case—and most insulting to Mouw's own standards of minimal competence—was the agent who insisted he was "psychologically incapable" of pronouncing any Italian names.

Mouw, at first at least, decided he would persevere. He would mold and shape his motley squad into fighting trim. After all, he could still remember the first time battle stations had been sounded on the *Lapon* and how his heart had thumped with fear. But he had come out of it a veteran, and the next time was easier. So, to build confidence, he announced a rule to his squad: Agents would be required to go out alone when conducting their interviews with members of the Gambino Family. And that was when his team started to whine and complain. They were afraid. It was only then that Mouw gave in to the mounting frustrations. "You're supposed to be agents of the Federal Bureau of Investigation," he bellowed, his anger rising out of control. "You represent the government of the United States of America. Where do you come off being afraid of a bunch of bums who don't even have an eighth-grade education?"

After that confrontation, Mouw turned ruthless. He made up his mind to replace nearly his entire squad. Let them retire, transfer, or simply disappear beneath their desks. Good riddance to all of them. He would recruit his own team. Agents who would go out into the streets. A squad that was up for taking on a gang of strong-arm Mafia hoods. A team he could lead into battle.

Only, he had a new worry: Where would he find them?

As it worked out, they found him.

Agent Andy Kurins had been christened Andris in Riga eight years before he and his parents arrived at a chicken farm in Indiana. Therefore, Latvian was his second tongue, Russian his third, and German almost a fourth. He wasn't happy, but he had to agree it made sense when the Bureau ordered him from its field office in Tampa, Florida, and assigned him to Foreign Counter-Intelligence in New York. It stopped making sense, though, when he arrived at 26 Federal Plaza and learned he would be working on the *Chinese* FCI squad. He spent a sulky couple of weeks trying to keep the squad's surveillance list with all its odd-sounding names straight in his mind, until, more infuriated than defeated, he decided to ask around about a transfer.

That was how he happened to be talking, complaining over a beer really, to Dave Steckle. He had known Dave forever, since the days when they had both wrestled for

Short Ridge High in Indiana. Only now Steckle, his days as a middleweight clearly long gone, was an agent heading a property crimes squad in New York. "Hey, I'll find room for you," he had immediately volunteered after hearing about his old teammate's slow torture on the Chinese squad. Kurins figured such an offer might be coming, and he hoped to deflect it without trampling over his friend's pride. But in the end, no diplomat, he just blurted it out. "I was sort of thinking about something more exciting," he said.

"Sure," Steckle said, stretching the word out so that it reminded Kurins of the sound of air hissing out of a flat tire. A bit curt now, he asked, "What'd turn you on?"

Kurins had been giving precisely this question some thought over the past few days. "OC," he blurted out. In Tampa, he told his high school buddy, he had been brought in to assist on a tail the Bureau had placed on Santo Trafficante. As it turned out, the elderly mobster had come to town simply to work on his tan. But Kurins, despite all their tricks, had managed to stay one step behind Trafficante and his boys for nearly a week. And even better, he found it was a game he liked.

Steckle listened and then took a pull on his beer. "Had yourself quite a war, the way I heard it?" he asked at last.

Kurins wondered where the conversation was going, but, he also noted gratefully, the edge was gone. So he nodded, and tried to keep it brief. He said that when he got out of Purdue, he had joined the air force hoping to fly jets. His eyesight, though, had done him in and he had to settle for a tour in Nam as a navigator on a B-52. And, he might have added, that when the Arc Light raids into Cambodia began, his plane had led the way. But that was a different story, and one he still didn't feel like talking about.

"Well," Steckle said after what seemed like another eternity, "there's this guy over in Queens putting together a new OC squad. Had himself a war, too. From what I hear he's still gung-ho. Determined to shake things up. Already making waves. The word's going around he's making all sorts of enemies in the Bureau."

"Well," Kurins said, "then he must be doing something right."

"I could give him a call . . ." Steckle began.

Kurins didn't let him finish. He simply reached into his pocket and handed his friend some change. "Let's," he said.

Bruce Mouw, in his shirtsleeves, a row of pens and pencils lining his breast pocket just above the JBM monogram, sat perched on the long walnut table in the Queens office conference room. Andy Kurins stood opposite him as if at attention. "We got nothing," Mouw said. "We got zero intelligence base. We got no cases worth squat. We don't even have any prospects of any cases. We're starting at the very beginning."

Kurins just listened, all the time sizing up the guy doing the talking. He liked what he saw: Mouw was very impressive. He had this quiet, almost soft voice, but at the same time he came across as very forceful and confident. A no-bullshit guy, Kurins decided instantly. A leader.

"It'll be a lot of hard work. Forget nine to five. We'll be working around the clock," Mouw continued. And as he spoke he too, no doubt, was doing his own appraising.

To look at Andy Kurins, he appeared harmless enough: about five-foot-eight in a baggy, dark suit, with a solemn, apple-cheeked face and a soup-strainer of a mustache. Similarly, a glance through his Bureau service record would only indicate he was a man who got results. But despite his dour appearance and deadpan gaze, his methods were generally one part invention to two parts mischief. As an Eastern District prosecutor who would spend a large portion of the next decade working with Kurins observed, "You tell Andy he'd need to walk on water to make a case, and he'd somehow do it. Only he'd be skipping the whole way across."

Mouw's first intimations of Kurins' spirited approach came as soon as he had finished his intentionally blunt speech. "Sounds like you could really use a guy like me," Kurins snapped back.

Mouw puffed on his pipe and thought about that. Then he said, "I'll put in the papers."

And yet Mouw was still not certain. He began Kurins' first day on the squad with a test. "I'm giving you the ticket on Joe Gallo," he told his new recruit. "Find out all you can about him."

"Will do," said Kurins. And he asked for the 92.

Mouw told him to dream on. All he had was a brief NYPD intell report. According to that, Gallo was the Gambinos' *consigliere,* the number three man in the Family.

"Well, you've got to have a photograph, right?" Kurins asked.

"Remember what I said about starting with zero?" Mouw reminded him. "I wasn't making that up."

"OK," said Kurins affably. "Now you've convinced me."

Over the next few weeks, Kurins rushed about the city. While Mouw, Sphinx-like in his office with its view over Alexander's toward the Long Island Expressway, silently waited. "Though," Kurins would later say, "whether Bruce was waiting for my report or for me to give up was, I've got to admit, going through my mind a lot of the time."

But Mouw's unspoken doubts, whether real or imagined, only egged Kurins on. He worked impossible hours. And one afternoon after trading war stories with a sergeant from the Manhattan D.A.'s squad, he latched on to a valuable bit of intelligence: Joe Gallo hung out at a luncheonette in Astoria, Queens.

Early the next day, Kurins went to the Bureau's camera shop on the twenty-sixth floor of headquarters in Manhattan and signed out a Canon with a three-hundred-millimeter lens. Then he went back down to his car, consulted his Hagstrom's map of the city, and still the navigator, carefully plotted out his route to Broadway Avenue and Crescent Street.

After driving through what seemed like a dozen foreign countries, he finally found Sperrazza's Luncheonette and parked his car a discreet block or so away. The sergeant had given him a grainy mug shot of Gallo that was at least twenty years old. Better than nothing, he told himself hopefully, and he propped it up on the dash. Then he reached under the front seat and took out a thermos filled with black coffee. Sharon, his wife, had made it before he left their house in Connecticut at six that morning. It was now nearly noon, but it was still warm. He poured himself a cup and stared out the window.

He didn't see Gallo that day. Or the next. But on the third day he spotted a short, elderly man with curly white hair shuffling down Crescent Street. The man was wearing jeans, his shirttail was hanging out of his pants, and he had a pair of bright blue Nikes on his feet. He could have been any grandfather on the way to the drugstore to pick up his Medicaid prescription. But Kurins took one long look at the mug shot on the dash, and then another straight into the old man's face just before he went into Sperrazza's, and decided he had found his *consigliere*.

Within a week he made his report to Mouw. His boss was sitting at his desk when Kurins walked into the small corner office. Without waiting to be asked, he plopped himself into one of the chairs.

"I spoke to Joe Gallo today," he announced.

"Yeah, right," Mouw mumbled, his voice soft and sarcastic. Whatever he was working on seemed to require his complete attention.

"Actually, I had coffee with him," Kurins continued. "He has angina. Takes pills. You know that?"

Now Mouw looked up from his desk. "You're not kidding, are you?" There was excitement in his voice.

"Hey, would I kid Chairman Mouw? Look at this," Kurins said. From a large manila envelope he took out four photographs and, as if he were dealing cards, dropped them one after another on his boss's desk. Each was a shot of the old man in Nikes.

"This is Joe Gallo?" Mouw asked. He was out of his chair and holding one of the photos in his hand.

"The Gambino *consigliere* in the flesh," said Kurins.

"This is great. Just great, Andy." In his elation, Mouw

47

began waving the photo in the air as if it were a flag. "Now we got a start. We got something to look at."

All at once Mouw had an idea. He grabbed the stapler off his desk and began to staple the photos onto the white plasterboard wall across the room. When he was done, the four shots formed a neat, eye-level row on the otherwise empty wall.

He admired his handiwork for a pensive moment. Then he spoke. "We're going to build us a family tree," he announced. "We're going to fill that wall with the faces of all the Gambino bosses. Each and every ugly one of them. How does that strike you, Andy?"

"Like a lot of fun," said Kurins truthfully.

# 7

BUT SURVEILLANCE WORK, HOWEVER INGENIOUS, COULD ONLY provide a part—and a small one at that—of the intelligence base Mouw required before he could go on the attack. He needed to know what the Gambino crews were planning. He needed someone on the inside: an informant.

The conventional Bureau wisdom, drummed into each new class at Quantico, held that "informants aren't born—they're groomed." And from his own tense experience helping to run Willie Boy Johnson, a violent half-Cherokee, half-Italian Gambino Family enforcer his team had inherited from the Queens D.A.'s office, Mouw could testify to its profundity. Persuading a wiseguy to turn on his *goombata*, to break his blood oath of silence, involved a lot more than demonstrating that there was something in it for him. The potential source, regardless of how self-serving and pragmatic his instincts, had to be brought along slowly. He had to learn to trust and respect his handler implicitly; after all, he would be putting nothing less than his life in a stranger's hands. And most importantly, he had to be somehow convinced that, despite all the irrefutable evidence, he wasn't simply a disloyal rat.

The recruiter, then, had to be part shrink, part tough guy, and part benevolent uncle. "Carrot-and-stick men," they called them with gruff understatement in the Bureau; and unlike informants, the best were born with the gift. Now where, Mouw wondered anxiously during those first difficult months of his command, would he ever find agents with such sly and intuitive skills?

Once again, they found him. Only this time with a little help from Andy Kurins.

It all began to be worked out one afternoon when, as was his increasingly obsessive habit, Kurins was staking out Joe Gallo on his home turf in Queens. But that day Gallo didn't head for the luncheonette. Instead, a black Lincoln was waiting for him in front of his modest, rent-controlled apartment building. At the wheel was a tiny man with a beaming smile on his round face and a large black fedora on his bald head; he was, Kurins would later learn, Frankie "the Hat" Distefano, a Gambino soldier whose specialty was busting kneecaps with a ball peen hammer. Without a word to the driver and with some obvious effort, the ancient *consigliere* climbed into the backseat and the big car drove off.

Kurins, always up for an adventure, followed. It was not until the Lincoln crossed the Verrazano Bridge and headed into the relatively foreign territory of Staten Island that he decided it might be wise to get a little help. Using his car radiophone, he had the Bureau switchboard patch him through to the Staten Island field office.

"I'm heading toward Hylan Boulevard in a gray Chevy and could use some backup," he said.

"On our way," replied a deep baritone that identified itself as belonging to Agent Matty Tricorico.

For the next twenty minutes or so, with first Kurins' Chevy having the lead and then a yellow Ford taking over, the agents played cat-and-mouse with the big Lincoln. Distefano was oblivious. He continued along at a steady pace until he pulled off into the block-long parking lot of a white stucco-faced restaurant. A small hill of broad stone steps, each step flanked on either side by a pseudo-Doric pillar, led to a massive, padded leatherette front door. On the flat roof was a red neon sign that identified the premises as J's Villa. The Lincoln found a space near the entrance; and only moments later, Kurins parked about twenty yards to its right, while the yellow Ford moved into a slot at the far end of the lot.

Frankie the Hat and Joe Gallo got out of their car. The old man now moved, Kurins observed and then quickly filed away for some future use, with remarkable spryness. All at once, another Lincoln pulled up next to them, and the agents waited rock-still in the parking lot for the new arrivals. First the driver stepped out, a tall, muscular man with an absurdly ill-fitting toupee. Tommy Bilotti, Kurins decided in an instant. *And where Billoti went . . .* , he was thinking. And then, as if on cue, a bulky figure with a distinctive hawklike nose emerged from the rear of the car. Paul Castellano, the Boss of Bosses, the head of the Gambino Family, was making his smiling way toward Joe Gallo.

Jesus Christ, thought Kurins as he watched the Don and his *consigliere* embrace, what have I stumbled into?

But before he could even begin to speculate, Tommy Bilotti was suddenly shouting to his boss and gesturing furiously toward the yellow Ford parked at the other end of the lot. The two Family leaders were quickly hustled back to their separate Lincolns; the heavy car doors slammed shut with an angry firmness; and in tandem, the two big cars screeched away from J's Villa and roared toward Hylan Boulevard.

Kurins watched it all with disbelief. Finally, he ran to the Ford. There were two men in the car. "How the hell they make you?" he yelled as the bald-headed man at the wheel lowered his window.

"How? I'll tell you how," the agent shouted back, just as angry. "Every wiseguy in Staten Island knows this piece-of-shit yellow Ford. They can spot us a mile away."

Kurins just stood there. He was near to shaking with frustration.

"No point in tailing them now," said the bald-headed man.

"We're blown," Kurins agreed, calming down. And thinking *if every wiseguy in Staten Island knows these two agents, couldn't hurt for me to know them too.* "This place any good?" he asked.

"Good enough for Big Paul," said a deep voice that Kurins recognized as Tricorico's. "That's the highest rating you can get on Staten Island."

"Well, I'm starved," said Kurins. "You feel like eating?"

"Always," said the tall, black-haired agent in the passenger seat. And he was bounding up the steps and toward the huge leatherette door before his partner had even gotten out of the car.

The dimly lit dining room stretched to nearly the length of an airport terminal, or so it felt to Kurins as they were led by the tuxedoed maitre d' on a long and twisting journey. The maitre d' stopped at last in front of a thickly cushioned booth that faced a mullioned stained glass window; a strip of the front parking lot was visible through a triangle of rose-colored glass. All the while, as they were marching across the acres of royally red carpet, Kurins was busily trying to decide on an opening gambit. He wanted to know more about the two agents, but he didn't want his curiosity to come off like the third degree. Dozens of subtle approaches galloped through his mind. But in the end, after they had settled into the booth and ordered from hefty menus that were bound in maroon leather like first editions, he simply asked, "You guys been together long?"

It was the *perfect* question. Once he asked it, the two men talked nonstop throughout the long meal. Except like a married couple, each partner spoke only about the other.

The short, bald-headed one was Frank Spero. After three years in the Marines, he had gone off to play a lot of football and, as long as it didn't conflict with practice, also attend a few classes at Wagner College in Staten Island. He was only five-seven, but he was built across the chest like an interior lineman, and, as Matty Tricorico told it, once he stepped onto the field, he played nonstop for four quarters with the ferocity of Bubba Smith. Tricorico, a star athlete in his own right, had been a lanky basketball forward at Wagner; "but all finesse, no muscle," taunted Spero. The two college jocks wound up pledging for the same fraternity and, perhaps for much the same reasons that opposites invariably attract, had been inseparable ever since. When Spero joined the FBI, it didn't take long for Tricorico, after a brief and depressing detour teaching junior college English on Staten Island, to follow.

Spero's career, Tricorico boasted, was the stuff of legends. He had been the first agent in the Bureau to go undercover against the Mob, passing himself off as a high-rolling, big-spending wiseguy. Chomping on a fat cigar, he would flash a roll of fifties and barrel his way into crap games throughout the city. He would trade small talk with the made guys for hours, and when the moment was right, saunter over to the window or the fire escape, give a discreet signal, and before anyone knew what was happening, the cavalry would come rushing through the front door. "Fearless" was the way Tricorico described his partner.

"Lucky" was what Spero had to say about Tricorico. A few years earlier the Bureau had been trying every which way to solve a $2.2 million bank robbery case; yet, despite a set of fuzzy pictures from the bank's surveillance cameras, there were no leads. When it was Tricorico's turn to have a look at the photographs, something caught his eye. He thought about it for a while, focusing all his attention on the face of one of the robbers. He looked, he paced the room, he looked some more from another angle, and all of a sudden, things fell into place. "I know that guy!" he shouted. It was one of the students from his junior college English class. And now that there was a distinct name to match the fuzzy face, the robbers—and the loot—were quickly rounded up.

Ever since then, the Bureau had been giving Spero and

Tricorico pretty much of a free hand to police Staten Island. "It might as well be Dodge City out here and we're Pat Garrett and Billy the Kid," Tricorico cracked.

Only, complained his partner, for reasons he pretended not to fathom in the least, everyone called them "the Twins."

"So," Kurins said as the long meal was winding down, "you guys are, I guess, sort of jacks of all trades. You never know what's going to pop onto your plate."

"If it goes down on Staten Island, we're there," Tricorico agreed.

"But a lot of that's OC work?" Kurins pressed.

"You know how in Rome there's a church on every street?" Spero said. "Well, in Staten Island we got a wiseguy living on every block."

"We know them, and they know the Twins," Tricorico added.

It was only as they were walking down the stone steps to the parking lot that Kurins decided to ask the question he had been silently formulating for a good part of the meal. He came to a sudden stop and for a moment leaned with the weight of his right arm pressing forcefully against one of the entranceway pillars. And, so very casually, he inquired, "How'd you two like to meet my boss?"

Tricorico and Spero did not speak. They looked at each other, not at Kurins.

"He's going to take down the Gambinos, the entire Family, starting at the top," Kurins continued quickly, realizing he sounded foolish but plunging ahead anyway. "We could use a couple of guys who know the ropes. What do you say? At least talk to him."

The Twins continued to stare mutely at one another. Kurins could only wonder at the secret communiqués that were, no doubt, being sent back and forth between the two men.

Spero broke the silence. "You think your boss could come up with something else for us besides that piece-of-shit yellow Ford?" he asked.

"He might," Kurins said, not sure if he was being put on, but ready to play along. "He might at that."

How did Mouw do it? Within a week of his meeting with the Twins he somehow persuaded the motor pool to assign them a battleship gray Oldsmobile Ninety-eight. Further, another resourceful bureaucratic triumph, he had the two Staten Island resident officers, special agents Matty Tricorico and Frank Spero, assigned to the C-16 squad. And from their first day as part of the team, their primary assignment was a crucial one. Get us someone on the inside, Mouw ordered in his quiet but direct way during a session in his locked office. We need someone who runs with the Gambinos. We need a spy.

Of course, the Twins realized such recruitments cannot be made on demand. Their approach, they told Mouw, would be long-term. "You never press," Spero explained. "You plant a seed, that's all. You let the wiseguy know, very carefully, very offhanded, that if he ever has a problem, if he ever needs help, then maybe I can come up with something that's mutually beneficial." Tricorico would even make a joke of it: "You pay your taxes," he would suggest with a provocative leer to any number of *goombata,* "or at least some of them. Why shouldn't the government give you some of that money back?"

The key was timing. You had to know when the moment was ripe, and then you had to strike. So when the Twins heard that the son of a Gambino loan shark had beaten up some guy in a bar pretty badly, and that since this was his third assault charge he was facing some stiff time, they went to talk with the father.

"Maybe we can help you out," one of the Twins suggested.

"I don't need any help," the father insisted stonily.

"Well," Spero said, "maybe we can help your son."

The next day the Twins told Mouw they wanted to open a 137 file. It was the initial bureaucratic step that was required before an informant could be placed on the federal payroll.

Mouw was elated. It wasn't that the loan shark was a TE

or even close; "Top Echelon" designations are, by Bureau custom, reserved primarily for made men. But, as he announced with uncustomary enthusiasm to his bosses in Manhattan, it was a start. His team now had developed—on its own—a registered informant. "We've turned the corner," he promised to anyone who would listen. "We're on our way."

And it seemed they were. Word of Mouw's squad began to spread through the Bureau grapevine; and the word, as one agent recalled it with blunt admiration, was that "some hard-nose out of Annapolis was putting together an OC team that was really going to kick butt." Such notoriety attracted some dedicated, and unusual, recruits.

There was, for one, self-assured, fast-talking Joe O'Brien, who had been a supervisor of a Foreign Counter-Intelligence squad. Only—as he told it, and others concurred—when his superiors began demanding that he promote a black agent he judged both lazy and unqualified, he chose instead to resign his post. Taking a cut both in pay and power, he decided to work for one of the few people in the Bureau he had come to respect. "Bruce Mouw didn't give a shit about office politics or public relations," he said later. "He just cared about results." Then there was curly-headed, blue-eyed Scott Behar, an incorrigible ladies' man with so many different women calling the C-16 squad offices and leaving beseeching messages that Mouw, who ran a tight ship, had to lay down the law. But Behar, to his boss's joy, also had a real passion and, better still, a knack for surveillance. And there was Mike Balen, who always seemed to be experiencing some imaginary but nevertheless frightening ache or pain or heart tremor; and yet, to Mouw's utter amazement, never connected all his various self-diagnosed illnesses to his incessant smoking. Still, Mouw was prepared to excuse all his personal gripes (and probably a lot more) as long as Balen continued to work backbreaking hours and eagerly volunteered for long and tedious stakeouts.

The core team, however, was not complete until George

Gabriel appeared. And, ironically, he had to be forced to report to C-16. Further, when Gabriel, an easygoing, muscular hulk with an endearing puppy-dog grin, first met his new supervisor, he was not won over. He found Mouw to be "a big, button-down, serious stiff."

Gabriel wanted action. He had grown up in Deer Park, Long Island, in a household where Greek was still the language of choice. Between religious school, guitar lessons, homework, football workouts, and shifts in his father's diner as either a busboy, waiter, or cook, his was an active and pleasantly fulfilling childhood. His proud father had important plans for his handsome son, who had grown, to his family's delight, so big and broad, so American. When Gabriel went off to Allegheny College in Pennsylvania, his father was determined his boy would return nothing less than a lawyer. But Gabriel, like many sons, had other plans. As an adolescent he had avidly watched the television series in which each week Efrem Zimbalist, Jr., playing a dashing, meticulously attired FBI agent, rounded up the bad guys with unfailing aplomb. From this celluloid seed, a vision of his own future had taken hold: He would join the FBI. He applied in his senior year, and after graduation, reported to Quantico.

As he had always anticipated, he loved the Bureau. He was, despite his lighthearted, affable manner, a bit of a tough guy, and one of his instructors, after watching him nearly destroy his partner in a hand-to-hand combat class, picked up on that trait too. He was selected for the FBI's SWAT team. Over a number of months, he was trained to a marksman's proficiency in a variety of deadly weapons, and his schoolyard street-fighting instincts were reinforced with an arsenal of arcane, yet brutal, tricks. He put in some time on a white-collar squad working out of New Rochelle, New York, and was yearning for an assignment worthy of his finely honed SWAT skills when his supervisor announced that he was sending him to the newly formed Gambino squad.

"I won't go," Gabriel said. Organized Crime, the way he

understood it, was little more than sitting in cars and taking down license plates. He saw himself busting down doors with a drug task force.

The supervisor argued that this crew was different. They were determined to get results.

"No way," Gabriel growled.

Finally, the supervisor, who like nearly everyone else could not help but like this big, bluff young agent, relented. Try it for six months, he conceded. If you're not happy, I'll see you get your transfer into drugs.

"Just six months," Gabriel warned.

But by the time six months had come around, Gabriel was hooked. Mouw, despite his often distant, always secretive approach to running his command, had managed to pull him into the thrill of the chase. And in the process, other, more complicated allegiances were beginning to be forged. Was it that Gabriel's strong-arm brawn meshed so instinctively well with Mouw's icy intelligence? Or perhaps it was simply the age difference, the ten years or so that separated them, that allowed the silver-haired Mouw to fall into the role of mentor, while Gabriel became his loyal protégé? Undoubtedly, respect, both professional and personal, had a bit to do with the intensity of the relationship, too. But whatever the various reasons, Mouw and Gabriel developed a deep friendship; and this, as much as anything else, energized their unwavering commitment.

And so, the inner circle was complete: Chairman Mouw, the resourceful Kurins, the street-smart Twins, the towering Greek. A gang of five. Against three thousand.

But even before his team was complete, Mouw was pushing to go on the offensive. Still struggling through those first disappointing months, he was determined not to wait too long before launching his first strike. He stayed in his office until all hours, poring over each new intelligence report and informant debriefing. Rather uncharacteristically, he initiated long, brooding talks with Kurins and the Twins. Thinking he might be missing an important nuance by reviewing only the dull prose of the 209s, he demanded to meet with Willie Boy and then with the Twins' loan shark. This was done, and at great risk.

Finally, toward the tail end of his first year in command, after there were now a half-dozen grim faces staring from the Family chart on his wall and the Twins had landed their first TE, he was ready to attack. He selected as his initial target one of the Gambino Family's most productive crews. They were, according to all he heard and read, a wild, hard-nosed bunch, into hijacking, loan-sharking, gambling, and murder. Their headquarters, the Bergin Hunt and Fish Club, was just a ten-minute drive from his office and this offered, Mouw realized, no small operational advantage. But the clincher was the multitude of reports that identified the crew's newly appointed capo as a comer, a man with both a talent for the trade and a ruthless ambition. "The most powerful captain in any Family," advised a source known as BQ 11766-OC.

The capo's name was John Gotti.

## 8

JOHN GOTTI WAS CRYING. LYING IN FRONT OF HIM IN THE OPEN, satin-lined coffin was his twelve-year-old son. Earlier, he had told the funeral director to get out, to disappear. He would take care of Frank; the boy was still his son, his responsibility. He would prepare his Frank for burial. So now only Gotti and some of his crew from the Bergin were in the back room of the Queens funeral home. Willie Boy, Tony Roach, Fat Angelo, Joe Piney, Skinny Dom, Joe Butch, Handsome Jack—the guys were huddled in a far corner of the windowless room, and they were quiet for once. It wasn't just the boy lying there in his dark suit and tie, his face so fresh and handsome. The guys were scared. They feared their boss was losing it.

For the last hour, Gotti had been walking in small, tight circles round and round the coffin. His eyes were fixed on his son, his sobbing uncontrolled and painful to hear. From time to time, he would lean over, reach into the coffin and touch Frank as if to see if the boy was only sleeping. Then things would completely fall apart. "Jesus Christ, who the fuck was supposed to do the hair?" he would bellow. And one of the crew would hurry over, comb in hand, to arrange the boy's black hair for the tenth or perhaps twentieth time, while Gotti ranted, "You fucked up the hair! I'll kill you, you stupid motherfucker!" Or Gotti, his powerful body shaking, would suddenly come to a halt as he reached the foot of the coffin. "Look at those fucking shoes!" he would scream. "You were supposed to shine the shoes! I'll fucking kill you if you don't get those shoes shined right!" It had been going on like that all morning. Gotti was a wild man, and the guys from the Bergin didn't like where this was heading at all. They had hung out with Johnny Boy for a lot of years, and they knew what he was capable of when he got this way.

It had all been so sudden, and so senseless. Late in the afternoon on March 18, 1980, young Frank, Gotti's middle boy, borrowed a friend's motorized minibike and rode off to have some fun. Howard Beach, the neat, middle-class Queens neighborhood where the Gottis lived, a sea breeze away from the Atlantic Ocean, was an enclave of solid, single-family homes. Ring any door, and the lady of the house might give you the grand tour: the basement rec room with the Ping-Pong table and Little League trophies; a wood-grained Masonite paneled den with its wide-screen TV wired for cable; and the living room with its matching sofa and loveseat protected by plastic slipcovers. Frank had gone as far as the chain-link fence that separated Howard Beach from the bustle of the Belt Parkway, and, evening closing in, turned down 157th Avenue, heading toward home and supper and homework. At the same time, John Favara, a fifty-one-year-old service manager for a furniture manufacturer, who lived with his wife and two adopted children in the house directly behind the Gottis, was also driving home to dinner. As Frank, taking a shortcut, darted out into the street from behind a double-parked dumpster, Favara's car slammed into him. Favara never saw the boy until the moment of impact. It was too late to brake, to swerve. And the son whose report card Gotti had only weeks before proudly shared with the Bergin crew—"Look at that, four fucking A's! Look at what this teacher says about him!"—lay dead in the street. Who could blame a father for losing control?

But there was more. There was another, keener dimension to the sorrow that was pushing him beyond control and distorting his grief. The timing, he ranted in his rambling way to the crew, was too malicious. "Why did it have to happen now?" he thundered. "I fought so hard for every fucking thing. Things are just beginning. Everything is coming together. Why fucking now?"

By the spring of 1981, Bruce Mouw was getting to be quite an authority on John Gotti. He had begun to assemble a background file on the man who, just one month before his son's death, had been appointed capo of the Bergin crew. Most of the entries were routine: police rap sheets, probation reports from Lewisburg and Green Haven, a telephone intercept that, by chance, had caught Gotti chatting with a targeted wiseguy back in 1969, 209s from informants, and cross-referenced surveillance reports. Still, all these terse documents, when read in a single sitting, did give him a sense that Gotti was a man on the move.

John Gotti had been born on October 27, 1940, the fifth of what would be thirteen children. "Nobody had it worse than I had it in life," he would later say, and his assessment, despite its street-talk absolutism, held a good deal of truth. His father, a Neapolitan immigrant, tried to keep his large family clothed and fed by working as a laborer for $1.25 a day and things only improved somewhat when, in his later years, he was hired by the Sanitation Department. It was always a stark, losing struggle, and one that sent young Gotti searching on his own for an easier way.

He found it in the streets. He was a bright kid, with a near-genius 140 IQ score; some of his teachers, in fact, were convinced he had figured out a way to rig the test. Not that he cared what they thought; he had no time or patience for school. His idol was Albert Anastasia, the self-styled mob king of Brooklyn, and Gotti knew you didn't need a diploma to run with Murder Incorporated. So at sixteen he dropped out of Franklin K. Lane High School, and took up with a tough-guy youth gang called the Fulton-Rockaway Boys.

They were punks, hot-wiring cars, looting the copper from construction sites, but Gotti, always looking for something more, managed to persuade some of the neighborhood wiseguys to hire the gang for contract work. Before long, Gotti, a husky, snarling teenager with a greasy pompadour, was running bets for the local bookies and the loan sharks were sending him out to collect the weekly vig. He was making a small reputation for himself on the streets of Brooklyn: Johnny Boy, the tough talker with the hair-trigger temper, the one who would show up at eleven in the morning dressed like he was going out barhopping, with his flashy wide-collared shirts and his tapered pants; the kid—and it was this quality more than anything else that convinced the local Mob talent spotters he was worth a second look—who had the other punks jumping when he spoke, a leader.

He was just seventeen, full of himself, convinced he was a real hard case, when he took a crazy chance and wound up making some important friends. A small-time hood owed Gotti some money. The deadbeat wasn't a wiseguy, but he did hang out with them. Not that Johnny Boy cared. When he got word that the guy was kissing him off, without thinking twice he came after him. He found the hood playing cards in the local wiseguy club, but Gotti was steaming. He flew in there, upending the table, kneeing the guy in the groin, jumping on him as he fell to the floor, and in a flash his thick hands were so tight around his victim's neck that he would have choked the lousy deadbeat to death if they hadn't pulled him off. It was quite a performance, and before the day was over the whole neighborhood was talking about it.

"You're a ballsy kid, you know that," Angelo Bruno, the Gambino soldier who ran the gambling operations in that part of Brooklyn told him. He had heard about the kid who had come roaring like a bull into the club and had sent for him. He was curious. "You could've been killed in there."

"Or I just might've killed somebody," said Gotti.

After that, Gotti started working for Bruno. The kid was smart, he was always ready to use his fists, he had a lot of attitude. It didn't take Bruno long to realize he had made a real find. He brought Gotti to meet his capo, Carmine Fatico.

Fatico, who had started out as a hijacker, was a no-nonsense wiseguy from the old school: dark suit, narrow tie, fedora on his head. He held court from behind a large desk in the back room of an East New York social club. When he saw the young punk Bruno had told him so much about come swaggering in, bright purple shirt open nearly to his waist, his pants tight as a girl's, his hair falling in a pomaded curl over his forehead, he started grinding his teeth.

"You look like a fucking guinea," the capo snarled.

Gotti tried to take the rebuke, but suddenly he found himself thinking, *Fuck him, and fuck that little fucking hat on his head!* So he shot back, "Yeah, but I'm a tough fucking guinea."

Fatico took a moment and then, at last, smiled. "I bet you are," he agreed with a quick laugh. And John Gotti was launched.

He became one of Fatico's boys, and using his mentor's connections, began hijacking trucks leaving Idlewild Airport. But from the start Gotti was looking to get his shot at some real money, and for that, he knew, he would have to become a soldier. So when Fatico wanted to make an example out of two black gamblers who were pocketing a share of the boss's take, Gotti and Willie Boy Johnson, eager to make their bones, went off to teach them a lesson. Both gamblers were found dead, shot in the back of the head.

And now that he was a twenty-year-old running with the mob, his ambitions focused, Gotti decided to get married; although the fact that his girlfriend was seven months pregnant had a lot to do with it, too. Victoria DiGiorgio was a pretty, raven-haired high school dropout, the daughter of an Italian builder and a Russian-Jewish mother. Their daughter, Angela, was born in April 1961.

Gotti worked as a truck driver's helper for the Barnes Express Company. But that was just a part-time job, a way to cover some of the pile of bills. Pretty soon, he had three more children—another girl, Victoria, and two boys, John, Jr., and Frank. Mostly, he was busy becoming a wiseguy. He earned a rep as a small-timer, someone into hijackings or break-ins. The word also got around that if you needed rough stuff, somebody to carry a piece of mail, as the guys would say, you could count on Johnny Boy to back you up.

The problem was, he just wasn't a very good thief. In 1963, he was arrested in a car stolen from Avis. That got him twenty days in a city jail. Over the next two years, he got busted two different times trying to pull off the jobs assigned to him by Carmine Fatico. Those bungled burglaries got him six more months in jail. And while he was doing the time, his angry wife, finding it just about impossible to feed the four kids and also wanting to make a point, filed for welfare. She gave the embarrassing knife in Gotti's back another sharp turn when she sued him for nonsupport in Domestic Relations Court in Brooklyn.

Still, after Gotti got out, the couple seemed to find a way to make the marriage work. And Gotti concentrated on his speciality—airport hijackings. It could be good money. On a lucky night, working with his brother Genie, he might grab, say, twenty thousand dollars' worth of TV sets. But in 1969, while out on bail after ripping off a shipment from the United Airlines airfreight terminal, he got caught trying to hijack two trucks on the New Jersey Turnpike. He pleaded guilty and was sentenced to four years at the federal prison in Lewisburg, Pennsylvania.

This was easy time, and a bit of an education. Gotti's cell was in the prison's "Mafia Row," and he stuck tight with the wiseguys, pumping iron, making friends, trading schemes. Carmine Galante, the squat, mean-spirited don of the Bonanno Family who was doing heroin time, took a liking to him, and Gotti—"a hoodlum's hoodlum" was one buddy's admiring assessment—was frequently invited to Galante's "Club Lewisburg": T-bones medium-rare, aged scotch, and all-night poker.

When Gotti was released after thirty months, he quickly hooked up again with Fatico. Only now Fatico had moved out of the increasingly black community of East New York and had set up headquarters in more congenial Ozone Park, a middle-class Italian neighborhood in Queens. He rented two adjoining storefronts on 101st Avenue, and inspired by an imagined yearning for a gentleman's life in the great outdoors, christened the bleak and smoky rooms the Bergin Hunt and Fish Club. But the Bergin, despite its name, was deep in gangland: the headquarters for a Gambino crew busy with gambling, loansharking, hijacking—and murder.

It was a contract killing that landed Gotti back in prison, but in his pragmatic world that was a small price, since the murder also got him "made." The assignment came from Aniello Dellacroce, a raspy-voiced, bull-necked, cigar-in-the-corner-of-his-mouth thug who was the Gambino underboss, and he was passing it on from the Boss himself, Carlo Gambino. A reckless Irish gangster, James McBratney, had thought he could make an easy hundred grand by kidnapping and then quickly ransoming Gambino's son, Manny. Except the ransom negotiations dragged on for over a month, and then understandably fell apart when Manny's corpse was discovered. McBratney was now a marked man.

Gotti and two of his buddies from the Bergin, the whale-like Angelo Ruggiero and Ralph Galione, whose lopsided Beatle-style toupee earned him the snide nickname "Ralphie Wigs," tracked McBratney down to a bar in Staten Island. They told him he was under arrest, even flashed police badges, but for some reason McBratney wasn't convinced the three men were genuine cops. A fight broke out, the three hitmen taking on an Irish bar; and while Gotti threw rapid punches and the hulking Ruggiero grabbed two drunks and banged their heads together like cymbals, Galione in a panic fired off three bullets at point-blank range into McBratney's chest. The Irishman fell dying to the barroom floor, as the three "cops" vanished.

Three months later, Gotti was arrested. "Who, me?" he asked with an incredulous grin when twenty cops, their guns drawn, rushed into a Brooklyn bar and surrounded him. As a "persistent offender," he was facing some serious time if convicted. However, Dellacroce told him not to worry. "Carlo says you take the fall, and that's it," Mr. Neil, as Dellacroce was called, ordered. Gotti obeyed. And contrary to either law or logic, Dellacroce's confidence proved justified. With the help of Roy Cohn, the attorney Gambino hired, a magnanimous deal was struck with an exceptionally understanding Staten Island District Attorney's office: Gotti was allowed to plead to attempted manslaughter. He served less than two years in Green Haven state prison.

The summer after he was paroled in 1977, Gotti, along with Fat Angelo Ruggiero and seven others from the Bergin crew, was inducted by underboss Dellacroce into La Cosa Nostra. He pledged his lifelong fidelity to the Mafia and to a new Gambino Family Boss. Gambino had died in his bed of cancer. His son-in-law, Big Paul Castellano, a former butcher with an eighth-grade education and a self-serving greedy streak, was now Boss of Bosses.

Yet Gotti, in allegiance as well as volcanic temperament, was always more closely identified as one of Dellacroce's boys. Similarly, Mr. Neil, who had inherited control of Fatico's Bergin crew as part of his share of the spoils after Gambino's death, took immediately to the new soldier. Gotti was rough, shrewdly respectful (at least outwardly) of the old-world Family traditions, and, perhaps most significant, he was a big earner. The relationship deepened, however, after Gotti, according to a Family story that was passed on by a number of sources to the FBI, played a role in saving Dellacroce from jail. The underboss, along with his alleged partner, Anthony Plate, had been indicted in 1979 for running a loan-sharking operation in Florida. Plate's testimony, Mr. Neil complained vehemently, would get both of them sent to prison. Soon Gotti was heard suggesting, "Maybe we should call Tony in for a strategy session." Then Gotti disappeared. And as events worked out, Tony Plate walked out of a Miami hotel and was never seen again, Dellacroce beat the rap, and Johnny Boy returned to the Bergin with a deep Florida suntan. "Neil and me," Gotti would tell people, "we're like father and son."

Still, many in the Family were taken aback when

Dellacroce, now that Fatico was a ragged sixty-eight and preoccupied with pending trials on hijacking and loan-sharking charges, appointed Gotti the acting captain of the Bergin crew. After all, Johnny Boy had just been "made" only two years before; such a rapid ascent, a lot of the talk on the street had it, was not just unseemly, but also unwise: the kid wasn't ready.

Johnny Boy set out to prove he was. He was determined to rule; and if necessary, to make his boys crawl.

So when Anthony Moscatiello, a particularly dim-witted soldier in his crew, dared not to return one of his calls, Gotti laid down the law. "I called your fucking house five times yesterday," he began slowly enough when he caught up with the hapless Moscatiello. But his anger kept building: "Now, if your wife thinks you're a fucking dunsky, and you're going to disregard my fucking phone calls, I'll blow you and that fucking house up!" Moscatiello did his best to sputter an apology, but Gotti was beyond listening. "This is not a game! My fucking time is valuable! And . . . if I hear anybody else calls you and you don't respond within five days, I'll fucking kill you!"

Or when he entered a Queens restaurant and Mike Coiro, a lawyer for the Bergin crew who was in the midst of a meal across the room, didn't put down his knife and fork and rush over to Gotti's table and offer his respects, Gotti took exception. The next day he summoned Coiro to the back room of the club: "When I found you, you were a fifty-dollar ambulance chaser. You're a piece of shit! You're supposed to *run* when you see me. You sit there . . . you don't even get up to say hello to me! I'll kill you!"

Or when Tony "Roach" Rampino absently tried to leave the Bergin after one of the weekly Wednesday night back-room dinners, Gotti at the top of his lungs sent a rocket across the room: "You dirty fuck! You don't go home until I tell you to!"

But more impressive to the Family's Administration than his power to command was his ability to make money. The Bergin crew, driven by Gotti's sense of urgency and tight-fisted management, was a gold mine. As an initial reward,

Gotti arrived at the Bergin one afternoon in the winter of 1980 to find a shiny black Lincoln Town Car with a red ribbon on its hood parked out in front. It was a present from Big Paul. A month later he drove the car to Castellano's pillared mansion on Staten Island where the announcement was made that Carmine Fatico had officially retired. John Gotti was now the captain of the Bergin crew.

Then, it wasn't long before he was driven in the Lincoln to his son's funeral. And, unknown to him, the C-16 team began compiling its Gotti file. In fact, one of the last entries in this early dossier was a small notice that ran in the obituary section of the New York *Daily News*. It went unnoticed until one of the squad's informants brought it to the Twins' attention:

Frank: The pain of losing you never leaves our heart. Loving you, missing you, always and always hurting.

It appeared on March 18, 1981, the first anniversary of Frank Gotti's death. Ten weeks later, Bruce Mouw, convinced his long tactical caution had served its purpose, would send his C-16 squad rolling into action at last.

# 9

AS THE RAID ON THE BERGIN HUNT AND FISH CLUB HAD BEEN first conceived and then carefully fine-tooled in a series of late-night sessions in Mouw's office, the battle plan consisted of three escalating stages, each designed to unfold in orderly succession.

In the first stage, Mouw's squad, accompanied by a burly group of city cops, would come charging into the Bergin ostensibly to confiscate the small mountain of illegal fireworks that, a TE had revealed, was being stored in the back room. But while the cops were carting out the boxes of Roman candles (and on Mouw's stern instructions, taking their time), the C-16 team would be casing the nooks and crannies of the club for the most ingenious places to hide a bug. Next, in the dead of night, a squad of FBI Tech agents would enter the Bergin and, guided by the intelligence the Gambino squad had gathered, would quickly and discreetly do their electronic dirty work. And once his team was eavesdropping on the daily machinations of the busy Bergin crew, Mouw was confident he would be able to march forward building cases. The Bergin thugs, even their new and ambitious capo, were not his primary targets. But he would climb on their shoulders to get a boost up the Family pyramid—until he could reach all the way to Big Paul Castellano.

As things turned out, Mouw's initial error was one of judgment. The fireworks cover provided his men with a search warrant to enter the Bergin; but however effective as a tactical premise, it was also a demoralizing pose. The C-16 team announced its presence to the Gambinos with a whimper, not a bang. "Big tough G-man worried somebody's gonna get hurt playing with firecrackers," one of the Bergin crew began taunting. Another sneered, "Ain't the Feds got anything better to do?" Soon everybody got into the act. The city cops were snickering too. And not bothering to hide it. "Respect is the name of the game on the streets," moaned Joe O'Brien. "And we came across silly. Like we were dogcatchers."

But that was just an embarrassment. Mouw could live with that. What happened next shook his confidence and gave him, for the first time, an understanding of how solidly entrenched his enemy was, and how diverse the forces conspiring against his team's success.

As the raid was winding down and the fireworks, about twenty thousand dollars' worth, were being carried off, Donnie McCormick, one of Mouw's new gung-ho recruits, picked up the receiver of a pay phone on the wall. He was going to phone in his field report to Mouw, who was directing the show from his sixth-floor office.

"Be careful what you say on the phone," Jackie Cavallo, one of the Bergin wiseguys warned. He shot a stagy wink and whispered, "Santucci's got a tap on it."

That really cracked the Bergin crew up, telling the Feds the Queens District Attorney had a tap on their phone. Always busting chops, McCormick figured, and he called Mouw.

But it was only minutes after Mouw got off the phone that he received another call. Remo Franceschini, the lieutenant who ran the Queens D.A. squad, was on the line. "Congratulations," he began. He had a lot of praise for what C-16 had accomplished, but it suddenly occurred to Mouw that Franceschini, in his own not-too-subtle way, had called to make another point. As well as maybe have a last laugh. *He had heard the conversation with McCormick.*

Which left Mouw stunned. And fighting mad. He had spent months planning to bug the Bergin, and the Queens D.A. was already in there. Why hadn't he been told? But worse, much worse, the wiseguys *knew* about the bug. How had they found that out? Did they have a hook in the D.A.'s office?

When he went to meet with John Santucci, the Queens D.A. wouldn't give an inch. The session, Mouw would say, had "a competitive air." The D.A., a loud, pompous career politician with a squinty glare, told Mouw he wouldn't think of pulling his bugs from the Bergin.

Mouw had a tendency to become quieter, more withdrawn, the angrier he got; it was a necessary trait in a junior officer. Sitting across from the Queens D.A., he kept his lips pursed, his back straight, his eyes fixed on some point in the distance. He didn't move a muscle. He finally spoke with perfect calm: "Then we'll just have to figure out a way to proceed on our own."

But all the time, his mind was in turmoil. When he returned to his own squad, he closed the door to his office, and alone with his inner circle, he let loose. Still, he didn't raise his voice. But his words had the force of a resigned anger: "We can't trust the D.A.'s office. They've got a leak and they don't even seem to care. Hell, we can't trust anybody. Even the cops were laughing at us. We're going to have to start again. From square one. Only from now on, C-16 is in this fight on its own."

As the team regrouped, there was something else driving them. John Favara, the neighbor who had had the misfortune to run over Frank Gotti, was missing. It wasn't likely, C-16 learned from their informants, he would ever be found.

At first, Favara had tried to offer his condolences to the

Gottis. He rang their doorbell and, before he could get any words out, Victoria Gotti came at him with a baseball bat. He took a couple of blows to the head and had to be hospitalized. When he was released, he decided to put his house up for sale.

Two days before Favara was to close on the deal, as he was coming out of the Capitol Diner and heading to his car in the parking lot, a man snuck up on him from behind and clubbed him to the ground with a two-by-four. Then the attacker picked Favara up by his belt and tossed him like a sack of potatoes into the rear of a blue van.

The diner's owner, Leon Papon, saw it all. He ran to the parking lot.

"Our friend is sick," the man with the two-by-four said. "We're taking him home." He spoke as if this was the most reasonable explanation in the world. He also had a size twenty neck and a plank in his hand. Papon watched the van pull away, then he called the police.

The next day three men came into the diner and took seats at the counter. One of them, Papon instantly decided, was the man from the parking lot. Only now he didn't have a board in his hand. And he was the smallest of the three. By a lot.

They ordered coffees, but they didn't drink. They just stared at Papon, slowly stirring their spoons in their cups. Until, without another word said, they left.

Papon sold the diner within the month. He moved to another state, and did not leave a forwarding address.

Of course the police questioned John Gotti. They found him sitting behind his desk in the back room of the Bergin. He was puffing a cigar and dressed in black: black loafers, black wide-lapeled suit, black open-collared shirt.

"You should be more circumspect in here," he began. The cops could tell he was pleased by his own choice of an adjective. When he was done milking the moment, he explained, "The place is bugged."

That cracked his boys up, so the police quickly announced this was no laughing matter. John Favara was missing, they said. Most likely murdered.

"You know I wouldn't be that stupid," Gotti said. "I don't know what happened."

Besides, he revealed, he had an alibi. Two days before Favara disappeared, he and his wife had gone down to Fort Lauderdale. It was a vacation, and they were away for a week.

"We'll check it out," the police promised.

But Gotti had the last word. "I'm not sorry if something did happen. He killed my kid."

The police learned that Gotti had been in Florida that week, and that he had driven down because he was afraid to fly. The FBI heard a bit more. Favara had, on Gotti's orders, been kept alive until the capo returned from his vacation. John Gotti wanted to be the one to chainsaw his son's killer into little pieces.

## 10

FOR MOUW, THINGS GOT WORSE. IN THE AFTERMATH OF THE Bergin raid fiasco, he found himself summoned to the Bureau headquarters in lower Manhattan. Jules Bonavolonta, the head of the New York Organized Crime and Narcotics division, wanted to speak with him.

Bonavolonta's office was on the twenty-eighth floor; and as soon as Mouw walked in, he was facing a wall of tall windows that gave him a view over jutting city towers, past a narrow, gray strip of the Hudson River, and all the way into New Jersey. The view put people in their place straight off and Mouw, who was not very sanguine about what was in store, had a rush of nerves: *So much was at stake.* He took a calming breath, and pulled himself up to parade rest.

Bonavolonta was seated at his desk, and he got up quickly when he saw his guest. It was a courteous gesture, but a lot of the people who had worked with him over the years thought they saw something else in his office manners. He was a short man, yet proudly sleek and as hard as a whippet. Perhaps, a few agents speculated, he had difficulty with people seeing him as just a little bureaucrat behind a big desk. Others, more kindly, said it was a wartime habit. Bonavolonta had been a genuine hero, a Green Beret who had led his squad at great risk behind enemy lines in Vietnam, and there were those who were convinced he pictured himself to this day as a wily stalker, a man on the prowl. Mouw, aware of his predicament, was not feeling judgmental. He simply took a chair, prepared to listen as Bonavolonta, striding back and forth purposely across the room, ran the show.

It was a dressing down. The bosses in Washington, Bonavolonta lectured in quick, punchy jabs, were asking questions, wanting results. The Gambino squad had been in business now for two years. What did they have to show for it? A truckload of fireworks? Where were the big cases? Hell, where were the little cases? A lot of time and money, not to mention man-hours, had to be accounted for. Now what was he supposed to tell Washington?

Mouw wasn't sure if he was expected to answer, so he kept his peace and let his superior's temper have its run. At last, Bonavolonta stopped pacing and, instead, found a seat for himself on the top of his desk. With this new position came a new mood.

"Bruce," he asked with what seemed like the utmost sincerity, "you know what you're doing?"

"Yes," Mouw said.

"Good. Then at least one of us does." He smiled at his own small joke, and in that instant Mouw understood that perhaps the worst was over. "OK," Bonavolonta went on reasonably, "why don't you tell me what you've got up your sleeve."

Mouw was infuriatingly vague. Perhaps he feared sharing his operational secrets with anyone not in his squad. Perhaps it was simply out of stubborn habit. Yet, he did talk for at least a quarter of an hour without pause. And however unspecific, he managed to touch on all the guiding principles of his attack: the need to build only "quality cases"; his commitment to "targeting the heads of the Gambino Family"; his plan to "look for opportunities, for weak links, and then to pounce"; and above all, his tactical belief in "patience, patience, patience." "When the right moment comes, then we'll strike. But not an instant before," he said.

Bonavolonta listened without comment. When Mouw finished, he rose and walked toward him. On instinct, Mouw rose too. The two men were suddenly standing face-to-face.

"Well," Bonavolonta said, "I've held off the desk jockeys for this long, I guess I can hold them off a little longer. I'll worry about Washington. You worry about the Gambinos."

To the astonishment (not to mention the envy) of many in the Hoover Building, Bonavolonta's confidence was soon justified—as was Mouw's patience. For just five months after he had suffered through the embarrassment of his ill-conceived attempt to bug the Bergin, he regrouped, found his opportunity, and then pounced. And this time he struck gold.

His course of action took shape slowly, however, almost coincidentally, and even then without great expectations. One of the team's low-level informants, George Yudzevich, a six-foot-nine, four-hundred-pound mountain of a man, had spent a few debriefings spinning stories about his occasional work as a collector for the Bergin crew. Usually, he told the agents with apparent pride, one look at him hovering about ominously was enough to persuade even the most recalcitrant debtor to pay up. But now and then, he would have to resort to rough stuff. "I'd snap their arms like they was chicken wings," he proudly boasted. "Or maybe I'd just pop one of their legs."

The 209s on these interviews reached Mouw's desk without fanfare. Interesting, but not crucial intelligence was the transcribing agent's evaluation. But Mouw read the reports and detected something more. For, he decided as he went back over the pages with building excitement, lurking between the lines of Big George's bemused and self-congratulatory tough-guy anecdotes was a very cogent description of the Bergin crew's gambling and loan-sharking operations. John Gotti, his brothers Gene, Richard, and Pete, his boyhood buddy Angelo Ruggiero—all of them, according to Big George, were involved. Mouw quickly decided this was his opportunity. There was sufficient informant testimony—especially with Willie Boy Johnson's additional insights on the crew's activities—to persuade a judge to authorize electronic surveillance of the Bergin's loan-sharking and gambling rackets.

But almost from the start, another operational worry began to tug at Mouw. Which of the players should he target? Time, he realistically understood, was not on his side. Jules Bonavolonta, however firm in his support and however valuable an ally, could not be expected to hold off cost-conscious Washington for too much longer. The bug would have to be productive from the moment it went "up." Mouw needed his "weak link."

Despite these pressures, Mouw was methodical in his approach. He considered, then rejected plans to move against John Gotti ("Too smart; he'd be cautious on the phone," the squad argued) and against his brother Richie ("Too stupid; nobody'd share anything with him"). Yet in the end, it was really just a tantalizing hunch that guided him. Angelo Ruggiero, an informant had once thrown out almost as an aside, had a phone in his Howard Beach home that was listed in his teenage daughter's name. It was, Fat Angelo told the snitch cryptically, his "safe" phone. In a burst of intuition, Mouw decided that what was safe for the bad guys might be a good bet for his team, too. One afternoon in the first week of November 1981, two FBI Techies dressed as Con Ed repairmen paid a visit to the Ruggiero residence to investigate the cause of a blackout that had mysteriously affected the entire block. By the time they left, power had been restored and a teenager's pink Princess phone had been wired. Now Mouw could only wait, and worry. His greatest secret fear: his agents would sit with their headphones on, listening shift after eight-hour shift to a string of gushy adolescent confidences.

So much for fears. From the first day it was activated, the tap produced fascinating, provocative results. There was, however, a short run of concern when the team learned Ruggiero was moving to a new home in Cedarhurst, farther

out in suburban Long Island; one informant reported that
Fat Ange had even been gloating that soon the FBI would no
longer know where he lived. But in April 1982, three
microphones hidden in the track lighting stretching across
the sunporch of the newly renovated Cedarhurst house were
switched on, and the C-16 team was once again eavesdropping. Only now, things were a lot juicier. Ruggiero was
boldly having business meetings over the dining table of his
new house. And the consequences of what was overheard at
these meetings, as well as on his phone, would soon propel
events forward in a manner and with a speed that was totally
unexpected.

"Wow!" Even Mouw, so grudging in his enthusiasm, so
controlled in his demeanor, couldn't hold back his excitement. "I mean it—wow!" he repeated. Wearing a pair of
headphones, he was sitting in his squad's "plant" in a
remote corner of JFK Airport. And at that moment, with
Mouw glued to every mumbled word, Angelo Ruggiero was
beginning his day with an 11:30 wake-up call to his capo.

"Wake up, Johnny Boy," Ange announced cheerfully.

"Fuck. Just let me sleep," growled Gotti.

"C'mon, Johnny Boy, rise and shine."

"OK. OK. I'm getting fucking up."

Mouw heard Gotti slam down the receiver, and his
emotions were still racing. After all this time, after all the
months of trying futilely to get a peek into the workings of
the Gambino Family, he was suddenly on the very inside. He
felt, he would later say, like an explorer who had finally
made his way after a rough journey to a long-sought land
filled with great riches.

Over the next busy stretch of months, the C-16 squad
discovered, to both their personal amusement and professional satisfaction, that Ruggiero was incapable of keeping
his mouth shut. He was on the telephone chattering nonstop
day and night. As a youth, he had picked up the nickname
"Quack-Quack," and the team had previously deduced it
was simply a snide comment on Fat Ange's thigh-scraping,
ducklike waddle. Now they weren't so sure. For day after

day, Ange was on the phone quacking frenetically about whatever crossed his mind. "Dial any seven numbers, and there's a fifty-fifty chance that Angelo will answer the phone," one of the Bergin boys, John Carneglia, was heard to complain with exasperation. To which the C-16 squad could only add, Amen.

He talked to everyone. One moment he would be ringing up Robert DiBernardo, the Gambino captain who ran the Family's porno business. Then he would put down the phone and call the Boss of Bosses, Big Paul himself. And the FBI was hearing it all.

The conversations were wide-ranging. Ange complained to Gene Gotti about Johnny Boy's out-of-control gambling binges; the capo had shelled out ninety thousand dollars over one painful football weekend. His losses for the month, Ange confided, were a "killing two hundred grand." (Which, the FBI noted, was indeed a "killing" sum since Gotti, at least according to his IRS 1040, was earning $25,000 a year as a salesman for the Arc Plumbing Company.) Or going against Family rules, and for that matter, common sense, he was on the phone disparaging Big Paul. Working himself up, he called the Gambino Boss a "milk drinker" and a "pansy," giggling that Castellano spent his evenings "whacking off with Tommy," his driver. Then, switching gears, he would confer with a couple of wiseguys and wind up warning them, "If I find out anybody's lying, a year from now, or six months from now . . . I promise youse this: Youse are gonna die the same way my brother died—in pieces!" Then at the end of his day he'd be a tickled father sharing a story about his daughter with his friend John Gotti: "So I told her about 'The Three Little Pigs.' And I forgot to tell her about the third little pig with the brick house. Would you believe, this morning when I woke up, she said, 'What happened to the other pig, Dad?'"

The clarity of the tapes was so precise, the intelligence he was gathering so valuable, that Mouw could not help but be impressed. And as the pile of transcripts grew, he came to a strategic realization. It would affect the methodology—or "handwriting," as they say in the trade—of his assault on the Gambino Family for the next decade. Whenever possible, he would pepper them with microphones. The wiseguys, despite all their often discussed fears of being bugged, were too undisciplined to be discreet. If he planted his equipment shrewdly, and if he waited long enough, Mouw was confident he would eventually reap the incriminating evidence he needed. Already, he was going ahead with plans to bug Paul Castellano's big white house on Todt Hill in Staten Island, as well as, blocks away, the bedroom where Neil Dellacroce, now broken by cancer, still struggled to conduct Family business.

And then, just as plans for these delicate operations were proceeding, Angelo Ruggiero suddenly stopped talking.

Not that there hadn't been hints. In April 1982, after Ruggiero spotted a team of agents following his car, he began to worry that the Bureau might also have targeted his home. He hired Jack Conroy, a burly former New York City detective, to "sweep" the Cedarhurst residence. Conroy worked for hours, and when he was done he announced that the place was clean. Which was true—up to a point. For just moments after the FBI had heard Ruggiero place his call to the self-styled electronics expert, they had shut down their microphones—only to turn them promptly back on when Conroy, after receiving Ruggiero's thanks and a thousand dollars in cash, walked out the door. And Quack-Quack resumed his chatter.

But then two months later, in late June, the house abruptly became silent. The microphones listened in vain. On Mouw's orders, the receiving volume was gradually increased, but there still was nothing to hear. Next, a surveillance team was dispatched and returned with a disturbing report. Dishes were piled in the sink, beds were unmade, clothes hung in the closets—but no one was home.

It took a week before the Ruggiero children and their mother were discovered to be staying with friends in Howard Beach. There was still no trace of the father. Ruggiero had, almost before his very eyes, a troubled Mouw felt, vanished. Could he have been hit, a victim of some unanticipated flash of mob violence? Or—another theory the team mulled—perhaps he had been ordered to take to the mattresses in anticipation of a new round of war?

Days later, Mouw's men, following up on a stray comment they overheard his wife making to a friend in the supermarket, located Ruggiero. He was clearly a troubled man. Surrounded by his own squad of thick bodyguards, he was camping out under an alias at Gurney's Inn in Montauk, Long Island. And when Mouw dug deeper and learned the story behind Fat Angelo's sudden, fearful flight, he found himself caught up in a mystery that left him shaken too.

**11**

"FAT ANGE," WENT THE LONGTIME BERGIN JOKE, "NEVER SAT
down for a meal he didn't like—or ever paid for." And as
Mouw discovered, after a rapid series of crash meetings
with his informants as he tried to piece together the events
leading to Ruggiero's sudden attack of nerves, this crisis,
too, had been set in motion by the promise of a free lunch.

It all started after Fritzi Giovanelli, an expansive Genovese capo who was celebrated in the mob for his valuable
ties into the Democratic machine, had invited Ruggiero to a
meal at an Italian restaurant on Court Street in downtown
Brooklyn. "I know the chef. We'll eat like kings," Fritzi had
urged. He had also promised, one informant noted snidely,
"On me."

Ruggiero arrived early and was busy studying the menu
when Giovanelli, followed by two of his men, strode to the
table. Immediately he handed his guest a manila envelope.

"With my compliments," said Fritzi as he took his seat,
according to the story that was passed on to the FBI.

Ruggiero, taken aback, put down the menu and looked
inside the envelope. There were about thirty pages, and on

the first page was the heading "In the matter of the application of the United States of America for an order authorizing the interception of oral communications . . ." When Ruggiero read on, he saw his name and the address of his home in Cedarhurst.

Fat Ange, for once, didn't stay for lunch.

Later that afternoon, with still another informant describing the scene for the FBI, a starkly pale Ruggiero was in the Bergin, frantically waving the document about and muttering to anyone who would listen, "I'm fucked. I'm really fucked." He called his wife from the club and told her to leave home immediately, and then Ruggiero—"shaking like a three-hundred-pound tub of Jell-O," said the amused informant—hurried off to Montauk. But not before he gave the balled-up document to one of his boys for safekeeping. Though which one, the informant apologized, was not clear.

Mouw received these reports and, as an agent recalled, "It was like watching a man take a blow to the gut." Or as Mouw himself later put it, "It was as if I had been personally betrayed." Yet by all accounts he acted quickly. He called an emergency meeting of his inner circle, and for once he was unable to contain the dimensions of his anger. How could they have gotten a copy of our authorization? he roared. Where was the leak? In the U.S. Attorney's office? In the judge's chambers? Or maybe—and now his voice rattled as if just articulating the possibility was a torment—in the Bureau? Perhaps even in our squad? He let that sink in. Then he issued an order: "Find that document. Do whatever you have to do. Pay whatever you have to pay. But I want that document. It's our only clue to the leak."

The precise amount that was paid was a closely held secret. But it was a matter of record that a blue slip signed by Special Supervisory Agent Bruce Mouw was hand-delivered to the attention of an obliging vice president at the Rego Park, Queens, branch of Citibank. The banker, who had been through the drill before, promptly cut a cashier's check (for somewhere between five and ten thousand dollars, suggested those who should know) with funds drawn from the Bureau's Field Service Account. Then he placed the check, signed with his signature, in a plain white envelope and gave it to the waiting messenger, who rushed back to the squad. Later that night, the cashier's check was handed to a Top Echelon informant as he sat having a room service steak dinner in a midtown hotel with the Twins.

Mouw, forgoing his own dinner, remained in his office waiting for their report. It was late when the call finally came, and he was on edge. But the news was promising. According to the TE, the Ruggiero wire authorization document had made its way intact—miracle of miracles! Mouw rejoiced—to a Bergin soldier. The TE was positive the papers were in Anthony Moscatiello's home in Howard Beach. Precisely where, he wasn't quite sure. But, he had suggested helpfully as he pocketed the check, if the FBI looked carefully . . .

"That you can bank on," Mouw told the Twins.

Eddie Woods, a short, compact agent who dressed like a dark-suited diplomat and whose every utterance seemed to be chiseled with an impressive grammatical precision, led the raid. By all accounts, his team tore the Moscatiello house apart. Of course, part of the problem was the agents couldn't reveal what they were really looking for. That might have blown the TE. According to the search warrant presented to the Moscatiellos, they were hunting for a cache of Walther PPKs that had been taken during a heist at JFK.

"Don't know any Walter," insisted Moscatiello straight-faced, as he went off to the privacy of his kitchen to phone his lawyer.

Quite quickly, to the surprise of all the agents involved, two of the guns were found in a cardboard box on the floor of a basement closet.

"How did those get there?" wondered Moscatiello, and then hurried back to the kitchen to call his lawyer once again.

The search party just pressed on. They kept at it for hours, until Woods, standing on a chair, carefully unwound the insulating tape holding two sections of an asbestos-covered ceiling heating duct together, stuck his hand inside, and came out with a thick wad of papers.

"I got it, gentlemen," he announced quietly after making sure that Moscatiello and his wife were out of earshot.

But it was not until Woods was putting the document into a plastic evidence bag that he had the opportunity to look carefully at the pages. Only then, in a terrible instant, did he realize just what it was that he had found.

"We've got a big problem," a somber Mouw confided to his inner circle in a locked-door meeting in his office later that day. The authorization document that had made its way to Ruggiero, he revealed, wasn't a photocopy. It wasn't the judge's typewritten original either. Nor could it have been taken from the U.S. Attorney's office.

Now his voice grew quieter, and his face rigid. It was the *handwritten* draft affidavit FBI agent Donald McCormick had put together for the squad's secretary to type. It could only have been stolen from one place—C-16's own files.

"Jesus," moaned Kurins. And, he would recall, he suddenly felt like getting very rough with someone.

Mouw, however, appeared to become more relaxed now that he had shared his revelation. He went on almost solicitously, in that odd, infuriatingly soft voice of his; it was as if he already had risen above—and beyond—the fray.

He had interviewed McCormick and the typist, he said. Both were, as expected, devastated. They insisted they had no idea how someone could have managed to walk off with the pages. And Mouw, "for what it's worth," he said, believed them. Still, he had conferred with Bonavolonta and the next morning a Bureau hypnotist would be arriving on the first shuttle from Washington. Perhaps that might stir some memories. Any other suggestions? he asked absently. He might just as well have been asking if they liked his tie.

"When we find the thief," spoke a voice from the back of the room, "we kill him."

"No," Mouw said, only now with a sudden icy deliberateness, *"I* kill him."

But they never found the thief. The hypnotist, to everyone's great annoyance, especially a frazzled McCormick, insisted on spending a week with the squad. In the end, he didn't even produce a hint of a lead. Naturally, the document was examined for fingerprints, and that too was a bit of a fiasco. Ruggiero seemed to have shared the pages with half the Gambino Family. As for Fritzi Giovanelli, the capo who had given the document to Fat Ange, he maintained that he had found the handwritten pages lying abandoned on the counter of a bar near the squad's office; and nothing the squad threatened or cajoled could shake him from that preposterous tale.

Then for an intense spell, all the team's angry attention seemed to focus on two likely traitors. One was a former agent who had helped transcribe the tapes recorded by the wiretap at Ruggiero's Howard Beach phone. His career in the Bureau had come to an abrupt end a month before after he was accused of molesting several of the players on the Little League team he coached on weekends. He might very well have had an opportunity to poke through C-16's files, and perhaps his bitterness over his snap dismissal was motive enough, some members of the team suggested. There was also an agent on the Genovese squad just down the hall from C-16 who had been recently fired. This veteran had had a run of bad luck in Atlantic City, and then got caught trying to play catch-up with some of his squad's informant funds. Perhaps he had been desperate enough to sell information, went the theory. Yet after a while, Mouw decided that these were dead ends too.

All he could do was put all the small clues he gathered into a new file. As the weeks went by, he added snippets of gossip, unproven suspicions, wild theories. He kept the Mole File locked in his office. It was a catalogue of his worst fears.

Even though he was not a suspect, Donnie McCormick, a freckle-faced father of five, seemed to have never-ending troubles. Now Angelo Ruggiero wanted to kill him. According to a report made by an always reliable TE, Ruggiero had read Agent McCormick's signature on the last line of the bugging authorization, and now he wanted revenge. He seemed to hold McCormick personally responsible. "I'm gonna kill that fuck McCormick! I swear I'm gonna kill him," Ruggiero had vowed wildly in the Bergin. "He broke into my house." And, said the informant, there was no reason to doubt Ruggiero's commitment. He had killed for smaller reasons in the past.

This cautionary piece of intelligence made its way to the team just as they were deep into their frustrating search for the traitor. It was a time when Mouw's energies were being pushed to an emotional edge. And perhaps that helped to explain his response. But the truth was, Mouw had been waiting for a fight. Someone had stolen *his* files. It was all becoming very personal.

When Ruggiero's threat was repeated to Mouw and Frankie Spero asked, "What now, boss?" Mouw's decision was almost automatic. "I'll take care of this," he said.

There was, he realized, little point in tracking down Ruggiero. That could take days; and, no small concern, in the churning mind of a psychopath like Fat Ange, a warning could be perversely transformed into a dare. He would commit the murder just to make a point. Mouw decided it would be more effective to speak to Ruggiero's capo. Besides, the time had come for him to confront John Gotti.

It was not quite ten in the morning when he rang the doorbell in Howard Beach, so Mouw knew he would catch Gotti at home. Sure, Johnny Boy would still be in bed, but that wasn't his problem.

Victoria Gotti thought it was. She answered the door and her face did not register anything when Mouw flashed his FBI credentials. My husband's sleeping, she explained flatly. If you don't have a warrant, maybe you had better come back another time. And, Mouw noticed, she didn't have a baseball bat this time. But there was a Rottweiler by her side, and the dog was already straining at the leash and growling deeply. The animal seemed ready to attack.

Mouw made a gun out of his hand and pointed it at the dog. *"Bang!"* he shot out loudly. *"Bang! Bang!"*

All at once the Rottweiler got a confused look on its face and then sat down on its haunches. Quietly. That was when Victoria Gotti decided to wake up her husband.

After a while, Gotti came to the door. He was in his pajamas and slippers, a silk paisley robe wrapped around him. Mouw was still standing in the doorway. The dog was by his side, and he was petting it.

It was a short conversation. Gotti listened impassively while Mouw said he knew all about Ruggiero's plan to kill an FBI agent.

"People say a lot of crazy things," suggested Gotti with a shrug. "Don't mean shit."

Mouw, however, was beyond playing around. The moment was intense and his words had an angry resonance. He told Gotti: "If anything happens to one of my men. If they get a scratch on their face. Anything. I'm going to hold you personally responsible. Something happens to anyone on my squad, I'm coming to get you. Forget the FBI. It'll just be Bruce Mouw coming after John Gotti. And believe me, John, you won't like that."

Gotti took it all in, his hands deep into the pockets of his robe. His face showed nothing. When Mouw was finished, he gave a small nod. "Your men got nothing to worry about," he said.

Mouw nodded back. An agreement had been reached. He turned from the house and started walking toward his car.

But Gotti called after him. "Hey, Mouw," he yelled, "you might as well take the goddamn dog with you. It stays here, I'm gonna kill the useless mutt."

Mouw didn't look back.

# 12

OTHER, UNFORESEEN CONSEQUENCES OF THE RUGGIERO BUGS also began to build ominously. Mouw had launched his operation with only the tactical hope of gathering the intelligence necessary to move against the Bergin loan-sharking and gambling enterprises, but he soon discovered something else. The crew was dealing drugs.

The evidence was all over the tapes. Sometimes Ruggiero would attempt to be careful, talking in an oblique, disconnected way about "bags of stuff." Or "furniture." Or even "shipments" and "mortgage payments." Other times, right on the phone with the FBI listening in, he would talk about handling "H." One evening a Jersey dealer came to dinner, and with the kids sitting at the table and the wife busy serving platters of spaghetti and meatballs, the dealer cheerfully announced, "I got thirty things of heroin. That's why I'm here."

Surveillance reports completed the picture. Mouw's men tailed Ruggiero and Johnny Carneglia to New Jersey, where in a hectic evening the pair managed to visit three different drug traffickers. On another afternoon, they caught Fat Ange making the rounds by himself as he checked in at a handful of drug-cutting dens throughout Queens. And the agents spent a lot of time snapping photographs of drug dealers leaving the Cedarhurst home with carefully wrapped packages nestled under their arms.

By the spring of 1982, a different pace, a different mood had taken over the C-16 team. For the first time, they felt they were finally closing in on their prey. It was a giddy, anticipatory time. The Twins, as if suddenly liberated, snuck in early one morning and devilishly put pepper in Mouw's pipe tobacco. To everyone's complete astonishment, this provoked only a rare smile from their boss. In fact, so steady was his confidence as the case against the Bergin crew progressed that Mouw even volunteered to share some of the details with Bonavolonta.

"Gotti?" Bonavolonta asked immediately.

"We got Ruggiero, Johnny Carneglia, Gene Gotti—all of them cold," Mouw said.

"What about John?" demanded Bonavolonta.

"Not yet," Mouw said. "We know he's involved. They wouldn't be dealing without his permission. But so far we can't prove it."

But could Paul Castellano?

That was the troubling question that was weighing heavily on the minds of many of the Bergin crew once they learned the Feds had bugged the talkative Quack-Quack's home. Because Big Paul had a simple, well-known Family rule. He called it his First Commandment: If you dealt, you died.

It wasn't a moral issue with the Don. It was a pragmatic one. He knew if one of his men got caught dealing *babania,* the soldier would be facing a life sentence. Wiseguys had become informants for a lot less reason. It would be better for the Gambino Family in the long run, he announced, to pass up the quick fortune that could be made trafficking dope.

It was his rule, and therefore it was inviolable. When Peter Tambone, a sixty-two-year-old grandfather, was fingered as a dealer by two soldiers from another Family,

Castellano convened a Commission meeting. On April 22, 1982, the heads of the Families met to decide Little Pete's fate. "Clip him," said Castellano without hesitation.

The Bergin crew knew their boss's edict. They knew about Little Pete's predicament. But they also knew they were pulling in at least three million dollars a month moving smack. They kept on dealing, and hoping they would never get caught.

So when Ruggiero had learned his house was bugged, he panicked. He fled to Montauk, surrounded himself with bodyguards, and was wild enough to talk about killing the agent who had drafted the intercept authorization. He was scared to death, but not of the FBI. He started thinking about Big Paul and telling people, "Maybe it's time to turn the tide."

It only got worse when, in the winter of 1983, a series of indictments based on hundreds of hours of FBI tapes were issued. Angelo Ruggiero, John Carneglia, and Gene Gotti were identified as the "organizers, supervisors and managers" of a heroin ring. John Gotti was not charged.

But Paul Castellano was still suspicious. He sent word to Ruggiero that as soon as the government made the tapes available to the lawyers, he wanted to hear them. And he told John Gotti, "Listen, Johnny, you'd better prove that you weren't involved."

All of which got Gotti thinking, one of his boys told the FBI, it was either kill or be killed.

Mouw, sitting behind his desk in his sixth-floor office on Queens Boulevard, found himself contemplating with some alarm what his team had set in motion. As he worked late one night, surrounded by his transcripts, his files, and a mayhem of suspicions, he began, he recalled, "to hear the winds of war whistling across the city."

In the tense, preoccupied months that followed the indictments, a small item ran in the papers, and it went unnoticed by both Bruce Mouw and John Gotti. It was a Metro Brief, and it told a tragic story. On the rainy afternoon of December 3, 1984, William Peist, a thirty-nine-year-old off-duty police detective, had agreed to drive his wife and mother-in-law to St. Barbara's Greek Orthodox Church in Manhattan. It was the eve of the church's name day and the two women were eager to join in the celebration.

They were driving in from Brooklyn, and as they crossed the rain-slicked Manhattan Bridge, their car stalled. Detective Peist tried to start the engine, but it wouldn't turn over. The cars backed up behind him were honking, so he decided it would be helpful to arrange flares around his Plymouth. A while back he had put a set in the car's trunk in anticipation of just such an emergency.

He got out and started walking in the rain to the rear of his car. At precisely that moment, a van pulled out impatiently from the lane of vehicles lined behind his Plymouth and sped forward. Suddenly, the driver saw Peist and tried to brake, but on the slippery roadway there was no traction. The van skidded into Peist.

That evening doctors at New York University Medical Center amputated his left foot up to the ankle.

That was where the newspaper account ended.

A follow-up story, if there had been one, would have reported that before the winter was over there would be two more operations. William Peist's leg was removed up to nearly his thigh. Six months would be spent in a body cast stretching to his waist.

It was while he was recovering at the NYU hospital that Inspector Aaron Rosenthal, his commanding officer from the Public Morals Division, came to see him. "How you doing, Billy?" he asked. It was, he immediately realized, a pretty stupid question.

"Getting by," Peist said.

"Sure." But Rosenthal didn't see how.

"You know, I'm going to get back on the job," Peist announced.

"Good for you, Billy." But don't count on it. The doctors had told him Peist would be lucky if he ever walked again.

"I will. You'll see. Though I guess it won't be to PMD. Figure they'll give me some sort of desk job."

"Probably." Rosenthal, who had a large and generous heart, figured it would be polite to play along. "Like what?"

"Oh," said Peist quickly, "I've been giving that some thought. Not much else for me to do." He laughed at himself. Then he said, "I been thinking a lot about Intelligence. I might really like that. The Intelligence squad just might be my ticket."

# 13

THE FUNERAL PARLOR HAD ONCE BEEN A TENEMENT. LIKE THE other narrow, slightly listing brick buildings on the block, it had been built, he estimated, at the turn of the century. In those days, it must have overflowed with the hectic lives of dozens of immigrant families: children bouncing balls off the stone stoop, fresh wash hanging across the fire escapes, the sweet smell of simmering tomato sauce wafting through the tin-ceilinged hallways. Or so Andy Kurins, crouching in the rear of his Dodge van, sketched the scene in his mind. It was an old watcher's trick. Boredom, not fear, was the worst enemy.

He had pulled into the parking space on Spring Street on the northern fringes of Little Italy at just after ten that morning. He was hours early, but experience had taught him to worry. What if he couldn't find a parking space? What if they made his van? What if his sight lines were obstructed? On the drive down to the city from his home in Connecticut, I-95 glistening for a brief moment when the weak December sun rose and then seemed to set immediately as the winter sky went quickly gray, he had found himself reciting the *what ifs* to himself with growing apprehension. The prospects suddenly seemed so dubious that he realized he might as well have been back zooming at three thousand feet, heading into Cambodia. And, as if on cue, an old flyboy's wisdom loomed once more as a comforting Major Truth: Time spent in preparation is not time wasted.

So, he was heartened when he realized that he had pulled into the city early enough to pick up a hefty sandwich to go from the Second Avenue Deli. Then he continued downtown and, more good timing, arrived in Little Italy just as alternate side of the street parking was taking effect. Quickly, he found a perfectly legal spot for his van that not only offered a direct view of the funeral parlor, but was also a prudent two blocks away. But all that had been accomplished hours ago. It was now nearly noon. His pastrami sandwich was long gone, and show time was still far off. He had no choice but to try to keep busy.

He parted the rear curtains—his wife Sharon's handiwork—another inch and continued his scrutiny. He decided that the building's crumbling facade must have only recently been given a coat of white paint, and that someone was fighting a losing battle. A dusting of city soot had already left its mark. The mortuary, he noticed, was in what had been the tenement's basement; he imagined that a catacomb of tiny apartments had been demolished to create the space. Nevertheless, the building, he joked feebly to himself, had found a new life. And after a while he found himself, tired and with time on his hands, pursuing a somewhat philosophical train of thought. Everybody wants to come home to die. The wiseguys spend a lifetime clawing their way out of their old neighborhoods and into the promised lands of suburban splendor, only to insist that on dying they return for a last good-bye to the scenes of their innocent—or at least relatively so—youth. Just as, he realized with a sudden shiver, he would want to be buried in Short Ridge, Indiana, a million miles away from a life that, to his constant astonishment, had become filled with a mortgage, and tuition bills, and wiseguys.

He did not like where these musings were taking him, so,

always the disciplined soldier, he simply stopped them. He returned once more to his mission. The entrance to the funeral parlor, he saw through his three-hundred-millimeter lens, was three steps below the sidewalk. He aimed his camera at a pair of amber, rippled glass doors. He had little doubt that there would be, as he had promised Mouw, quite a crowd. It was a rare intelligence opportunity. The entire Gambino Family, not to mention *amicas nostrum* from the four other New York divisions, would emerge from the shadows long enough to make a respectful appearance at this wake. All the wiseguys would come to say good-bye to Aniello Dellacroce.

By two o'clock, the first few somber faces from the Bergin crew began to arrive. Next, a black limousine pulled up. Dellacroce's common-law wife, Rosemarie, was helped from the rear seat and escorted down the steps by two huge footmen, one gingerly holding on to each elbow. Her daughter, Sandy Grillo, the wife of Ernie Grillo, a Family member doing time for a murder rap, and, by common knowledge, Dellacroce's only soft spot, followed. No one escorted her, or, Kurins thought, dared. Even in mourning she was, he observed with a keen eye as he snapped away, quite regal: jet black hair, cat eyes wet with tears, a delicate, pale complexion. A true Mafia princess. Soon, the entire street was jammed. On this frigid, leaden gray afternoon, December 4, 1985, just two days after the Gambino Family underboss had succumbed to cancer at seventy-one while sleeping in his bed at Mary Immaculate Hospital in Queens, they all came. The crowd of mourners filled the subterranean doorwell, continued up the steps, and in a snaking but orderly line, down the block and around the corner.

Kurins finished one roll of film and without pause added another. Yet, oddly enough, as he worked away, he grew quite disturbed. Angry, even. He knew Mouw would be angry too. He put off checking in for as long as possible.

"Alpha-Kilo to base," he finally broadcast over his walkie-talkie.

Mouw answered immediately, "Base here." And he barked, "Where you been, Andy? What's going down?"

"It's a mob scene," Kurins announced, delivering the line he had rehearsed.

But Mouw knew his troops. "What's wrong, Andy?"

"Bruce, we got company."

To which Mouw sneered, "For a change." It was a rare display of sarcasm; the boss really must be ticked off, Kurins thought.

Kurins had seen the first car arrive around four and within the hour they were all in place. Dutifully, he made his report to Mouw. The NYPD was double-parked across the street from the funeral parlor in a black sedan that had four whiplike aerials jutting from its rear. "Might as well have sent the Goodyear blimp!" Kurins exclaimed. The State Organized Crime Task Force guys had not one, but two cars constantly driving around the block, with two brazen madmen aiming their long-lensed cameras through rolled-down windows. Why they thought such frantic behavior would be more surreptitious than simply double-parking was, Kurins declared, anybody's guess. But the prize, he said, went to the Manhattan D.A.'s squad. They had a big, fat van parked directly in front of a fire hydrant just a yard from the mortuary door.

"We got more cameras clicking here than at a Hollywood opening," Kurins said. "That's what's going down, Bruce."

Mouw said something, but the transmission was garbled. When Kurins asked him to repeat, all he heard was static. The link had gone dead.

But as Kurins sat in the van, the more he thought about it, the more he grew certain that he had heard his boss's sign-off message. And that it had consisted of three distinct words: "Shit! Shit! Shit!"

Mouw's frustrated, even fierce mood had been building for a long time. By the afternoon of Dellacroce's wake, he had spent an angry year watching prosecutors rush up to the evening news microphones to announce their latest headline-grabbing forays in the war against the mob. And by now, to his way of looking at things, the competition among law enforcement agencies had gone way beyond territorial disputes. Or grandstanding. Or politics. It had become, Mouw and his team were firmly convinced, reckless. Years of work were being jeopardized. And, much more unforgivable, so were lives.

In Mouw's orderly, very patient world, it looked like this. His troops, after all the false starts, were now on the offensive. The Ruggiero bug had already produced unexpected results—and a handful of indictments against the core heroin traffickers. Next, as he had envisioned in his original battle plan, C-16 had begun working its way up the Gambino Family pyramid. In March 1983, the Techies had snuck past the Doberman pinschers and the complex alarm system that protected Paul Castellano's house on Todt Hill on Staten Island and had planted microphones in the Boss of Bosses' living and dining rooms. Then, while still busy analyzing the three thousand pages of transcripts the Castellano bugs had generated, the squad had another success. For two fruitful months, starting in June 1985, the mikes had gone "up" in Neil Dellacroce's sickroom in his house on West Fingerboard Road on Staten Island. An invisible net, Mouw felt, had been cast over the key players of the Gambino Family. It would only be a matter of time before C-16 collected all the evidence it needed, and then, triumphant, hauled in the harvest.

But the prosecutors had refused to wait.

In February 1984, the Manhattan Organized Crime Strike Force had moved against Roy DeMeo, a psychopathic Gambino Family capo who ran a profitable luxury car-theft ring; the thirty-seven people he had ordered killed were, he apparently felt, just part of the price of doing business. Yet, to the dismay of many in the Bureau, Paul Castellano's name had been tacked on almost coincidentally to the indictment. The Family head was charged with profiting from the stolen cars and with having knowledge of the murders the DeMeo crew had committed. Which, went the uneasy consensus of the C-16 team, was no doubt true—but also was no doubt going to be difficult to prove.

Not long after that, a squad of IRS agents arrested Neil Dellacroce at the Ravenite Social Club. They found the frail underboss hiding in the toilet. But despite his fears, the FBI was less than sanguine about the eventual outcome of the case. The U.S. Tax Court had ruled just a month earlier that the IRS had incorrectly assessed Dellacroce's taxes on an unreported bribe.

Then, in February 1985, Rudolph Giuliani, the calculatingly ambitious U.S. Attorney in Manhattan, announced to carefully orchestrated fanfare the indictments of the bosses and underbosses of the five New York Families. They were charged with operating an illegal RICO enterprise—the Commission. It was a complex, wide-ranging case and the Bureau—including C-16—was cooperating with Giuliani's office. But still, the grumbling, warily articulated feeling among Mouw's men was that Giuliani had moved too quickly against Castellano and Dellacroce. A better case was still to be built.

Yet these indictments, however precipitous or unpredictable in their ultimate results, were, Mouw and his team believed, at worst only small setbacks in their attack on the Gambinos. Win or lose, C-16 would still have a chance to present its cases—airtight FBI cases—against the Family. But then, as the team moved forward, they learned about a grand jury probe by an assistant U.S. Attorney in Brooklyn, Diane Giacalone, that threatened to undermine irrevocably all they had so far done. Her target was the Bergin crew.

At first, C-16 tried to discourage Giacalone. Joe O'Brien, full of Irish charm, was sent on a mission to placate her. In between the broad smiles and the rogue's blarney, he did his best to convince her of the efficacy of Mouw's operational philosophy—patience. Wait until there's a solid case, then take it to the grand jury, he counseled. When this line of reasoning failed to impress Giacalone, Mouw tried a less subtle approach; he was, after all his years in the Bureau, no stranger to bureaucratic battles. At his urging, Edward McDonald, chief of the Organized Crime Strike Force in the Eastern District, wrote an October 23, 1984, memo to Giacalone's superiors in the Justice Department. Her case, he flatly stated, had "little likelihood of success." When she still plowed ahead, he waited a few months and then fired his next rocket. This second confidential memo, written on March 8, 1985, was harsher than the first, and therefore even more unprecedented. McDonald warned that Giacalone's case "was especially weak." Further, if the Bergin crew was acquitted, and he was confident that they might very well be, they could be "immunized" against future RICO prosecutions. Under federal double jeopardy statutes, they could not be tried for the same enterprise crimes again.

That was Mouw's great fear. After having climbed so far up a steep and slippery mountain, his team would have to start again at the base.

But Giacalone would not be deterred; and, more troublesome, her superiors were not inclined to pull her back. She was a brittlely thin, intense woman, a native of Ozone Park, Queens, an Italian by birth and, she would boast, by temperament. She marched into each encounter, whether in or out of the courtroom, determined to give as good as she got. When one frustrated member of C-16, James Abbott, appeared in her office to proclaim, "If you were a man, I'd hit you in the face," she jumped up from her desk. "Don't let that stop you," she challenged. "Take your best shot." And to her credit, no one doubted that she was less than serious.

Another bit of gossip that made its way around the Brooklyn courthouse insisted that as a schoolgirl she had had to pass the Bergin on her way to Our Lady of Wisdom Academy. Each day she was made to suffer a barrage of the wiseguys' taunts and now she was out for revenge. And while the story might be apocryphal, the simple fact that it was circulated was revelatory. People found it necessary to look for explanations for her zeal. For, even to her friends and supportive colleagues, Giacalone was "driven," a "workaholic"; while to the C-16 squad, she was, as more than one agent would complain, "out of control." Mouw, by nature a gentleman, would make sure to take a calming breath when asked about her; and then, very tactfully, suggest, "Diane had her way of doing things. We had ours."

C-16 refused to cooperate with her as she, despite protests, continued to present her case to the grand jury. The Ruggiero tapes, as required by law, had already been turned over to the defendants' lawyers, but the Bureau refused to share the transcripts with Giacalone. "Security issues" was the vague but adamant explanation offered to the U.S. Attorney's office. And Mouw, his head already at sea with suspicions, never even considered disclosing the existence of the Dellacroce bug. So what if the underboss was her lead target? It was not an FBI case.

But Giacalone persisted. She was determined to get her indictment. She relied on city police detectives, Drug Enforcement agents, and even postal inspectors. On March 25, 1985, a sealed indictment, *United States of America v. Aniello Dellacroce, et al.*, was voted against the Gambino Family underboss and nine of his men.

Dellacroce was in the hospital at the time for chemotherapy treatments; it was his third federal charge in five months. On March 28, city detectives and DEA agents began rounding up the others. It was four in the morning when they hit the Bergin, and they found three of their targets playing cards. John Gotti, his younger brother Gene, and their longtime buddy Willie Boy Johnson were sitting around a table in the back room.

"What'd we do?" Gotti asked innocently.

"Your crimes have caught up with you," solemnly replied DEA agent Edward Magnuson.

That just cracked the guys up. But within hours, by the time the arraignment and bail hearings were completed later in the day, nobody was laughing anymore. Not John Gotti. Not Willie Boy Johnson. And certainly not Bruce Mouw and his team.

# 14

THE PROCEEDINGS IN JUDGE EUGENE H. NICKERSON'S wood-paneled courtroom in Brooklyn had all gone pretty routinely. Dellacroce, still in his hospital bed, pled not guilty by telephone. Anthony "Tony Roach" Rampino, a cadaverous, hollow-cheeked member of the Bergin crew, was released to the facility where he had been arrested—a Bronx heroin detoxification center. John Gotti, his brother, and the others were all released on bail. And then it was Willie Boy Johnson's turn. Giacalone told the judge that he should be jailed immediately. "No conditions of bail would secure his appearance," she said.

Members of the C-16 team watching from the back of the courtroom were stunned. It was one thing to indict one of their Top Echelon informants. But it was another, very dangerous thing to reveal his role. "She'd never go that far," Mouw had predicted just days earlier.

But then she did. Giacalone looked up at Judge Nickerson and, her voice steady, announced, "The reason is that Mr. Johnson has been an informant for the Federal Bureau of

Investigation for a period of over fifteen years, including a period up through the present time."

John Gotti turned toward Johnson. He spoke quietly, in almost a whisper, a hiss through clenched teeth: "So you're the reason we're here, huh?"

Willie Boy did not answer. He continued to look straight at the judge, his hands clenched very tightly. Tattooed on the knuckles of one fist was the word "True"; on the other was the word "Love." He was fifty-one years old, a former boxer, a man the Family used when they wanted to teach somebody a lesson. And he could not stop shaking.

Giacalone continued without pause. She told the judge she had explained to Mr. Johnson that identifying him as an informer "was a legal issue that we had resolved reluctantly in this way." Earlier in the day, she said, she had offered him the opportunity to enter the Witness Protection Program. He had refused.

He had also refused to testify.

"I will be killed," he said. "My family will be slaughtered."

Then it was the judge's turn to ask questions. "Did you give information to the FBI about Messrs. Gotti and those?"

"No, sir," said Willie Boy firmly.

The judge pressed. "You never mentioned Mr. Gotti?"

"No, sir," he answered, although less convincingly this time. After a moment, as if a faint memory was just beginning to surface, he added, "I might have mentioned the name. Yeah. Mr. Gotti. They mentioned it to me."

But Willie Boy still refused to testify.

Judge Nickerson remained concerned for his safety. "It would be irresponsible of me, it seems," he ruled, "to release him on bail . . . and so I order his detention."

Willie Boy was sent to the Metropolitan Correctional Center in Manhattan. He was kept away from the other prisoners and confined to his cell for twenty-three and a half hours a day.

He still refused to talk.

But Mouw knew it hardly mattered. Giacalone had gone

too far. "Whether she wins or loses the case, she's given Willie Boy a death sentence," he told members of his team.

It was a very depressing time. Mouw began jogging longer distances. He took up tennis again and found himself returning shots with a previously unimagined ferocity. He started going with a new girlfriend who, for reasons he never understood or even asked about, seemed always to be dressed in cowboy clothes. But he could not shake his mood. He felt besieged. Wiretaps had been leaked. Affidavits had been stolen from his files. Indictments had been rushed. And now his informants had been betrayed.

On his orders, C-16's operational detachment from the rest of law enforcement intensified. And the truth was, the team preferred it that way.

Yet all the while, in those frustrating and combative months before the Dellacroce wake, the FBI microphones continued to do their job: They listened. There was one awkward moment which, if some of the members of the squad had had their way, would have given them a small last laugh on Giacalone. Judge Nickerson had announced that since Dellacroce was too sick to travel to Brooklyn for a pretrial hearing, he would bring his court to the underboss's house. Let's get her on tape, they urged. That'll really drive her up the wall. But Mouw showed great restraint. Besides, he explained, they would also be secretly recording a federal judge, and that was another matter. He ordered the microphones shut off as Dellacroce, clad in white embroidered pajamas and propped up on his king-size bed, began his testimony.

But the bug had been "up" when Angelo Ruggiero and John Gotti came on June 8, 1985, to confer with their ghostly pale and fragile underboss. Their concern was the Ruggiero heroin tapes. They had been released to Ruggiero's attorneys and Big Paul Castellano still wanted them.

"If you two never bother with me again . . . I ain't givin' them tapes up. I can't," insisted Fat Angelo.

Gotti's voice was even. "While he's the Boss, you have to do what he tells you."

"You don't understand La Cosa Nostra," Dellacroce lectured from his sickbed.

"Angelo, what does 'Cosa Nostra' mean?" Gotti demanded, playing along.

But it was the old man who answered: " 'Cosa Nostra' means that the Boss is your Boss."

Ruggiero was beyond all that. If Castellano got the tapes and heard he was dealing drugs, Big Paul would have him killed immediately. Or maybe first he would whack Gotti. Then him.

"I won't do that," Ruggiero announced firmly.

"Forget about it," Dellacroce warned.

"I won't do that," Ruggiero repeated.

Finally, Dellacroce just sounded weary. He was seventy-one years old, the chemotherapy had taken its toll and, he had to realize, was still not doing enough. "I've been tellin' Paul, 'The guy can't give you the tapes because his family is on there,' " he explained to Ruggiero and Gotti. "I've been trying to make you get away with these tapes, but Jesus Christ Almighty, I can't stop the guy from always bringin' it up. Unless I tell the guy, 'Why don't you go fuck yourself?' "

No one spoke for a moment. Until Dellacroce, his voice suddenly stronger, deliberate even, went on, "Then we know what we got to do then. We . . ." And then he stumbled; it was if he was daunted by what he was about to say. But in an instant he continued, "We go and roll it up and go to war."

After he said it, he tried to take it back. His tone was conciliatory. "Let's wait. Let's take it easy. That's the last stage."

But it was too late to retreat, he realized. "If it has to come to that, it'll come to that," he predicted.

Gotti and Ruggiero agreed.

And so did Mouw when he heard the tape the next day.

But Castellano was oddly unaware. Later, there would be many theories offered for Big Paul's seeming unconcern. Certainly, he was preoccupied with his own problems. Two indictments, after all, were pending against him. And now that he had been notified by the government that his house had been bugged, he had still another genuine worry. "I must've said so many things," he moaned to friends. Then there was also his relationship with his wife's Colombian kitchen maid. Not only was he having an affair with Gloria Olarte, but he had also gone through the trouble of having a penile implant to make it all possible. A further distracting complication: He was in love with her. Or, another explanation: Perhaps he simply thought he didn't need to trouble himself about John Gotti. The two men had met on June 12 to discuss "a peaceful transition" after Dellacroce died. It could have been that Big Paul thought he could tell Johnny Boy he was planning to close the Ravenite, decimate Neil's crew, and that would be that. Or maybe Castellano felt he could simply do as he pleased. He was head of the Gambino Family, the Boss of Bosses.

But whatever the reason, on the day of Aniello Dellacroce's wake, Paul Castellano made a grave miscalculation. And it was Andy Kurins who first brought the ill-timed transgression to Bruce Mouw's attention. The information, as Kurins remembered it, was shared the day after the wake.

"So who'd you catch yesterday?" Mouw asked when Kurins, carrying a stack of freshly developed prints, walked into his office.

"Wrong question," said Kurins.

Mouw just gave him a look. He had no times for games.

"It wasn't who was there that's so interesting," Kurins said. "It's who wasn't—Castellano didn't show."

"The fool," Mouw said.

But that was small criticism compared to what John Gotti was saying, according to informants' reports, about the head of his Family. "I told you the fuckin' guy's a bum," he declared to anyone who would listen. "He don't even come to his own underboss's funeral."

There was still another clue that "the last stage," as Dellacroce had presciently predicted it from his sickbed, was getting closer. At the time, however, it was simply accepted by the FBI as one more stray piece of intelligence to add to its growing file on John Gotti: a small entry, and a comical, even farcical one at that.

It seemed that three nights after Dellacroce was buried, at about one in the morning, Gotti's black Mercedes 500 SEL pulled up in front of the Barbizon Plaza Hotel on Lexington Avenue in Manhattan. While he waited in the backseat with a black-haired woman, his bodyguards, Iggy Alogna and Dominick Pizzonia, went into the hotel.

"I want a room," Pizzonia told the desk clerk, according to the interview the clerk later had with the FBI.

"Shall I put that on your credit card, sir?"

"No," Pizzonia said. "Cash." And just to make sure the clerk understood, Iggy Alogna approached the desk and glowered.

"Cash it is," agreed the clerk quickly. "Now if you'll just fill out this registration form, sir." The clerk pushed the form across the counter.

"No," Pizzonia said. He pushed the form right back.

"We ain't signing nothing," Alogna said. He now stood shoulder to shoulder with his buddy Dominick. The clerk might just as well have been facing a wall.

But he was persistent. "I'm sorry, sir. It's hotel policy. If you'll just fill out the registration form." Once again, he pushed the form across the counter.

And once again, Pizzonia pushed it back. "I won't fill out nothing."

To which Alogna added, "This is America. We don't have to fill out nothing." He ripped the card in half and let the pieces fall to the lobby carpet.

That was when the clerk pressed a silent alarm and the night security chief, a former homicide detective, hurried over. He took one look at the two bruisers by the front desk and thought to himself, as he later told the FBI, "This is gonna make my day." He was giving them a hard time, telling them very politely how there were hotel rules they had to follow, and they were going on with loud indignation about how this was America, when John Gotti and the woman walked into the lobby.

"What the fuck is going on?" Gotti demanded of his boys.

Pizzonia tried to explain but Gotti cut him dead. "Just sign your fuckin' name to the fuckin' sheet. What's the big fuckin' deal?"

And so Pizzonia did. Although, as the FBI later learned, he gave, perhaps out of habit, a false address.

The desk clerk handed Pizzonia the key. Pizzonia and Alogna led the way. Gotti and the black-haired woman followed, hand in hand.

"Need help with any luggage, sir?" the clerk asked with a smile.

No one answered.

Later that night, the security chief, curious, made it a point to happen to go by the room. The two bruisers were leaning against the wall. They just stared as he walked down the hallway.

The next day, the security chief called the FBI with "something that might interest them." Since Dominick Pizzonia's name was on the registration form, the tip eventually made its way to the C-16 squad. Later that week, two agents came to the hotel. They brought with them a folder full of the photographs Kurins had taken from his van.

The clerk picked out Gotti, Alogna, and Pizzonia. But the real surprise came when he picked out the black-haired woman. She was Sandy Grillo.

When the ID was called in to C-16, a lot of the team thought it was pretty interesting that Gotti was seen in a hotel with Dellacroce's common-law daughter just days after his mentor's death. But the larger significance of the incident did not occur to Mouw for at least another week: If John Gotti was feeling confident enough to flout La Cosa Nostra's strict prohibition against carousing with a fellow wiseguy's wife—if the clerk's ID was accurate and that was what was going down that night—he was also no doubt prepared to break at least one other of the Family's inviolable rules.

But by the time Mouw had worked this out, it was already too late.

# 15

A WOODEN SHOE, A GIFT FROM HIS MOTHER, HAD THE PLACE OF honor in the center of Mouw's living room mantel. Certainly, it was not a particularly valuable object, or even a very decorative one. Yet years ago, Jan Mouw had given her departing son the present on a a hopeful impulse. "I thought Bruce should have something to remind him of his roots as he went out into the world," she would explain. It was a heritage that was Dutch: "My dad was born in Holland," she said. "I could speak Dutch as a little girl." And pious: "The Reformed Church is very strict, and very much a part of our lives." And small-town: "Here in Orange City, everybody knows and cares for everybody else." Without thinking too much about it, a dutiful Mouw had lugged the wooden shoe with him to all his billets, to the Manhattan highrise, then to the tiny apartment in Washington, and most recently to the slightly down-at-the-heels house within jogging distance of Oyster Bay. He had positioned it, for lack of a better place, on the mantel when he had first moved in. And there it sat, grandly displayed, and largely ignored.

Only now, as Jan Mouw had hoped, it was turning out to be a very potent symbol.

It was a time when Mouw had become convinced he was fighting a multi-front war. It was challenge enough to dismantle the richest, most powerful organized crime family in America without also having to protect his back against prosecutors who would indict their grandmother for a headline—and then frame her for a conviction. Or without bumping into squads of Keystone Kops at every turn. But there were also, he knew too well, other forces still at work. C-16 was being hampered by more than mere idiocy or ambition. The duplicity ran much deeper. There would be days, then, spent isolated in his corner office, the door locked, and the Mole File spread across his desk. He searched, he analyzed, he theorized—and in the end he was left only with questions, not answers.

To these worries was added another frustration: operationally, things were on the back burner. His wires were "down." His burrowers were still mining the rich pages of the Castellano and Dellacroce transcripts for hidden nuggets, but the urgency had subsided. Castellano had two indictments pending, and Dellacroce had—rather shrewdly, it seemed—died. Yet even though Giacalone's lead defendant was gone, the case persisted. A grab bag of Family members, including John Gotti, remained charged under her indictment. It would be more productive to see how that case played out in the court before he intensified his efforts against Gotti, the comer, and his fast-track Bergin crew.

To add to his woes, lately Mouw found his equilibrium shaken by a smaller, and definitely more personal, concern. After nearly five years, the job was getting to him—and in a way he had never anticipated. One afternoon he had launched, for reasons long since forgotten, into a tirade and wound up calling a hapless agent "a dunsky" and "a punk." Also, he was finding it increasingly difficult to talk without gesticulating with his hands; he caught himself chopping at the air after nearly every word. Next thing he knew, he teased himself, he would be greeting the Twins with a kiss on the cheek or wearing his Academy ring on his pinkie. He joked about it, but it bothered him.

Struggling through this low and brooding period, Mouw would come home from the office late at night and find himself, as he sipped a Coke, glancing at the wooden shoe on the mantel. And it got him thinking that, as the Christmas of 1985 approached, maybe it was time to go home for the holidays. He would fly into Des Moines, spend a day or two with Happy, his younger sister and her family, and then rent a car and drive up to see his mom in Orange City. Get together with some old friends, play some snooker, catch up on all he had missed. C-16 would have to get along without him for a week or so. Besides, Christmas was always a quiet time in gangland.

John Gotti was also making plans for the holidays. His world, too, while always precarious, had grown increasingly strained. Big Paul was still demanding the Ruggiero tapes, and perhaps an even more troublesome concern, had begun threatening to disband Gotti's crew. In the anxious days following their underboss's death, the whole Bergin gang began to feel the Family tensions mounting dangerously. "Everybody's running scared, John," his brother Gene complained as the two men sat in the Bergin a week after the Dellacroce wake. "Well, fuck 'em. We ain't," Gotti announced. And it was true. His mind was set. He had decided to make his move.

But shrewdly, aware that with this decision his very life was now on the line, he for once reined in his volcanic temper. It would not be enough to rush in guns drawn like some street-corner punk. The magnitude of his ambitions required a more thoughtful, carefully political strategy. For John Gotti was not only setting out to assassinate Paul Castellano, he was also determined to replace him. Gotti would be the Boss of Bosses. Or he would be dead.

And so in Gotti's world, as in Mouw's, it was the Christmas season. In Howard Beach, where Gotti started his days, the houses were festooned with twinkling lights and rooftop Santas. In Manhattan, where he and Sandy

Grillo, to the FBI's eyes an apparently comfortable couple, ate at Da Noi's on York Avenue or sat sipping Remy's until late in the evening at a corner table at Régine's, the big stores had unveiled their holiday windows and a star of peace shined from the top of the tall tree at Rockefeller Center. In Ozone Park at the Bergin, there was even a dwarfish, white-needled plastic tree standing near the bar. And it was here, in the seclusion of the back room, that Gotti continued to spend his afternoons. Discreetly, yet methodically, he was lining up support from the other Families. He chose not, however, to reach out directly to his potential conspirators. Instead, for those hushed, initial discussions, he dispatched his emissaries. He was already, it was said, acting like the Boss.

For a newly upbeat Bruce Mouw, now that he had bought his ticket for Des Moines, it was also a hectic time. There was so much to do, and there were less than twenty shopping days left until Christmas.

## 16

THE SHOOTERS HAD ALREADY GONE TO THE MATTRESSES. THE word had been passed just days after the Dellacroce wake. "John says it's getting serious" was the oblique, guardedly whispered message. Once they had heard that, they packed their bags, took the "clean," untraceable pieces from their hiding places, and told their wives and girlfriends they were going away for a while. They wanted to be where Johnny Boy could quickly reach out to them once a plan was set. And they wanted to be somewhere Big Paul couldn't find them in case he started looking first.

That was a real concern. Now that the plot to kill Castellano was moving forward, the circle of Gambino Family conspirators was expanding. There were five factions committed: Gotti and his Bergin gang; Sammy "the Bull" Gravano and the crew of hard cases who hung out with him at Tali's in Brooklyn; Joe "Piney" Armone, a gray-haired capo who had promised to bring the old Gambino guys around when the time came; Robert "Di B" DiBernardo, who didn't have a crew, but was a prodigious money-maker; and Frank DeCicco, a happy-go-lucky captain who was one of Castellano's *goombata*—or so the Boss believed. Together, these plotters had formed a coalition they called "the Fist." They wanted to believe they were that tough. But, they also understood, let enough time go by and even the tightest of fists will become unclenched—or pried apart.

Gotti, however, was not a general to be rushed. The prospect of finally making a move seemed to fill him, the street fighter always ready to come out swinging, with a newfound hesitancy. One of the soldiers from the Bergin would look back at his boss's reluctance and decide, "John was like one of those shit-kicking linebackers who catches up on his Z's just before a game, and then goes out to rip the quarterback's head off." That might have been one explanation. But it was also true that Gotti was wisely being very careful.

From the start, he had said they would only get one chance to take Castellano by surprise. The hit had to be timed perfectly. The main problem was that Big Paul was under double guard. Not only did he have his boys, chiefly his driver Tommy Bilotti, a muscle-bound oaf with a jet black toupee that he took to angling raffishly over his watermelon-sized head; but also the FBI was giving Castellano a lot of heat. There was a genuine possibility that at any moment the Feds might be playing I-Spy from the back of a van or a rooftop. A plan, then, to whack Big Paul early one morning as his Lincoln was pulling down the driveway from the white pillared house on Todt Hill was seriously argued, and vetoed at once by Gotti. Suppose the Feds still had Paulie's home staked out: Smile, *goombah*, you're on "Candid Camera." Forget about it, he had ruled.

In desperation, Sammy Bull soon came up with another scheme. Each morning, on his way into the city to stand trial in the car-theft case, Castellano and Bilotti stopped off for breakfast at a local diner on Seventh Avenue and Sixty-fifth Street. Five days running Sammy's men had clocked it: same time, same booth in the rear, same order of eggs over easy and bacon crisp. Why not have someone come into the diner, make like he's heading for the john in the back, only on the way he reaches under his coat, pulls out a .357

Magnum, pops Castellano, and then, for good measure, puts one smack in the middle of Bilotti's forehead. For a while, the plan was seriously considered. Sammy even spoke with Joe Paruta about doing the job. But in the end, Gotti decided there were too many impracticalities: you would be relying on only one shooter; he would have to be one hell of a quick-draw artist; there was no telling how many waitresses would be running up the aisles—and into the line of fire. No, Gotti concluded after mulling it over thoughtfully, the diner wasn't their best opportunity.

So the plotters waited. By now they were bunking together, two or three guys to a group, lying low in party pads in Manhattan or crashing at friends'. Sammy Gravano had told Joey Watts that he and a couple of guys needed his rec room. Joey didn't ask why, he just told his wife to stay out of his friends' way, not to speak to them or even go downstairs. Sammy and Frank DeCicco and Frankie Botz made themselves at home in the pine-paneled basement of the house in Grassmere, Staten Island. Watts had a set of weights and, a real surprise, a sauna. They played a lot of poker, ate a lot of Chinese takeout. One night, Joey and his wife and baby daughter were told to find someplace to go, and Frank DeCicco took over the upstairs kitchen. Sammy and Frankie Botz had done all the shopping, and they had a feast—veal and peppers, pasta with a homemade tomato sauce that had bubbled for hours, and a lot of Chianti. But mostly, they waited. They waited for Johnny Boy to send word, to tell them it was a "Go." There was no longer any shrinking back, no space for hesitation. Hang loose, Sammy told the two Frankies. The way he figured it, either they would be home for Christmas, or they wouldn't be going home at all.

Sammy Gravano had been hanging loose for quite a while now. Last spring, when Gotti was still just coming around to the idea of raising his hand against the head of the Family, he had sent Di B, the porno king, over to Sammy's club with a message.

Tali's was on Eighteenth Street in Brooklyn. Until a few

years back it had been, as its owner was fond of calling it, a cocktail lounge. That meant it was one of the few bars in Bensonhurst where you could take your date out for a cozy Friday night and they wouldn't give you a puzzled look if she ordered a White Russian. But now it was Sammy's joint, and while it was still an intimate sort of place with the same black Naugahyde bar that curved like an *S* and the same round, knee-high, black-topped tables, these days he ran it as a private club for his crew. In the back room, Sammy had put a pool table—a lot of hookers had partied with a lot of wiseguys on that green felt, according to the stories that were going around—and it was there, with a cue in his hand, that Di B found him.

They went, on Di B's suggestion, for a walk along Eighteenth Street. That way they would not be overheard by a wire, or by an informant.

"I want to speak to you about serious business," Di B began.

"I'm listening," Sammy said. They continued to stroll down the street. The people in Bensonhurst knew Sammy Bull; they always gave him room.

"It's about Paul."

"Yeah."

And now Di B, as Sammy would later recall, seemed to be having trouble getting the words out. Di B had made a fortune skimming from the unions and pedaling porno. It wasn't easy money, but Sammy knew Di B was no tough guy. Talking the talk was not the same as walking the walk, Sammy liked to say. He figured that was why Di B, with his suit and tie and razor-cut hair, was having a hard time.

"I'm listening," Sammy prodded. No reason why he should make this easier; Di B, after all, wanted something from him.

"It's John," Di B managed to go on. "I got a message from him. He wants to know if you want to meet with Angelo. To discuss things." Then he added, perhaps unnecessarily, "About Paul."

In addition to this terse invitation, Gotti, very shrewdly, was also sending a couple of unspoken messages. By having chosen DiBernardo as his messenger, he was telling Sammy that Paul was already in a lot of trouble. Everyone in the Family knew Di B was one of Castellano's boys. Paul was always having him come up to the house on Todt Hill, inviting him to those prime rib dinners, the beef, Paul would boast, personally selected from the rows of hanging carcasses at the butcher company he and his sons owned. If Di B was backing Johnny's play, then support for the Boss must be wearing pretty thin.

And having Di B on his side also demonstrated that Gotti had his priorities straight. This was more than something personal. The Family business was business. The purpose of the Brotherhood was to make money. If Di B was on board, a guy bringing in millions each year, then when the dust settled the Family was going to keep on pulling in big money. Only now Sammy Bull might be able to get his hands on some of it.

Sammy, who had a very pensive, even analytical side, was weighing all this before he answered. He had a habit of swaying his head back and forth very slowly when he played with an idea. His eyes, usually just calm and sleepy like a junkie's, would narrow. But with Sammy it was easy to miss these little tics. A steady regimen of steroids and Nautilus had pumped him up cartoonishly; he was built like the Incredible Hulk. That was what a lot of people noticed first, although it was also fairly disconcerting that so much extravagant muscle was being constantly flexed by a guy standing barely five foot five.

"Sure," Sammy said after he had thought it all through. "Tell Johnny I'll meet with Ange." But he didn't say what else was going on in his mind: I'll talk all right, but I'm not committing myself to anything. Not until I'm convinced they can really take down Paul. And not until I know for sure what's in it for Sammy Bull.

## 17

THE ODD THING WAS, JOHN GOTTI HARDLY KNEW SAMMY BULL. They had first met just after Gotti was paroled from Greenhaven, during the summer when he got made. It was in an after-hours club in the city, and Frank DeCicco and his dad had brought Sammy over to the table where Johnny was holding court. "Like you to meet Sammy Gravano," Frankie's dad had said. And straight off he explained, "He's a friend of ours." That way Gotti knew Sammy had earned his button too; if he hadn't, the old man would have referred to him simply as a "friend of mine." Still, that had been eight distant years ago, and as their lives and careers moved on, things had never worked out to bring the two men together. They would have run into each other at weddings and funerals, or every now and then at a dice game Johnny ran in the city, since Sammy also liked a bit of action. But they never hung out or, although in the same Family, did any business. It was only a twenty-minute drive from Tali's in Brooklyn to the Bergin in Queens, yet for those in the life it would have been like taking a voyage to another country.

119

Sammy stuck with the guys in Toddo's crew, and Johnny had his Bergin gang. There was plenty up for grabs, and everyone knew his place.

But now that Gotti had decided to rule a larger realm, he came around to thinking that he wanted Sammy Bull on his side. Part of it was that Gravano, like Gotti himself, was young, not quite forty. Not, as Johnny Boy derided them, "one of those old-fart Mafiosis." He was also a big earner. And, again like Gotti, he was a take-no-crap tough guy. But while all these qualities were admirable, even vaguely promising, there was something else that convinced Gotti he desperately needed the Bull: Gravano was a killer, a stone-cold Iceman.

Like everyone else in the Family, Gotti had heard the stories about how Sammy, never flinching, had plain whacked out anyone who crossed him. Back in 1982, Frank Fiala had thought he could just waltz into the Plaza Suite, a disco Sammy was running in Brooklyn, and announce he wanted to buy the place. Fiala initiated the conversation by explaining that he was connected to a lot of gun-toting Colombians, to which Sammy only blankly nodded. When Fiala offered a little over $1 million for the club, Sammy decided maybe a deal could be struck. A $650,000 down payment was even deposited in an escrow account. But one evening Sammy walked into his office and found Fiala smoking a big cigar and sitting with his feet up on the desk. *His desk.* Sammy started to say something, and Fiala began waving a machine gun right under Sammy's nose and talking again about all the coked-up killer Colombians he knew. That was when Sammy decided Fiala was history. He whacked him that night. He got his desk back, and he kept a large chunk of the down payment. As for the Colombians, they took one look at Sammy the Bull and backed off.

A few years before that, his wife Debra's brother, Nick Scibetta, had made the mistake of borrowing a hunk of money off Sammy and then boldly refusing to repay it. Some people said what happened next was simply business; Sammy had a lot of money on the street, and it was a dangerous precedent to let anyone, even a relative, stiff you.

Others would whisper that the relationship between the two men was more complicated, and that this, as much as the money, had provoked Sammy. According to this way of looking at it, Sammy and Nicky had been teenage buddies, the two friends making it a longtime habit to hang together until closing time on adjacent barstools at Doc's on Seventeenth Avenue. But then Nicky had started tooting serious amounts of coke and Sammy, more focused in his aspirations, got made.

For a while, Nicky had disappeared completely from Bensonhurst. But one evening he reappeared at Doc's—only now his hair was hennaed and there was an earring in his ear. Nick's style grew more outrageous over the next months, campy and flirtatious; and Sammy, now moving up in the Family, couldn't handle that. There were a lot of late-night barroom squabbles, Sammy going after his brother-in-law, punching and kicking him with an out-of-control fury. "People will say you're in love," Frankie Stillitano teased Sammy after observing one vicious, noisy quarrel at Doc's. The rebuke seemed to push Sammy's anger further. He stormed out of the bar, oddly silent, beyond even offering up a comeback. Later, the word in the neighborhood would be that maybe Frankie was onto something, and that Sammy was trying to put an end to a lot more than a bad debt.

But whatever the ultimate provocation, Sammy had the final say. He shot his brother-in-law and friend twice in the back of the head at close range. Then he had the body chopped up and the incriminating pieces buried around the neighborhood. It would have been an effective method of disposal, except that one evening, while the Scibetta family was sitting in their living room watching "M*A*S*H," their dog scampered in with Nicky's hand clutched in its mouth. It was the only remains of their son the Scibettas ever found, so they had the hand placed in a silk-lined coffin and buried with sacred rites. Sammy stood in the church next to his wife for the entire service. Afterwards, he promised the Scibettas he would try to find out who had murdered their son.

Over the years, as the bodies piled up, Sammy earned a reputation as a man who wouldn't back off, no matter who was in his face. Shaking with indignant anger, he had even stood up to Big Paul at a Family council. Dellacroce, who had witnessed the scene, first with stunned amazement as the moment escalated and then jumping in tactfully to defuse it, later gave Gotti an admiring summary of the confrontation. "The little guy's got a hell of a pair of balls," the underboss told Johnny.

Sammy's anger had, at its onset, not been directed toward Castellano, but at another Gambino soldier, Louie DiBono. The two men had been partners in a scam known in the construction trade as "lumping." DiBono, who ran a large and ostensibly legitimate drywall company, would receive multimillion-dollar Federal housing rehabilitation contracts that specified union laborers. Only he would bring in Sammy's nonunion Stillwell Avenue Construction Company to do the actual drywalling. And Sammy, always persuasive, would cut his own deals with the unions. He paid off the top officials, and he made certain that the union workers on the site realized what they would be getting into if they reported his crew to the authorities. Beginning in 1981, Sammy had "lumped" on to several of DiBono's jobs, and it had been a very profitable arrangement for both men. After a couple of years, however, Sammy began thinking that maybe it was too profitable for DiBono. He compared what he was taking each week to what DiBono was making, and he came to the unshakable conclusion that his partner was robbing him.

That was when Sammy went to DiBono's office on Long Island and had it out with him. There were a lot of people hanging around the office, and perhaps that was why DiBono, who also had an arrogant, quickly ignited temper, decided to play it cool. Sammy, he cajoled, nobody's ripping you off. We're both making money. Relax. But Sammy was not buying it. He didn't care who was around, who heard him. He just listened, and when DiBono was done he shot back: "I guarantee you, if you rob me, you won't enjoy the money. I'll kill you." Then he turned and walked off, and the clicking tattoo of his high-heeled boots on the linoleum floor was suddenly a large and ominous sound in the silent room.

DiBono was all at once at a loss. A threat from Sammy Bull was as good as a promise. In a panic, he went to his captain, Patsy Conte, and together they came up with a plan to strike first. They went to Castellano and put up a "book" against Gravano. By threatening a fellow member of the Brotherhood, Sammy Bull had violated the oath he had taken when he joined La Cosa Nostra. As punishment, he should be killed. Castellano considered the complaint and decided to haul Sammy before a Family meeting.

Things weren't looking good for Sammy. That was what Frankie DeCicco, who managed to move among the different and competing Family cliques with a politician's easy friendliness, told him when he delivered Castellano's summons. And since he genuinely liked Sammy, DeCicco also gave him a succinct piece of advice—lie. Say you never threatened anyone.

But by the time a gruff Tommy Bilotti picked up Sammy as arranged in front of the Country Diner and without a word drove him in the big Lincoln with the tinted windows to some strange house in a remote corner of Staten Island, Sammy had made up his mind that nobody was tough enough to spook him. Nobody was taking him down without a fight.

So when he was led into the basement of the house and saw the entire Gambino Family Administration staring at him like hanging judges from behind a long table, Sammy didn't flinch. Castellano asked him if he had threatened DiBono and Sammy didn't even attempt to back off. He just looked the Boss of Bosses in the eye and, his voice steady and firm, agreed that, sure, he had threatened DiBono. Louie was a liar and a cheat and a thief. He deserved to die.

And with Castellano's fleshy face turning a fiery red, his eyes bulging with anger, Sammy walked down to the end of the table where DiBono was sitting. His arms were by his sides, but he was clutching his fists so tightly that every vein in his muscular body was popping. He leaned across the table until his face was just a knuckle's width from DiBono's, so close that DiBono must have felt his heavy, panting breath. Then Sammy, with the entire Administration listening, spoke so softly right into DiBono's terrorized face that his words might have been a sweet whisper. Except he said, "Let me kill him. I'll shoot him fuckin' dead right here and now. He'll never walk away from this table. Let me kill this fuck right here and now."

Castellano exploded. Gravano, he ranted, had gone too far. Now he was threatening to whack a Family member in front of the Administration. Maybe Gravano was the one who should be killed right on the spot, he said.

For an unsteady moment, it was a real possibility. But fortunately for Sammy, Neil Dellacroce, the practical underboss, intervened. He carefully calmed Big Paul, persuaded a grim Sammy and a very rattled DiBono to shake hands, and the dispute was, for the time being at least, defused.

But it was not forgotten. And when just about a year later John Gotti began looking for the sort of man who could help him take down the Don, he thought of Sammy Bull. Yet, considering all he knew about Gravano's narrow, self-important way of looking at the world, as well as what he had heard about the Bull's tendency to take insult both quickly and personally, Gotti made a surprising miscalculation when the day came for the initial meeting his emissary, Di B, had arranged.

John Gotti didn't show. When Gravano arrived at the Bergin, Angelo Ruggiero alone was there to greet him. That didn't seem right to Sammy. He had come to discuss "serious business." He wasn't going to cut a deal, put his life on the line, for Fat Ange. Still, he kept his peace. There would be plenty of time to make it clear he didn't take to being treated so disrespectfully if things fell apart. Meanwhile, it was Ruggiero's meet, and he let him run it.

They walked along 101st Avenue. It was after four in the afternoon and the street was crowded. But Ruggiero, in his breathy way, jumped right into the heart of the matter.

"When the time comes to hit Paul, you gonna be with us?" he asked.

Gravano avoided answering the question by asking a couple of his own. "Where's John? What's his opinion in all this?"

Ruggiero was a huge Humpty-Dumpty shaped man, and when he got excited he would shift his weight from one foot to the other. It was an unconscious mannerism, but it made him look slightly ludicrous, like one of those jiggling dolls displayed in the rear windows of cars. As he hurried to explain that Gotti was fully backing this piece of business, directing it even, his grossly fat three-hundred-pound hulk was no doubt tilting to and fro. But Gravano, as he would always remember the discussion, was silently focusing on one increasingly angry thought: If this was Johnny's big play, why wasn't he here?

Yet too much was at stake to make things personal. So Gravano posed another question: Where did Frankie DeCicco stand in all this?

Hey, you want to talk to Frankie, talk to him, Ruggiero said.

"I will," Gravano promised.

"Look, you with us or not?" Ruggiero pressed.

Gravano considered his response. "I'll get back to you," he told him after a moment. But he might just as well have said: Don't hold your breath.

It just didn't seem right that Gotti hadn't shown.

Truth was, by the time Gravano went to talk with Frank DeCicco at the capo's club on Bath Avenue, his mind was set. He was going to take a pass on this piece of business. The more he thought about it, the more he doubted Gotti could pull it off. If John and Fat Ange were sweating over Big Paul's getting his hands on the tapes the Feds had recorded in Ruggiero's house, that was their beef—not Sammy Bull's. Besides—and this was no small factor in Sammy's mental equation—it still rankled that Gotti had not shown him the respect of appearing for the meet at the Bergin.

But as Gravano and DeCicco talked for hours in the rear

of the Bath Avenue club, espressos appearing in front of them as if by magic after each nearly imperceptible flick of the capo's index finger, DeCicco proved to be a most persuasive campaigner. In years of Family meetings, he had honed his method of argument into a bantering style that was easygoing, affable, even self-deprecating. It was also relentless: a constant shrewd tapping of the same spot. That afternoon and into the evening, he zeroed in on Gravano's famous greed.

First, DeCicco outlined with infuriating detail how Castellano was selling out the Family—and by extension, Gravano—to line his own pockets. The Don, he explained, had established Metro Concrete for his son-in-law and himself, and in one swift maneuver had taken millions of dollars of business away from the Family companies. Equally costly to the Family fortunes, Castellano was holding on to the kickbacks from many of the construction unions and refusing to pass the moneys on to his soldiers. The Don also—and this was a matter of honor, too—was not above making deals with the Genovese Family. Castellano had allowed them, to cite one notorious case, to hit Frank Piccolo, the Gambino capo in Connecticut, as long as he, personally, would continue to get a share of the state's immense gambling and loan-sharking revenues.

"Green-eyed motherfucker," Gravano swore at his Boss.

So DeCicco, after having rubbed Gravano's avarice raw, now sprinkled the salt. He suggested, quite authoritatively, that not only would the Family be wealthier without Castellano's voracious skimming, but there could also be a lot more trickling down directly to Sammy Bull. Stand with Gotti, you'll have a real future. And, I promise you, a very rich one.

Before Gravano left Bath Avenue that night, he and DeCicco had contacted DiBernardo.

"You tell Johnny, me and Frankie will back his play," Gravano instructed.

But killing the Boss was one thing. Getting away with it, Gotti understood, was another. Now that he was determined to whack Paul, now that his Fist of conspirators was clenched, his great concern was over what would happen after Paul went down. If the other Families turned against him, there would be war. It would be long and bloody. And, he had little doubt, in the end a united Commission would swat him dead.

Unless he won the Families over first.

Therefore, not long after Gravano came on board, Gotti convened a meeting of the leaders of the plotting factions. In a gesture that was wisely meant to be both diplomatic and to erase any lingering ill will, he asked Sammy Bull to pick the place for a meet. Sammy chose Joey Watts's wood-paneled basement rec room.

The night of the meeting, seated around the room on a hide-away bed, a Barcalounger, and a couple of bridge chairs were the key conspirators: John Gotti, Angelo Ruggiero, Sammy Gravano, Frankie DeCicco, and Joe "Piney" Armone. Only DiBernardo, the businessman pornographer, was missing; all he was expected to deliver to the cause was a chunk of his earnings.

Gotti chaired the meet. He had turned a bridge chair around, so that when he sat in it his heavy chest pressed against the chair's straight back. Look, he said, we can't expect the other Families to back us at this stage. But, he went on confidently, there's no reason we can't reach out, test the waters. See which way they would go if Paul got hit.

"Makes sense to me," Gravano agreed.

When they left Joe Watts's rec room, each of the conspirators had an assignment. It didn't take them long to make their reports to Gotti.

Joe Piney had talked with Joe Gallo, the Gambino Family *consigliere,* and with some of the Genovese crowd on the West Side. "I'll be able to control them," Armone said, which, however boastful, was good enough for Gotti. He knew that Armone and Gallo went back a long way together, all the way to the 1930s when Piney had earned his nickname by giving away Christmas trees to the poor on the Lower East Side. If Joe Piney said he could deliver, it was a done deal.

Sammy Gravano and Frank DeCicco reached out to Vic Amuso and Anthony "Gas" Casso of the Luchese Family. "You won't have a problem with those people," they told Gotti.

Gotti himself contacted Joe Messina, the underboss of the Bonanno Family. They had done business together in the past, and Messina said there was no reason they wouldn't be working together in the future.

When Angelo Ruggiero contacted Gerry Lang, the Colombo Family underboss, Lang said he had to discuss things with his Administration. A day later Lang sent a message to Gotti: "What the hell you waiting for?"

It was, no doubt, in the increasingly tense days after Dellacroce's death, the very question that was weighing heavily on all the conspirators' minds. They couldn't keep to the mattresses forever. And, a real heart-racing danger, Castellano was certain to hear something before long. "No time like the present," Gravano told Gotti.

But Gotti would not be rushed.

Yet just when it seemed their moment would never come, an excited Frankie DeCicco announced that Castellano had summoned him to a dinner next week at Sparks, a steak house in Manhattan.

What do you say? DeCicco demanded of Gotti. He argued that Big Paul would be coming with only Bilotti in tow. He wouldn't be expecting anything. The guy would simply be stepping out for a prime rib dinner with some friends at his favorite restaurant.

Still, Gotti hesitated. "Let me play around with it," he told DeCicco.

Later he would say it wasn't the best opportunity—just better than all the others. By the end of the day, he sent word: The moment had come.

# 18

NUMBER 1809 STILLWELL AVENUE WAS A SQUAT, RED BRICK BOX of a building. A pair of small windows, protected by heavy iron bars, flanked a tarnished, once white reinforced metal door. It stood, as impenetrable and inviting as a fortress, near the corner of a glum, low-rent commercial block, one more squat, flat-roofed structure in a motley Brooklyn neighborhood filled with auto body shops, restaurant supply companies, and tire warehouses. There was no clue as to what sort of business was conducted behind the closed door of 1809. In fact, from the outside, the only suggestion that the building was even occupied was a sign which nearly obscured one of the windows. It was commercially printed, Day-Glo orange letters on a black background, and the vertical iron window bars cut through it like exclamation points. *No Trespassing,* it warned.

At night, the neighborhood was quickly deserted. After all the daytime open-air tumult, the high-pitched sounds of car engines racing, power tools whirring, and the constant background drone of so many competing radios, the heavy quiet was startling. And a little furtive. A watchdog was usually prowling somewhere deep inside a padlocked warehouse, and its menacing growls carried for blocks. It was the only noise in the still of the night.

Yet on this frigidly cold evening—December 15, 1985—there was a great deal of activity at 1809 Stillwell. Within minutes of each other, cars packed with men suddenly began to arrive on the dark street. The men hurried to the doorway, their voices low. They did not want to attract attention. There was no need to knock. Sammy Gravano was already waiting by the metal door. It was his building. The first floor served as the offices for his construction company. He ran his other, more private enterprises from the basement.

As soon as a group arrived, Gravano swung the door open quickly. Each time, the light from the front room escaping for that instant into the street, he took a moment to look carefully into the shadows. He was searching the street for a parked van, or perhaps a telltale glow from a warehouse window across the way. The FBI, he worried, could be hiding out there. Or worse, Castellano's men. Tucked into his belt was a .357 Magnum. From time to time, as was his habit when he was packing, his hand would come to rest on the revolver's heavy butt.

But Gravano saw nothing disturbing, and when they all had arrived, he bolted the door and led them down a stairwell to the basement. It was very narrow, dimly lit, and they had to walk single file. A stack of Diet Pepsi cases created another bottleneck at the bottom of the stairs and, again, they had to pass through the doorway one at a time.

They walked into a startling bright light. Fluorescent tubes hung from the ceiling and ran the length of the room. A long, richly polished wooden conference table had somehow been wedged into the small space; it seemed inappropriately grand in the windowless basement with its linoleum floor.

Waiting for them, seated at the head of the table, his silver hair almost sparkling under the intense glow of the overhead lights, was John Gotti.

They took their places without delay. Ten faces stared at

Gotti from around the table. Seated close to him, near the head, were the original conspirators—Sammy Gravano, Angelo Ruggiero, and Frank DeCicco. They already knew the score; they had met with Gotti earlier in the day and had helped him formulate the plan of attack. But the hard cases down at the end of the table—Eddie Lino, Fat Sally Scala, Vinnie Artuso, Johnny Carneglia, Tony Roach Rampino, Joey Watts, and Iggy Alogna—could only guess what "serious business" was at hand. Gravano glanced at them, checking them out, and decided on one word—"Antsy." Not that he blamed them too much. You didn't have to be a whiz kid to know that whatever was going down, it would all be over very soon. One way—or another.

It was Gotti's show, and he would run it as somberly as a board of directors meeting. He did not resort to temper, nor did he attempt to lighten the occasion with his charm. From the moment he began, he settled into a steady staccato and kept it at that sharp level. "We're gonna do a piece of work tomorrow," he announced right off. "We can't miss. It has to be done."

He went on in this unembroidered way to say there would be two targets. The plan was to hit them at five in the evening as they arrived for an appointment at a restaurant in the city.

Then he rose and began walking around the table.

"Eddie," he said, and put his hands firmly on Lino's shoulders. It was an affectionate gesture, but its suddenness seemed to take Lino by surprise. For an instant, an apprehensive shudder crossed the man's face.

Gotti moved on to Fat Sally, Vinnie, and Johnny Carnegs. He stood behind each of them, and, one after another, brought his large hands down on their shoulders. He could have been choosing sides for a basketball game.

"You guys are the shooters," he said when he had completed his circuit around the table. He told them they would wait outside the restaurant.

Everyone else, he said, would have a backup role. If, say, one of the targets managed to slip off and make a run for it, then they would jump in and finish him off. He would give out the exact assignments tomorrow afternoon. They would meet at a park on the Lower East Side, near the East River, at three. There would be plenty of time, he said.

He didn't ask if there were any questions. Or any comments. Gotti just concluded by repeating five words he had said at the start: "It has to be done."

Then he rose to leave without identifying who the hit tomorrow evening would target or explaining why. He did not even mention the name or the location of the restaurant. Perhaps he reasoned that the hit would be more secure if the details were closely held until the last possible moment. Or perhaps he thought it went without saying who the targets were. But the way Gravano looked at it, there was no reason the shooters should need to know anything else. John Gotti and Sammy Bull were telling them to do something. That should be reason enough to risk their lives.

It was a long night.

Sammy Bull and Frank DeCicco went back to Joey Watts's rec room. Sammy took the foldout bed. Frankie had brought in a cot. It must have been 3:00 A.M. when Frankie heard a noise. He woke up with a start to find Sammy, in his shorts, a barbell in each hand, grunting as he did curls in front of the bathroom mirror. Sammy was still going at it as Frankie fell back asleep.

Meanwhile, John Gotti, according to the report a TE later filed with the FBI, left Stillwell Avenue and, with Alogna at the wheel, immediately drove into Manhattan. He went straight to Régine's on Park Avenue, where Sandy Grillo was waiting. They held hands for a while and then left. The informant did not know where they went. All he could add to his report was a curiously introspective thought he had overheard Gotti sharing with Sandy. Gotti had just downed the last sip of his Remy and was making his way slowly through the crowded nightclub toward the door, his arm linked possessively through Sandy's, when he turned to her. "You never know what's down the road. Your number could come up any day," he said. "You never fucking know."

# 19

ON DECEMBER 16, 1985, AT JUST BEFORE NOON, PAUL Castellano kissed the maid (and his mistress) Gloria Olarte good-bye, walked across the black and white checkerboard marble floor of the front hall, and out the oversized double doors of his mansion on the top of Todt Hill. Tommy Bilotti was waiting in the circular drive in his black Lincoln with the tinted windows. The Boss of Bosses waved one final time to Gloria, now standing on the balcony outside the second-story master bedroom, struggling to secure a Christmas wreath to the wrought-iron railing. She interrupted her work to wave back, and now satisfied, he got into the front seat. Bilotti put the car in gear and they headed down the hill. They were going to the day's first sit-down.

That morning, Bruce Mouw was sitting in his office above Queens Boulevard contemplating how to extricate himself from one particularly unappealing piece of business. There was a seminar at NYU law school later in the day. Professor Robert Blakey of Notre Dame was in town to present

133

another of his RICO dog and pony shows. But just the thought of sitting through the inevitably high-pitched session gave Mouw, he had confided days ago to members of his team, the willies.

It wasn't the professor that filled him with such dread; in fact, not only did he appreciate and endorse his inventive philosophy, but Mouw also got a kick out of Blakey's no-holds-barred histrionics. It was, to use the fraternal phrase of the announcing flyer, his "fellow law enforcement community" that he wanted to avoid.

The Giacalone indictment remained a sore point. The betrayal of Willie Boy Johnson would always be unforgivable. The presence of so many different agencies on his turf was a constant irritation. And his mind continued to rage with suspicions; the Mole File was a steadily growing inventory of serendipitous coincidences. Mouw, no matter how inchoate and unproven his theories, knew one thing for sure: The last thing he wanted to do was share his strategy—and his hard-won street knowledge—with a room full of self-styled gang-busters.

But how was he going to get out of it? True, it wasn't a command appearance—yet close enough. His Bureau supervisors would be there. They expected him to show too. Still, after years of devising cover stories for his agents, how hard would it be to come up with one for himself? Besides, it would be Christmas Eve in eight days and he had a lot to get done before he caught the plane to Des Moines.

Across the borough, just a ten minute ride away, John Gotti was having his own rough moment. Only it had brought him to a full-blown rage.

Now that the defining day had finally arrived, the weeks of waiting ended, there was an urgency to every moment. Gotti had arrived at Bergin at the ungodly hour of noon. Today there had been none of the usual *goombah* banter with the guys. Instead, he had crossed quickly into the back room and taken his seat in the barber's chair; "the throne," his crew called it with no attempt at irony. He had looked into the wall mirror for a while, lost in some private thought or, perhaps, taken by a rush of sudden fear. When it passed, he summoned Angelo Ruggiero and it was while going through a last-minute checklist with Fat Ange that he erupted.

"You call this white?" Gotti screamed. "You fuckin' color-blind? This is yellow, you fuckin' idiot. Yellow! *Fuckin' yellow!*"

Days earlier, Gotti had come up with the idea that all the shooters should wear the identical disguise. It would make it more difficult, he explained, for a bystander to identify any one individual. They would all look alike. Get them raincoats and some kind of hats, he had ordered Ruggiero. The same outfit for each of the guys. But nothing crazy, he had insisted. I want them to blend in. I don't want them standing out there like they're wearing a sign saying *Hitmen*.

Ruggiero had done a resourceful job with the headgear. Somehow he had come up with four bulky, Russian-style fur hats. Sitting in the barber chair, Gotti looked them over and nodded his approval.

Ruggiero had also provided suitable coats. They were a neutral, tannish color and three-quarter length: long enough to hide a weapon. The problem was that Fat Ange had been able to come up with only three identical coats. The fourth was approximately the same length and cut, but it was also definitely a bright yellow.

Gotti took a long look. "You fuckin' kiddin' me?" he demanded.

"John," Ruggiero hurried to explain, according to the report a TE would share weeks later with the FBI, "I couldn't find anything else. It's almost the same."

It was the only time in all the months of planning that Gotti, previously so controlled, so calculated, gave in to all the pressures that had been building. His attack on Ruggiero was enormous, ferociously out of proportion. Every word was overheard by all the boys in the front room. Gotti was screaming incoherently about *"yellow! motherfuckin' yellow!"* and they were afraid even to speak.

But after a while Gotti was once again in control. "It'll fuckin' have to do," he told Ruggiero finally. "What the hell," he decided with some resignation. A further calming silence; then, as if to emphasize that he had moved back from the edge, he was abruptly one of the guys again. "Who the fuck knows when we'll get a chance to eat?" he said to Ruggiero. "Hey, let's get some lunch."

Paul Castellano, meanwhile, was finishing a business lunch at the Country Diner on Staten Island. His guests were John Riggi, the Boss of New Jersey's DeCavalcante Family, and Jimmy Failla, a Gambino capo. Riggi was having some problem holding on to his lucrative position as business agent for a laborers' union. He wanted Big Paul's advice.

"Got to show 'em who's boss," Castellano lectured. "Don't take any shit."

By two, with Bilotti doing the driving, Castellano left the Staten Island diner for Manhattan. The black Lincoln crossed the majestic Verrazano-Narrows Bridge, took a right turn onto the Gowanus Expressway, and then entered the Brooklyn-Battery Tunnel. The car emerged at the southern tip of Manhattan, and then, after taking a connecting underpass, proceeded up the East River Drive.

At nearly the same time, Sammy Bull Gravano and Joey Watts took the identical route into Manhattan. Sammy had his .357 stuck into his belt, and Watts, too, was packing. Both men also had walkie-talkies. It was Watt's car, so he was driving. He pulled off the East River Drive near South Street. He went along a service road that paralleled the highway until, just past Henry Street, he saw the park.

"Pull over anywhere," Gravano ordered.

Watts found a space near a chain-link fence directly across from a cluster of tall brick apartment buildings. It was a federally subsidized housing project not unlike the ones where Sammy and his nonunion construction crews had done a lot of illegal, big money jobs. The two men walked quickly toward the handball court inside the park. A lot of the guys were already there, waiting in the cold.

* * *

At around 2:45, Bilotti pulled up in front of a sleek black tower on Madison Avenue near Twenty-fifth Street. Castellano, with Bilotti at his side, took the elevator to the twenty-second floor. He had come, full of holiday cheer, to his lawyer's office to distribute Christmas envelopes to the staff of secretaries assisting on his stolen-car case. He was pleased with how the trial was going, and he was grateful for everyone's help. The Godfather believed that no good deed should go unrewarded, and no evil one unavenged.

Castellano had arrived without an appointment, but as soon as his lawyer, James LaRossa, learned the head of the Gambino Family was chatting with the secretaries, he hurried to greet him. LaRossa, who had a courtly, ingratiating manner, led his client into his office. He sat behind his large desk, and Castellano and Bilotti sat down in the black leather chairs opposite him. From this vantage point, Castellano was able to look beyond his lawyer, through a wall of windows, and across the city toward the Hudson River and the sun that would soon be setting over the apartment towers huddled on the New Jersey Palisades.

At around three that afternoon, Bruce Mouw, after considerable procrastination, placed a call to Jules Bonavolonta's office at the Manhattan FBI headquarters. He did not attempt to speak with Bonavolonta. Instead, he left a message with one of the secretaries. He wouldn't be able to attend the Blakey lecture, he said. Before making the call, Mouw had planned to offer an oblique yet somewhat exculpatory "Something came up" as an excuse. But when he finally got the secretary on the line, he found to his mild embarrassment, he couldn't bring himself to mouth even such a small untruth.

John Gotti, hatless, the collar of his double-breasted camel hair coat turned up around his neck for some protection against the cold wind blowing off the East River just yards away, was standing in front of a handball court backstop. Spread out in a ragged semicircle around him were the men who had attended the Stillwell Avenue meet less than twenty-four hours ago. Only Frank DeCicco was absent; and he had a five o'clock dinner appointment at Sparks.

Ruggiero, on Gotti's signal, distributed the fur hats and the long raincoats to the shooters. As they put them on, Gravano, who had not previously known about this twist, was struck by Gotti's cleverness. We just might pull this off, he silently decided.

It was slowly beginning to turn to dusk; the streetlights along the East River Drive suddenly blinked on. And for the first time, Gotti, talking softly, as if afraid of being over-heard, revealed to the shooters the details of the hit. "Paul and Tommy are going," he said tersely. The restaurant, he continued without emotion, was a steak house, Sparks, over on Forty-sixth Street, between Second and Third Avenues.

It was growing late, the conspirators still had to drive nearly a mile uptown through city traffic, but Gotti insisted on once more, very carefully, very patiently, going over precisely where each shooter, each backup gunman, was to position himself.

Come on, come on, Gravano's inner voice urged. It's getting late, John.

Yet Gotti made certain he was satisfied that everyone knew his place before he wrapped things up. His concluding words were the same pragmatic appeal he had offered to the conspirators on the previous night: "It has to be done." Those five words, Gotti seemed to believe, were sufficient: a rationale, and a benediction.

Without a further command, the men hurried to their cars. "You're riding with me," Gotti told Gravano.

It was only then, as Gravano walked silently by Gotti's side out of the park and toward the car, that he was struck, as if for the very first time, by the enormity of what they were attempting. They were going off to kill the Boss of Bosses.

"We were in a vacation mode," LaRossa would later recall. "A holiday mood." Castellano and Bilotti, in no apparent hurry, chatted in the lawyer's office until after four. Still, when they left nearly an hour remained until the appointment at Sparks, and Castellano reasoned he might as well do some Christmas shopping. Gloria had been talking recently about "high-class ladies" and "the way they smell like money," so Castellano, taking the hint, decided to buy the woman he loved some perfume. Bilotti drove him uptown to a store on West Forty-third Street one of LaRossa's secretaries had suggested.

Bilotti pulled the Lincoln into a no-parking zone. Then he opened the glove compartment and removed a shiny blue-and-gold New York City Patrolman's Benevolent Association card. Issued to a police sergeant, it had somehow made its way to the head of the Gambino Family. Bilotti placed the card in the middle of the padded dashboard. That way, a traffic cop would be sure to see it. Then the two men joined the moving crowd of holiday shoppers making their way along Forty-third Street.

The store was jammed and it took them longer than they had anticipated. It was past five and dark when, carrying a large, gift-wrapped bottle of Chanel No. 5, they returned to the Lincoln. A fifty-dollar parking ticket had been placed under the windshield wipers. Still, things could have been worse. If it hadn't been for the PBA card, the car might have been towed. That would have really screwed things up. As it was, they were already late for the dinner at Sparks.

John Gotti was having his own parking headaches. He couldn't find a space. He had managed to pull his Lincoln into a small space on the northwest corner of Third Avenue and Forty-sixth Street; from the driver's seat he could look diagonally across the street toward the long entrance canopy leading to the restaurant. The problem was that the hood of his car was sticking out into the crosswalk. All he needed was for some traffic cop to tell him, "Move it." Then what would he do? He could be driving around the block, caught in rush-hour traffic on Second Avenue, when Big Paul showed up. Or, just as likely, the cop might insist on writing a ticket, and he would be handing over his license and registration when the guys across the street broke out with the artillery. Of course, next thing the cop would be asking was for him to step out of the car, and things would get really sticky when he tried to explain why he and Sammy Bull were loaded for bear. Not that the walkie-talkie Sammy had in his lap wasn't incriminating enough.

But it was already after five. Where the fuck were they? Was there enough time to drive around the block and maybe find a better spot?

"I'm going to circle," he told Gravano when the light turned green. Gotti nosed the Lincoln across the intersection and headed down Forty-sixth Street, toward Second Avenue.

There better not be any traffic, Gravano silently prayed.

Further west on Forty-sixth Street, the traffic was bumper-to-bumper. Castellano sat in the Lincoln, the car not even inching forward. He was at least fifteen minutes late. It would be quicker to walk. But he knew his guests would wait. He was the head of the Family.

As Gotti drove his Lincoln down the block, he passed Sparks. The evening sky was pitch-black and a jangle of brightly colored Christmas lights reflected off the store windows and the passing cars. The sidewalks were filled with people, hurrying home from work, going off Christmas shopping, heading out for a night in the city. Down Third Avenue, closer to Forty-second Street, a Salvation Army Santa was ringing his bell. From somewhere else, near Fifth Avenue perhaps, an amplified recording of "Silent Night" carried across the busy city streets.

Gravano looked out of the car's tinted windows and saw two men in light coats, fur hats pulled low on their heads, huddled near a street lamp on one side of the Sparks canopy. A similarly dressed pair was standing casually on the other side.

The car proceeded down the block, and for an instant Gravano glimpsed a familiar figure standing across from the restaurant. The Christmas lights strung from a row of bare beeches had caught the gaunt features of Tony Roach.

The car continued to move toward Second Avenue, and, a colossal bit of luck, they made the traffic light and turned right. But not before the headlights had picked up, for just a moment, three more backup shooters. They might have been Christmas shoppers weighing the merits of Nikes or New Balances the way they stood fixed in front of the Athlete's Foot window. Except, as Sammy noted, their eyes were focused across the block, toward Sparks.

We got him sandwiched all right, Gravano silently congratulated himself. Now if only we can get around the damn block and back into position in time.

The traffic moved freely, and Gotti once more drove down Forty-sixth Street. This time, his luck continuing, there was a space on the corner. He parked effortlessly.

The two men sat in the car waiting. The engine was running. Gotti's hands were on the steering wheel. Sammy gripped the walkie-talkie; in his belt, beneath his unbuttoned leather jacket, was the .357.

Where the hell was Castellano?

A well-dressed, elderly gentleman was walking across Forty-sixth Street to a Korean market for a quart of milk when he passed Sparks and noticed the men in the light coats and the fur hats. Bodyguards, he thought. Some United Nations diplomats must be having dinner at Sparks, he quickly concluded.

"What's keeping them?" he heard one of the men in the fur hats complain to his companion.

Yes, he decided, that had to be it. He continued to the store, congratulating himself on how well he knew New York.

Then all at once Gravano looked out the tinted passenger-side window and there they were. A Lincoln had stopped for a red light at the intersection of Forty-sixth Street and Third

Avenue. The dome light was on inside the car, and he could see Castellano and Bilotti talking. Bilotti was *this* close to him; Gravano could have opened his window and snatched the toupee off his head. It was eerie.

He motioned to Gotti.

"About fuckin' time," Gotti said.

Gravano spoke into the walkie-talkie. "They're the first car," he said. "They're stopped at the light."

The light turned green.

"They're coming through," Gravano said into the walkie-talkie.

The Lincoln crossed Third Avenue and stopped directly in front of the restaurant. There was a No Parking sign on the street lamp, but Bilotti ignored it. He turned off the engine and hurried out of the driver's seat. He was going to hold the door open for his Boss. But Castellano was impatient. He opened his own door.

The moment Castellano stepped from the car, two men in raincoats and fur hats rushed toward him. They had their arms extended. One man held a .32-caliber semiautomatic revolver. The other, a .38. And they were firing rapidly.

From the driver's side of the car, Bilotti saw the men moving toward Castellano, and on instinct, he hunched slightly to look through the car window for a better view. At that instant, the two other men in fur hats who had circled quietly behind him began firing.

Bullets ripped into Castellano. He was shot five times in the head. Blood oozed furiously from his ears, his nose, his mouth. A bullet caught him in the chest, just above his tie clip. He slumped to the sidewalk, a dead man falling back against the car door. One black leather glove was still clutched in his right hand.

When the shots broke out, people on the street started screaming. "Oh my God! Oh my God!" a woman cried. Two men and a woman took cover behind the stone lions guarding the entrance of a nearby Chinese restaurant. Another group ran frantically into the lobby of an apartment building. Others just fell to the ground, hoping to get out of the line of fire.

And still the shooting continued. Four bullets smashed into Tommy Bilotti's skull. Another four shots sliced through his back and into his chest.

He fell like a giant tree, teetering at first, swaying slightly, and then landing flat on his back with a thud. He lay with his arms spread wide, a dead man, his blood soaking the street.

One of the shooters still came at Castellano. He got to one knee and pressed his revolver directly against the dead man's temple. He fired once, a coup de grace, and the final bullet exploded into the skull of the man who was no longer the Boss of Bosses.

A bartender inside Sparks called 911. "Someone's been shot," he shouted into the phone.

A 10-10 transmission went out over the police radio. "Shots fired, vicinity of Forty-sixth and Third," announced the dispatcher. All over midtown, police cars hit their flashing lights and sirens as they sped through the city traffic.

Three minutes. That was all the time after the first shot, John Gotti had warned, they could safely count on before the cops would arrive. Yet he waited until the shooters were running up the block to the escape cars before he drove across Third Avenue toward Sparks.

Even then he was in no hurry. The car moved forward deliberately, slowly, as if out of synch with all the fast-paced commotion that was rushing around it. When he drove past the restaurant, Gravano looked out the window at Bilotti's body. It was lying face-up.

"Tommy's gone," he said.

Gotti, satisfied, suddenly gunned the engine, and the big car moved quickly forward. They were turning onto Second Avenue, heading to the East River Drive, by the time they heard the first sirens. Then they saw the flashing lights going in the other direction, passing them by.

* * *

Inside Sparks, at table number 94, a waiter rushed over to the three men who had been waiting and told them that Mr. Castellano would not be joining them tonight.

"Jesus," said a very rattled Jimmy Failla, "I could've been in that car."

"You wouldn't have been hurt," Frankie DeCicco told him with authority.

And without another word, Failla understood what had happened.

Bruce Mouw's beeper went off as he was driving home. Probably somebody wondering why he hadn't shown at the Blakey lecture, he imagined as he looked for a street-corner phone booth. Then he heard the radio announcer's voice: Paul Castellano, the head of the Gambino crime family, had been gunned down on a midtown street just minutes ago.

Mouw immediately made a U-turn. He was driving back to his office on Queens Boulevard, speeding, he would later tell his squad, like an ambulance driver hauling a cardiac case. And two troubling thoughts were occupying his mind.

First: Was this war? Was the Castellano hit just the beginning of an all-out conflict?

And second, but not by much: How was he going to explain to his family that they shouldn't count on his coming home this Christmas after all?

At the NYU seminar, so many beepers rang out in unison that they formed a steady hum. Soon the news was all over the room: Someone had whacked Big Paul Castellano. The seats emptied quickly. Professor Blakey was left alone on the podium, staring silently into space.

In the basement at 1809 Stillwell Avenue, John Gotti and Sammy Gravano were also oddly muted. There was no shouting, no congratulations. Both men understood that there would be time for that down the road, when things were clear and settled. When John was Boss.

They waited around, sharing a bottle of Chivas that

Gravano had produced from a desk drawer, until Frankie
DeCicco joined them.

"Went off without a hitch," he said. "Everyone got away."

"Great," said Gotti, but, Gravano noticed, without any
real enthusiasm. "Now let's get the hell out of here."

John Gotti was at home in Howard Beach, in his silk
pajamas, watching a movie on cable television when,
around ten o'clock, two homicide detectives rang his doorbell.

"Paul got hit?" he repeated incredulously to the two cops
at his door. "Gee, that's too bad." He showed, they reported, no emotion.

But when they left, John Gotti's mind might very well
have been racing with the same concern that was keeping
Bruce Mouw up that night—Would this mean war?

# 20

ANDY KURINS TOOK THE HAT OFF HIS HEAD AND PUT IT ON THE dashboard of his Oldsmobile. The hat was wool, a tobacco shade of brown in a herringbone pattern, and its crown snapped rakishly into the visor—not at all his sort of look. It was too sporty, he felt; but it had been a gift one Christmas from his wife and because of that he always wore it when the weather turned cold.

This morning, he pushed the hat forward slightly until it was resting against the windshield. It was the safety signal and he wanted to make sure it would not be missed. It said: Come on in. Everything's warm and cozy. Then he checked that the visor on the passenger side of his Oldsmobile had not slipped down. It was an unnecessary worry, he knew, but he liked to be certain. A lowered visor was the counter-signal: Keep on going. Don't stop until you're back in your own home with the door double-locked behind you. The visor, of course, was up.

A gesture of hospitality was also expected when you met with a Top Echelon informant, and now that the contact procedures were in order, Kurins turned to the food. He

146

opened the white McDonald's bag on the seat across from him and he took inventory: one large coffee, black; one large coffee very light, extra sugar; and two Egg McMuffins. All there.

And very tempting. He thought about starting in. It was not quite seven in the morning, he had been up for hours, his stomach was growling, and he could certainly use a jolt of caffeine. But that would be rude, a sign of disrespect. An informant already had enough doubts about what he was doing; it would be foolish to jeopardize such a tentative allegiance by giving the TE any cause to think his control was dumping on him. Anyway, it wouldn't be much longer.

Kurins had told him seven, which meant the TE was supposed to show at 7:07. Their prearranged word code translated into a real time that was precisely seven minutes after whatever hour Kurins announced over the phone. It was another safeguard they had drummed into him at Quantico: never on the hour, always odd times. That way if you're spotted, there's a chance—a small one, but still a chance—you'll be able to pretend it was an accidental encounter.

So Kurins, tired, hungry, and anxious, waited. He was parked in a far corner of the lot behind the McDonald's on Myrtle Avenue in Brooklyn. His car's hood was facing out. Someone driving by could easily spot the brownish hat on the dashboard; or, if he had to, Kurins could make a quick getaway. Also, one more precaution, he had his gun out of its holster and resting on the seat beside him. Kurins usually didn't do this, but today he was being very careful. Paul Castellano had been shot last night. He didn't know what was going to happen next. He just hoped the man he was waiting for would be able to tell him.

Mouw's timing had seemed diabolical. Last night Kurins had just sat down for dinner, Sharon was bringing the roast chicken over for him to carve, and even the two girls, for once, were sitting more or less peacefully at the table, when the phone rang. Kurins and his wife immediately exchanged pregnant looks: If it's important, they'll certainly call back after dinner. The phone continued to ring. After what must have been the seventh or eighth ring, Kurins ran to the hallway. "I'll get it," he apologized. "Be back to carve in a sec."

"Here's the news," Mouw said as soon as Kurins, rather snappishly, answered the phone. "Somebody shot Castellano. About two hours ago. In midtown."

"Jesus," Kurins said. "Tell me more."

"That's it," Mouw complained. "Now you know all I know." He went on rapidly, and with an urgency that Kurins found surprising. His boss was usually so controlled.

"What's going down, Andy? We *got* to find out," Mouw insisted. "If the Families are going to go to war, we need to know."

"I'll be right in," Kurins volunteered.

But Mouw had another plan. The Twins were poking around Staten Island. Phil Scala was already at the scene. He wanted Kurins to reach out to his informant and pump him. "See if he knows who ordered the hit. Was it the Gambinos or some other Family?"

"Got you, boss," Kurins agreed.

"If this means war, it's going to be one hell of a Christmas in New York. Get back to me ASAP."

"Will do," Kurins said, but Mouw had already hung up.

When Kurins returned to the dining room, he was wearing his topcoat. He saw that Sharon had carved and the girls were eating.

"Something's come up," he said quickly, as he kissed his wife on the top of her head and at the same time pulled a wing off the chicken. "I'll try not to be too long."

Sharon shot him a stony, unforgiving look. There would be time enough to deal with that later, Kurins guiltily decided as he, never breaking stride, attacked the chicken wing and hurried from the house. He was closing the front door when, a small wish fulfilled, he heard his wife call after him, "Just be careful, Andris."

It was nearly a twenty-minute drive from Kurins' home to the Howard Johnson's by the interstate. The Connecticut

backcountry roads were scenically twisting and maddening-
ly unlit, but Kurins drove quickly. The prospect of solving a
mystery energized him. He kept his foot steady on the
accelerator, silently praying he wouldn't hit a patch of ice.
But he was also wondering with a building sense of anticipation, just what does Frankie know?

Frankie was the code-name for the TE Kurins had been
running for the past thirteen months. He was a beefy, darkly
handsome, happy-go-lucky wiseguy, a man who once had
truly believed that although only thirty-four years old, he
already had it all: a pretty wife, a prettier girlfriend, and a
future as solid as money in the bank. He was tight with both
Frankie DeCicco on Bath Avenue and Sammy Bull's crew
over at Tali's; he had been told it was only a matter of time
before he got "made." But on the morning when Andy
Kurins had first caught up with him, Frankie's prospects
were beginning to sour.

They met in a holding room at the Manhattan Correctional Center. Frankie had been picked up on a hijacking charge,
which in itself was not too promising since he had already
done time for grabbing a truckload of dresses. But things
had quickly gotten worse. The bullets fired from a gun
discovered in his car matched, ballistics announced with
considerable satisfaction, the bullets recovered from the
victim of a long-unsolved gangland execution. When Mouw
heard about Frankie's woes, he had sent Kurins over. "Feel
him out. See which way the wind's blowing," he had
suggested.

The wind was blustery and frigid. "Get out of my face,"
Frankie had barked as soon as Kurins introduced himself.
"They got nothing on me. I'll make bail and I'll give you
odds the gun case never comes to trial. I don't got to talk to
you, so leave me the fuck alone."

Ten days later after Frankie had, as he had predicted, been
released on bail, Kurins ran into him at a Brooklyn diner.
"Hey, Frankie, how you doing?" Kurins greeted him cheerfully. "Don't you just love this place? I come here all the
time. Funny meeting you here."

Of course, there was nothing "funny" about it at all.

Kurins had been tailing Frankie all day. And Frankie, Kurins never doubted, suspected as much. But if Frankie had any suspicions, he was keeping them to himself.

Kurins, eager not to lose momentum, quickly said, "Hey, mind if I join you?" He was in the booth before Frankie could protest.

When Frankie finally got around to talking, his mood was pitifully less confident than the one he had strutted out while awaiting bail in the MCC. Since he had been released, he said as he began to enumerate his problems, things had been "going straight to hell." First his lawyer had predicted his future in no uncertain terms: He was going to do heavy time. Then his wife had started asking who was going to pay the rent, buy the food, if he went away for life. His girlfriend, too, was snarling the same questions. Only she, Frankie was convinced, was already checking out the local talent to find herself an answer. How long after he got shipped upstate to Attica before his wife would be hitting the same bars, he moaned.

Kurins simply nodded consolingly. Always let the mark dig his own *deep hole* was another slice of Quantico wisdom. But Kurins judged Frankie had hit bottom when he heard him sigh, "I wish I never got involved in the life."

That was when Kurins, wise and authoritative, offered, "Maybe I can help."

By the end of the month, the gun charges had been dropped after the prosecutor volunteered that he had some problems with the legality of the search that had found the gun, the hijacking case had been postponed, Frankie had found a new girlfriend, and he was receiving monthly checks from C-16's special account.

It had been, both Mouw and Kurins agreed, money well spent. Frankie got around, and better still, he remembered what he saw and what he heard.

So now when Kurins pulled up to the Howard Johnson's, he headed straight to the row of phone booths near the rest rooms. A stroke of luck: The third booth was vacant. If it hadn't been, he would have had to wait; the phone in the third booth was the nighttime call-back line Kurins had made Frankie memorize months ago. But Kurins had a small fit of temper as he cursed his own stupidity for not thinking to keep an Out of Service sign in his glove compartment. With a shrug, he took off his coat and draped it over the phone. It was the best he could come up with on the spur of the moment. Still, he told himself, it should keep people out of the booth for a couple of minutes. Or less, if somebody ripped off the coat.

Then, in only his shirtsleeves, he jogged across the freezing parking lot to the lobby of the adjacent motel and placed a call to Frankie's beeper. When Frankie saw the Connecticut area code, 203, flash across the miniature screen, he would know who was calling, and where to return the call. And if Frankie's beeper had happened to fall into the wrong hands, there would be no way, even if the bad guys somehow traced the number in a flash and hightailed it up I-95 to Connecticut to see who was waiting for the call-back, to tie Kurins to the call.

Because Kurins wouldn't be in the motel lobby. A moment later, the chill now seeping into his bones, he was jogging once again across the parking lot. He hurried inside the Howard Johnson's and returned to the third booth by the rest rooms. He retrieved his coat with a good deal of relief, took a seat in the booth, and shut the door. And he waited.

When the phone finally rang, it woke him up. For an instant, he had forgotten where he was. Let Sharon answer it, he told himself. But on the third ring, he was wide awake.

"Federal Express," he said into the receiver. It was the code they had agreed on in case anyone was listening on Frankie's end.

"I got a package," Frankie said. Everything, therefore, was fine. If he had a letter, Kurins would have hung up immediately and summoned the cavalry. Still, Kurins did not waste time. "The Arches. Tomorrow morning. At seven."

"You got it," Frankie said, and then he clicked off.

* * *

Frankie didn't show at 7:07. The fall-back time was forty minutes after the hour. Kurins sat behind the wheel of his Oldsmobile and, growing more uneasy with each glance at his watch, tried to concentrate on the passing traffic. It was only a small concern that Frankie had missed his primary contact time; it had happened before. But if he wasn't there at 7:40, Kurins would know something was very wrong. Maybe the Families had already gone to war and Frankie was lying low, making sure he wouldn't be caught in the crossfire. Or maybe he was off doing an early morning piece of business, part of a Gambino hit team that was retaliating for the murder of their Boss. Or maybe it was too late and Frankie was face down in the gutter with a bullet in his back.

Kurins' mind was troubled, and very fertile. The waiting was always the hardest part. But then at precisely 7:40, he saw a black Cadillac drive by the McDonald's once, a circumspect twice, and then continue down Myrtle Avenue. Kurins breathed a genuine sigh of relief.

Frankie, an old hand after all the months, knew the drill. He parked a few blocks away and walked to the lot; it was safer not to have his car near Kurins'. Then he climbed into the backseat; there was a lot more room in the rear in case someone unexpected drove by and he needed to do a duck-dive.

"I overslept," Frankie explained sheepishly as he locked the car door.

Kurins was in no mood to issue reprimands. Instead, he turned in his seat so that he was looking Frankie straight in the face and, without even an attempt to disguise his concern, asked, "What's happening, Frankie? We got a war on our hands?"

Frankie smiled very broadly, a large, even mischievous grin. It taunted: I know something you don't know.

"Hey," warned Kurins, "cut the shit, all right?"

Frankie gave in a little. Still, when he spoke, he sounded amused. "Everyone in the Family's being very quiet about Paul getting whacked. Very quiet. Like they don't care. Like nobody cares. It's all business as usual."

"No war?" Kurins repeated.

"A coronation's more like it," Frankie said drolly.

"Who?"

Frankie continued to enjoy his advantage. He waited a melodramatic moment before announcing, "John Gotti."

"Jesus," said Kurins.

But Frankie went on, eagerly now, "The word is he whacked Paul. Now he's going to try and take his place."

"Gotti?" Kurins challenged incredulously. "He got the weight to pull this off?"

Frankie shrugged philosophically. "Everything's very quiet," he said. "John's looking very good."

It had been a long day after an even longer night for Bruce Mouw. By the time Andy Kurins walked into his office, twenty hectic hours had passed since the Castellano shooting, and a beleaguered Mouw felt as if he had spent every frantic minute of each of those hours with a phone in his hand. More dispiriting, he had little to show for all his work.

The squad, along with homicide detectives from the 17th precinct, had been combing the streets around Sparks, ringing doorbells in nearby apartment buildings, going into stores up and down the block, as they searched for witnesses. They weren't having much success. Even the restaurant staff contended they had seen nothing. Quite coincidentally, it was insisted, a waiters' meeting had been taking place in the kitchen at five-thirty. For all his squad's efforts, the only clue Mouw had was a vague, although provocative, report that a Hasidic man in a long black coat and black wide-brimmed hat had been seen talking with a very blond woman in a luxurious fur just a yard or so down from Sparks as Castellano's Lincoln had pulled up. And of course, there were the eleven bullets, fired from three different guns, recovered from the two bodies.

But there were plenty of theories. Walter Mack, an assistant U.S. Attorney in Manhattan who was coordinating the murder investigation, had been on the phone to Mouw early that morning to share what he had heard. Roy DeMeo's crew, Mack revealed, had done the job on Big Paul. It was their misguided hope that with the Boss of

Bosses no longer a defendant, the prosecutorial heat would be turned down on the car theft case. A senior investigator from the State Organized Crime Task Force had with considerable fanfare offered a conflicting yet equally definitive assessment to the press: The four rival Families had ordered the hit on Castellano because he had vetoed a lucrative narcotics venture proposed at a recent Commission meeting. The investigator warned a mob war was imminent, and, he predicted, the struggle for control of the Gambino Family would be long and bloody. Mouw, naturally enough, had worked out a few grim predictions of his own. When Bonavolonta pressed, he had no choice but to share them. The old guard, Jimmy Failla, say, or Tommy Gambino, would soon be running the Family. Unless, and this he said was a real possibility, someone stepped up to pop them too.

So, when Kurins came into Mouw's office and made a big show of closing the door behind himself, Mouw was immediately intrigued. Kurins, however, was in no hurry to surrender his advantage. Without a word, he sauntered across the room to the wall chart that Mouw had so diligently constructed over the years. As Mouw watched with mounting anger, Kurins, clearly relishing the moment, ripped the mug shot of Castellano from the top of the pyramid. And in its place, he put the photograph of a capo he had removed from the third row. It was a headshot of a smirking John Gotti.

"You're kidding me," Mouw burst out. "Gotti?"

Kurins nodded.

But Mouw was still not convinced. "The Family will never let him get away with it."

# 21

MOUW'S FIRM PREDICTION WAS, IN THE END, NOTHING MORE THAN wishful thinking. John Gotti's control was masterful. He had formulated his plan with careful foresight in the long weeks before the shooting, and now he followed through with a focused dedication that swung, as the circumstances required, between diplomacy and ruthlessness.

His first move was to solidify his support within the Family. Yet with shrewd restraint, Gotti let the uncertainty, the rumors of war, run wild for two tense days. Then, just as this edgy brew threatened to boil over, he had Joe Gallo, the cranky seventy-one-year-old *consigliere* who was ostensibly head of the Gambinos now that both the Boss and underboss were dead, call for a sit-down. It was a summons that provoked fear.

The meeting held a mine field of possibilities. It might turn out to be, the captains worried, a call to battle. Gallo would issue his orders to avenge Castellano's death. Or it might be a free-for-all; they would be forced to choose sides, either with Gotti or with the old-timers—and only those who made the right decision would get out alive.

Gotti, of course, counted on all these concerns; they
would make his intervention, the peacemaker stepping in to
head the Family in a time of turmoil, so much easier. In fact,
when he heard that two of the captains, Joey Arcuri and
Mike Mandaglio, had immediately sent contrived regrets,
Mandaglio even checking himself into a hospital in New
Jersey so he would have an excuse not to attend the
sit-down, Gotti's spirits soared. "They're sweating bullets,"
he gloated to Sammy Bull.

The meet was held in Caesar's, an ornate Italian restaurant on Third Avenue and Fifty-eighth Street in Manhattan.
It was not more than a ten-minute stroll from Sparks; and if
this wasn't sufficient to send an anxious chill through the
invited guests, the identity of its owner certainly was. It was
Sammy the Bull's place.

The captains came in twos for protection, but Gotti was
prepared. Four of his thick-necked crew, all with telltale
bulges under their sport coats, were waiting by the door to
enforce the evening's protocol. The capos, a deferential Iggy
Alogna explained, his exaggerated civility reminding one
guest of "the headwaiter at one of those fuckin' French
places," would dine downstairs. He suggested that their
"drivers" wait by the bar. "Anything you want, it's on the
house," Iggy promised graciously. But as the "drivers"
headed to the bar, Iggy, without apology, took a small
liberty. He frisked them. Very quickly, an arsenal of blue-
steel revolvers were piled high on a chair in the coatroom.

Downstairs, the capos were led into a room that was very
rococo, perhaps someone's vision of a Venetian palazzo.
The walls were a gold-flecked stucco, and heavy, antique-
looking bronze-colored sconces held flickering electric candles. There was also an overhead chandelier, many-tiered
and very bright, and it was positioned directly over the
center of a long table set for dinner.

At the head of the table, waiting for the twenty-one capos
to take their seats, was Joe Gallo. And flanking him like
bookends were John Gotti and Frank DeCicco. The two
men had the resolute look of fighters waiting for the referee
to give his final instructions.

But it was Gallo's evening. This, too, was on Gotti's orders and it was another inspired tactic. The fact that the Family *consigliere* was running things allowed the appearance of an orderly transition to be maintained. Gallo did not wait for dinner to be served. As soon as the men were seated, he gave a small, unaffected speech, and later everyone agreed he did it well. He spoke like a weary man caught up in a great and perplexing mystery. We don't know who killed Paul, but we're investigating it, he began.

All at once, the tension seemed to slip out of the room.

So that's the way it's going to be, the captains immediately realized, most with relief. No taking to the mattresses. No cowboying through the streets. Just business as usual.

Of course, as the old *consigliere* went on, full of querulous wonder about who could have assassinated their boss, the captains understood that he was laying it on pretty thick. His ignorance was preposterous; it was as if, one guest at the dinner was later quoted to the FBI as saying, "FDR had scratched his head after Pearl Harbor and said, 'Gee, this is a rough business. I wonder who could've had it in for us like that?'" Still, however fraudulent his questions, the old man's bottom-line logic was unassailable. If the Family didn't know who had killed their boss, how could they be expected to put the shooters to death?

Gallo ended his brief comments with a plea for calm. Don't overreact, he told the captains. There's no need to carry guns. No need to be on guard. Nobody is in trouble. Nobody is going to get hurt. The Family will survive and prosper.

When he was done, he sat down. And waited.

The room was quiet with anticipation. If anyone was going to challenge the old man's version of events, they would do it now. If any bullheaded capo, full of righteous anger, was going to declare, Cut the crap! We know Gotti killed our boss and he and his crew got to pay!, now would be the time.

A moment passed. Then another. No one said a word or made a careless sound. The silence was intense.

At last Gallo spoke again. How about we get something to

eat? He clapped his hands loudly and a flock of waiters quickly emerged from the kitchen carrying platters of pasta.

When the wine was poured, it was John Gotti's glass that was filled first.

Not that Gotti had taken the Family's support for granted. For during the entire time Gallo had the floor, and in that long, quiet pause after he had concluded, Sammy Bull Gravano and Fat Angelo Ruggiero were prowling the room. They had walked back and forth on either side of the long table, the grips of their revolvers sticking out prominently from their waistbands, their footsteps loudly treading behind the backs of the seated captains.

But what about the other Families? A Commission rule had been broken. The head of a Family had been hit without permission. The punishment was death—unless, Gotti realized, he moved very quickly. For—and this was the key to his diplomatic strategy—it was one thing to extract vengeance against John Gotti, a renegade capo, but it would be another to challenge the Don of the Gambino Family.

Yet despite the urgency of his ambitions, he also understood that he could not simply proclaim himself Boss. The other Families would not tolerate such a rebellious disregard of La Cosa Nostra rules. For his position to be accepted by the Commission, he would have to be elected.

The day after the Caesar's sit-down, Gotti convened a meeting of the Gambino Family inner circle to discuss the procedures for electing a new Boss. They met in the basement coffee shop of a Manhattan hotel. It was about four in the afternoon, and a sign on the coffee shop door read *Closed*. Fat Ange Ruggiero, without any hesitation, gave the door a forceful push and it swung open. He held it as Gotti, followed by Frankie DeCicco and Sammy Bull Gravano, walked in. The room was empty and dark. Ruggiero quickly found the light switch, and Gotti led the others to a booth in the rear. The walls were made of glass, and he chose a booth that he hoped could not be seen by someone strolling through the basement shops. Ruggiero stood by the door until Joe Gallo and Joe Piney Armone arrived. While they made their way to the back of the coffee shop, Ruggiero locked the door. He was about to sit down when Gotti ordered, "Check the kitchen, Ange."

Ruggiero went through a swinging door, and when he came out he announced, "It's clean." Only then did the meeting begin.

This time, now that they were in private, it was Gotti's show. He did most of the talking. Repeatedly, he kept on insisting that the election had to be soon, and that it had to be held "La Cosa Nostra way." All the captains, he said, must be contacted. He didn't want anyone later claiming they weren't notified and that that had prevented them from coming to the vote. "You make it clear to each and every one of them," he told Sammy Bull with a stern and fiery precision, "that I, John Gotti, want them there."

Then, jumping topics quickly, he addressed the more immediate problem of the other Families. "We got to buy time," he said. He ordered that messages be sent that day to the heads of the other groups. Tell them, he said, that we don't know what happened to Paul, but that our Family is intact. That we have no internal problems. Tell them that we're in the process of electing a new Administration and in the meantime we don't want anyone to get involved in our problems.

Only Joe Gallo, the rock-hard, wizened old man who had managed to survive three generations of rough-and-tumble Family politics, offered a dissenting thought. "You really think they're going to buy that?" he asked.

"Sure," said Gotti quickly. But Sammy Bull wondered if Johnny had his doubts.

Gallo must have, too. He pressed his point. "You know, sooner or later we're going to have to come up with a story about who killed Paul. We won't be able to keep on saying we're investigating forever."

"After I'm Boss," shot back Gotti, "we won't have to say *anything.*"

The election was held just days before Christmas. Jackie "Nose" D'Amico, the capo who ran the Diamond District for the Family, kept a party pad in a new high-rise apartment building in Tribeca near the southern tip of Manhattan. The building was crowded with yuppies, lots of young lawyer and stockbroker types who were attracted by the easy commute to Wall Street, and there was a large room in the basement the management made available for TGIF beer blasts and the occasional toga party. On a Wednesday evening in December, Jackie Nose told the manager he needed the room for a Christmas party he was throwing for some of the guys from his office. "Don't do anything I wouldn't do," the manager said; it was a tease which he later admitted to the FBI with considerable chagrin.

Once again, Joe Gallo presided. He sat at the head of the table, and when all the captains arrived he pointedly called the meeting to order. His tone was formal, full of the solemnity of the occasion, and he moved quickly to the heart of the matter. The purpose of the sit-down, he said, was to elect a new head of the Family to replace Paul Castellano. Who would like to begin the nominations? he asked.

Frankie DeCicco shot up from his chair, and all eyes in the room fixed on him. It had been Gotti's idea that Frankie should be the first to speak; he knew that there were some people in the Family who would prefer Frankie with his ties to the old guard as Boss and he wanted to let them know straight off where Frankie's loyalties lay.

"I nominate John Gotti," Frankie said.

When he sat down, everyone understood a deal had been made and it would be foolish, even dangerous, to oppose it.

Now Joe Butch rose: "I nominate John Gotti."

Then Frankie D'Apolito: "I nominate John Gotti."

One after another the capos stood, until everyone at the table, twenty-one loud voices, had spoken. Each of the men had nominated John Gotti.

It was unanimous. Within eight days of the murder of Paul Castellano, John Gotti, a forty-five-year-old hijacker from Queens, had replaced him as Boss of the Gambino Family.

* * *

The Christmas Eve party at the Ravenite was a coronation. The iron fire escapes of the tenements along Mulberry Street were draped with gaudy seasonal displays of lights that illuminated the clusters of men crowding the narrow sidewalk as they waited to get into the club. They would be there for hours. By seven, the front room, a cave of dense noise and smoke, was packed. A kid from the neighborhood who had a day job with the Sanitation Department was working the bar; he had one bottle of scotch in each hand, pouring two drinks at a time, and still the wiseguys were lined three deep. There were elaborate trays of food, all donated by restaurants throughout the neighborhood, on a long table across from the bar, near a soda machine. The immense spread was soon gone and Joe Butch sent one of his boys to his place, Café Biondo, down the block for more. "You tell 'em to haul ass," he ordered. "It's for John."

But John was in no hurry. He sat sipping Chivas in the back room, under a picture of his mentor Aniello Dellacroce. Across from him was his newly appointed underboss, Frank DeCicco; proud of his reputation as a stand-up guy, Gotti wanted the word to get around that he had moved quickly to cover his debt. The two men sat alone in the room, regally isolated from all the noise and confusion just steps beyond them. Earlier in the day, as he was going into the club, Gotti was overheard telling DeCicco proudly, "They've got to come to me." But now that they had come, captains and soldiers from all over the city and Jersey and up into Connecticut, Gotti let them wait.

Perhaps he was intent on making a point—he was head of the Family and his whims would have to be suffered. Or just as likely, he was exhausted. The last few days had been very busy. He had moved swiftly on many fronts. Other debts had been generously repaid: Sammy Bull and Fat Ange had been made captains. He had also handpicked and then dispatched a delegation announcing his appointment to each of the four other Families. Their responses had been swift: John Gotti has our blessings; he may represent his Family on the Commission. There was, however, one small, cautionary demurral. The Genoveses, who had done a lot of business with Big Paul, had taken care to explain to Joe Piney that a Commission rule had been broken. Someday, they promised, someone would have to pay. But other than that, things had moved just as Gotti had planned when he first started seriously thinking about taking out Castellano more than nine months ago. Maybe even better. So it was also quite possible that John Gotti sat quietly sipping his drink because he was, at last, enjoying his long and hard-fought triumph.

Just before nine, he put down his Chivas and gave the order: Send them in. One by one, the capos were led in to pay their respects to their new Godfather. They kissed John Gotti on each cheek and vowed their eternal loyalty. In return, the new head of the Gambino Family gave them his blessings.

Before each man was ushered into the back room, he handed an envelope to Gene Gotti. Inside was a Christmas present for his new Don. If his crew had run an average year, a capo would fill his envelope with as little as fifty thousand dollars. If his boys had made a few big scores, or if he wanted a favor from Gotti, or if he was worried some careless wisecrack he had mouthed years ago might still be held against him, he would be more generous. It didn't take long until Genie's hands and pockets were full. Ruggiero had to take his place at the door while he cleaned house. When he returned, Ange's pockets were full and the line still stretched across the room.

By the time the evening was over, Gotti had received nearly $2 million in cash. And that, he knew, was just the beginning.

# 22

"NOBODY ROLLS SEVENS AND ELEVENS FOREVER," JOHN GOTTI was fond of saying and it didn't take long for the new Godfather's run of luck to come skidding to a halt. Just as, it seemed, Diane Giacalone's streak was beginning. While as for Bruce Mouw, he wasn't having any luck at all.

Last March, nine long months ago, Gotti's name, as well as those of eight other wiseguys who hung out at the Bergin, had been tacked on to a federal indictment aimed at Neil Dellacroce. Who could have predicted that by January, as the case finally moved toward trial, both Dellacroce and Castellano would be irrelevant, both men dead and buried? Or that there would be a new head of the Family and that Diane Giacalone, the assistant U.S. Attorney who had revealed that Willie Boy Johnson was an FBI informant, would be bringing him to trial? Certainly not Bruce Mouw, not even in his worst nightmare.

Yet on January 13, 1986, when the principals in what had been *United States of America v. Aniello Dellacroce, et al.* had to appear for a pretrial hearing at the U.S. District Courthouse in Brooklyn, John Gotti, the head of the Family for just three weeks, found himself identified as the lead defendant. The press, hoping for a look at the man rumored to be the new Godfather, was waiting. Gotti, his unbuttoned camel hair overcoat draped over his shoulders like a cloak, his double-breasted gray flannel suit faultlessly pressed, his husky face youthful under a warm, butternut brown tan, his brushed-back silver hair as carefully styled as any anchorman's, was ready. And, more to their surprise, even eager.

"They say you're the Boss of the Gambino Family," a reporter challenged as microphones and tape recorders were shoved toward John Gotti's face.

"I'm the Boss of my family . . . ," he agreed quickly. And all at once the reporters wondered what was up: Who *is* this guy?

But in the next instant, his timing perfect, Gotti flashed a coy, twinkling smile and went on: ". . . my wife and kids at home."

Without breaking stride, cheered on by the appreciative laughter of his entourage of lawyers and bodyguards, Gotti continued his walk to the courtroom. Many of the reporters were smiling too: *This was too good to be true!* The man from the *Times,* an old-time police reporter farmed out after a distinguished career to the tedium of the courthouse beat, would look back at that moment and say, "From the start you could tell Gotti wasn't one of the usual tight-lipped Mustache Petes. He was what you pray for—good copy."

As Gotti reached out to open the door of courtroom 11, a rather pretty radio reporter from WCBS also grabbed for the door handle. "I was brought up to hold the door open for ladies," Gotti said with a warm smile, while, very gingerly, he opened the door with one hand and showed her in with a gracious wave of the other.

Then, his face beaming like a man who was enjoying a very good joke, the new Boss of Bosses disappeared inside the courtroom. He and his codefendants were accused of taking part in three murders.

* * *

The trial finally began in April. But after four argumentative days, in the midst of jury selection Frankie DeCicco managed to get his boss one more postponement. He was blown up.

It was a warm, spring Sunday, April 13, 1986, and DeCicco had spent the afternoon at the Veterans and Friends Social Club, Jimmy "Brown" Failla's place, on Eighty-sixth Street in Brooklyn. When he left the club, Frank Bellino, a Luchese soldier and an official of the concrete and cement workers' union, walked him to his Buick. The car was parked across from Tommaso's Italian Restaurant and DeCicco got in on the passenger side. There was a card in the glove compartment he wanted to pass on to Bellino; a friend was thinking about building a home in the Hamptons and maybe Bellino could give him a call with the name of a contractor who would do the right thing. No problem, agreed Bellino. He was leaning against the Buick, while DeCicco reached into the glove compartment.

At that moment, someone watching them pushed a button.

And the Buick exploded.

The force of the blast propelled DeCicco through the windshield. He landed on the sidewalk across from the restaurant. In pieces. One foot was found up the block, hooked around a parking meter. An arm landed on the awning above a bakery, the hand, all its thick fingers intact, raised as if in a final wave.

The news was passed on to John Gotti very quickly, and he, loyal and curious, rushed from his home in Howard Beach to take a look at what had happened to his second-in-command. It was a mistake. By the time he drove up, Bellino was in surgery at Victory Memorial Hospital and DeCicco was in the morgue. But he saw enough to leave him shaken. The Buick looked like a tightly sealed can that had combusted inside a furnace.

An hour later, surrounded by his guys at the Bergin, Gotti was still reeling. "The bomb was fuckin' something," he was muttering, going on, it seemed, more to himself than anyone in particular. "The car was bombed like they put gasoline on it . . . put a bomb under the car . . . you got to see the fuckin' car, you wouldn't believe the car."

Ruggiero, full of vengeful passion, tried to get his boss to focus on a more strategic issue. "We've just got to get to the bottom of it, that's all," he kept on repeating, his voice not at all steady.

But Gotti had already decided he knew who had ambushed DeCicco. He took one look at the charred and twisted car and the message Joe Piney had passed on months ago from the Genovese Family suddenly seemed very important: *Someday, someone will have to pay for Big Paul's death.*

That was why he was so rattled. He could not stop wondering if one piece of flesh, one body for one body, was enough to even the score. Or was this war?

The newspapers were wondering too. It was all over the six o'clock news. It got so that Judge Eugene Nickerson felt the publicity was "contaminating." He ordered the trial delayed until August.

Which should have cheered Gotti. Except the way things were going, the trial seemed the least of his problems.

No doubt about it, the new Don was taking a lot of hits.

It wasn't long before an informant shared with the Twins the snide nickname a lot of the guys were starting to whisper behind their boss's back—John-Paul Gotti. The TE said that people were making book Johnny Boy couldn't last. After less than six months as head of the Family, he was reminding some of his soldiers of that pope, John-Paul something or other. You remember, Spero and Tricorico were told in case they had not grasped the historical reference, the white smoke goes up and there's John-Paul standing on the balcony of St. Peter's waving to the crowds; the next day he drops dead and they're electing a new pontiff. Only, the TE added without even a show of sympathy, he didn't think John-Paul Gotti would be fortunate enough to get off by simply dropping dead.

When the Twins ran this scenario by their boss, Mouw

was skeptical. He had underestimated Gotti's ability to survive all the vindictive forces lining up against him in the days after the Castellano assassination, and he was reluctant to make the same mistake twice. Besides, he was getting to know Gotti better. Now that his smirking face was staring at him each day from the top of the pyramid of Gambino Family photographs arranged on the wall across from his desk, Mouw was burrowing with a renewed intensity through the Gotti files. They were remarkable testimony to one man's malicious ambition. Gotti had, against all odds, clawed and murdered his way up from the bottom, climbing from low-life hijacker to Boss of Bosses in just a few years. John-Paul Gotti? No, Mouw decided. No way. Mouw's instincts told him that Gotti would, somehow, hold off his gangland opposition, as well as have the last laugh on Giacalone. Gotti would survive; and in the end, Bruce Mouw and C-16, now pacing impatiently on the sidelines, would be waiting.

Still, even an optimist like Mouw had to see that Gotti was under siege from all sides. And the fact that he was now being forced to defend himself while sitting in a nine-by-twelve-foot prison cell didn't seem to help his prospects at all.

When a bemused Mouw tried to make some sense of it, he decided it was just as much a dispute over proper manners as over anything else. Nevertheless, a small argument with a rudely impatient refrigerator repairman had set in motion the events that wound up landing the Don, just one month after Frank DeCicco's death, in jail.

The incident itself was trivial street-corner stuff, and years old, played out in Maspeth, Queens, a rough-and-tumble part of the borough, on a September afternoon in 1984. Romual Piecyk returned to his car from cashing his $325 paycheck and found a double-parked Lincoln blocking his way. Immediately, his anger started to build. It wasn't so much that he was in a hurry, although that was part of it. It was really something else that was ticking him off: *That Lincoln got his nerve.* It didn't take long for Piecyk, who was six-foot-two, and a bruiser to boot, a guy who had been busted in his time for possession of a weapon and assault, to work himself into a real state: *Nobody was going to get away with this kind of crap.* He got into his car and started pounding on the horn. When no one rushed out to move the Lincoln, he just leaned on the horn. He put all his weight into it and let it blast.

That got Frankie Colletta's attention. He was sitting in the Cozy Corner Bar and he went out in the street to investigate. He didn't like what he saw. Who did this jerk think he was, pounding his horn like that? You see a car parked in front of the Cozy Corner, a Lincoln, you got to know the guy's connected; everyone in the neighborhood would figure it that way. Or maybe this big oaf didn't care. Colletta decided to teach him some manners. And while Piecyk was a guy who earned his living fixing walk-in refrigerators, the sort of units that were used to hang animal carcasses, and he liked to think of himself as a hard-ass, Colletta was the real thing. His friends *hung* people in walk-in refrigerators.

Colletta just walked on over to the car, reached through the open window, and caught Piecyk with a left jab in the face. That got Piecyk to stop pounding the horn. And to teach him a lesson, Colletta deftly grabbed the wad of bills he saw sticking out of the stunned man's shirt pocket.

Colletta was strolling back to the bar when Piecyk rushed him. He came at him like a charging bull, but Colletta stood his ground, and his arms moving like pistons, he threw a couple of sharp combinations. That shook Piecyk up, but he didn't go down. He came at Colletta again, but this time more slowly, and with caution. There was no change in Colletta's expression. His fists were raised, ready.

At that moment, John Gotti came out of the Cozy Corner. "What the fuck is going on?" he demanded.

For some reason, maybe it was the authority in Gotti's voice, or maybe he caught something in the way Colletta was looking at him, Piecyk backed off. Instead, he turned to the well-dressed man and began complaining that his cash had been stolen.

Gotti walked right up to him and looked him in the face. For a moment Piecyk might have hoped he was going to get his money back. But Gotti slapped him, open-fisted but with all his might, across the face. Piecyk's nose started bleeding.

"Get the fuck out of here," Gotti ordered.

Piecyk stood motionless. He could feel the blood dripping down his face. Who was this guy? He wanted to rip him apart.

Gotti did not move an inch. He held Piecyk without mercy in a rock hard, expressionless glare. His voice was controlled, not very loud, but full of warning: "You better get the fuck out of here." In case Piecyk still hadn't gotten the message, he reached underneath his coat as if he were preparing to draw something out.

Piecyk, at that moment, decided he should forget about the money and just leave. But ten minutes later he was on the corner of Seventy-second Street and Grand Avenue complaining to Officer Raymond Doyle and Sergeant Thomas Donohue.

"Two guys just beat me up and took my money," Piecyk said.

"All right," said the officer, "we'll make out a report."

"No, no," insisted Piecyk, once again full of rage. "They're still here. Over there."

He led the two cops to the Cozy Corner. The bar was empty. But when they were back on the sidewalk, Piecyk happened to glance toward a restaurant down the block. "There they are!" he shouted.

Gotti and Colletta were sitting at a table by the window when Piecyk walked in with the two policeman. Eight other large men also sat around the table. "Those are the two," said the refrigerator repairman, pointing to Gotti and Colletta. For a moment it looked as if he was going to tap them on the shoulder, tagging them "caught" like in a children's game. But Gotti nailed him with a hard look and Piecyk retreated.

"Stand up," ordered Sergeant Donohue, gesturing to the two men. "You're under arrest."

The whole table stood up.

"Just those two," insisted the sergeant, pointing.

The ten men stood there, hands at their sides.

"I'm warning you," the sergeant said.

The ten men did not move. Finally Gotti spoke. "Finish your food," he ordered. The men sat down.

Then he turned to the sergeant. "Do you know who I am?" he asked.

The sergeant didn't. And he didn't care to find out. "Step out," he told Gotti.

When Gotti walked into the street, he handcuffed him.

"Let me talk to this guy," Gotti asked, waving his handcuffed wrists at Piecyk.

The sergeant just wanted to get this guy to the precinct before the eight big guys having lunch decided to skip dessert. "Forget about it," he told Gotti.

At the precinct, Gotti was booked and quickly released. But within the week a grand jury indicted Gotti and Colletta for felony assault and theft.

The case did not come to trial for nearly two years. In those two years, Castellano had been murdered, Gotti had taken his place, and Romual Piecyk had figured out whose Lincoln had been blocking his car. Just days before the trial, Sergeant Anthony Falco of the Queens District Attorney's detective squad paid a routine visit to the star witness.

Falco, as his report to the D.A. detailed, found a man being destroyed by fear. All Piecyk's feistiness was gone. He had lost weight and his eyes darted about nervously, trusting nothing. He told the detective that he had been receiving calls at odd hours of the night, deep voices warning him not to testify. After he found the brakes on his van cut, he got himself a gun. He didn't care if it was illegal. He worried about his wife, and he worried about himself. He kept on having the same dream. He would be found dead in one of the meat refrigerators he repaired.

"I ain't testifying," Piecyk said with conviction.

Later that week Piecyk gave an interview to the *Daily News*. If the D.A. forced him to testify, he would have no choice but to take the stand. But, he promised, "I'm not going to go against Mr. Gotti. I'm going to go in his behalf. I don't want to hurt Mr. Gotti."

On March 24, 1986, he took the stand. He wore dark glasses, and he was biting his nails.

The assistant district attorney was a young man, blond and dignified. He asked Piecyk if he saw the two men who had "punched and smacked" him in the room. "I ask you to look around the courtroom," he demanded.

Piecyk looked quickly to his left, then to his right. Then, with no place else to turn, he looked directly at the defense table, straight into the calm, unsmiling faces of Frank Colletta and John Gotti.

"I do not," he said.

When the prosecutor tried to press the witness, Piecyk sounded like a man begging to be left alone. "To be perfectly honest, it was so long ago I don't remember," he nearly moaned.

A front-page *New York Post* headline the next day incisively, and a bit archly, summed up Piecyk's testimony: "I FORGOTTI!" Still, the judge had no choice but to grant the defense motion to dismiss the charges. The Boss of Bosses emerged from the courtroom a free man.

But not for long. Diane Giacalone, as she prepared her federal racketeering case, had become concerned that her witnesses would wind up as jumpy—and as useless—as the refrigerator repairman unless she moved quickly. In April, on the very day Judge Nickerson had ordered a postponement of the trial due to all the complicating attention the DeCicco bombing had focused on the case, Giacalone moved to have Gotti's bail revoked. She argued that while free on bail, Gotti had managed to intimidate a state witness—Romual Piecyk.

The judge's written opinion was issued on May 13: "The court concludes that there is substantial evidence that John Gotti, after he was admitted to bail, intimidated Piecyk and that if continued on bail John Gotti would improperly influence or intimidate witnesses in this case. . . . The court revokes the release of John Gotti and orders that he be detained. . . ."

On May 26, at a few minutes after three in the afternoon, Gotti, all his appeals denied, surrendered to the Brooklyn court. He was wearing Reeboks and a tan safari suit: his prison clothes. "Let's go," he told the marshals. "We're ready for Freddy." Freddy was the grim undertaker who lurked about the Li'l Abner comic strip. The "we" was strictly royal: John Gotti, the Boss of Bosses.

The marshals put him in leg irons and handcuffs and, along with five other prisoners, he was driven in a gray van to the Metropolitan Correctional Center across the bridge in Manhattan. It would be his home for the next ten months.

# 23

BUT HE WAS STILL THE BOSS.

John Gotti might be off the streets, living in a cell about the size of one of the closets where he kept his racks of double-breasted suits, but he was also determined to make sure his Family did not forget who was in charge. When Ange and his brother Genie told him that some of the guys were talking cocky behind his back, the John-Paul Gotti jokes and stuff, he made up his mind to teach someone a lesson; and at the same time, to teach them all a lesson. Sitting in his cell, with lots of time to think about it, he decided to make an example out of Robert DiBernardo.

The more Gotti mulled it over, the hotter he got. Where did Di B, a blow-dried hustler, come off bad-mouthing the head of the Family? But, as was so often the case, there was also a practical side to Gotti's rage. Di B was sitting on a fortune. He was into porn, pulling in millions of dollars each year, and he was also making money hand over fist by shaking down the construction unions, especially Local 282. With Di B out of the way, Gotti could put his own management team into place, one that would be a lot more generous with the CEO's compensation package. Stuck in his tiny cell, Gotti gave his pragmatic anger full run. It was high time, he quickly decided, for a very hostile takeover of Di B's varied enterprises.

On a visiting day at the Metropolitan Correctional Center during the last week in May, Gotti took his guest, Angelo Ruggiero, for a stroll. The two men walked in a direction that, as it happened, led them away from the guards; the prisoners did not have to be told to give them room. When they were certain they could not be overheard, not even by a hidden microphone, Gotti leaned over as if to share a joke with his friend. Di B must be whacked! he whispered. Now!

Ruggiero, before a day passed, shared the Boss's order with Sammy Gravano. After all, Sammy was the Iceman.

But Sammy, for once, was reluctant. It wasn't just that he and Di B had worked together to keep the unions in line, but they were also friends, *goombata*. He reminded Ange that when Johnny was putting together his team to take down Paul, he had used Di B to recruit some of the players. You owe him, Sammy argued.

Ruggiero shrugged. "That was then. This is now," he said.

So Gravano, who could think quickly on his feet, tried another tack. "Di B just talks a lot. He don't mean nothing by it. He's harmless."

"This has to be done," Ruggiero said flatly. It was John's orders.

If it has to be, it has to be, realized Gravano. At the same time, it no doubt crossed his shrewd mind that with Di B gone, Sammy Bull would be single-handedly running the unions for the Family.

Where do I come in? asked Gravano obediently.

Ruggiero said his plan was neat and quick; there was no time to lose. He would invite Di B to a meet in the basement of Tony Lee's mother's house. He wanted Gravano, in case Di B had a rush of the worries and checked with him, to reassure his friend; tell him that he was going to the sit-down too. Sammy, in fact, would be there. He would be sitting in the basement watching while whoever was walking down the steps behind Di B put a hollow-nose into the base of the pornographer's skull.

A day later, a frantic Ruggiero appeared at Sammy Bull's office on Stillwell Avenue. There was a problem, he told Gravano. They couldn't get the house. John was fuming. He wanted this piece of business taken care of right away. "Could you take care of it?" he asked Sammy.

Gravano thought about that. Di B was his buddy. John was his boss. "If it has to be done," said Gravano, "I'll kill him right here."

Most wiseguys never get up before noon. But DiBernardo, with his ranch house in Hewlett Harbor, Long Island, his Saturdays as a Little League coach, and his three-piece suits from Barney's, liked to think of himself as a businessman. He even kept to a suburban commuter's schedule, leaving the house at eight and returning in time for dinner with the wife and kids. The fact that his business involved selling magazines and videos showing children intertwined with barnyard animals was, he wanted to believe, irrelevant.

Sammy Bull was also a morning person. He, too, would be out the door of his Staten Island home at eight. His motivation, however, was to get his day off to a healthy start. He would be out on a five-mile jog, or going a couple of rounds with his trainer at Stillman's gym, and then he would fit in an hour or so of pumping iron. The fact that he supplemented his wholesome exercise regime by shooting a fortune in steroids—Deca-Durabolin was his drug of choice—into his Terminator body was just one of the many contradictions he lived with easily.

Since both men were up early, their routine was to meet a couple of mornings a week, at around eleven, at Sammy's place on Stillwell Avenue. They would have a few cups of decaffeinated coffee and, full of indignation, discuss which construction job–sites were behind on their payoffs. But when Di B showed up at Stillwell Avenue on the morning of June 5, Sammy had no time for his friend. "I got an appointment," he apologized. "How about you come back later, say five-thirty, six. We'll have a cup of coffee. Discuss things." Sammy was careful not to make too big a deal about it.

"Fine with me," Di B said.

As soon as Di B drove off to Manhattan in his white Mercedes, Sammy was on the phone. He called his brother-in-law, Eddie Garafola. "Round up Huck and Old Man Paruta," Sammy told him. "We got a piece of business to do this afternoon."

When Di B returned to Stillwell Avenue shortly after five, the secretary was already gone. Tommy Carbonaro, "Huck" to his friends, was waiting by the door. "How ya doin'," Huck said. "Sammy's waiting for you downstairs."

"I know the way," Di B said.

Huck's mind immediately started racing: *Is he being friendly? Or is he telling me to keep my distance?* Huck figured the best thing to do was just smile and let Di B keep walking.

Di B found Sammy, along with Joe Paruta, sitting at the long table in the brightly lit basement office. He took a seat across from them, his back toward the door.

"How about a cup of coffee?" Sammy asked.

"Black," Di B said. He was watching his weight, but he was too vain to mention it.

Sammy, who was a capo, told the old man to serve.

Paruta got up and went to the Mr. Coffee machine that was on a gray steel file cabinet behind Di B. He reached for a mug. And then he looked at Sammy and Di B. The two men were busy talking. So he put down the mug and, as if it was the most natural thing in the world, opened the cabinet. Inside was a .38 revolver fitted with a silencer. The grip was covered with black masking tape, and the gun felt heavy in his hand. He started walking toward Di B.

"Sugar?" the old man asked.

Before Di B could answer, Paruta shot him once in the back of the head.

The noise was muffled, just a *ping!* and Huck upstairs would later say he never heard a thing. Still, instantly it seemed, there was a red hole about the size of a nickel just below where Di B's hair was starting to thin.

The next shot tore his skull apart. Pieces went flying all over the room as if a ripe melon had been smashed with a sledgehammer.

"Jesus, that was fucking messy," complained Sammy as he picked pieces of his friend's brain off his clothes.

While Huck and the old man cleaned up the office, Sammy and his brother-in-law drove over to the Burger King on Coney Island Avenue. Ruggiero was waiting, eating a Whopper.

"It's done," Sammy told him.

Fat Ange, between bites, said he would send a couple of guys over to pick up the body and Di B's Mercedes later that night.

"Just make it sooner rather than later," said Sammy. He was heading back to his car when he turned toward Ange as if an important thought had just occurred to him.

"How can you eat that greasy shit?" he asked with disgust. "It'll kill you."

"Hey," said Ange after he stuffed the last bite into his mouth. "When you gotta go, you gotta go. Just ask Di B."

He was still laughing when Sammy drove off.

And, Sammy was told, John Gotti was smiling too when, on the next visiting day, he got the news.

The Don, it seemed, was making it a point to smile a lot. It was as if he wanted to get the word out that despite his heavy load of troubles, John Gotti would have the last laugh. So, the months in jail didn't seem to bother him. "Easy time," he bragged to the press. "I can do it standing on my head."

And, when the trial finally began in August, he didn't seem at all threatened by the government's wide-ranging case. He was charged with being involved in three murders. He was facing life imprisonment. There were three wiseguys who had cut a deal and were now waiting to testify against him. One of his codefendants, Neil Dellacroce's son, Armond, had already pled guilty. But Gotti, full of swagger, his tight-lipped grin curling into a snarl the moment he saw a photographer, did not appear to be intimidated.

Each day, he rode to the Brooklyn courthouse in the same van with Willie Boy Johnson. Willie Boy, as Diane Giacalone had revealed at an early pretrial hearing, had been informing on Gotti and his crew for fifteen years. But Johnny did not seem to mind. "Hey, Willie Boy," he could be heard yelling across the courtroom, "wait till you hear this." Then he would launch into some elaborate joke one of the lawyers had just shared with him, and with the whole courtroom watching in astonishment, the two men would wind up laughing heartily together. Bygones were indeed bygones. Apparently, the Boss of Bosses could truly forgive and forget.

The only bothersome aspect of his imprisonment, it appeared, was that life at the Metropolitan Correctional Center made it difficult for the Don to dress suitably for court, and of no less importance, for his public. "My client takes great pride in his appearance," his lawyer had appealed to the judge. "Physically coming into court haggard and worn and not impeccably attired does him a disservice when he is fighting for his life." But Judge Nickerson, whose tastes ran to button-down shirts and club ties, was unsympathetic. He refused to allow Gotti two preparatory hours each morning in his lawyer's office. Nevertheless, Gotti somehow managed to appear in court each day with a new, crisply pressed suit and shirt. His silver hair was always perfect, and his tan never faded.

After the jury was selected and the opening arguments were about to be delivered, Gotti's confidence continued to remain unshakable. "They got no case," he told the dozens of reporters who surrounded him, notebooks open, tape recorders humming, during one recess. "If my kids ever lied as much as these guys lied, they'd have no dinner." On another occasion, his head held high, his deep brown eyes narrowed as if he was taking aim, he greeted the reporters with a vow. "I promise you," he told them, "we're walking out of here."

And all the while, Bruce Mouw watched from a distance and wondered what ace John Gotti had hidden up his sleeve.

# 24

THERE WAS AN AUTHORITATIVE RAP ON THE DOOR, A VOICE CALLED out, "Room service," and immediately the two FBI agents inside the hotel room drew their revolvers. Mouw raised his hand, palm high like a cop stopping traffic, and motioned toward the Twins. He was saying, without a word: I'll take care of this. You watch the woman.

He moved quietly to the door and listened for a moment. He heard nothing. That troubled him; there were none of the stray, intrusive sounds he would have expected to echo through a busy hotel corridor. The silence seemed controlled, deliberate.

Matty Tricorico, his gun still drawn, caught Mouw's concern and, turning toward the black-haired woman, raised a finger to his lips; it was a gesture a parent might use to try to shush a cranky child. She nodded that she understood. Still, he took her firmly by the hand and led her into the bathroom, and out of the line of fire.

His partner, Frank Spero, was at the same time moving away from the bed. He settled into a narrow, carpeted aisle

179

between a desk and a hutch designed to conceal a television set. His back was up against the windows. Behind him rose the illuminated towers of Rockefeller Center. But now he faced the door. That was where, gripping the revolver in a two-handed combat stance, he aimed his gun.

Mouw silently mouthed, "One . . . two . . ."

At "three," he jerked the door open with all his might.

A startled waiter was standing there with a rolling table loaded with silver-colored chafing dishes. He found himself looking directly into the muzzle of Spero's revolver.

"Police?" the waiter asked hopefully.

Spero, his gun going swiftly back into his holster, grimaced as if he had been rudely insulted. "Mafia," he corrected sternly.

The waiter did not say another word. He seemed uninterested in Mouw's elaborate apology, or even in the exceedingly generous tip he added onto the check. Only when Mouw explained that they would serve themselves did the waiter seem at all grateful. He quickly left the room, firmly shutting the door behind him.

Inside the room, the agents could hear his footsteps running down the hall. Later, they would laugh about the waiter, and about their own high-strung behavior. But at the time, the night had its own imperatives, its own tense discipline. The Twins had been in this cautious—and ferocious—mood ever since they had heard, earlier that very day, the latest report from the doe-eyed beauty identified in the Bureau's informant files as code-name Easter. So unsettling was her information that they had reached out to Mouw and convinced him he had to come into the city for a crash meeting. They would be waiting with the woman from seven on at the usual spot, the Sheraton on Seventh Avenue and Fifty-third Street. They wanted Mouw to hear Easter's news for himself. It shed a great deal of light on John Gotti's trial strategy; and at the same time, it confirmed one of Mouw's troubled suspicions.

Informants, as a rule, were recruited only after the most delicate and subtle of seductions. But as with any rule, there were valuable exceptions. That was the fortuitous case with code-name Easter. She recruited herself. When she demanded a meeting with the FBI, her mind was already set. The Bureau, she had come around to deciding after several sleepless nights, would *have* to be her salvation. She had already run through the alternatives like so many unfulfilled wishes. Everyone else had only used her: her boyfriend, the mob, and even the city cops. If she didn't get someone on her side soon, the way things were going she would wind up in jail—or, no less likely an ending, shot dead.

Looking back at her predicament, Easter would blame it all on men. Yet while it was true that hers was not a solitary journey, she had worked very hard at attracting their company. She was a coffee-skinned Puerto Rican with a pile of jet-black hair, warm bedroom eyes, and very languid moves. She kept the first three buttons of her blouse undone, and her skirts were always stretched tight across her hips. She was petite, maybe five-three, but she wore stiletto heels. She would walk across a room, the click-click-clicking of her heels announcing her progress, the fabric of her skirt rustling as she moved, her head held high while, as if to keep her balance, she thrust her chest forward, and a lot of eyes would be checking Easter out.

There were many boyfriends, but in that crowded field she remained loyal, in her fashion, to two steadies. One was rich and powerful and, she would come to complain, "a creep." The other was just a creep; but, she would make sure to add since she felt an explanation was necessary, he was also *"mucho* sexy in bed." She had met them both—and although she preferred not to make too big a deal of it, a few others—through her job. She was a receptionist for a group of gem dealers whose offices were in the heart of the midtown Manhattan Diamond District, one flight up from the street.

The sexy boyfriend worked as a messenger, and he had shown up at her office one day with a package, and a cute smile. He left with her phone number. The rich man was Italian and she had met him at an office holiday party. He was standing with Jack D'Amico, and straight off that told her something. Everyone in the Diamond District knew about Jackie Nose: He was connected. Maybe that was why she stared. And, she couldn't help but notice, he was taking her in, too. She was getting a drink from the bar when he introduced himself. Later, as she was heading to the ladies' room, her boss called her over and whispered that her new friend was a very important man. "Like Mr. D'Amico?" she asked. "Bigger," said her boss; and it was only months later that she realized it had been a warning. But that night his cologne smelled wonderful, his white shirt was, she was certain, real silk, and his silver-gray suit was perfectly cut. It must have cost, she guessed wildly, five hundred dollars. They went home together.

Easter and her "important" friend were soon seeing each other once or twice a week. He had an apartment downtown, a sparsely furnished place in a white brick high-rise in Greenwich Village. She would stretch out in his big bed, her skin cool against the taut black silk sheets, a sparkling glass of Perrier et Jouet in her hand, and look uptown, toward the floodlit spire of the Empire State Building. *I've got it made,* she would congratulate herself.

Of course, she knew he had a wife and maybe even children somewhere on Long Island. But that didn't bother her. He was very generous, buying her dresses and, for Christmas, a handbag from Gucci's. He also told her that he was a very powerful man, with many important friends. He mentioned John Gotti a lot, and once he had even called him while she listened and that gave her a thrill; after all, she had seen Gotti's picture in the *Daily News.* The only thing that bothered her about her friend was that he kept a pair of handcuffs ("I stole 'em from a cop," he had bragged) in the nightstand, along with a few other of what he called his "toys." Some mornings, her body throbbing dully, she would wake up and feel very glad that she wouldn't have to see him again until the next week. But as if he could read her mind, after a particularly skittish night there would always be a present, something from Gucci's, delivered to her office, and she would tell herself no relationship was perfect.

They had been seeing each other for months when he

finally got around to asking the question she had been expecting. For a while he had been hinting, his tone off-handed enough, but his interest was still very pointed. She was pretty sure she understood what he was driving at. But then one night, as they were lying naked in bed, he finally asked, "They tell you when they're sending the diamonds out?" "Of course," she answered.

The rest was arranged fairly quickly. There was a ship-ment of uncut diamonds, nearly $160,000 worth, being sent across town by messenger later that week. Perfect, he told her. He had friends who would be able to fence small change like that without working up a sweat. When everything was settled she would, he offered generously, make ten grand for her information. Ten thousand dollars! She hugged him with delight.

Still lying in bed, he breezily sketched out his plan. When the messenger leaves, my boys are waiting by the elevator, they bop him once or twice, and we're home free. The only downside risk, he went on, talking as much to himself as to Easter, was the messenger. Never know how they're going to react. Some guys will play hero. You'd think it was their own diamonds they're protecting.

Easter considered that, and she thought about what ten thousand dollars could get her. I can handle the messenger, she abruptly volunteered. I guarantee you, I ask him, he'll play along. He'll hand over the diamonds with a smile. You just tie him up and he'll tell the cop he didn't see nothing.

Could work, the man agreed. We'll do the right thing by your friend too, he assured her.

Easter was very excited. In her mind, she was already spending her fortune. That evening, she was the one who, bold and enthusiastic, opened the drawer filled with all the toys.

But on the afternoon of the heist, the messenger—Easter's sexy boyfriend—didn't hand over the diamonds. While two Italian guys with guns and a rope were waiting in the stairwell, he very coolly took the elevator to the lobby. He continued down the block, a manila envelope filled with $160,000 of uncut diamonds in his satchel: a messenger going about his business. But Easter had given him an idea. What was good for the Italians would be just as sweet for the Puerto Ricans. All of a sudden, he made a pained face. That's what you get for drinking cup after cup of coffee, he mimed to anyone who might be watching. I'd better find a john fast. As luck would have it, he was in front of Charley O's restaurant. He hurried inside in search of the men's room. He picked the stall farthest from the door. When he opened the door, there was a man named Luis with a rope in his hand. He gave Luis the satchel, stuffed a handkerchief in his own mouth, and put his arms behind his back so Luis could tie them up. Hours later, a reelingly inebriated patron stumbled, quite literally, over him in the stall. The messenger was very convincingly out of sorts when the police arrived. The cops never suspected that it had only been the presence of a couple of large, inquisitive mice, scooting closer and closer as he lay there bound and gagged, that had left him so shaken.

At the precinct house, he told the detectives he could not describe the robbers. They had worn ski masks. Sure, he would be glad to go through the books of mug shots, not that he thought it would do any good. One thing—could he call his girlfriend first? He wanted to tell her he'd be late for dinner.

Use my phone, said the friendly detective. What's the number?

When Easter answered, he couldn't really talk because the detective was across the room, but he told her not to worry. Everything was going to be just *fine*.

There was no way she could believe that. She had just lost ten thousand dollars. What the hell happened? she screamed.

I'll see you tonight, he said sweetly, and then hung up.

It was nearly eleven when he rang her door. She thought about not getting out of bed. He kept on ringing, so she finally gave in. Before she could say an angry word, he handed her the satchel. "Lot better than a lousy ten grand, huh?" he said.

Easter thought about that for a moment, then threw her arms tight around his neck and kissed him deeply. It had all worked out better than she could have ever expected.

Except that two days later, the messenger was on his way to work when, according to what the police were able to learn from a startled crowd of witnesses, two big men came up to him as he was about to enter a Bronx subway station and, without a word, started shooting. He was hit six times. Four of the bullets went ripping through his face. When the police came, they didn't call an ambulance. Just the city morgue.

That night, the Italian met with Easter. I want the diamonds, he insisted. We can still be friends. You can still get your ten grand. But I want the diamonds. His voice was calm, friendly even, but his flat eyes drilled through her. It was the same detached, yet menacing look that would mask his face when he was getting carried away with his toys. The memory made her shiver. "Don't fuck with me," he warned, his voice as soft as a shadow. "I want those diamonds."

The next day two detectives came to see Easter at work. Both were full of sarcasm, and very threatening. The messenger's being shot full of holes had left them, she was told, feeling very foolish. Puzzled, they went through their interview notes and found that he had made one call from the precinct. So they traced the number, and what do you know—it belonged to a woman who just happened to work at the very jeweler's that had lost a package full of diamonds. Quite a coincidence, one of the detectives taunted. She was, they warned, in big trouble. Grand theft. Maybe even accessory to murder. If she knew anything, she had better come clean. Cut a deal. Or a pretty little thing like her was going to do some very heavy time.

When they left, Easter ran into the john and vomited up her lunch. That night, nearly trembling, she went to see the Italian. This time she brought the manila envelope filled with the uncut diamonds with her. "I knew I could count on you," he said sweetly, and for the first time in days Easter thought that maybe everything was going to be all right.

They were lying in bed, huddled together comfortably on the black silk sheets, when she finally dared to ask about the ten thousand dollars.

He smiled without hostility. Then he said, "You're lucky I don't kill you."

"But you promised." Her indignation flew from her before she had time to consider what she was saying.

"You bitch," he erupted. He slapped her hard across the face. "You fuckin' tried to rip me off."

As she was lying there stunned, he locked the handcuffs around her wrists.

In the morning, her body was so sore that it hurt her to put on her dress. Even he must have realized he had gone too far. As she was leaving, he gave her five one-hundred-dollar bills. Better than nothing, he said with a grin.

Sure, she lied.

After another visit from the detectives and several fitful nights, it wasn't so much that Easter decided to call the FBI as that she realized she had run out of alternatives. The police were threatening her with jail. The Italians had gunned down her boyfriend and wound up with the jewels. All she had to show for it was five hundred bucks and a few very ripe black-and-blue marks. The hell with them all, she vowed. She picked up the phone.

In her brief call to the Bureau, she mentioned John Gotti's name, so it was no coincidence that her promise of "some very valuable information" made its way to Bruce Mouw's desk. Or that Matty Tricorico and Frank Spero were dispatched that very day to interview her. They sat across from her on the plastic-covered sofa in her Queens apartment; and according to those who were familiar with what became known in the Bureau as "the landing of code-name Easter," she was, considering her situation, very self-possessed, as well as infuriatingly coy.

She would not be rushed, and the two agents, full of discipline, gave her free rein: The informant is always right. For over an hour, she led them through a more or less accurate version of her biography (she lied baldly about her age, among other things), her job in the Diamond District, her mobster boyfriend. When she finished, she had so artfully managed to avoid mentioning any names that in other circumstances it might have passed unnoticed.

Well, she was finally asked, How can we help you? *Tug the string gently,* was the Quantico wisdom. *In time, the whole ball of yarn will follow.*

So she told them about the stolen diamonds. About the messenger who had been killed. And about the police.

Who has the diamonds now? they prodded.

"Maybe I shouldn't get involved," she said. But her doubts, everyone in the apartment knew, were the opening of negotiations.

You're already involved, one of the Twins pointed out. Any more involved and you'll be in jail. Or dead.

Who has the diamonds? his partner repeated.

In the end, she broke down and told them what she had planned to reveal from the moment she made the call to the FBI. She told them her Italian boyfriend's name.

The name belonged to a capo in the Gambino Family, one of a handful of John Gotti's closest *goombata.* He would check in once a day with Johnny Boy, maybe more frequently when something was brewing. He wasn't just one of the boys, he was on the inside, a player who was very tight with the whole Administration.

And the Twins were sitting with his mistress.

Once the name was spoken, the rest fell into place. A deal was proposed, seconded by Mouw, and—despite some last-minute, slightly hysterical sobbing—agreed to by the woman. She even signed a formal contract drafted by a Justice Department lawyer. It was Good Friday when they registered her in the C-16 squad's 137 File, so, for lack of a better name, she was dubbed, then and forever, code-name Easter.

It never occurred to any of the agents that a code-name which evoked a festival commemorating sacrifice and redemption would be disturbingly appropriate. Still, no one in the Bureau would deny that in order to stay out of jail and to earn a monthly government check, code-name Easter was expected to spend one night a week in bed with her Italian friend and his toys. And then to report to the FBI every careless thing he said.

Easter had been making these reports for nearly a year when she finally delivered the one small bit of gossip that led to the crash meeting at the Sheraton with the Twins and Bruce Mouw. After they had finished both the room service steaks and all the necessary small talk, Mouw took over. He wanted to hear what had gotten the Twins so excited.

Code-name Easter, a born reporter, told it all simply and directly. So much anticipation, and then it was over in a moment; her story could have fit on the back of a postcard. She had, Easter said, asked her lover about John Gotti's court case. Her inquiry had not been premeditated. She wasn't fishing for information. She was simply curious. It had been in the papers every day after all. "Looks bad?" she had suggested.

"Forget about it," he laughed. "It's in the bag."

"You never know," she tried, now intrigued.

"I know," he shot back. "It's in the fuckin' bag. *We bought a juror!*"

Neither code-name Easter nor Mouw knew at the time which juror had been bribed, or how the Family had reached him. It would be years before Mouw would learn the whole story. The facts, as they later would be pieced together by C-16, were these: Juror number eleven, a fifty-three-year-old ex-Marine named George Pape, happened—and for once, this was the work of pure coincidence—to be the lifelong friend of a man named Bosko Radonjich. And Radonjich, a Yugoslav born thug who headed a bunch of Irish contract killers known as the Westies, happened to be an occasional business partner of John Gotti. The trial had just begun when Radonjich went to see Sammy Gravano and suggested a deal: For a price, his friend would vote to acquit.

Gravano promptly relayed the proposal to Gene Gotti, and Genie, who was also on trial in the case, gave the good news to his brother. A day later an elated Genie got back to Sammy Bull. "Do what you have to do," he told Gravano.

As the trial continued to be played out in the Brooklyn courtroom, Gravano delivered $60,000, in three $20,000 installments, to Radonjich. The Family would have paid more—"whatever it takes" was the order Gotti had sent from jail—but Gravano, out of habit, felt he had to negotiate. He got, it was agreed, a real bargain. And it looked even better once it was learned that the jurors had chosen juror number eleven to be their foreman.

Yet even if Mouw had known all these details, it was still unlikely that he would have decided on another course of action. His detractors—mainly a vocal assortment of angry prosecutors—would later insist that his actions had been unconscionably circumspect. After receiving Easter's report, he should have, they argued, informed both Diane Giacalone and Judge Nickerson immediately. A mistrial would have been declared. A new jury selected. A full-scale investigation would have been launched. And, they pointed out with rancor, a dangerous precedent would have been avoided, one that to their way of looking at things would have truly unforgivable repercussions as Mouw's determined pursuit of John Gotti intensified.

His supporters—an equally strident group—would argue that Mouw's hands were tied. How could he announce he had learned a juror had been bribed without revealing his source? Giacalone had already demonstrated her willingness to sacrifice informants. Who could guarantee that she would not reveal code-name Easter's identity in open court? An extremely productive source of information on the Gambinos would be shut off, and a life would be put in jeopardy. Operationally *and* morally, Mouw had no choice but to keep his peace. Besides, they pointed out, he did share code-name Easter's bombshell with his superiors in the Bureau, chief district judge Jack B. Weinstein, and the new U.S. Attorney in the Eastern District, Andrew Maloney. And while Maloney, a former West Point middleweight boxing champ who was partial to sporting metaphors, raged about the inequities of an "unlevel playing field," in the end he, as well as the others, went along with Mouw's decision.

But there was also a school of thought, one shared by both

Mouw's friends and enemies, that believed his motivation was, to a large degree, very personal. He was rooting for Gotti to beat the Giacalone case. He wanted his own shot at the Don.

Yet whatever the ultimate reason, and however moot its wisdom, Bruce Mouw sat back, and without even dropping a hint at how the deck was impossibly stacked against her, he let Diane Giacalone slug it out with a very confident John Gotti.

# 25

WHILE FEW FBI FIELD AGENTS RELISHED COURTROOM DUTY, George Gabriel's distaste for such a static, tedious assignment was especially strong. He was a hard-muscled FBI SWAT-team veteran, built, the joke in the squad went, "like one the twin Towers," and Gabriel saw his role in C-16 as that of a snarling, in-your-face gangbuster. It was precisely these hard-edge qualities that, in part, persuaded Mouw to send the young agent to observe the Gotti trial: Just let one of those silk-suited greaseballs try giving Gabriel the evil eye. But there was another reason. It was high time that Gabriel, the new agent on the squad, got to watch John Gotti in action. It was important that this tough young Greek understood just what sort of man Mouw would soon be asking him to go up against.

Still, it was with a reluctance that felt like defeat that George Gabriel obeyed Mouw's order and reported to courtroom 11 on the second floor of the United States Courthouse in Brooklyn. From the start, the assignment was a series of surprises. It did not take Gabriel long to realize all his firmly held preconceptions were not applicable to this

191

strange, fierce trial. And, also very quickly, he got his chance to go head-to-head with John Gotti.

The first small shock came during the opening arguments. Gabriel, who had excelled on the brutal hand-to-hand course at Quantico, took one look at Bruce Cutler, Gotti's handpicked lawyer, as he strode over to face the jury and thought, There's a fighter. It was in Cutler's walk, the way he bent slightly at the waist, dropped his broad shoulders, and even clenched his thick fists. And indeed, as if from the first bell, Cutler came out swinging. He marched over to the blackboard where Diane Giacalone in her opening statement had very meticulously sketched a Gambino family tree and, with one swift swipe of a heavy hand, cut a wide path right through it. It was a brutal gesture, and it succeeded in capturing the jury's attention. The government's case, he bellowed, was "fantasy." He had erased Giacalone's handiwork because "it tells you about a secret world that doesn't exist."

As he continued, Cutler let his indignant anger push him into a rage. He seemed truly out of control, his big bald dome of a head jutting toward the jury provocatively, his hand jabbing through the air as if he were flailing away at an opponent caught in the ropes, the veins in his ham hock of a neck bulging. The indictment, he proclaimed at the top of his lungs as he waved it wildly about, "stinks." RICO, he taunted, was just a "fancy wine dressing." "It still is rancid! It's still rotten! It still makes you retch and vomit! This is where it belongs!" With all his might, he slammed the sheaf of papers into a wastebasket. Then, his fury apparently spent, he took his seat. But not before his beaming client, John Gotti, rose to shake his hand.

The next day, as the trial moved on, John Gotti caught George Gabriel's eye, made his hand into a gun, and mouthed, "Bang!"

Gabriel, sitting in the first row, did not hesitate. He simply caught the imaginary bullet in midair; and then, a Man of Steel, he defiantly crushed it in a viselike fist.

That brought a smile to John Gotti's face. And during a

recess he motioned for Gabriel to come over to the defense table. "You a cop?" he asked.

"FBI," Gabriel corrected.

The Don took a moment to consider that; it was as if he was looking at Gabriel from another angle. "What's your name, Fed?" he finally demanded.

Gabriel told him.

"Well," Gotti said evenly, "you know who I am. Now I know who you are. It's better when everyone knows everyone else." The Godfather let that sink in. Then he asked, "Mouw send you?"

Gabriel smiled cryptically. He was much taller than Gotti, and from the way he stood, his head held high, it was apparent he was trying to make the most of this advantage.

"Well, you tell Mouw," Gotti went on, suddenly angry, "that I'm going to beat this case. When I walk out of here, I want him to come and see me. You tell him, just him and me. We'll settle things."

All at once Gabriel's smile was gone. "Bruce Mouw isn't your only worry, John. Don't forget about me. You walk out of here, I promise you, I'm going to be all over you."

The two men were inches apart, eyes locked. *Take your best shot,* Gabriel's rigid demeanor was challenging. *Make my day.*

But Gotti simply slipped into another mood. His hostility seemed to evaporate. "Hey," he told Gabriel, "you just sit back and enjoy the trial. It's going to be quite a show. That I guarantee you."

Gotti, this time at least, was a man of his word. The trial was "quite a show." Diane Giacalone never succeeded in persuading Willie Boy Johnson to testify against Gotti, but she still managed to keep the witness stand filled with a sordid procession of mob turncoats. She led these bornagain thugs through a well-rehearsed series of questions, and the jury listened raptly as an incriminating noose of evidence seemed to be tightening around Gotti's neck. But then it was Bruce Cutler's turn. Shoulders down, fists clenched, he lumbered toward the stand and began his attack. His pounding style was that of a barroom brawler; kneeing, eye-gouging, kidney-punching—whatever it took to take the man down and keep him there. He would not rest. "Brucify him," Gotti urged his lawyer on with delight.

First there was Edward Maloney. Giacolone had used his testimony to help establish that Gotti, a decade earlier, had helped kill a man in a Staten Island bar; it was an act, Maloney said under the oath, of Family vengeance. But, Maloney was to learn, vengeance takes many forms. Cutler set out to destroy him. Slicing the air with Maloney's rap sheet, he got the witness to concede that he had spent half his life in prison.

"You'd agree with me, sir, you are a menace and have always been, haven't you?" Cutler said, his voice booming across the courtroom with all the fiery indignation of an Old Testament prophet.

"No."

"Were you a menace to society when you went into jewelry stores and held people up with a loaded gun?"

"Yes," Maloney conceded, finally surrendering under the barrage.

But Cutler was not satisfied. "Does it refresh your recollections that you received from the government in total some fifty-two thousand dollars—well, let's put it this way, Mr. Maloney, that it cost the United States of America some fifty-two thousand dollars to give you a new identity, to give you a new home, to give you a new job, to cut your hair, and give you a suit, a menace and a bum like you."

"Objection!"

"Sustained."

But Cutler kept on coming, while the trapped Maloney looked desperately to the judge, to Giacalone, to stop the slaughter. "You used," Cutler said, "expletives like fucking cocksucker and bum on the tapes quite often, didn't you."

"Yes."

"Is that what you are?"

"Objection!"

"Sustained."

Maloney was quivering by the time he left the stand, and the jury was openly smirking at him.

Cutler's verbal assault of Giacalone's next witness was a short, nasty piece of business, but no less effective. In no time at all, he was referring to "Crazy Sally" Polisi, a robber who used to hang out with the Bergin crew, as a "yellow dog" for participating in a prison race riot. His rapidfire cross-examination was tenacious. He seemed energized by each low blow he was able to slip by the judge. And he soon had the ex-con staggering, agreeing that Gotti was "loved and revered" in the streets of Ozone Park, the same neighborhood where "yellow dog" Polisi peddled drugs. All Giacalone could do was watch in mute anger, her thin, sorrowful face drawn as tight as a deathmask.

Her moment seemed to come, however, with the testimony of James Cardinali. "Jamesy," as he was known around the Bergin, was a heroin addict and a convicted murderer, but in the courtroom, with his steady, even thoughtful tone and detailed responses, he came across as a model witness. He very convincingly implicated Gotti in the three murders specified in the indictment.

Gotti sat at the defense table listening to Jamesy, a *goombah* he had first met when they were both doing time in Lewisburg, and for once seemed unable to disguise his emotions. The audacity of the betrayal seemed to overwhelm him. As if to vent his boiling mood, he grabbed a pen and quickly wrote a note that he insisted be immediately circulated to each of the lawyers seated around him. One after another, as Cardinali continued in his direct, reasonable way to describe Gotti's role in the murder of James McBratney, each of the defense lawyers read the Don's instruction: "I WANT THIS GUY MOTHERFUCKED!!" And Gotti was serious. When his brother Genie's attorney, Jeffrey Hoffman, began a slow, circling cross examination, Gotti lost patience. He interrupted the questioning to pass Hoffman a note. It said: "SIT DOWN OR YOU'RE DEAD." Gotti wanted his Iceman, Bruce Cutler, to take care of Jamesy.

He was not disappointed. Cutler charged toward the stand and forced the witness to recall a telephone conversation he had from jail with none other than—Bruce Cutler. It was made during one of Jamesy's low periods, when he was having second thoughts about the deal he had cut with the government. Naturally, Cutler gloatingly revealed, he had taped the call. Then he began to punch away.

"You made up with Ms. Giacalone, did you?"

"Yes."

"So she's no longer the same individual you described in May of 1989, is that correct? In other words, she's no longer a slut, is that right, in your mind?"

"Correct."

Judge Nickerson had not interrupted, so Cutler took things even farther. "She's no longer a blow job in your mind?"

"Correct."

"She's no longer a liar, isn't that right?"

"Correct."

Finally, Nickerson, as though he was just beginning to understand where the conversation was leading, dared to intervene. "Excuse me a minute," he said politely. "Please keep your voice down."

"Yes, sir, sorry, sir . . . I apologize to the court," said a contrite Cutler. But after a short lull, the Brucifying resumed. When Cardinali, his previous confidence in tatters, left the stand, Giacalone heard voices from the defense table hissing across the open courtroom. She listened carefully. "The rat is dead," they promised.

And when the defense lawyers weren't tearing into Giacalone's witnesses, they came clawing after her. It was as if they were daring her to step outside the halls of justice; and then they would settle things, once and for all, in the streets.

A call by Judge Nickerson for a sidebar conference precipitated a free-for-all. As the team of defense lawyers rose and approached the bench, Cutler, without a measure of restraint in his voice, advised, "See if the tramp will give us an offer of proof."

Giacalone rushed to the judge to complain. Cutler's voice was, she said, "loud enough for the jurors to hear."

But Cutler refused to retreat. The venom curled around his words like barbed wire, and he told the judge, "I'm ashamed that she is part of this government in this courtroom . . . this is a dangerous woman. She's trying to inhibit me and intimidate me and she is not going to do it, Your Honor. I beg the court to open your eyes, Your Honor, and I say it most respectfully, to see this woman for what she is. I'm not ashamed to see it."

Judge Nickerson, a snowy-haired patrician, struggled, in his measured way, to be above the fray. Calm down, he, full of meek reason, advised both sides. It was a suggestion that was, after all the high-pitched battling, impossible.

So when the defense complained that Giacalone had not turned a necessary document over to them, Giacalone wagged her finger sternly at defense attorney George Santangelo and cried, "You're lying!"

To which Santangelo responded, "Get your finger out of my face and stick it up your ass."

They kept going at Giacalone for the entire trial, and she, a scrapper, refused to yield. But her will seemed to collapse after Matthew Traynor took the stand. He was the defense's final witness, a plump, smirking bank robber and drug dealer; and as soon as he began to testify, it was clear Gotti's lawyers' rude assault had been, from the first hot personal exchange, a deliberate and escalating strategy.

Giacalone had once considered using Traynor as a prosecution witness. However, after catching him in a series of lies, she'd had no choice but to turn her back on him, and on his prospects for a reduced sentence. When he took the stand, there was a sense of joy in his eyes. He was eager to even the score. Cutler was suddenly deferential; he stepped back from the stand and let Traynor rip.

Traynor portrayed himself as a disillusioned man; a mere mortal, he desperately wanted the jury to understand, who was more sinned against than sinning. In a singsong voice, his pitch rising as he shared each new indignity, he recounted his ruthless victimization at the hands of none other than Diane Giacalone. She had fed him drugs and kept him "zonked" to win his cooperation. "I was so stoned I didn't want to go home," he admitted with a wide, hangdog grin, as if now ashamed of his own behavior.

But that was not all. He, his eyes shining mischievously, offered another, even more remorseful confession. He had confided to Giacalone that he "wanted to get laid." He said this with a small shrug; he was only human, after all. But how did Giacalone, "the woman with the stringy hair," as he called her, respond? The assistant U.S. Attorney, he testified with convincing mortification, "gave me her panties out of her bottom drawer and told me to facilitate myself. She said, 'Make do with these.'"

And why was he so abused? So tortured? Because, Traynor said with tormented anger, Diane Giacalone "wanted me to frame Mr. Gotti and the others."

From her seat, Giacalone gripped the table in front of her. She was rigid, and silent. It was as if she was no longer capable of speech, so intense, so paralyzing was the hate that had, in the course of this long trial, metastasized within her.

Then at last it was, mercifully, over. After seven months and ninety witnesses, on March 6, 1987, the case went to the jury.

"We're walking out of here," Gotti insisted once again, both to the press and to his codefendants. "You can bet on it."

To which Mouw thought, That's one way to cover the cost of buying a juror.

The verdict came a week later, on Friday the thirteenth. John Gotti and his codefendants were acquitted on all charges. The announcement was made in open court by juror number eleven, the ex-Marine who had been chosen as foreperson.

"Shame on them!" Gotti snarled across the courtroom at Giacalone and her associates. "I'd like to see the verdict on them!"

It was left to Andrew Maloney, the new U.S. Attorney, to

face the press. The strobe lights from the TV cameras held him in a harsh arc of light, and his words came slowly, like a dirge. "The jury has spoken. Obviously they perceived there was something wrong with the evidence," he lied. It was, he would say, the most painful moment of his life. But he had no choice but to lie. He rumbled on, mouthing pious sentences he didn't believe at all, as an inner voice was devoutly praying: "Just give me one more time at bat. Please God, just one more in ...."

As soon as he heard about the verdict, George Gabriel decided he had to see Gotti. He had made a promise to the Don in the trial's opening days, and now he felt it was very important to keep it.

He guessed that Gotti, in his first moments of freedom after nearly a year in jail, would go directly to the Bergin. The triumphant Don would want to celebrate with his men. Gabriel rushed across Queens, driving, he would say, "like a madman." He wanted to be there to greet Gotti too.

Gabriel's timing was perfect. His Ford pulled into 101st Street just as the gray Cadillac carrying John Gotti turned the corner. Gabriel jumped from his car and moved toward Gotti. At the same time, two huge men flung themselves from the Caddy and put themselves directly in Gabriel's path.

He didn't care. *He wanted to hit someone.* He took off like a halfback who knew the goal line was just a yard away and the game was on the line.

Just then Gotti stepped from the backseat of the car. "Forget about him," he told his boys. "He's a Fed."

In an instant their wariness was gone and Gotti, too, was full of cheer. "Agent Gabriel," he called out, "how ya doin'?"

But Gabriel still had his edge. "Remember, John, I told you how I'd be all over you the day you got out."

Gotti took a step toward the agent. He did not speak.

"Well," Gabriel said, "I always keep my promise. I'm going be right on top of you from now on."

It was just a joke to Gotti. "It's a free country," he said with a large shrug. His boys enjoyed that one.

Gotti waved good-bye, the way one might to a child; and then, surrounded by his amused entourage, he disappeared inside the Bergin.

When he came out an hour later, Gabriel was still there. "Hey, John," he called, "long time no see."

The Don walked rigidly past him. It was as if he had neither heard nor seen Gabriel. But, as he could not help but notice, Gotti was biting down hard on his lip, and his thick hands were clenched into hard fists.

Before he went home to Howard Beach that night, the Godfather had spoken with his men in the Bergin. He was, by all reports, elated; and his mood was understandable. He had taken out Big Paul; he had won the support of the Commission; he had done a year in jail; and he had walked away from two trials. He had taken them all on and he had won. The Family, at last, was his to rule.

"I told you guys we're the toughest fuckin' crew in the whole fuckin' world," he proclaimed with total conviction. "Nobody can touch us now!"

The meeting that took place at nine the next morning in Mouw's office was more somber. The entire C-16 squad was there, everyone punctual for once, but Mouw sitting at his desk, his arms folded, seemed reluctant to begin. The day before, as soon as he had gotten the news from the courtroom, he had started a new case file, number 183-35-07. It was a small, bureaucratic step, but he wanted to do something. It didn't help. He felt diminished by how empty the file was, by all that needed to be done.

For months Mouw had been anticipating this moment. For months it had worked away at him, at all he believed in, that Gotti had bought a juror. But now that the case was once again his, and the attack was his to lead, his own anger did not seem relevant. It was personal, and today only the mission mattered.

When he finally stood up, he gave it to his men straight, the way, he would say, they did in the navy when they were sending you off on something that, whatever the risk, had to be done.

"We're only going to get one chance," he began. "Just one. So we're going to do it *our* way. By ourselves. However long it takes, we'll wait. Whatever we have to do, we'll do.

"But," he said solemnly, "we will do it. It's our number one priority. *We will get John Gotti.*"

# 26

TWO MONTHS AFTER THE THIRD OPERATION, A FEW DAYS AFTER the body cast had been removed, he was given the prosthesis. The artificial leg was a hearty pinkish color as if it were human flesh. But it was ice cold to the touch, and if he tapped it with his fingers there was a vacant, hollow sound. It was fabricated from laminated polyester resin and fiberglass.

His left leg, just below the thigh, had been beveled by the surgeons into a cylindrical mass. The stump was swollen, and there was a great deal of edema; his body fluids, unable to flow to his foot, had flooded the rounded joint. The stump felt heavy, and it throbbed.

Before the prosthesis could be attached, a stump sock had be stretched over what was left of his left leg. The purpose of the sock was to prevent abrasions and blisters. If, as the day progressed, his edema become too severe, or if he wore the wrong ply stump sock, the prosthesis would, he was warned, cut into his skin and the pain would be excruciating.

There were no straps or screws to keep the prosthesis in place. He had to raise his stump up in the air and slide the lips of the artificial leg over his supracondylar, where the knee would normally bend. When he lowered it, the bone contracted, and the stump was locked into the socket of the prosthesis.

The prosthesis, he was assured, would support the weight of his body. Go ahead, he was told, take a step.

It seemed like the most impossible thing in the world.

Yet, on November 3, 1986, twenty-three months after the rainy afternoon when a van had slammed into him on the Manhattan Bridge, Detective William Peist reported for his first day of duty at the New York City Police Department's Intelligence Division. He was assigned to Organized Crime, and when he walked to his desk there was hardly the trace of a limp.

But he had not forgotten what he had been through. In fact, in February, he had sued the city for $75 million, arguing that its negligence had contributed to the unsafe conditions on the Manhattan Bridge. The suit was still pending, working its long, slow way through the meandering twists and turns of the legal process. His suit against the Police Department, however, had been handled with alacrity. He had sued for a tax-free, line-of-duty pension. His claim: When he had attempted to arrange flares around his stalled Plymouth on the rainslicked bridge, he had, even though off-duty, been acting as a police officer. The pension board's decision: Denied.

"The P.D. screwed me royally," Peist told one of his fellow detectives at Intell. "But," he said philosophically, "what can you do?"

Detective Peist had been working at Organized Crime for nearly a year when Bruce Mouw found himself considering a small, new mystery. He was not sure how, or even if, it fit into his pursuit of John Gotti. It was just something, he told a few of his agents, that bugged him. "A bee in my bonnet," he had said somewhat self-consciously.

The city police, it seemed, had managed to plant a microphone in the head of a parking meter outside a Gambino social club on Myrtle Avenue in Brooklyn. The mike had been "up" for only a couple of days, however, before the operation hit an unanticipated snag. Louie "Ha Ha" Attanasio, according to what the police department's brief postmortem was able to uncover, had found a parking ticket on his Caddy and, furious, had run back into the club—only to emerge with a sledgehammer. His anger would not be satiated until he had pounded a parking meter to smithereens. The police report moaned that it was just bad luck that he had chosen to attack the one meter with the microphone in its head.

But Mouw, while he had been raised in Orange City to believe in the forces of predestination, could not rid himself of a certain uneasiness. On his own, he began, most discreetly, to do some poking around. He could not find a record of any parking ticket given to a Caddy belonging to a Louis Attanasio. And a quick drive by the club showed him that there was a long row of meters stretching along Myrtle Avenue. What were the odds, he wondered, that a vengeful Louie Ha Ha would just happen to assault the lone, doctored meter? Slim, in a perfect world. And none, he told himself, in the real world.

The incident became another entry in his Mole File. Another troubling mystery that, Mouw realized with considerable dissatisfaction, he so far didn't have the slightest chance of solving.

# III

## Tickling
## the Wire

# 27

THE NIGHT SKY EXPLODED. PLATINUM TRACERS ARCHED OVER-
head. Suddenly, there was another deep boom, only to be
followed by a suspended moment—and then, as if bursting
from heaven itself, a magnificent red star filled the sky. It
burned like a supernova. It was at this instant, just a few
minutes before midnight on July 4, 1987, that John Gotti
walked out the door of the Bergin and toward the street. He
was surrounded by eight bulky men, and he stood, illuminated by the blood red afterglow of the fireworks, in the very
center of this circle of bodyguards. His head was high, his
shoulders squared.

The crowd stretched for six blocks down 101st Avenue.
There were at least two thousand people, and as soon as
those closest to the club realized the Godfather was in their
midst the news rushed about. It traveled quickly and
excitedly through the streets, the way a small flame might
catch the corner of a piece of paper and then spread out
across the page.

It was John Gotti's party. He was the host and benefactor

of this open-air celebration of America's two hundred and eleventh birthday.

That afternoon, his men had stripped to their tee shirts and, working under the hot summer sun, had shoved at least a dozen massive green dumpsters into position down 101st Avenue. Six long blocks—more than a quarter mile—were cordoned off; a traffic-free mall now led to the front door of the Bergin Hunt and Fish Club. The carnie barkers and the cooks soon arrived to set up their booths. By six, as the first group of neighborhood kids were starting to fill the street, there were sausages grilling and roulette wheels spinning. An oversized American flag, easily large enough to drape over a car, was hung in a celebratory display across the length of the Bergin storefront. When it grew dark and the high-spirited crowd was nearly shoulder-to-shoulder along the avenue, the fireworks began. It was a long and elaborate production. Roman candles, weeping willows, blazing comets—each new and ingenious bit of pyrotechnics exploding in the sky above Queens elicited an appreciative rumble of oohs and aahs.

It was quite a Fourth of July party. And it was entirely illegal.

A permit had not been obtained from the city to block off the busy Queens thoroughfare. There were no temporary licenses granted to the food stalls or the games of chance. And most flagrant, if not audacious, of all, official permission had never been given, or even applied for, to shoot off such a monumental display of fireworks. The Ozone Park Fire Department, in violation of state and city laws (as well as common sense), had never been warned about the many rounds that would be exploding in the sky above hundreds of wood-framed homes.

And yet the police did nothing. They remained outside the wall formed by the dumpsters. They milled about in their blue uniforms and merely looked in, a mute, impassive, and benignly curious presence.

Staring down on all this from his makeshift surveillance post on a railroad trestle two blocks west of the club, Andy

GANGLAND

Kurins boiled with rage. The refusal of the city police to enforce the law left him stunned. In his rigid, admittedly sentimental immigrant's way of looking at things, the police, as much as Gotti, were guilty of twisting Independence Day into a mockery of the democratic values the holiday was meant to celebrate. Restrained either by their apathy or, no small possibility, their fear, they were admitting that John Gotti, the head of the Gambino Family, was beyond the law: a force and a power who lived by his own rules.

Kurins, his indignation growing into disbelief, watched as Gotti stepped into the crowd. The Godfather, still surrounded by his regal circle of eight bodyguards, still bathed in the electric glow of the fireworks, moved forward, and the crowd responded by surging toward him. Hundreds, perhaps thousands, of voices rose in unison to cheer him. "John-*nee!* John-*nee!* John-*nee!*" they chanted until the Godfather, his smile radiant, had no choice but to acknowledge their greeting. He raised his left hand slightly; his palm was held out flat to the crowd, and a bit of white cuff fastened by a heavy gold-colored cufflink was exposed. The crowd would not be subdued. Their enthusiasm ran wild. "John-*nee!* John-*nee!* John-*nee!*" they continued to chant, as another round of illegal fireworks erupted into a brilliant flash of white light across the nighttime sky. The Godfather, his unguarded expression full of delight and pride, took it all in: a Caesar accepting his tribute.

If there was ever a period in John Gotti's life that fulfilled his adolescent, street-corner tough-guy fantasies, it was the incredible time following his courtroom victory and his release, after eleven dour months, from the Metropolitan Correctional Center. His triumphs were complete, and they moved forward on many fronts.

His most visible success was, undoubtedly, the least expected: He had become a folk hero of sorts. The press, long weary of trying to extract even a nugget of a story from the gangland escapades of inarticulate and privatistic Don Cheeches, realized from the bombastic start of Gotti's

RICO trial that they had struck a journalistic mother lode. Here was a real-life Don who, in his studied public demeanor at least, was as compelling as any fictive Godfather. It was love at first sound bite. So what if Gotti was an accused murderer and a reputed narcotics trafficker? He had—and this only added to the legend—walked away from all the government's charges a free, if not totally innocent, man. A small-time, sharply dressed hijacker from Queens was quickly catapulted into a front-page Dapper Don. And as Gotti appeared on the cover of *Time,* his portrait painted by none other than Andy Warhol, *People,* and *The New York Times Magazine,* his notoriety was in many not too scrupulous minds transmuted into celebrity. When Gotti and his entourage of men with necks as thick as tire rims showed up at Régine's, his bodyguards had to hold off the groupies and the autograph seekers. Best of all, Gotti relished the centerstage attention. From his elegant DeLisi suits to his trademark last-laugh smirk, he packaged and polished his image as carefully as any politician. And it worked. A fascinated press followed his every public move.

Off-camera, Gotti was also active. This was his first sustained opportunity to consolidate his power in the Family and he acted with startling firmness. Just days after he strode out of the courtroom, he sent three of his captains—Joe Butch, Sammy Bull, and Frankie Locascio—around the city to meet with the twenty other crew leaders. The message this no-nonsense committee conveyed—and no one ever doubted they spoke from a script prepared by their boss—was terse and hard-edged. Gotti, his legal problems now history, would immediately begin to reshape the Family. He was determined to rid the Gambino organization of the old-fashioned Castellano way of doing business. The days of "selling wagon wheels," as many of the new-breed Mafiosi sardonically referred to Big Paul's out-of-touch commercial practices, were over. The Family, Gotti's Family, was going to be young and tough and obedient. The capos could either give him their full support or, without too much trouble or delay, he would crush them.

If more tangible demonstrations were needed to reinforce the bluster of the committee's words, Gotti did not wait long to provide them. When he had planned the Castellano hit, he had courted Joe Gallo, the Family's ancient, white-haired *consigliere*. But now that he was Don, he did not want a competitive senior statesmen in his Administration; or, more threateningly, waiting in the wings in case he stumbled. Gallo's days as a force in the Family, Gotti quickly decided, were numbered.

Gallo, his instincts for once failing him, did not even see it coming. At seventy-seven years old, the *consigliere* not only overestimated his own strength, he also underestimated Gotti's ruthless political skill. Things started moving to a showdown when, at a Family meeting, Gallo openly challenged the new Boss by suggesting, now that Castellano was gone, the captains should resign. It was his plan, although of course he never articulated it this badly, to select crew leaders who would owe their positions—and their loyalty— to Joe Gallo.

"I'm right," Gallo insisted forcefully. "I can break the captains, I can break the underboss anytime I want."

There was an anxious silence as the Family members waited to see how Gotti would react to this power play by his *consigliere*. "Joe," Gotti shot back, "don't flatter yourself. You ain't no Paulie [Castellano]."

"What are you talking about?" Gallo, clearly flustered, asked.

Gotti did not back off. "I'll get you voted in or voted out," he said coolly. "Joe, you think you're dealing with a fool? I break them twenty-three captains. I put in ten captains I promote tomorrow . . . They vote you down . . . And you ain't no *consigliere*."

After that public confrontation, it wasn't long before Gotti forced Gallo to resign his position as the number-three man in the Family. In his place, Gotti appointed the Iceman—Sammy Bull Gravano. And that, too, helped to underscore the message the committee had been sent out to promulgate. First, it emphasized Gotti's commitment to bringing young blood into the ruling hierarchy; Sammy was a babyfaced forty-one-year-old. Equally important, it warned that Gotti was not just talking tough; it was well known in the streets that Gravano was a one-man murder machine. Guilt never troubled Sammy Bull. He would go off to whack someone with a genuine, detached nonchalance. He made doing a piece of business seem as emotionally complicated as pulling the tab off a can of beer. And the Iceman rarely missed. He was the perfect hitman.

So, when Gotti was just starting out to show what kind of Family he was going to run and his new *consigliere* came to him with a beef about a crew member who was shooting too much heroin to be trusted, the Godfather issued his decree without hesitation: You have my permission—ice him.

The murder of Michael DeBatt, a former Wake Forest football star turned mobster, was designed by an inventive Gravano to look like the consequences of an ill-conceived robbery. DeBatt was told to report to Tali's, Gravano's club. When he arrived on a November evening in 1987, a couple of Gravano's boys greeted him warmly, and then when his back was turned, opened fire. By the time the police showed up, the shooters were gone, but the bartender, a conscientious witness, explained that this lug had burst in, gun drawn, trying to rob the place. "Guess this'll teach him crime doesn't pay," he observed, remarkably straightfaced.

No one in the Family had any doubts that there would be a lot more punitive lessons in the months ahead.

There were also, now that Gotti was back in hands-on control, lessons in, of all things, etiquette. The guys at the Bergin, Gotti fumed, had to realize that he was no longer one of them. He was the Boss of Bosses, not their old *goombah* Johnny Boy. So, no doubt with a bit of pride, he would chide his childhood buddy Fat Ange Ruggiero, "You got to forget them liberties you take. Take 'em when we're alone." Or sounding both weary and exasperated by his new burden of responsibility, he would complain, "You got to make your men know their fuckin' place." The guys, he would lecture, "have to learn, listen, nobody talks to the

Boss . . . Want to talk about baseball, it's different. When we talk about sandwiches, it's different. Girls." However, he went on with some force, no one could simply go up to him and talk about Family business. "I'm a Boss, you know what I mean? I got to isolate myself a little bit," he added, sounding almost sorrowful.

But all things considered, John Gotti was having the time of his life enjoying the rewards and fulfilling the responsibilities of being the Don. He even, according to a report a TE made to the C-16 squad, appeared at the christening in a Staten Island church of Sandy Grillo's new son. On the priest's command, he rose to his feet and announced in a booming voice that he would serve as the boy's godfather. The boy, to Gotti's apparent satisfaction, was christened John, Jr.

There was in John Gotti's world only one small problem as he moved ahead determined to rule his Family and make his mark: The Genovese Family wanted him dead.

Before the meeting could begin, Louie Manna, the Genovese capo who was in charge of the hit, had to clear out the ladies' room. He started banging impatiently on the locked door, making a real racket, until a female voice called out, "Just a minute, OK?"

"Go piss in the street, lady. We got to have a fuckin' business meeting," he snarled back.

That got her moving. The guys could hear the toilet flush, and after just another moment she came marching out, her heels clicking on the tiles. Snickering like schoolboys, the four men watched her walk off in a huff. Then with Manna leading the way, they stepped into the pink-tiled ladies' room of Cassella's Restaurant in Hoboken, New Jersey, to plan the murder of John Gotti and his brother Gene.

The order had come down to Manna from the head of the Family himself, Vincent "the Chin" Gigante, who was convinced that Gotti was planning to make a run on the New Jersey construction unions the Genovese Family controlled. Already there had been reports that Gene Gotti,

acting for his brother, was shuffling around the state intro-
ducing himself, trying to make friends. The way Gigante
figured, he could either call Gotti on it and listen to a lot of
half-baked denials, or he could just whack him. With
millions of dollars in labor union kickbacks at stake, he
decided, why should he take any chances? Besides, he had
never liked Gotti that much anyway.

Gigante reached out for Manna, the head of the Family's
Jersey operations, and on a steamy August afternoon in
1987, the capo began plotting with his team. Crowded along
with Manna into the narrow, windowless ladies' room were
Motts Cassella, the Genovese soldier who owned the restaurant; Frankie Danello; and Bocci DeSiscio. The plan they
worked out was straightforward. DeSiscio, dressed in a
disguise, would rush out of a parked car and begin firing as
John Gotti and his brother left the Bergin. It had the
element of surprise, and DeSiscio was a genuine triggerman.
It might have worked.

Except for one miscalculation. The Newark office of the
FBI had bugged the restaurant's men's room. *And* the ladies'
room. They heard the entire plan.

Not everyone agreed with Mouw. There were many agents
who, citing a higher operational priority, insisted that it
would be imprudent to blow an ongoing and highly productive wire just on the *possibility*—and they took care to
emphasize the uncertainty—that a murder might take
place. Others in the Bureau took the pragmatic low road and
had no qualms about it. As one agent argued with a
philosophical shrug, "Hey, the way I look at it, the bad guys
want to save us a lot of time and money by killing each
other—more power to 'em." But Mouw was adamant. From
the moment he received the report from the Newark office,
his mind was made up. For him, it was not an issue; there
was nothing to debate.

His decision was explained in moral terms. "The FBI has
a responsibility to save lives—not to risk them. It doesn't
matter who the intended victim is." Nevertheless, there

were many in law enforcement who speculated that whatever Mouw's articulated reason, there was in this instance, as well as in others, also something else at work: John Gotti was *his* alone.

Without delay, he dispatched George Gabriel to warn the Don.

It was another of those early—in John Gotti's day, that is—morning conversations in the doorway of the Howard Beach colonial. Gabriel, with Agent Mark Roberts standing at his side, explained in careful detail to the pajama-clad Gotti just what the FBI had learned about the plot to kill him.

Gotti, no longer sleepy-eyed, listened attentively; but when he spoke, his tone was narrow, almost petulant. "No big deal," he said.

"Well," said Gabriel, who had felt that going off to save Gotti's life was a rather incongruous mission to begin with, "don't say I never did nothing for you."

"Yeah," Gotti said with a small laugh, "I owe you."

"No, John," Gabriel corrected, "I'm just doing my job."

"Well," taunted Gotti just before he shut the door, "keep up the good work."

"Listen to me! I want the Chin dead! Kill the fuck."

When John Gotti was caught by surprise, he turned mean. That was when things would get out of control. According to the informant report filed with the C-16 squad, from the moment Gotti stormed into the Bergin just hours after his meeting with Gabriel, that was the way things were: vengeful and ferocious. He was kicking over chairs, slamming his thick fists into the wall, and ranting nonstop: "The fuckin' FBI had to come to my door to save my ass. Incredible! I want the Chin dead! Kill the fuck!"

But for once, his men couldn't follow orders. Gigante had anticipated Gotti's rage and had surrounded himself with an army of bodyguards. They formed a beefy cordon around him and relentlessly shadowed his every move. It would require, Gotti was informed with some trepidation, a battalion to take out Gigante; and even then, it would be a dicey piece of business.

Gotti's rough, impetuous mood slid back into control. He, as compliant as any politician, would accept a compromise. Before the week was over, Jimmy Rotondo, Gigante's underboss, was shot dead in his car. A bag of rotting fish was left on his lap. It was a Sicilian touch, meant to enrage the Genovese Family. It sneered: Revenge is sweet.

In the aftermath of Rotondo's death, the Chin thought things over and finally sent word that the two Families should make peace. Gotti, realizing that he had nothing to lose, agreed. But his men were still edgy and battle-ready.

And William Ciccone paid the price. Ciccone, a mildly retarded young man who lived in the neighborhood, made the mistake of standing directly across the street from the Bergin and, for hours on end, staring intently at the front door. His fascination with the club got on some of the guys' nerves. The kid was up to no good, or maybe he was trying to spook them. Either way, it was rapidly decided, he should be taught a lesson. Armed with baseball bats, they came charging out of the Bergin. They didn't care who was watching, they tore into the kid. Ciccone had his hands up over his head, yelping senselessly like a wounded animal, but they kept slamming the bats into him, his bones cracking until he crumpled to the sidewalk. His body was thrown into the backseat of a car. Later that day, William Ciccone, a bullet in his head, was found in the basement of a Staten Island candy store.

His murder was never solved. But nobody stared into the Bergin anymore.

The Godfather, then, had everything under control. It was a philosophical, even hopeful Gotti who shared his prospects for the future with his old *goombah* Joe Messina as the two men strolled outside the Bergin.

"If I can get a year run without being interrupted," Gotti said wistfully. "I get a year, I can put this thing together

GANGLAND

where they could never break it. Never destroy it. Even if we die," he added, his voice full of iron, "be a good thing."

"It's a hell of a legacy to leave," Messina agreed.

The Godfather just hummed thoughtfully.

"We got some fuckin' nice thing," he said at last, "if we just be careful."

# 28

As John Gotti forged ahead, determined to establish his "legacy," a dispirited Bruce Mouw had to admit that his team was "back at square one." All their previous strategies aimed at the Gambino Family had become, as they tactfully said in the Bureau, "inoperable" with the murder of Castellano. Then, just as frustrating, had come that taxing period when the C-16 team had no choice but to pace on the sidelines as the Giacalone trial meandered to its rigged conclusion. Mouw had found this forced idleness particularly painful. Out of desperation or boredom, he had fallen into a short-lived but most unsuitable relationship. When he abruptly broke things off, squad gossip had it, the woman got her vengeance by marrying a low-level wiseguy.

But now Gotti was a free man. And Mouw and his team were back in the chase, compelled to forge a new strategy. Mouw was purposeful, ready to roll up his sleeves, eager to resume putting in killing hours. "If it takes years," he told his men prophetically, "we're going to stick this one out. We're in this for the long haul."

Searching for a point of attack, Mouw, like Gotti himself,

moved on many fronts. Part of his attention was focused on the Castellano murder investigation. It was one thing to have the word of an anonymous TE, however reliable, that Gotti had engineered the hit, and it was another to be able to prove that beyond a reasonable doubt to a jury. So, working with the detectives from the 17th precinct, his team set out to locate and interview witnesses to the shooting.

From the start, it was a troubled partnership. The C-16 agents were never eager to play a subordinate role to the homicide detectives who were running the show, and they quickly made more enemies when they began to complain loudly that the city police had "screwed things up royally from the get-go." Worse, police officials were forced to admit there was a good deal of rude truth to C-16's unfraternal charge: The DD-5s transcribed in the aftermath of the murder were missing the names and addresses of many of the people who had been in Sparks. One potential eyewitness was simply identified as "a good-looking woman waiting to meet someone for dinner." It was only after months of detective work, and a good deal of luck, that she was traced to the Barbizon School of Modeling. And then, to both the Bureau's and the Police Department's astonishment, she was able after looking through C-16's photo file to announce she definitely remembered seeing Anthony Rampino lurking about on the street. "Those spooky, deep-set eyes," she said with a shudder as she looked at a surveillance photo Kurins had taken years earlier, "how could I ever forget them?"

Still, the small sense of triumph and teamwork this fortuitous ID produced was short-lived. A strained relationship fell further into shambles when Phil Scala, a squat agent whose gruff, street-talking demeanor seemed contrived to disguise the fact that he had written a decidedly literate master's dissertation in psychology, received permission from the Bureau to follow a lead on his own. He headed off to the Caribbean in hot pursuit of a Sparks busboy who might have witnessed the entire shooting. The police were not informed of Scala's lead or his trip until he returned and filed his report; and by then, many of the detectives were too angry even to read it. After working together on the case for a combative year, the task force's assembled evidence was still slim enough that it had little choice but to beg for help. A team of agents and police, to their mutual embarrassment, found themselves distributing an imploring flyer to Christmas shoppers in the neighborhood surrounding Sparks:

"If witnesses to the killings would only come forward, these murderers could be brought to justice. We need your help to solve this crime. We need your participation to keep the streets of our city safe for all. It is imperative for the maintenance of a civilized society."

It was also a time when Mouw focused, once again, on the possibility of a Gotti spy in law enforcement. To the list of clues in his closely held and growing Mole File—the blown wiretap at the Bergin; the handwritten FBI affidavit found in a mobster's ceiling heating duct; the jury-tampering strategy; the bugged parking meter fiasco; the tantalizing informants' gossip that speculated about the Don's "high-level connections"—he now added a new one. On one of the tapes that had been secretly recorded in the kitchen of Castellano's Staten Island home, a perplexed Tommy Bilotti suddenly asked his boss, "What's 'superceded' mean?" Dutifully, like a father helping a slow child, Big Paul struggled through an approximate definition. Yet, at the same time, he also managed to drop a few hints that suggested the Family was receiving advance warning of pending indictments in Manhattan.

It was only a small clue and, even Mouw would concede, it raised the possibility of only a correspondingly small leak. Nevertheless, he pursued it with a dogged determination, and after an intense session in his office with Andy Kurins and Joe O'Brien, he came up with a plan to trap the culprit: A phony indictment charging Joe Butch Corrao with loan-sharking would be filed in the Southern District of Manhattan.

The "indictment," its progress carefully monitored by Kurins and O'Brien, worked its way uneventfully through the twists and turns of the judicial system until it reached the desk of Mildred Russo, a deputy court clerk in Manhattan. By all appearances, she was an unlikely conspirator; "granny" was the dismissive, one-word description that crossed O'Brien's mind as he flipped through a drawer of courthouse index cards while keeping a watchful eye on whoever was handling the bogus indictment. Yet to his amazement—and mounting rage—he saw the petite, gray-haired woman, with not the least hesitation or fuss, slip the indictment into her desk drawer. Moments later, she bent down as if to retrieve a stray paper clip; only, as O'Brien observed from his post across the room, there was nothing on the floor. She was very discreetly slipping the indictment into a large brown folder. Then, the brown folder under her arm, she marched to the Xerox room at a distinctly military clip. That evening, the agents learned, and thereby salvaged at least a small laugh from an otherwise disheartening episode, Joe Butch Corrao took off for Florida on a chartered jet without even pausing to pack a bag. He was fleeing at great expense and haste from an indictment that, except in the world of Mouw's scheme, did not exist.

It was not long, however, before Mildred Russo was removed from her job and was herself the target of a genuine indictment. Yet, oddly, this success brought Mouw little satisfaction. In fact, it only served to aggravate and infuriate him further. Despite all the invention and attention he directed into making the case against her, it was never Mildred Russo, court clerk, who concerned him. She was just a small, well-placed hook the Gambinos had into the system. By the nature of her job, she was of limited value to the Family. Still, if she was out there, so, he had to believe, was someone else. That was the way the Family operated. Russo's existence was, to Mouw's conspiratorial mind, further proof that somewhere beyond his reach, with an identity most probably beyond his wildest suspicions, there existed a mole who protected Gotti; and whom Gotti, when cornered, would depend upon.

* * *

Although he was preoccupied with these other, corollary mysteries, the main thrust of Mouw's attention was to find a way to jump start his operation against John Gotti. There were late-night sessions with his inner circle, laborious reviews of all the case files, crash meetings with informants to try to identify, as Mouw put it, "Gotti's weak link." Months passed; and when "the suits" at 26 Federal Plaza (responding, no doubt, to pressures from the Organized Crime officials in the Hoover Building in Washington) started getting antsy, Mouw put them off in no uncertain terms. "For every week that nothing happens," he found himself repeating so often that it wasn't long before his men would jump in to complete the sentence, "Gotti will grow more secure. And when that happens, he'll make a mistake." Or so Mouw hoped.

Finally, after much internal debate, after rejecting as too dangerous (if not impossible) a scheme in which an agent would infiltrate Gotti's crew, as well as a suggestion that they sit back and let Kurins' and the Twins' informants do all the work, Mouw announced his battle plan. He decided to employ the same operational strategy that had worked first against Ruggiero and then against Castellano. He would pepper John Gotti's meeting places with bugs.

His plan to "go electronic" was immediately challenged. In meetings at 26 Federal Plaza, as well as with his own squad, voices were raised in strong protest. These agents said that Gotti, after having listened to tapes at his own trial and having seen the repercussions from both Fat Ange's and Big Paul's talkativeness, would now be particularly prudent in his own conversations. He would expect the FBI to be listening in. Mouw, they insisted, would be squandering time and, no less important, resources—running a wire required a small army of men, the bureaucrats were quick to point out—if he set out to eavesdrop on John Gotti. We're only going to get one shot, they reminded the head of the Gambino squad, shrewdly repeating Mouw's own words: Don't blow it.

Mouw readily conceded that Gotti would no doubt be careful. But—and this was the key to his strategy—*Gotti had to talk.* Overriding the dissenting agents on his squad and rashly ignoring the complaints from headquarters, he argued that Gotti was, after all, the head of the Gambino crime family. The Boss and his Administration needed to share their plans and schemes. They were running a multimillion-dollar business. The problem, then, was not would Gotti talk, but *where.*

Once they decided on a strategy, a new sense of purpose, even urgency, animated the C-16 squad. They were back in the streets, and back in the hunt. Their new mission: to find the one corner in the sprawling city where John Gotti and his men felt sufficiently confident and protected to discuss Family business. Just how the Bureau Techies would enter undetected and surreptitiously plant their equipment in such a well-protected inner sanctum was never discussed. It would have been too discouraging.

# 29

IT WAS JUST A BOXY CHEVY VAN, A COUPLE OF YEARS OUT OF date, well dented and a soot-streaked royal blue. Typical government issue transportation. But after Kurins rigged up a long tube with mirrors at both ends so they could hunker down in the back, curtains tightly drawn, and with the device jutting up unobtrusively through the partially opened sunroof, still check out the street, one of the agents came up with a fond nickname: "the submarine." It stuck at first because Kurins' makeshift creation did indeed function like a periscope; and, no small consideration, the agents enjoyed paying homage to their boss, an old submariner. But by the end of a tour of extended surveillance duty, the nickname took on a harsher meaning. Being cooped up in the back of that airless van for hours on end, day after day, was like being trapped in the hold of a sub deep in a dark sea. It was rough duty. Only Kurins, who was a bit of a loner anyway, seemed to like it.

But now that the decision had been made to "go electronic," and the sub, by operational necessity, had become a second home of sorts for the team, no one was complaining about the cruel hours. The teams of watchers were glad for the chance to throw themselves into the case. There was a new sense of purpose, of things finally moving forward after a long lull. Anger was a common motivator too: Gotti's buying a juror had left them eager to even the score.

Mouw had spelled out the significance of their task in a closed-door meeting for the entire squad. It was held early in the morning, the sleepy-eyed agents crowding into his office with their coffees in hand. And there was their supervisor, his sheer energy almost electric, pacing back and forth across the room as he waited for the squad to assemble. "It was as if Bruce was some kind of animal dying to break out of his cage," one agent observed. Which made sense: How else to describe a fieldman who found himself confined to a desk when the action was heading out into the streets?

Despite the importance of the occasion, Mouw spoke in his soft, downbeat voice. Operationally, he explained, their mission was two-fold. First, they had to collect sufficient firsthand information—names, dates and times of meetings —to persuade a judge to authorize an oral intercept order. It would be careful, demanding work. They had to stake out all of Gotti's haunts, record everyone who entered and exited, until they were able to establish that there was, as the speculative but legally binding language went, "probable cause to believe the subjects are utilizing the premises in connection with their criminal activities." Informant reports, he emphasized, were not enough; judges tended to look on them as collateral confirmation at best. "There's no getting around it," Mouw said. "Seeing is believing." It was his shorthand way of saying that the team had to stick it out in the sub until they saw with their own eyes (or binoculars) what the TEs were reporting.

But that was only one aspect of the surveillance mission —and although essential, arguably the part that would be of lesser significance in the long run. As Mouw admitted to his squad, if you stuck to form, made sure to dot all the *i*'s in your affidavit, judges handed out wire authorizations pretty routinely. What was genuinely rare, however, was a *produc-*

*tive* wire. Imagine spending six months eavesdropping on Johnny Boy's home—and all we've got is tapes of our man fighting with his wife and kids. It was Mouw's worst nightmare. When the Techies go in, he said, we've got to make sure we send them off to spike the right place.

He had made his point, and now he was winding down. "If we succeed," he said, "we'll be laying down the first pieces in the puzzle. We'll be setting down the base around which we can build our entire case." And he ended his speech with a businesslike but urgent order. Find me, he instructed his squad, the answer to one question: Where does John Gotti go to meet with his top men?

Ironically, it was Mouw, the deskman, who made the first major breakthrough. True, both the Twins' TEs, Kurins' Frankie, and even code-name Easter had reported pieces of the story. Nevertheless, it wasn't until Mouw had stitched them together into a coherent whole that the value of these reports became clear. He had worked it all out in the energetic days following his instructions to his squad. While the team was parked in the sub a few blocks down from the Bergin, he had squirreled himself away in his office reading and then rereading a tall pile of informant 209 reports. When he found enough facts to put together a fairly convincing theory, he summoned his inner circle to another one of the early-morning meetings that, now that the team was on battle alert, were becoming increasingly frequent. Gentlemen, he announced, John Gotti has moved his base of operations.

He proceeded, shuffling through the pile of 209s scattered across his desk, to quote stray underlined remarks and circled tidbits as supporting evidence. But what it came down to was this. Like many people who had first found success in the outer boroughs, Gotti was stepping into the brighter lights and bigger promise of Manhattan. The Bergin, tucked away in the back alley obscurity of Queens, had been a suitable hangout when he was just a capo running a crew of wiseguys, but now that he was Boss of Bosses, the head of the entire Family, he required a headquarters that reflected his new position. The Dapper Don, as the tabloids were now calling him, headed over the Manhattan Bridge and into the heart of the city. He was, all the clues seemed to suggest, working out of his old mentor Neil Dellacroce's headquarters in Little Italy—the Ravenite Social Club.

It was raining the first night they parked the blue sub adjacent to the cemetery on Prince Street in Little Italy. The small cemetery, surrounded by a high brick wall, was on church property; the dark Gothic spires of Old St. Patrick's Cathedral rose up as gray silhouettes in the evening sky above the faded headstones. In the back of the van, the curtains were drawn and the rain was pinging on the metal roof. The agents were deep in enemy territory, and silence was the rule. It was as spooky, Kurins imagined, as being laid out in the cemetery itself.

But even on that first night, it was worth it. The Ravenite was hopping with activity. Gambino soldiers and capos were hurrying through the rain up Mulberry Street. With their attention largely focused on protecting their often carefully arranged hairdos, no one seemed to notice the blue van parked up a block by Old St. Pat's. But the agents looking through the periscope—and when they dared to part the curtains, through a long-lensed Canon camera—caught it all.

They even watched as Gotti's black Mercedes—the Lincoln Town Car was no longer suitably regal—pulled up to the front door of the club. When one thick-necked bruiser rushed from the front passenger seat, umbrella in his hand, to open the rear door for his Don, they saw Gotti ignore the man, and with a graceful little leap, step from the car to the sidewalk. Hands in his pockets, he jogged through the downpour to the front door. No doubt about it, they decided, they were in the right place.

Only, it was the worst possible place.

During a strategy session the next day at the Queens office, it was agreed that the Ravenite would be a difficult target not simply for the team to monitor, but also for the

Techies to penetrate. Maybe impossible. Part of the difficulty was the neighborhood. Little Italy was alive with a bustling army of plainclothes watchers. As an exasperated police report that had crossed Mouw's desk put it: "The denizens of that area are very alert to the presence of strangers and strange vehicles. The fact [that] even law-abiding inhabitants of that area will report the presence of strangers to the organized crime figures who frequent it is legend in the NYPD."

Also well known was the list of surveillances mounted against the club in Dellacroce's day that had quickly turned sour. There had been the time when one inventive police intelligence officer had come up with the brainstorm of hiding in the trunk of a parked car so that he could eavesdrop on the passing parade of wiseguys—only to nearly drown when someone opened a slew of fire hydrants and flooded the street. And the time when, the day after the police set up a video camera and a parabolic microphone in an apartment overlooking the club, a note was pushed under the door threatening to burn the entire building down unless "you rats" left.

Then, when the cops tried to break into the club in the middle of the night to plant a microphone, they were rebuffed by a ferocious German shepherd. They returned the next night, planning to drug the dog, only to find a half-dozen baseball bat–wielding thugs waiting for them. Leading the charge was the club's elderly caretaker, Mike Cirelli, who lived with his wife in an apartment on the building's second floor. The next morning, according to a report a detective filed, Cirelli was ordered to forget about baseball bats. If the cops broke in again, he was instructed to shoot first and ask questions later. We can always say we thought they were burglars, the old man was told.

To make things worse, all these fiascos had occurred before the security-conscious Gotti took over the Family. Now that the Ravenite was his headquarters, he had transformed the club into what appeared to be a fortress. The large storefront windows had been ripped out and replaced with red brick walls. The two windows that remained were not much bigger than portholes and were guarded by iron bars. There was also a new front door at least half a foot thick and no doubt as solid as a tank. And, the agents feared, who knew what the Don had installed inside the club? Motion detectors? Surveillance cameras? It was anybody's guess.

The team, it was generally felt as a sense of frustration seemed to take hold, had come this far, to the very threshold of Gotti's world, only to realize that the Don was still very much beyond its reach. George Gabriel, to whom Mouw had assigned the demanding responsibility of writing the affidavit that would be submitted to the judge, would later remember afternoons and evenings spent staring at the white storm door of the Ravenite and wondering if he would ever even come close to knowing what went on behind it.

All the C-16 team could do was to sit in the blue submarine, watching and waiting. And mostly hoping, as Mouw put it, "for something to land right in our laps."

Meanwhile, on weekends, the team discovered, Gotti, like any suburbanite weary from all the daily commuting, preferred to stay closer to home. He shifted his court back to the Bergin. Naturally, the blue submarine followed. The van would pull into what was a rather conspicuous position underneath the railroad trestle two blocks up from the club, but no one ever disturbed them. From this vantage point, they could watch as Family members, mostly Johnny Boy's longtime *goombata,* started arriving at about noon on Saturdays. Like clockwork, the hardworking Don would make an appearance himself sometime after three in the afternoon.

One Saturday, out of curiosity as much as strategic instinct, Mouw decided to have Gotti followed from the moment he left his white colonial in Howard Beach. He assigned only one car to the task, and he had just a slight flicker of interest when the agent, at about 12:30, radioed in that Gotti's Mercedes had quickly and expertly succeeded in shaking him. Mouw decided Gotti had risen early for once and was having some fun with the agent as he headed to the Bergin. But when more than two hours had passed before Gotti's car pulled into Ozone Avenue, Mouw found himself wondering if the Don had a more clandestine weekend meeting place tucked away in another corner of the city.

The next Saturday, Mouw peppered Howard Beach with unmarked cars. The operation was, in the prideful Bureau shorthand, "strictly top shelf": backup cars, parallel tailing in case the front team overran, no dashing through lights, everything nice and neat. And although Gotti tried his resourceful best to shake the tail, they succeeded in following him to his destination. The black Mercedes made its way through the baronial, wrought iron gates of a cemetery.

Watching through their binoculars, a team of FBI agents saw the Don emerge alone from his car. He had a bouquet of roses in his hand. Walking rigidly, he went to his son Frank's grave and bent to place the flowers on the headstone. He took his time, arranging the flowers very carefully. When he stood up, he looked at the arrangement for a moment and, the agents thought, offered a nod of approval. For the next thirty minutes or so he sat on a stone bench across from the grave, staring at it, his shoulders hunched. From time to time, he talked softly, like a man holding a conversation; but from the agents' vantage point, whether Gotti was speaking to himself, or to his son, or simply to the heavens was anyone's guess. Finally, he stood, uttered a long, audible sigh, and like a man just awakened from a deep sleep, he shuffled off listlessly to his car. Yet twenty minutes later when the Mercedes pulled up in front of the Bergin, there he was jumping from the car with a youthful bounce and strutting, cool and imperial, across the sidewalk to the front door.

With that small mystery solved, the team now concentrated all its weekend efforts on the Bergin. It would be, Mouw decided confidently as the surveillance reports detailing busy Friday and Saturday afternoons at the club mounted up, a relatively easy piece of business for the Techies to spike the place. It was nothing like the seemingly impregnable Ravenite. And the Queens neighborhood, he

noted with relief, was pretty much deserted at night. But
most encouraging of all, the State Organized Crime Task
Force guys had planted mikes in the place back in 1985. The
only tricky part, he reasoned, lay in deciding just where
inside the club would be the most productive spots to hide
the little devils.

For a long stretch of late nights, the submarine also took
up a watchful position near Tali's, Sammy Bull Gravano's
headquarters in Brook... Once again, it was rewarding
duty. The club was hopping with wiseguys, especially on
Tuesday nights when Gravano's crew was under orders to
show up. Nevertheless, Mouw soon found himself forced to
make a command decision. He had only so many men, and
the team was working double shifts as it was. He simply
could not afford, logistically or even temperamentally, to
scatter his resources across the city. Besides—and this was
no doubt the clincher—his primary target, John Gotti, had
never, as far as Mouw could tell, made even a brief
appearance at Gravano's club. So, although weighed down
by plenty of second thoughts, he decided to pull the sub off
Tali's.

Instead, he ordered his surveillance teams to intensify
their efforts at the Ravenite. It was, he was convinced, the
key to the entire operation. After all the months, every
surveillance report he read, every informant he debriefed,
every, as he would say, "bone in his body" was telling him
that what he needed to know was going on somewhere
inside that club. If he could only figure out a way to get in.

Then one night a team of watchers, much to their
annoyance, found themselves trapped inside the blue submarine. They had been staking out the Ravenite since
around four that afternoon, and now that it was after eight
and Gotti had left for his customary night on the town, they
were planning to head back to Queens. Except they couldn't.
Someone had double-parked directly in front of the van,
and then vanished.

The car couldn't have succeeded in blocking them in

more effectively if it had set out to do exactly that. As the hours passed and the double-parked car still hadn't budged, that anxious thought became in some of the agents' minds a convincing possibility. Maybe it was a trap. Guns were checked, and minutes later double-checked. There was even a brief discussion about calling for backup. But that was quickly vetoed. It would blow months of surveillance work, maybe even the entire operation. Pounding on the horn, summoning the thoughtless driver to come out from wherever he was holed up and move his damned car, would also be equally disastrous. They had, the agents realized, no choice but to sit tight and wait.

And while they waited, they also watched. They were watching when the lights inside the club were shut off and, as was the practice, the last man out locked the front door for the night. The man with the key was, just as they expected, their old friend Norman DuPont. He had first come to the squad's attention months before when they had begun monitoring the club. A small background file was quickly assembled, but it contained nothing too remarkable. DuPont, in his late twenties, broad-shouldered, movie star handsome, and a self-styled tough guy with an assault charge on his rap sheet against an off-duty cop to prove it, was a nephew of Mike Cirelli, the Ravenite's elderly caretaker. During the day, DuPont worked for the Sanitation Department. At night, he worked as the club's bartender; if one of the guys wanted a scotch or an espresso, DuPont fetched it. He also, now that Cirelli was getting on in years, had been taking over some of his uncle's responsibilities. He was the one who showed up at four to unlock the front door, and he was always the last to leave. To the agents, it didn't seem like a very significant job, but it must have had its benefits. DuPont was probably the only garbage collector in the city who drove a gold Jaguar. Still, the agents didn't take him too seriously. He wasn't a made guy, only a hanger-on. They were stalking bigger game.

But that night, stuck in the back of the van with nothing better to do than to check out Mulberry Street, the agents turned their attention to DuPont. At around ten that night, he returned to the club. And he was not alone. A woman was with him. Very stealthily, it seemed, looking to his left, then his right, DuPont put the key in the lock and quickly ushered the woman into the Ravenite. He closed the door behind him, and the agents waited but the lights didn't go on inside. Perhaps he just forgot something, one of the agents suggested. They'll be out in a bit. But ten minutes passed. Then fifteen. There was still no sign of DuPont and the woman. And the place remained dark. What was going on? the agents wondered. Was DuPont ripping off the club? Could he be that reckless? Or, someone suggested, maybe he was bugging the club. Was that possible? Was he a double agent working for the cops? The DEA? Hell, maybe even another Family?

It was a long night, and there were lots of theories.

The couple did not emerge from the club until just after one in the morning. They were holding hands. An hour later the driver of the double-parked car returned, and the submarine could finally head back to its garage near the Queens Boulevard headquarters.

The following night there was no car blocking the van, but the watchers stayed late anyway. At around ten, DuPont returned to the club. And again, a woman was with him. But as DuPont was unlocking the door, one of the agents caught something in the woman's smile. It was a different woman. She had black hair and was shapely like the woman the night before. But she was years younger and really special: alive, lots of bouncing flesh, and very sexy.

This couple, too, stayed in the pitch-dark club for hours. And the agents began to grapple with a seemingly impossible theory. Could DuPont really be up to what they thought he was up to? *In John Gotti's headquarters?*

The next night nothing happened. Then it was the weekend, so the team headed out to the Bergin. But on Monday the van was back across from Mulberry Street, and DuPont was back to his old tricks. Only now there was a *third* woman with him. A redhead, the punkish color clearly out of a bottle, and not nearly as pretty as the other two. She was dressed all in black and looked only pudgy in a pair of tight stretch pants. The agents, for no good reason, felt disappointed.

But they had worked up a plan and, at some risk, decided to stick to it. They watched as the couple disappeared into the club, waited a disciplined fifteen minutes, and when they were sure Mulberry Street was deserted, one of the agents slipped from the back of the van to reconnoiter.

First he strolled down the block, walking nonchalantly past the club, and yet he thought he heard something. It was a muffled sort of sound, like someone banging on a wall or a table. Maybe they had been wrong. DuPont and his harem really might be spiking the place after all.

He was concerned, and intrigued. And the street was, for once, providentially deserted. That was why, he later explained, he broke with the plan, with all his training really, and instead of returning directly to the van went to the doorway of the club.

The first thing he did was unzip his fly. It was the perfect cover story if anyone came by. It was midnight, he had had too much to drink, and he was taking a piss in a doorway. But no one came by, so he could just press his ear against the door and listen.

What he heard was more of that muffled pounding, and some whispers, and a lot of . . . moaning. It got louder, building in intensity until he heard a very distinct, triumphant, and familiar yelp. And he no longer had any doubts about what Norman DuPont was doing late at night with all those women in John Gotti's headquarters.

# 30

BINGO!

All along Mouw had been preaching, "Find the weak link." And now, like an answered prayer, they had found it. There was no doubt in Mouw's mind that his team had stumbled on the soft spot that, when pressure was judiciously applied, would get them inside the Ravenite.

"Talk about unsafe sex," Kurins, a bit impressed by the audacity of it all, had marveled. But his point was well taken. The Ravenite might be a social club, but it was not Plato's Retreat. Anyone who dared to party after hours in the Don's headquarters did so at considerable risk. If Gotti, a stickler for respect, ever found out what was going on, the consequences of all that reckless passion would be significant. Perhaps even fatal.

Still, the word "blackmail" was never used by anyone on the team. They preferred to speak of "pressures" and of "squeezing." But from the moment Mouw had heard the watchers' excited report, his plan of attack was certain. He would make sure Gotti received a few revealing eight-by-ten glossies snapped of the loving couples sneaking into the club in the dead of night. Unless, of course, one of the lovebirds was willing to cooperate with the FBI.

Yet, one more example of the self-discipline that characterized his command of the entire operation, Mouw did not rush off to threaten DuPont or the women. His hesitancy was not an attack of moral squeamishness; after all he knew about Gotti and his crew, he was prepared to play hardball. His only concern was one of tactics. Which one of the late-night revelers should he target?

Squeezing was always a tricky business. You could never predict who would play hero and who would, in Mouw's often-repeated metaphor, fold "as quick and as neat as a tortilla." All the team needed was for someone to tell Gotti that the FBI was asking a lot of questions about the Ravenite. That would be warning enough. Johnny Boy would stop talking inside the club about even the weather, and the squad would be back to square one. Only this time, with Gotti on the alert, they might be stuck there for good. Therefore, Mouw said, we've got to be very confident before we even make our initial contact. We've got to pick the one who will play along.

There were only four possible accomplices and, methodically, the team focused on each one in some detail. On Mouw's order, they first concentrated on Norman DuPont. An approach scenario was plotted, refined over a couple of days, and in the end it worked out like this. An offer would be put to DuPont that he could not refuse. It would be a strictly big stick approach; a hard case like DuPont would only interpret a conciliatory carrot as a sign of weakness. They would simply shove a few of the compromising photographs under his nose and tell him either he could behave like a good boy and follow orders, or the Don would find the snapshots in the backseat of his Mercedes. And once Gotti saw how the bartender was taking advantage of his responsibilities, tough guy Norman could kiss his job and his future with the Family good-bye. Of course, the agents would be sure to point out, he still would have his work with the Sanitation Department. If he could handle it with a broken arm or leg.

Yet there was, it was generally agreed, a troubling element in this carefully drafted plot. DuPont was a very stubborn character; he would be hard to direct. He might just be foolish enough to think he would be better off taking his chances with the Godfather than with the FBI. Besides, he was Mike Cirelli's nephew and that bloodline might indeed be enough to help get him off with just a stern warning from the Don. Or, another real possibility, a street guy like DuPont might stoically accept whatever punishment came his way rather than become a rat.

A decision was finally made to steer clear of DuPont. He was too risky. Instead, the squad would search for their "weak link" among the women. A delicate problem now presented itself: Which member of the harem should they choose?

Meanwhile, John Gotti was spending a good deal of his time attempting to shore up the weak links in his Family. But unlike Mouw, he did not bother sorting through the candidates. Nor did he resort to the relative nicety of blackmail to coerce cooperation. His approach was much more direct, foolproof even. He began killing anyone he felt might be a problem.

Tommy DeBrizzi, a soldier in Tommy Gambino's crew up in the Bronx, first caught Gotti's attention after "the Breeze," facing some serious time, got a slap-on-the-wrist sentence. As Gotti, who knew his way around the courts, figured it, either Tommy had a hotshot lawyer or he had cut a deal. The Godfather had never heard of the attorney.

Then, when he got out of jail, the Breeze didn't rush to the Bronx to pay his respects to his capo, Tommy Gambino. He just made some excuse. He said because of his parole he was restricted to his home state of Connecticut. Gotti went to the trouble of having that one checked out and, to his surprise, it was true. But was the truth really good enough with so much at stake? Why take a chance?

Ice him, ordered a suspicious Gotti.

They caught up with DeBrizzi in Connecticut, in his car, and even though his body was riddled with bullet holes, the medical examiner said he had probably died very quickly. A bullet from a .38, one of the first fired, had caught him directly in the eyeball, and after that he was more or less dead. The shot through his mouth, going straight out the back of his head, was probably not even necessary. But the hitmen, like their boss, must have thought: Why take a chance?

As soon as C-16, systematically working down *its* list, began checking out DuPont's date with the garish redhead —"Little Miss Punk," the agents had immediately christened her—alarm bells started ringing in the squad's offices on Queens Boulevard. She had a record. A long one. It started with a couple of busts for amphetamines and cocaine when she was a teenager, went on to a serious rap for dealing heroin that was dismissed after she agreed to enter a methadone clinic, and had trailed off more recently into a string of convictions and fines for prostitution. She was twenty-four years old; and, the team noted judgmentally, looked at least a washed-out decade older.

All of which made her the perfect candidate for a burn. She was a longtime loser, a woman accustomed to being used and manipulated. Apply a little pressure, just offer a low-keyed hint or two of what the Boss of Bosses might do if he knew a junkie was screwing around after-hours in his private club, and she would fold in seconds flat. You name it and she would agree to do it.

But could you trust her? The problem was precisely that Little Miss Punk *was* a junkie. Her allegiances and her promises would be sworn on some very shaky ground. One moment she might be pledging her soul to the Bureau. The next, in a stoned panic, she might be pouring her heart out to DuPont. There was just no telling what she might do. She was simply too mercurial and unpredictable a player to be cast in a starring role. All things considered, maybe she wasn't the best possible candidate. And with that grudging realization, Little Miss Punk disappeared without a further mention from the case file.

Gotti, too, continued moving down his list. The time had come to get his house in order, to settle scores. When Sammy Gravano, his new *consigliere,* came to him with a beef that Louie Milito was bad-mouthing the Administration, the Godfather agreed that they had better take him out. You could never tell where all that loose talk would lead. Besides, with Milito there was a lot more to worry about than one-liners. He was a dangerous guy. Gravano seconded that. He had done enough hits with Milito to know firsthand just how nasty Louie could get without even any provocation.

Once Gotti gave the OK, Gravano wanted to do the piece of business himself. The Iceman was looking forward to getting it over with. It made him jumpy knowing a stone killer was cutting him down behind his back, questioning his judgment. Gravano had run with Milito since the days when they were both teenage hoods hanging out on street corners and now he was a business partner. But Gravano felt that Milito had betrayed him with his loose-lipped criticisms.

That bothered the Don. His new *consigliere* was taking something that should be strictly a business decision all too personally. Gotti was uncomfortable with vendettas. When things got primitive, he liked to say, they had a tendency to get out of control. It would be better, he instructed Gravano, if his brother Genie and his crew took over.

But Genie was sympathetic to Gravano's anger. The two men were strolling down Mulberry Street when he offered the Bull a compromise. Genie, as his brother had ordered, would provide the shooter and ditch the body. There was no getting around that. But Johnny hadn't said anything about who should set up Milito. If Sammy wanted to, the job was his. He could even stay around and watch the hit. That should satisfy his sense of honor.

The deal was done in moments.

But Gravano, still the Iceman, was clever, and by instinct

cautious. It wouldn't help things at all if Milito got suspicious. He had Milito's capo, Big Lou Vallario, send for him and pitch a story that they were setting up a hit on Johnny Gammarano. It was an artful touch; everyone in the Family knew that Gotti had a real hard-on for Johnny G.

Milito was told to show up on Tuesday night at Big Lou's club on Seventeenth Avenue in Brooklyn and help the crew work things out. When he got there, Big Lou, grinning genially, was behind the bar. Sammy, Genie, and Arnie Squitieri were playing five-card draw over in the corner. Johnny Carneglia was spread out across the sofa, eyes closed, catching up on some sleep.

"Hey, Louie," Big Lou greeted the new arrival, "what you drinking?"

Milito, who had a happy-go-lucky way about him when he wasn't carrying a grudge, walked over to the bar. Johnny Carnegs, suddenly wide awake but not making too big a deal about it, slipped into the other room. When he came out, he was carrying a revolver with a silencer. The gun was by his side, close to his body.

Milito was still talking to Big Lou when Johnny Carnegs pulled the trigger. He fired once and the bullet struck Milito in the back of the head. Milito was a hefty man, fat really, but he crashed as if pole-axed to the floor. Carnegs, still as silent and detached as death itself, knelt down next to Milito and pressed the barrel of the gun up against the dying man's chin. That shot blew Milito's skull apart.

By 8:30 that evening, Milito's body had been stuffed into the trunk of a Chevy and Genie and Sammy Bull were on their way to Tali's. Sammy made it a point to hang around on the sidewalk in front of his club for a while. He knew the FBI was checking out the place, and he figured what better alibi could a killer have than the U.S. government.

After just a quick perusal, the woman the watchers had spotted with DuPont on the first night had seemed to be a very likely candidate. She was thirty-four, a reassuringly mature age: She would listen to reason. Divorced: which the agents decided was simply further indication she would understand the power of a legal threat. And she was a secretary: a woman accustomed to taking and following orders. She was perfect, they reported back to Mouw.

It was only as they were intensifying the background check in preparation for their initial approach that the team discovered something that brought their inquiries to an abrupt halt. She was connected. Her father was a made guy, and her mother's brother, her favorite uncle, was a capo. They would be asking her to betray not just DuPont, or even Gotti, but the entire world she was raised in. And that, very possibly, would be asking too much. At the very least, it was a genuine risk. And one that Mouw felt he couldn't comfortably take.

After this discouraging development, there were some on the squad who argued that too much time had already been wasted. Let's introduce a girl to DuPont, they suggested. Say, code-name Easter or even a curvy agent. Certainly DuPont's tastes were eclectic enough to be attracted to whomever we could come up with. At least we would have a shot at getting someone we could count on deep inside the Ravenite.

It was a provocative proposal, and one that Mouw considered quite seriously. But in the end, the image of sending some woman off with DuPont, a seductive lamb tethered to catch a sharp-toothed wolf, was too disturbing. Besides, he told the squad, there was still one last candidate remaining on their list.

It didn't take John Gotti long to agree that the Oliveris, the father and the two sons, had to die. When Johnny Gambino, a crew leader from Brooklyn, showed up at the Ravenite and told his don that the Oliveris had bumped off one of his soldiers, Giuseppe Gambino, that was all Gotti needed to hear. It didn't matter why they had whacked Giuseppe. Justice, even revenge, didn't enter into it. The only thing that counted was that Giuseppe was a made guy, a friend of ours. You kill a member of the Family without permission, you had to die. It was a rule, La Cosa Nostra way, and that was that. You start looking for ways around the rules, then the next thing you know there's nothing a man can count on, nothing he can pass on to his children. They're history, Gotti flatly told Johnny Gambino. Take them out.

But murdering the Oliveris would be a nervy piece of business. There were three of them, after all. Johnny Gambino was a gambler, a guy who made his living playing the angles, and he didn't like those odds at all. Anyway, he wasn't a killer, or at least not an executioner. Two weeks later he was back at the Ravenite, and looking a little sheepish, he told his don he was having some trouble doing this piece of business.

That was when Gotti, who didn't like the way this was dragging on at all, gave the contract to the Iceman. And just to make sure there weren't any more delays, he told Sammy Gravano to reach out to the Jersey crew for Bobby Cabert. Bobby was a ballsy guy. He might come in handy if there were complications.

Gravano went to Queens the next day to check things out. That was the way he always worked. He liked to be prepared, to know who he was going up against. It was about ten in the morning and he just marched into the haircutting place where the two Oliveri boys worked and gave them a story about how he was looking for a florist. It was the first thing that popped into his head, and as soon as he said it he worried that maybe it sounded a little odd. There he was, this guy built like the Incredible Hulk, looking bright and early in the morning to buy a dozen roses or something. But the brothers didn't seem suspicious. There's a place across the street, one of them announced helpfully.

When Gravano left, he met with Bobby Cabert. "I could've done it right then and there. The place was empty." He just didn't see what the big deal was in taking out two hairdressers.

Only now there was another rub. Johnny Gambino's boys had come around to thinking that maybe the two brothers had nothing to do with Giuseppe's murder. The father, sure, he was guilty; no doubt about that. But the sons, that was another, murkier matter altogether.

OK, Gotti ruled agreeably, so we just do the old man. It was fine with Gravano too. As he would say, "John told me to bark, and I bit." It didn't matter whose name was on the list. Except, he noted with some satisfaction, killing one guy should be a lot less work than doing three.

So Gravano and Cabert returned to Queens, and this time they took up positions outside the apartment house where the old man lived. The two hitmen were in separate cars, both stolen the night before by Johnny Gambino's crew. They parked at either end of the block, but they had walkie-talkies to keep in touch. It was about six in the morning, and the plan was to wait until Oliveri came out to move his car because of the alternate-side-of-the-street parking regulations. Whoever was closest to him would take him. They waited until noon, but Oliveri didn't show. "Maybe he's onto us," a worried Gravano ten-foured Cabert, just before he gave the order to head back to the Ravenite.

They were in Manhattan, trying to figure out what had gone wrong, when one of the guys hanging around the club quickly provided the answer: It was some sort of Jewish holiday; alternate-side-of-the-street parking had been suspended. "Maybe I should check with a rabbi before I go off and do a piece of business," Gravano joked. But he felt pretty stupid.

Two days later, after making sure the parking regulations were in effect, the two hitmen returned to the Queens block. Just before seven, Francesco Oliveri came out of the red brick building to move his car. It was cool that May morning, but all he had on over his shirt was a V-necked sweater decorated with diamond shapes in lots of bright colors. He walked up the block toward where Cabert was parked, and Gravano watched as Cabert quickly, but without any fuss, got out of his car. Cabert had on a leather jacket and Gravano could see him reach inside and come out holding a gun. Suddenly there was a muzzle flash, then another. And Oliveri was down on the ground, crawling toward a spindly tree; perhaps he thought he would be able to raise himself if he could just hold on to something. But he never got the chance. Cabert fired once more, and the old man lay there dead, his hands reaching out hopelessly, the tree forever beyond his grasp.

Walking outside the Ravenite that night, Gravano told Gotti he could cross another name off his list.

Meanwhile, in the offices on Queens Boulevard, there was finally a growing sense of optimism. The team was beginning to feel that they had saved the best for last. As soon as the background check was completed on the remaining woman on their list—"the Looker," they had admiringly dubbed her—there was a general agreement that their search was over.

Even the cautious Mouw had to agree that, on paper at least, it seemed to be a match made in heaven. She was young, just twenty-three, and that, to the team's manipulative way of looking at things, made her easily compliant. She was Hispanic, so there were certainly no Family members lurking in her closet. And—the clincher—she was a clerk for the Internal Revenue Service on Church Street in lower Manhattan: *She already worked for the government!*

Yet even after the decision had been made to recruit the Looker, there was still a good deal of discussion about how the approach should be made. Some thought the team should take her by storm, pounding on the door of her apartment, badges out, and then dragging her down to 26 Federal Plaza where, reinforced by the visible power and authority of the Bureau, they would make their pitch. Another view was that they should pounce on her early one morning as she made her way home after spending the night with DuPont; the theory here was that she would be at her most vulnerable after sneaking into the Ravenite. But Mouw, instinctively a gentleman, believed that if you're going to propose a marriage, it doesn't hurt to do a little courting first.

So for the first date, as the initial meeting came to be known, he sent just one man—George Gabriel, tall, handsome, and, when he tried to be, a charmer. It was to be very low-key. A supervisor was sent to the Looker's desk to

announce that she was to report to a room upstairs. Someone wanted to see her, the supervisor explained cryptically;
but the truth was, that was all she knew.

The room upstairs was small, windowless, and painted a
dull, bureaucratic gray. There was a metal desk where on
other occasions an IRS auditor would sit imperially, and
opposite it a straight-backed chair from which the unfortu-
nate taxpayer would beg for understanding and perhaps
even mercy. But for this confrontation, Gabriel made a
point of avoiding any symbolic trappings. He was standing
against the wall when the Looker came in, and he introduced himself with one of his boyish grins. Please, he told
her, you sit at the desk. He'd make do with the chair. She
thanked him with a dazzling smile, and he would later
confess it was at that moment that he couldn't help but
think: You're a very lucky man, Norman DuPont.

By all accounts, that first meeting and the one that night at
a midtown hotel, when the Looker was introduced to Mouw,
were a stunning success. Within moments of Gabriel's
making his pitch, she agreed to cooperate and meet Mouw.
She might have been swayed by their attentions, intrigued
by the prospect of doing undercover work for the FBI, or
simply eager to do in DuPont, whom she was quick to call "a
bastard." The possibility of getting a significant promotion
as well as a raise—both were offered—might also very well
have played a part in bringing her around. Whatever her
motivation, by the time an elated Mouw left his interview
with the Looker that first night, he had advanced the
operation beyond his expectations.

First, she had provided him with a sketch of the layout of
the two small rooms that made up the Ravenite.

Second—and this was pure gold—she, as Mouw watched
open-mouthed, had drawn in the precise location of the
table in the back room where she insisted John Gotti always
sat. How did she know? Because, she explained with a flash
of embarrassment, Norman always made a point about it.
We always make love lying across that table. I think it turns
Norman on. You know, screwing on the Godfather's table.

Third, she had drawn in a back door to the club. It was in

the same room as Gotti's table, and it opened out onto a hallway that was shared with the rest of the tenement building. How was the door secured? Was there a lock? Alarms? Surveillance cameras? No, she said with some amusement. There was just a bolt up by the top. Norman was always checking it, making sure it was in place before he left each night. Said they'd kill him if he ever forgot.

Fourth, and perhaps most remarkable of all to Mouw's mind, was that he now had a source inside the Ravenite—and one whom Gotti would never suspect. He told Gabriel to hurry up and get the eavesdropping affidavit ready for a judge's signature. The time had come to spike John Gotti's headquarters.

As the operation, thanks to the Looker, now moved on to a higher footing, Mouw paid little attention to a single-page TE debriefing report that crossed his desk. It was filed just days after Mike Cirelli's funeral, sometime during the week of January 16, 1988. According to the TE, the entire hierarchy of the Gambino Family had turned out for the funeral mass at Old St. Patrick's Cathedral in honor of the Ravenite's longtime caretaker. As the crowd was leaving the church, the TE noted, Gotti made his way to Cirelli's nephew. He offered his condolences, and then told Norman DuPont that he wanted the locks changed immediately on his uncle's apartment above the Ravenite.

It was not until more than a year later, after he first began wondering if that overheard snippet of a conversation was perhaps of some larger strategic significance, that Mouw would discover the Looker, too, had been at the funeral. And then her true value to the case would finally become clear.

# 31

SOMETHING WAS OUT THERE. CROUCHED INSIDE THE TALL REFRIG-erator box, John Kravec, the Tech team supervisor, could hear it coming toward him. It was pitch-dark in the carton; he was doing his best not to move a muscle; and in that careful silence every sound was amplified. He could hear someone, as if on tiptoe, softly walking around his hideout.

Before Kravec could prepare himself, there was some kicking against the side of the box. No, not really kicking, Kravec decided. More like tapping. Checking it out. Very quietly, Kravec reached down for the nine-millimeter revolver he kept in his ankle holster. Where the hell was the backup? his mind was screaming. Were they sleeping? Or had they already been taken out by Gotti's men? He flicked off the safety on his gun and, his body tensed, aimed at whatever was on the other side of the cardboard carton.

Just that morning, at the operational briefing where he had shared his plan for getting into the Ravenite, Kravec had been so confident. Sure, he had told the assembled agents, egress—as he referred to breaking-and-entering— was always the most dangerous part of any bugging mission.

But, he had said, we've got this one fairly well worked out. It should all go down like this:

At some time after one in the morning, a city garbage truck will pull up, quite routinely, to 247 Mulberry Street. Besides the Gambino club, more than a dozen Italian families make their home in the tenement, so it will be a busy stop. The garbagemen will be busting their backs lugging trashcans from the sidewalk to the truck and emptying them. In all that clanging commotion, why should anyone notice that a tall Sub Zero refrigerator box is brought *from* the truck to the sidewalk? Or that the box just happens to be left directly in front of the doorway of number 247, just a yard or so away from the Ravenite, which has its own front door opening onto the street. Damn thing won't fit in the truck, the garbagemen will be sure to mutter since you never can tell who is listening or watching. The truck will continue on down Mulberry Street, its mission accomplished; but since good cover requires consistency, it will also stop at the next building and collect its trash, too.

Meanwhile inside the box, "your hero, John Kravec" (it was his habit to talk about himself in the third person; perhaps it was a way to dissociate himself from all the danger) will be slowly counting to 500. If he can make it to 499 without a flash warning bursting from his walkie-talkie, he will peel off the tape that is holding the makeshift back of the refrigerator box in place; and—presto!—find himself an arm's length from the tenement's front door. All any insomniac staring out from a window across the street will see is a discarded refrigerator box.

The front door to the residential part of the building will, of course, be locked. But this shouldn't be a problem. Kravec, under the tutelage of a team from the Bureau's lock shop, has become a master at picking the very make of lock that secures the tenement door. Shielded from curious eyes by the bulky refrigerator box, he will have all the time he needs.

Next, with the front door open, Kravec, now joined by two of his ablest wiremen, who have hurried from a Bureau car, will saunter down the hallway; make a right; and, lo and behold, there's the back door to the Ravenite. And, neatest trick of all, *the door will be unlocked.*

Mouw himself had guaranteed this impossibility, and Kravec had not asked for details. Not that Mouw would ever have disclosed the Looker's vital role in the operation. All he told Kravec was that he would not be able to give the bugging operation a definite "go" until late that night. All of the Looker's intrigues—how, after a spirited session across Gotti's table with Norman DuPont, she would linger in the rear room just long enough to throw the bolt—were carried out without Kravec's knowledge. He would be unaware of how much was riding on the Looker's finding the right moment, or of her silent prayer that DuPont would not hear the soft sound of the bolt being slipped. Or of the anxiety that gripped the C-16 team as they waited for her to call to say it had all gone down without a hitch.

All Kravec knew was that the back door to the Ravenite would, as if by magic, be unlocked. His biggest concern, he was told, would be that it might require a bit of artful prying with a crowbar to swing it open. Still, on the outside chance that the bad guys might be waiting in the hallway or in the club that night, Kravec had taken a precaution. A dozen of the Bureau's match-quality marksmen, guys who could shoot a smile into a target from forty yards, were scattered up and down Mulberry Street.

Only now, an hour or so after midnight on an icy night in February 1988, before Kravec had managed to count much beyond 200, the operation had fallen apart, his backup troops had vanished, and he was standing with his gun drawn, ready to shoot blindly at whoever was hanging around his hiding place.

But at the very moment when Kravec's imagination was racing with all the possibilities of what might have gone wrong, as his finger grew heavier on the revolver's trigger, water began to seep through the cardboard box, an acrid smell drifting upward.

Only it wasn't water, he suddenly realized with disgust.

Kravec knew at once what was on the other side of the box. And what the backup teams were up to. They were laughing their asses off because a stray dog was pissing on his hiding place.

So much, Kravec summarily decided, for counting to 500. In an instant, the false back was off the carton and he was going at the front-door lock. It took only a minute or two before he heard a comforting click. Then he turned the knob and walked into the fluorescent-lit, white-tiled hallway of 247 Mulberry Street.

Without waiting for any signal, the two Tech team wiremen dashed out from the car and joined their boss. Now there were three men in the tenement hallway but they made no effort to sneak about; the theory was that a stray noise at two in the morning would draw less attention than a muffled sound. And their clothes—chinos, windbreakers, and sneakers—were, also by design, ordinary. But anyone looking out an apartment peephole might have wondered why each man had a black canvas backpack, not much larger or bulkier than a hardcover book, slung over his shoulder.

They walked in single file down the narrow hall; Kravec led the way. Weeks earlier, Mouw had passed on a floor-plan drawn in scarlet ink by his TE, and Kravec, who made it a practice always to doublecheck, had also requisitioned architect's drawings from the City Buildings Department. In his mind he had walked down this hallway dozens of times. But now that he was finally doing it, the hallway was brighter than he had imagined, illuminated, he worried, like a movie set; and the sound of each step against the tile floor seemed to reverberate, bouncing like an echo off the tin ceiling.

But when at last he came to a fork in the hallway and, as memorized, made a sharp right, he found just what he had expected—a metal door, painted a deep, grim brown. It was the back door to the Ravenite.

A child's red bicycle was leaning against the door, and Kravec motioned for the men to move it. They did, picking the bike up from each end as gingerly as if it were a ticking bomb.

Kravec saw that a crowbar would not be needed. There was a handle on the door. It was painted the same ugly brown as the door, so it was easy to miss. But it was there. One pull, and if Mouw was right, the door would open.

Yet for a moment he just stood there. He knew that as soon as he gave the handle a tug, it would be like taking a leap off the high board: There would be no turning back. The door would open, or it would not. Alarms would ring out, or the early-morning silence would remain unbroken. Gotti's men waiting inside the club would open fire, or that, too, would be just one more unrealized fear. He would be alive, or he might very well be dead.

Kravec reached out for the handle and pulled. There was a creaking noise from hinges that desperately needed oil. But that was all. Nothing else. The door swung open.

Kravec took a bold step into the darkness, and as the metal door closed behind him, he found himself standing in the headquarters of John Gotti and the Gambino crime family.

It was a hard room, a wireman's nightmare. Kravec realized that immediately as he swept the beam from his Mini-Mag flashlight along the wood floor, up a plaster wall, and over the metal-plated ceiling. The soda machine in the corner, humming away even in the dead of night, was the clincher. It would be like trying to listen in on someone talking in a tin can—with a bass drum pounding in the background. The sound waves would bounce all over the place, getting more twisted and distorted as they crashed against each hard surface. And if Gotti kept to a whisper, the mikes would have a hell of a time picking up anything at all.

Yet all the time Kravec was worrying, he was also working out a plan. That was the way it always went. A wireman never knew precisely what he was going to do until he was inside the target. He had to see with his own eyes what he was up against, what options he had. And since he never knew how much time he had before a burst came shrieking over the walkie-talkie advising that he had better clear out *now*, he also had to figure things out in a matter of very tense minutes.

Still, Kravec had done enough black-bag jobs to know

there were only two ways, really, to spike a room effectively. He could go RF, which meant using a radio frequency transmitter to support a miniature microphone. It would be the fastest and easiest bug to install: Just flick it on, hide it, and run. The problem with RF, however, was that while the best mikes are as small as a matchstick and can catch a whisper from twenty-five feet away—Kravec had a handful of miniaturized mikes in his backpack that boasted just such a capability—even the most sophisticated microphones still have to be powered by a battery-run transmitter. The batteries for a state-of-the-art Bureau quartz transmitter, although small enough to fit in a Walkman and conveniently much flatter, would give out in about seventy-two hours. That meant he would have to sneak into the Ravenite once a week to replace the battery pack.

Or he could go hardwire. The advantage there was that he wouldn't have to rely on batteries to power the mike. He could use what was already in the room—the existing Con Ed electrical current. All he had to do was splice the two thin black wires that ran from one of his miniature mikes into the room's wiring and the conversations would be transmitted back to the Bureau listening post through the electrical lines. It was roughly similar to rigging up a sophisticated version of a store-bought baby monitor: Plug the mike into an electrical socket in one room, the receiver into a socket in another, and the sound travels instantly and distinctly over the existing electrical current. The one drawback to going hardwire was that it took time. He had to find an appropriately unobtrusive place to hide a microphone that was not much larger than the eraser on a number-two pencil, then run a line from the mike into the existing power, and finally, camouflage all the chipped paint, scraped walls, and often yards of hair-thin wire involved in the process. All that was demanding work, especially in a pitch-dark room with the bad guys likely to burst through the door at any moment.

Kravec looked at the luminous dial on his watch. More than twenty minutes had passed since he had climbed out of the refrigerator box. The plan had called for him to be in and out of the club in less than an hour. It was taking longer than he had anticipated. Come on, get moving, he was shouting to himself.

He aimed his flashlight on the table where, if Mouw's information was accurate, the Don always sat. It was covered with a white tablecloth. *Nothing doing there!* He let the beam climb up the wall. It settled on a framed portrait, actually two hand-colored photographs in a single mahogany frame: John Gotti and his mentor, Neil Dellacroce, both men dressed for the occasion in somber suits and ties, and both gazing threateningly into the distance—co-conspirators keeping a stern watch on their domain. And all the while Kravec's mind was racing. He could plant a mike behind the frame, run a wire through the wall, and then piggyback onto the current in a nearby electrical outlet. *It would work!* But just as quickly he also figured that there would be at least three feet of wall to be replastered and paint to be matched, and who the hell knew what would happen if the bad guys ever took the picture down for a dusting.

So now Kravec played the beam of light along the floor, using Gotti's table as his starting point. The light was making its way toward the rear door when he discovered a rectangular metal grill just above the baseboard. It was a heating duct, he realized. He moved in closer with the Mini-Mag and saw that the grill was held into the wall by a screw in each corner. He looked once again at his watch. *Come on! Time's running out!* "Help me unscrew this thing," he ordered his men. "We're going hardwire."

They worked with surprising speed, yet carefully. They knew just a scratch on one of the brown-painted screwheads could catch someone's attention. Meanwhile, Kravec sorted through the collection of miniature mikes he had in his backpack. He decided on one and, using just his thumb and index finger, inserted it into the screwhole in the grill's upper right-hand corner. The color was off; the mike was a jet black while the screws were a mud brown, and the hole was too big. But right away he knew that after a dollop of bee's wax from his caulking syringe and a dab of paint, no one would ever notice. He gave his team a thumbs-up.

Without further comment, Kravec was on his hands and knees snaking No. 38 gauge wire—about as thick as a strand of hair—down the back of the grill and along the interior of the wall above the heating duct. This was the part of his improvised scheme he liked best. All the wires would be out of sight. He worked with what was known in the trade as a wirelaying tool, a gunlike device, much smaller than his nine-millimeter, that "shot" out wire from a preloaded spool. The tool had been originally designed by the CIA for their wiremen and the Bureau had appropriated it. He ran the wire in a snaking path for about three feet until he reached an electrical outlet. The rest was easy. Just a matter of removing the outlet cover, twisting the wire about the proper terminals, and then soldering the connection. It took only seconds to screw the outlet cover back over the socket.

When the grill was replaced and the brownish paint was drying, Kravec stepped back to admire his handiwork. A final touch was needed, he decided. He scooped up a ball of dust from the corner of the floor and spread it around the mike and the genuine screws.

It had taken him, Kravec saw as he looked at his watch, thirty-four minutes to hardwire the room. No doubt about it, it was getting late. He had been warned that a man living in a third-floor apartment was a baker and that he left for work at 5:00 A.M. Kravec definitely did not want to bump into him on the way out. It was time to leave. He had placed a mike less than a foot from Gotti's table. That should make Mouw happy. But Kravec hesitated. He still had an RF kit in his bag.

*It's your lucky day, Bruce Mouw,* he decided.

Without any more deliberation, he went across the room to an orange sofa. In an instant, he was flat on the floor, aiming the beam of his flashlight into the eight-inch clearance beneath the couch.

"Exacto," he requested.

When he was handed the knife, he began cutting out a small flap, a six-by-six-inch tongue, more or less, from the bottom of the sofa. He removed a wad of stuffing and put in its place an RF transmitter. Usually he would have used upholstery glue—there was, in fact, a tube in his backpack —to cement the fabric seamlessly back into place. But now he glanced at his watch. It was after four. *Maybe this isn't anybody's lucky day,* he suddenly worried.

"Stapler," he nearly shouted. As soon as he said it, he was embarrassed that he had not been able to control his rising panic. Still, each staple seemed to take a lifetime to hit its target.

But all at once Kravec was up on his feet and they were ready to go. There was one final task to be done inside the club. Kravec went to the back door and with one strong and quick gesture threw the bolt. It was now locked from the inside, just as DuPont was certain he had left it.

They left by the club's front door. It was the most natural way, and therefore the least suspicious in case anyone was looking out a window. But just to be sure, they went one at a time, at two-minute intervals. They had been told to walk, not run, up toward Prince Street. A waiting car would flash its lights; the back door would be open.

Kravec was the last to leave, and it was his job to work on the front door so that it, too, would be locked as DuPont had left it. The faint winter sun was threatening to rise and he seemed almost lackadaisical as he stood for a frozen moment, holding the door of the Ravenite, contrary to both operational tactics and common sense, wide open. "It was a long and busy night," his boss, Jim Kallstrom, would later suggest as an explanation. "He must have been bushed." Or he might have been taking one last prideful look at what he, to his own amazement, had accomplished. Whatever the reason, he recovered in a flash. He closed the front door of John Gotti's headquarters firmly behind him and played with the lock. Then without looking back, he made his way up the block to the waiting car.

# 32

Now that they were "up" inside the Ravenite, Mouw could not wait to get to work each morning. He arrived at the office on Queens Boulevard, often after only a fitful sleep, by six, sometimes even earlier. It did not take him long to start a pot of strong black coffee ("navy grog," the agents sneered, and learned to avoid it at all costs). While it was brewing, he carefully turned the dial on the black combination safe across from his desk. Inside was a reel of tape. It had been dropped off at around midnight by the plant manager, as the agent who was running the listening post at 26 Federal Plaza was known, and it was the work copy of what had been recorded just hours earlier inside the club. The original, sealed and dated, remained locked away in the ELSUR—Bureau-speak for electronic storage—room at headquarters in lower Manhattan.

Mouw realized, of course, that if anything the least bit incriminating had been overheard, the plant manager would have called him immediately. Still, these were remarkable mornings. He was consumed by listening to each new tape. The squad room was quiet, in fact, usually deserted when he arrived; but after he threaded the lead of each new reel through the machine and put on his headphones, his mental transposition was so complete that it would not have mattered if the entire C-16 team was pounding on his door. He was inside the Ravenite.

Morning after morning, Mouw sat in his office, his tall, lanky jogger's body hunched over, the smoke from his pipe curling about the room, listening to each new tape with a deep and studious intensity. When he heard a door slam, or the booming echo of footfalls as a gofer made his way into the back room of the club, in his mind's eye he would sketch in the details of each scene: the way Gotti aimed a single .38-caliber finger to order an espresso; how the Don, at ease yet imperial, leaned back in his chair as he held court; or how Sammy Bull approached his boss's table, his head high in the air to make himself look taller, and the slow, distinctive patter of his child-size feet as, another compensatory habit, he walked forward on his toes. And the voices! There were so many, but he learned to recognize a few: Gotti's deep, drawling mumble; Frankie Locascio's tentative stammer; and Sammy Bull's odd, high-pitched whine.

Mouw was fascinated. He could put on his headphones and enter into the very heart of Gotti's private world. Every morning brought new insights into his enemy. And yet, he had to acknowledge that operationally the tapes were a colossal disappointment.

Part of the problem was technical. Kravec's fears had proven accurate, even cautious. It was a hard room and the tapes were very difficult to understand. For starters, the RF transmitter in the couch was a total disaster. Trapped between a grinding soda machine on one side and a constantly blaring TV on the other, whatever the little mike managed to pick up was effectively drowned out in a thick rumble of discordant sounds. After its batteries died, Kravec did not even consider returning to the Ravenite to replace them; and the exhausted listeners breathed a sigh of genuine relief. The hardwire reception was better— marginally. Still, when the building's ancient heating system coughed and wheezed into action, it was almost as if the mike in the heating duct was at Ground Zero: You had better remove those headphones quick or you might never hear again.

And when the transcribers in the windowless audio room on Queens Boulevard were not wearily writing *IA*—for inaudible—across a page, they found themselves writing *UM:* Unknown Male. That was the other frustrating problem. Most of the time, they weren't sure who was speaking. On a slow night, the Ravenite might be filled with perhaps thirty different voices; when things were jumping, the club would be jammed with fifty, maybe sixty, rapidly talking tough guys. At first the agents tried to make a joke of the challenge they were facing. "Name That Goon," they called it. But after a week of sitting in the audio room, headphones on, staring into a vista of off-white acoustical tiles, the struggle to decide whether the Jack trying to ingratiate himself with the Boss was Jack the Actor or Jackie Nose or perhaps some other upwardly mobile Jack quickly lost its charm. They grew to hate transcription duty.

But—and for many of the agents this was the truly discouraging part—even when a conversation came across loud and clear, even when the identities of the participants were apparent, the transcripts still were of little intelligence value. Not an incriminating word was ever heard. At least not after the first tedious month of listening. The Teflon Don emerged from all this scrutiny without a deep scratch. There was nothing on any of the reels that a prosecutor could play to a grand jury, no glaring admission that could lead to an indictment. And while Mouw was intrigued— "addicted" was the more emotional word one of his agents used—by the opportunity to learn even a few gossipy details of Gambino family life, not all his superiors in Washington shared his limitless curiosity. Dump the operation, they yelled. It was obvious that Gotti conducted the nastier Family business at some other, still unknown location. The Ravenite bug was not delivering; it was not worth the time, money, and manpower it was costing the Bureau.

Mouw, however, was prepared to fight. And, a necessary trait in any commander embarking on what might very well turn into a long siege, he was also optimistic. Sooner or later, he told his bosses at 26 Federal Plaza, Gotti or one of his henchman will get careless, the heating system will be off, and the mike will pick up every word. We're in the back room of the Gambino Family headquarters, for God's sake, he nearly yelled at both Jules Bonavolonta, the headquarters OC supervisor, and the head of the New York office himself, the patrician Jim Fox. We're too close to walk away. And before they had a chance to argue, Mouw upped the ante. He asked for permission to man and outfit an observation post within strolling distance of the Ravenite. If we can keep track of who enters the club every evening, he said, it will make identifying the voices on the tape that much easier.

He did not give his bosses an opportunity to react to the audaciousness of his request; the meeting, after all, had been convened to consider pulling the Ravenite bug, not enlarging the operation. Mouw simply announced he was very busy. He was needed back at Queens, and he would appreciate their getting back to him with a decision about the OP as soon as possible. Then, without further discussion, he left.

When Gabriel heard about Mouw's performance, he decided that his friend, finally succumbing to all the pressure, had overplayed his hand. Well, he told himself philosophically, at least we went out with a bang, not a whimper. A few days later, when Mouw summoned him to his office, Gabriel was prepared to do whatever was necessary to help his boss get over the disappointment of what he was certain had been a stunning reprimand. He would offer condolences. They would go off on a bender to end all benders. He would even, regardless of whether there was the slightest chance of success, fly to Washington to try a personal appeal to some higher suit if Mouw was game. Instead, Gabriel found himself taken by complete surprise as Mouw quite matter-of-factly informed him that not only had the wire been extended, but also his request for an observation post had been approved. He ordered Gabriel to get on it right away.

\* \* \*

Finding an apartment in New York is always a difficult task, but Gabriel's criteria made the hunt particularly complicated. He required a space that was roomy enough for a pile of high-tech surveillance equipment as well as at least two agents. It had to be secure enough so that there would be no special need to worry about someone ripping off the cameras and binoculars during the long stretches when the apartment would be vacant. It had to be in a building that was sufficiently laid back so that the comings and goings of different pairs of men at all hours would not attract gossipy attention. Most essential of all, it had to have an unobstructed view of the Ravenite. And there was one small additional concern—he couldn't pay much.

Nevertheless, after only a month of playing a sad-eyed advertising man who was moving in from the suburbs to the Big Apple following the collapse of a marriage that had been financially devastating and was still too sore a topic for him to discuss, Gabriel found his dream apartment. And, proof that all the news reports about the collapse of the New York City real estate market were not exaggerated, he rented the 1 bdrm., 2 bths., lv/dng rm. apartment for only about $1,500 a month.

The apartment smelled of fresh paint and plasterboard, but as an observation post it could not have been improved on. It was at 298 Mulberry Street, a boxy and newish light brick high-rise just two city blocks up from the turn-of-the-century Little Italy tenement that was home to the Ravenite. It might just as well have been in a different city. The incongruity of these two adjacent communities reminded Kurins, who had once spent a vacation on the West Coast, of a Hollywood studio back lot: Every time you turned a corner, you entered a different world. North of the great divide of Houston Street was a neighborhood that had been christened with the trendy sounding acronymn of NoHo and was filled with NYU undergraduates and yuppie ac-count executives. It was a community of roommates; no one paid the slightest attention when, inevitably, the faces kept changing. Number 298 Mulberry was also distinguished by a bit of uptown pretension, its doorman. And its views.

From the living room and bedroom of the sixth-floor corner apartment, you could look out the wide Thermopaned windows straight down Mulberry Street to the front door of number 247.

The team moved in during the first warm week of April 1988. They brought with them their video cameras, night surveillance binoculars, long-lens cameras, even Nagra reel-to-reel machines. It was all packed in plain brown cardboard boxes identified on the outside by only a discreet, catch-all phrase—"Household Items." But even if any of the neighbors had noticed all the high-tech equipment, it probably would not have created much of a suspicious stir. Down in NoHo, who wasn't a video artist? Who didn't have a state-of-the-art sound system? Perhaps that was why when two very professional-looking locksmiths came to supplement the front door of the apartment with an alarm system that required a cipher code to be punched in before it would open, no one thought it particularly odd or paranoid. (If the neighbors had known that to enter the bedroom another set of cipher alarms had to be deactivated, *that,* however, might have raised a few eyebrows.)

It all went very smoothly. There was even, the agents were quick to discover, a yuppified pool hall on the corner and, the real surprise, plenty of free parking available in the side streets surrounding the building. Gabriel, sticking to his advertising-man cover, had rented furniture—a jaundice-yellow couch, a couple of narrow beds with stony mattresses, and a few very functional tables. While no one thought he had any future as a decorator, the place was comfortable enough. The only discordant note, in fact, was raised by Doug Grover, one of the federal prosecutors assigned to audit the squad's books. He took one look at the price of the living room and bedroom blinds and went ballistic. He and his wife had recently done the windows for an entire Brooklyn Heights brownstone for just about what the Gambino squad had spent on two windows in an observation post. Gabriel, who considered the youthful Grover not only an ally but also a friend, was taken aback. He explained patiently that the two windows were exceptionally large, a *custom* size, and that vertical blinds, always more expensive, were an operational necessity. It wouldn't do to raise and lower the blinds whenever they had to aim the video camera out the window.

However, any lingering concerns on either side about the cost of the blinds were quickly put aside after the screening of the first surveillance videotapes. It was a four-star show. The clarity, even when the camcorder was rigged up with slow film and a Night Vision light-intensifier tube, was phenomenal. As Jim Kallstrom proudly noted, "You could see the curled lip when Gotti smirked."

Further, it didn't take long for the observation post to make an important intelligence contribution. For a while the team had been receiving vague but provocative reports from Kurins' and the Twins' TEs that Gotti, worried about bugs, had many of his most incriminating conversations on the sidewalk outside the club. And now they had a series of these "walk-talks" on videotape. There was Gotti nearly bending in half as he stooped to confer with an intense Gravano, Sammy keeping pace by taking two steps for each one of the Don's. Or Gotti and Joe Butch Corrao walking up Mulberry and laughing exuberantly over some private joke or scheme. And Gotti lecturing a perplexed Frankie Locascio, the older man looking as befuddled as if his boss was holding forth on some principle of theoretical physics. On each occasion bringing up the rear were the same two doorway-sized bruisers, their presence a none too subtle reminder to the locals to keep a deferential distance. What better verification could Mouw have hoped for?

Mouw was so encouraged that, despite his continued disappointment over the audio surveillance inside the club, he decided late in May that the time had come to plant another bug. He sent Kravec into the back room of the Bergin, reasoning that perhaps Gotti would be more loose-lipped on the weekends.

Spiking this club was a snap. The Queens neighborhood was deserted in the evenings and the locks were no challenge. Kravec was in and out of the Bergin within an hour.

The mike went up on June 5, and the sound was a lot clearer than the ongoing Ravenite tapes. Yet it, too, caught little that would interest a court of law. As one of the agents complained, "About the only thing we have on these guys is bad grammar."

Their boss, too, was frustrated. "We were getting these truly brilliant pictures," Mouw would later say, "only we weren't hearing anything worth a damn. We were so close, yet so far. All we needed, though, was one stroke of luck. Each morning when I went into the office, I went in believing that today would be the day. That things would get a lot better."

George Gabriel was in Kravec's office when the call came. It was a hot July afternoon nearly five weeks after the Tech team had spiked the Bergin, and the two men were discussing what to do next. Gabriel wanted the Techies to go back inside the Ravenite; if they could plant a mike in some other spot in the club, perhaps the reception would be better. Impossible, Kravec bellowed. It'll be the same anywhere in that room. You might as well ask me to bug a tin can. Besides, he continued grimly, the place is a total mine field. It's not worth the risk.

Gabriel kept his peace. He had learned it was best to let the man have his say. Impossible, in fact, was nothing more than Kravec's usual morose assessment of any challenge. It was his typically hopeless preamble until he got around to saying, "Well, maybe there is *something* we could try." As Gabriel had told Mouw, "If Kravec wasn't such a genius, he'd be a real pain."

That was why when Kravec interrupted his monologue to answer the phone and his face seemed to deflate as if he was hearing about a death in the family, Gabriel was unconcerned. For all Gabriel knew, Kravec was listening to someone go on about the weather. Or he had just heard he had won the lottery.

But then Kravec replaced the receiver, leaned back in his chair, threw up his hands, and announced, "We're blown."

He told Gabriel that it had been the listening post at 26 Federal Plaza on the phone: Gotti had found the bug that had been hidden in the Bergin.

"Yeah, right," Gabriel shot back. He still didn't believe Kravec was serious.

"Call him yourself," Kravec said and he handed Gabriel the phone.

That was when Gabriel knew Kravec was serious. "As serious," he would say, "as a heart attack."

But simply because the mike in the Bergin had been discovered was no reason for Gotti to suspect a bug had also been planted in the Ravenite. He would never believe anyone had penetrated his Manhattan headquarters. Or at least that was the wishful theory that sustained the C-16 team over that long summer weekend.

On Monday afternoon when the Ravenite heating duct mike was scheduled to go up again, Mouw and his men were waiting anxiously by the phone. Finally, at about four thirty, the plant called in. The mike was alive. It had not been discovered.

A loud, thankful cheer went up from the agents assembled in Mouw's office.

Around five, the plant called back. They were getting a lot of static on the mike.

"Static?" Mouw challenged.

"Well, actually," the plant manager said, "it sounds like a waterfall."

Mouw tried not to sound concerned. "Call me when you know something definite."

The plant called back just before six and reported that a few minutes ago the waterfall noise had stopped. Everything was suddenly coming over loud and clear from inside the club. That was when he had heard a deep baritone voice boom out, "Rewind the fuckin' tape, for Christ sake." And in an instant, it was as if the mike was once again underneath Niagara Falls.

Mouw slammed down the receiver. It didn't matter whether Gotti ever found the mike. After the discovery at the Bergin, the Don was not going to take any chances. From now on every conversation inside the Ravenite would be drowned out in a cascading sea of white noise.

There was one more blow. It had little operational effect on the case. It did not undermine Mouw's entire strategy as the collapse of the Bergin and Ravenite bugs had done. Yet, on a purely emotional level—which was the pitch that Mouw found himself working on most of the time—it was the most painful. It was another score that however long it took, C-16 would have to settle.

Nearly six weeks after the Bergin mike had been discovered, on August 29, 1988, at seven in the morning, Willie Boy Johnson was on his way to his car. It had been revealed at Gotti's racketeering trial that Willie Boy had been informing on the Gambino Family for fifteen years, first for the police and then for the FBI. At the time Gotti had been icily pragmatic, promising his longtime buddy that if he refused to testify at the trial, the past would be past. Johnson accepted the deal. He did not take the stand. When the trial was over, Willie Boy returned to his job with a Gambino-controlled union. He hung out with the guys from the Bergin. He had been, it seemed, forgiven. But the past was never past. And on that summer morning, almost two years after his betrayal of the Family had first been revealed, four men formed a circle around Willie Boy and opened fire. And they kept on shooting. The coroner found nineteen bullet holes in Willie Boy Johnson's body.

"Well," Gotti explained with a wistful shrug hours later to a reporter, "we all gotta go sometime."

The quote appeared in the *New York Post* the next afternoon and an agent showed the paper to Mouw. He read it, handed the paper back and even thanked the agent, then he stormed out of the squad room. He didn't return that day. None of the agents knew where he went. Or dared to ask.

It was a very rough stretch for Mouw and his team. And there was no reason to believe things were going to get any better.

# 33

FOR JOHN GOTTI, LIFE WAS GETTING BETTER ALL THE TIME. THE money was rolling in. He didn't even need to ask for it because everyone in the Family knew that if it came to that, the Don sent his special collection agent—the Iceman. The associates and the soldiers would routinely turn in half of whatever they were making on the streets to their capos; and the capos would pass the money, small change in the multifaceted scheme of Family businesses, up to the Administration. Still, there were about three thousand men in the Gambino Family and every one of them, except for the guys doing time, was earning for John Gotti. It added up.

One Sunday a month the big money was collected. It was the Don's older brother's job, and Pete Gotti was chosen no doubt for his loyalty, although he would have received high marks for experience too. Petey had, like their father, worked for the city Sanitation Department, his career ending with a disability pension after he had managed to hit his head against a garbage truck. "Hey! What's the big deal? It's not like it was working so well before" was the running put-down of Petey's infirmity at the Bergin, and nobody was joking. There was a goofy, out-of-touch quality to Petey. He talked slowly and always seemed confused; it was as if he couldn't quite understand the complex plot life was spinning around him. But thanks to his kid brother, Petey was back in the carting business. He was hauling cash.

Petey started out early on Sundays and would try to get back to Gotti's house in Howard Beach before whatever game the Don was watching on the big screen TV in his den was over. Most of the time, Petey never made it. There were just too many stops. He made pickups from Sammy Bull, who was handling the construction business—building companies and unions—for the Family; from Jimmy Brown, who controlled the private garbage haulers throughout the city and their union; from Sonny Ciccone, who ran the piers and the longshoremen's union; from Tommy Gambino, who represented the Family in the Garment District; from Tony Pep, who was in the oil and gas business, running a scheme for the Family that skimmed off a hefty chunk of the sales tax consumers paid on these products; and, if they had accumulated a significant sum, he also visited the smaller earners like Joe Butch who had a lot of loan shark money out on the street and Tony C. who was running the Family's gambling operations up in Connecticut. Everyone paid up in cash, the money handed over in shoeboxes, plastic bags, whatever was convenient. The capos would keep twenty percent of the action for themselves, a generous tax-free nest egg, but the rest went straight to their Boss. By the end of the day, the trunk of Petey's Lincoln was jammed with bundles of loose bills.

How much money was coming in? From Sammy Bull, a big earner, Gotti received about $100,000 a month: $1.2 million in cash a year. A gambler like Ralphie Bones turned in about $60,000 over the same Family fiscal year. Then there were the tributes, the envelopes stuffed with cash that the Don received from his capos on his birthday and Christmas. The Bureau accountants, after reviewing the C-16 informant report summaries and going over the bank records obtained in a case against Tommy Gambino that showed he had $12 million in a checking account, tried to come up with a figure. They estimated that Gotti received about $10 million in cash each year. But that might be too generous, they admitted. Or just as likely, they said with an embarrassed shrug, he might have an annual personal income of $20 million. In cash.

Not even John Gotti knew precisely how much money was rolling in each week. It was all, by necessity, disposable income. Unlike Tommy Gambino who was a capo *and* a high-powered businessman, Gotti was in the life full-time. He had no legitimate earnings other than $75,000 or so he received from no-show jobs as a plumbing supply salesman and as an executive for a friend's zipper company. There was no effective way he could make deposits into a savings account or a retirement fund. He would never be able to leave a mansion or a trust fund to his children. The government, he knew, was just waiting for him to make sizable investments or start accumulating the flashy possessions of a sweepstakes' winner—and then they would jump in to confiscate whatever they could grab. As it was, he was already stonewalling the IRS. He simply refused to file. At least that way, he reasoned with warped logic, they would never be able to catch him in a lie. How he was going to avoid the criminal penalty for failure to file, though, was a problem he preferred not to think about.

Meanwhile, he was busy spending. The money went out as fast as it came in. He bought a speedboat which, with one more last laugh, he named *Not Guilty*. There was a house in the Poconos he dared to put in his son's name, nothing too fancy, but with big picture windows, a hot tub, and a Jacuzzi. A condo overlooking the ocean in Montauk, Long Island, decorated in pastel shades like a desert sunset was in the name of another of his children. And still a third condo in Fort Lauderdale, along with a big cabin cruiser docked across from it, were both in another relative's name. Then, he had a Family to support, and his crews ran up outrageous legal fees; $300,000 for the defense in a single case would cause the Boss to moan, but he would pay it. Mostly, he spent the money on living a mobster's life. He might lose $200,000 by betting against the spread in a busy football weekend. Or he would take a crowd of thugs and their party girls out to dinner and then on to Régine's, and by dawn he would wind up covering in cash a tab the size of a college tuition payment. And, a conscientious Romeo, he bought lots of jewelry for his girlfriends. He even set up one of them, the FBI was convinced, with a Manhattan restaurant. That affectionate gesture cost him, it was estimated, a million bucks.

There were also formidable black Mercedes sedans with windshield wipers on the headlights, and iridescent double-breasted sharkskin suits he had custom-made at a shop down the block from the St. Regis Hotel in Manhattan with buttons on the jacket sleeves that could be undone. Trusted Petey, wearing his orange-tinted aviator glasses and his perpetually bemused look, brought him the cash, and the Don would spend it. As long as he didn't suspect he was being ripped off—that was a certain death sentence—Gotti really didn't focus on how much precisely was coming in. He was an old-school tough guy when it came to business. He never thought about how to leverage his Family's fortune into institutional power. He was very shortsighted, even feudal that way. The soldiers earned, he spent. Why should he save for a rainy day? The way he looked at it, it was *his* Family. The money would just keep on rolling in.

Mouw was stymied, his operation at a standstill. Once again he was back at a depressingly familiar spot—square one. But even though a microphone had been literally ripped out of the Bergin wall, even though the sound of cascading water continued to flood the Ravenite, he insisted on keeping the mike up in the Manhattan club for another two months, until September. Then, in what was promptly criticized by a chorus of Justice Department officials as a last gasp, and a doomed one at that, Mouw decided to go back up in the Ravenite. The mike was turned on for the holidays, from Thanksgiving to Christmas, 1988. When that, too, produced nothing, the carping about squandered Bureau funds and the demands for results grew ominously louder. Mouw could not help but sense the bureaucratic wagons circling. It seemed that only Jules Bonavolonta and Jim Fox were unequivocally willing to stand by him; however, for all he knew, their jobs were, thanks to his failures, now on the line too.

It was a characteristic stubbornness that had convinced Mouw it made operational sense to keep the Ravenite mike alive. The Observation Post, after all, was still active. Its videos continued to be a daily treasure. To walk away and simply close up shop when the squad was that close, with its eyes and ears in place and focused on the club, seemed foolish. Mouw still very much wanted to believe that if C-16 waited long enough, its patience would be rewarded.

And there was something else motivating his reluctance to abort the Ravenite bug. It was a rationale his critics in Washington would never have guessed; and for that matter, one he would never have risked sharing with them. But however unarticulated, it was also his most powerful reason for continuing the operation. He desperately wanted the chance to prove a long-kindling theory—a traitor was in their midst. He saw an opportunity for two negatives to create a positive. In the wake of the Bergin fiasco, the unproductive Ravenite audio operation now took on additional purpose. It became the perfect trap to catch a mole. And the mike in the heating duct was the dangled bait.

After the discovery of the bug in the Bergin, an embarrassed Kravec had immediately launched a damage-assessment investigation. He read informant reports, listened to the tape of the moments immediately preceding the prying of the mike from the wall, and he came to a very consoling conclusion—the Bureau bug had not been detected. At least not at first.

According to the testy report Kravec wrote for a limited internal distribution, it was the State Organized Crime Task Force that was to blame for the setback. In the course of routine telephone repair work at the club, a long dead bug the Task Force had left behind years ago had been uncovered. Once this was found, the furious Gambinos began following telephone lines and tearing apart walls until they stumbled upon the Bureau mike. There was no way you could protect against that kind of scrutiny, Kravec insisted. It wasn't, he said in an angry conclusion, an error by the Tech Squad that had led to the operation's being blown. It was the incompetence of a fellow law enforcement agency. And in case anyone missed the point, he made sure to mention that the Bureau always went back when an operation was over to remove the evidence.

Kravec's analysis, with its vindication of the vaunted Tech Squad as well as its swipe at a rival agency, was welcome news, and therefore quickly accepted within the Bureau. Mouw wanted to believe it too. He wanted things for once to be what they seemed to be. He wanted this—his most recent failure, and the Teflon Don's most recent great escape—to be simply one more knot in a string of bad luck. If the Bergin phone had not needed to be repaired . . . If the Task Force wiremen had removed their bug . . . He wanted to believe it was that simple.

But he couldn't. He had been on Gotti's trail too long to confuse coincidence with a pattern. He had a file in his black safe that documented too many abruptly dead-ended operations, too many fortuitous discoveries. Perhaps, he found himself wondering, it wasn't phone trouble that had led to the Bergin bug's discovery. Perhaps it was the knowing whispers of a traitor into Gotti's ear. Perhaps the phone trouble and the madcap search with sledgehammers for the bug were all an act staged for Mouw's benefit. One more attempt to protect Gotti's great secret. An act to protect the mole.

So Mouw, confiding only in his inner circle, came up with his plan. He would keep the Ravenite bug alive for as long as he could, dangling its existence provocatively in front of the spy. And he would wait. He would wait until Gotti just happened to call in repairmen to check the Ravenite's boiler. He would wait until someone happened to unscrew the heating duct and, what do you know, look what was found. Then he would have his proof. There are no accidents, he would proclaim. He would, after all the time spent building his file, of living uncomfortably with his suspicions, have the evidence he needed: Someone at the highest level was helping the Don.

But the plan failed. Perhaps Gotti's instincts persuaded him to be careful. Perhaps he felt the constant white noise was a dangerous enough admission; why risk betraying the extent of his knowledge by attacking an ineffectual mike. Or perhaps Kravec had been right all along: Gotti had simply lucked out. But whatever the reason, by Christmas nothing had happened. And Mouw ran out of time. Totally dispirited, he had no choice but to pull the Ravenite bug. The third anniversary of the murder of Paul Castellano and John Gotti's coronation as head of the Gambino Family came and went, and Mouw was not one step closer to making his case.

# 34

WHILE BRUCE MOUW WAS STILL TRYING TO FIGURE OUT WHAT TO
do next, the Manhattan District Attorney arrested John
Gotti for assault. City detectives burst into the Ravenite and
handcuffed the Don on a frigid evening in January, 1989. It
was only days after Mouw had finally pulled his bug, and
this stinging irony was not lost on the Bureau's Organized
Crime bosses. Neither was the distressing possibility that if
Gotti was convicted and sentenced to twenty-five years as a
"predicate felon," all of the Gambino squad's costly efforts
over the past three years would have been wasted.

That possibility did not escape Bruce Mouw either. Not
for a moment.

The D.A.'s charges were revealed at a standing-room-only
press conference, and even in the indictment's unembel-
lished prose the story unfolded with all the drama of an
episode in a TV series. According to the prosecution, in
February 1986, John O'Connor, the vice president and
business manager of the carpenter's union, had appeared at
a restaurant that was under construction. He looked around
and then speculated that since the work crews were non-

union, there could be "a problem." The owners of the Bankers & Brokers restaurant were worldly men. They offered O'Connor five thousand dollars to solve this "problem." It wasn't enough. Before the week was out, a team of crowbar-wielding thugs trashed the place. More than thirty thousand dollars' worth of damage was done in one rampaging hour.

The restaurant, however, had a silent partner—the Gambino Family. When Angelo Ruggiero reported the incident to the new Don, Gotti didn't remain silent for long. "Bust him up! Put a rocket in his pocket!" Gotti ordered Fat Ange, and that incendiary command was overheard by the State Organized Crime Task Force bug at the Bergin. (And another uncomfortable irony was not lost on the Bureau. It was the same mike that had, according to Kravec, derailed Mouw's operation. Now it might very well finish off Gotti.)

Fat Ange gave the job to the Westies, the Irish mob that occasionally took on enforcement assignments for the Family. In May, they attacked. O'Connor was cornered by four gunmen. They weren't out to kill him, only to make a point. He was shot in the buttocks and both legs. After a month spent recuperating in the hospital, O'Connor told police that he had been waylaid by "Puerto Rican gunmen." Why, he insisted, he just did not know.

The D.A.'s office, however, was certain it knew, and could convince a jury. Not that the prosecutors weren't wary. They had seen how Gotti and his in-your-face legal team had mauled Diane Giacalone during the trial in Brooklyn federal court, and they were determined to prevent another embarrassing debacle. Michael Cherkasky, the special assistant D.A. who was directing the prosecution, might have had the rumpled, other-worldly, forelock-tugging air of a grad student pondering the wisdom of the Romantic poets, but in the courtroom he was a tough guy. And he had a 40-and-1 felony trial record to prove it. As further ammunition, the prosecutors also had the FBI in their corner—or so they thought. When the indictment was announced, a beaming Jim Fox sat to the left of Robert Morgenthau, the Manhattan District Attorney. Then, just to make sure that

Gotti wouldn't succeed if he attempted a behind-the-scenes run on the jury, Morgenthau, a master at playing the old-boy network, took Jim Fox to lunch. Over pasta and martinis at Forlini's in Little Italy, Morgenthau extracted a promise that the FBI would "be on the lookout for jury tampering." And as if to cement the arrangement, Morgenthau for once abandoned the stinginess that is second nature to many who are born into the comfort of inherited wealth—his father had been both a distinguished financier and Secretary of the Treasury—and to Fox's surprise he picked up the modest check.

Despite either the evidence or the institutional forces that were being lined up against them, the Gambino Family seemed unruffled. Of course, by the time detectives caught up with Fat Ange he had other, more immediate problems. He was dying. He was in a hospital bed, his once bloated body now decimated by cancer, when the police came to arrest him for his role in the assault on O'Connor. "You are in a world of trouble, Angelo," Detective John Gurnee said. The mobster responded with the weary shrug of a prisoner who knew he was already a condemned man.

John Gotti, however, was full of his usual, take-your-best-shot cockiness. "Three-to-one odds I beat this case," challenged the Teflon Don.

Bruce Mouw found himself caught in a storm of contradictory passions. It was not as if he didn't know which side he was on. When he looked at things as a detached member of the fight against organized crime or even simply as a citizen, he understood he should be cheering on the D.A. As soon as Gotti was arrested, that became the airy, objective peak from which he watched the proceedings. He wanted Gotti to lose. He wanted the jury foreman to announce, "Guilty!" and the judge to lock up the Don and throw away the key.

Still, there were other observers who suggested that Mouw's fight against Gotti had become too personal a feud for him to want anyone else to get in first for the kill. And that, in light of what happened, would become a very persuasive theory. Certainly one that both Bob Morgenthau and Mike Cherkasky, two perceptive and bitter men, would endorse.

And so with the D.A.'s case against Gotti moving confidently forward and his own operation in a shambles, Mouw appeared to have been beaten. He had no new plan to put in motion, no new attack to launch. The long winter of 1989 seemed to be a ceasefire, if not a period of hibernation. Only later would Mouw describe it as "the turning point."

He had not given up. His mind refused to rest. He was goaded on not so much by his animosity toward a powerful enemy, but by his revulsion at that enemy's unrestrained methods: the bribed juror, the vengeful murders, and—he was increasingly certain—the mole Gotti had recruited and nurtured. He could not surrender even if he had been ordered to. For what must have been the dozenth or the two dozenth time—the case had so many twists and turns that even he could no longer keep track—Mouw regrouped. He returned once again to "square one."

His was a solitary journey, and a time-consuming one. He retraced every step he had taken so far in his long march against Gotti. Alone in his office, the huge Alexander's sign outside his window often his only reminder that there was a world beyond gangland, Mouw combed through every piece in his archive. He read through the case files. He digested a mountain of 209 informant reports. He scrutinized the transcripts of every recorded conversation, and still not satisfied, replayed many of the actual reels. He viewed all the old surveillance videotapes. And he kept up with the new ones, for without too much fuss he had, even though the mike at the Ravenite was down, kept the Observation Post operational; it was an instinctive decision—you never touch capital.

When he was done, Mouw reached what he had to feel was a very reassuring preliminary finding. He had been right all along. His tactic of trying to bug the Don was not only operationally sound, it was also, he was more convinced than ever, the most effective strategy possible. Informants, undercover operatives, surveillance—no matter how he tried to invent an attack scenario using only these ploys, he came up short. But—and this was both his insight and his challenge—he now realized he had spiked the wrong locations. He had no doubt that Gotti was meeting somewhere with the rest of the Gambino Administration to run the Family. He just needed to find where those secret meetings were held. Then he could strike.

So, additional testimony to his patience, Mouw began his journey once again. Only this time, since he had an idea of what he was looking for, his path was not linear. He shook up all the pieces. He went forward, then backward, and then forward again through the archives. He made columns of notes on legal pads, hoping to see where solitary facts might intersect and form a pattern.

First, there was a December 1988 209 from Frankie, Kurins' long-time TE. Frankie had moved up in the world. These days he was a regular at the Ravenite and he reported that now that it was winter the thin-blooded Gotti was reluctant to go for walk-talks along Mulberry Street. Instead, he and his Administration huddled in the hallway outside the club.

So, Mouw went back to the Ravenite tapes. And there it was. Little was said; that was why he had missed it all the other times he had listened. But now that his ears were pitched to the sounds, he heard it quite clearly. The mike in the heating duct was a perfect witness. There was Gotti at his table whispering to Sammy Bull; then the sound of a chair scraping against the floor; the pounding of footsteps; and a squeaking whine as a door swung open and a cannon blast as it slammed shut. It was a stage direction that had been omitted on dozens of the transcripts, but without it the drama was incomplete: *Exit stage left.*

Without the slightest doubt, but still scrupulous even in his excitement, Mouw reread the Looker's description of the club and Kravec's 302 report. Then he was certain. The backdoor to the club, the same one that the Looker had left unbolted for Kravec, led to the isolated hallway where Gotti and his men secretly discussed Family business.

But Mouw did not stop there. He knew, or at least felt,

there must be other meeting places. He once again went through the Looker's file. He was still restless when he finished, so, in a logical progression, he reached for Norman DuPont's. The brief TE report filed after Mike Cirelli's funeral caught his eye. There was Gotti, still in church, making a point to tell DuPont to change the locks on the dead man's apartment upstairs over the Ravenite. And that got Mouw wondering: What was so important about that apartment?

So, again he searched the 209s. And he found it: vague, carelessly unspecific, and therefore also previously overlooked. One of the Twins' TEs had reported he had heard a rumor that Gotti had a place, maybe an apartment, where he conducted important meetings. It was in Little Italy, he thought. But he wasn't sure.

Mouw read on, pushing aside more of the verbal brush to expose a narrow—but distinct—trail that ran through the 209s. Another TE had also in passing made a reference to an apartment. Shortly after becoming Don, Gotti had met with representatives of the Bruno Family of Philadelphia. The meeting had taken place, the TE had reported, in an unknown apartment. Mouw had always assumed the apartment was in Philadelphia, but now he was no longer sure.

Slowly, his theory began to take root. But the conclusive piece in the puzzle did not surface until he was already far along in his search. Frankie reported that on April 26, 1989, on the very day when Tommy Gambino was arrested on state charges, Gambino had quickly made bail and then hurried to meet with his Don. The meeting, according to the scuttlebutt Frankie had overheard, had been in an apartment somewhere.

Reining in his excitement, as rigorous in his approach as any scientist, Mouw looked at the Ravenite surveillance tape for that day. There it was: Tommy Gambino, pencil-thin and dapper, a silk square puffing out of his suit jacket breastpocket, going into the front door of the club. And yet—just as Mouw expected—there was no video of his leaving. But to make sure, Mouw also checked the surveillance log. It revealed the same mystery; although none of the agents on surveillance duty that day in the Observation Post had picked up on it. Tommy Gambino had been logged going into the front door of the club. *But he had not been logged out.* There was no record of his ever leaving the club.

And Mouw understood why. Gambino had accompanied Gotti out the back door of the club, into the hallway, and then up the tenement staircase to the Cirelli apartment. When the meeting ended, Gambino walked down the stairs and out the front door of the tenement. He never went back into the club. That was why the camera, aimed only at the Ravenite door, never saw him leaving.

With that deduction, Mouw for the first time in many months felt a surge of his old confidence. A new weapon, he realized, was within his grasp. He now knew where Gotti held his most secret meetings.

The summer of 1989 was a period of intense activity as the C-16 team swung back into action. It was just as well since, as Mouw himself would say, "they were chomping at the bit." In a closed-door meeting in his office, Mouw had announced the new targets. They would return to the Ravenite, although this time John Kravec promised he had a few tricks up his sleeve to improve audibility. They would spike the hallway and, somehow, the Cirelli apartment. And there was one more impossible mission: If Kravec could come up with a feasible plan, they would monitor the walk-talks along Mulberry Street.

The first step, however, was to put together an affidavit that would persuade a judge there was probable cause to eavesdrop on John Gotti and his men at these locations. The team threw themselves into the task. But it did not take them long to collect some very discouraging intelligence. Mike Cirelli's seventy-eight-year-old widow still lived in the two-room apartment. She was gray-haired and stooped, but she was also alert and rather spirited. And she hardly ever left the apartment.

Well, Mouw asked with some irritation, doesn't she go shopping?

George Gabriel agreed to look into that one himself.

Within a week, he reported back to Mouw. I got good news and bad news, he told his boss. The bad news, he explained with an ominously deadpan expression, is she doesn't go out much. She usually has someone from the neighborhood do the shopping for her.

Mouw simply puffed on his pipe. He wasn't going to beg.

So Gabriel jumped in with the good news. You know who does the old lady's shopping? The Looker.

# 35

THE FIRST TIME JOHN KRAVEC SNUCK UP THE CREAKING STAIRS TO the Cirelli apartment, he took one look around and immediately called the operation off. His two wiremen were right behind him on the landing. A dozen or so marksmen were scattered in the shadows along Mulberry Street. The quiet in the building was nothing less than reassuring. And, most opportunely of all, Mrs. Cirelli was in Philadelphia for a niece's wedding. But Kravec studied the door to apartment 10 for just a moment before he curtly whispered to his men, "We're out of here."

It was only when he was in the backup car returning with a mystified Jim Kallstrom to 26 Federal Plaza that he revealed what had caused him to abort: C-16 had gotten approval to bug the wrong apartment.

The affidavit signed by the judge, he pointed out in a blast of temper, was for an apartment on the building's second floor. The Cirelli apartment was two floors above the club, all right. However, that was the tenement's *third* floor. If he had proceeded, he later said, "It would've been a monumental fuck-up. It wouldn't matter if we overheard Gotti pulling the trigger. Without all the i's dotted, his lawyers would dropkick any evidence out of the courtroom. I had no choice but to run out of there like a virgin bride from the altar."

That fiasco was still raw in his mind when weeks later, on the night of November 21, 1989, after a new authorization had been signed by District Court Judge Kevin Duffy, Kravec prepared to return to apartment 10. And as if that wasn't unsettling enough, his pre-launch nerves had been further ruffled by an odd talk earlier in the day with Bruce Mouw. He had known the head of the C-16 team for years and had always judged him as a seasoned warrior: the casebook cool customer. But that day Mouw had been, just as Kravec was trying to settle into a zone of determined concentration, a jangle of impatient nerves. "So much is riding on this," Mouw had said, nearly begging. "I'm counting on you to get us up inside there."

Kravec, a bit petulantly, attributed Mouw's uncharacter-istically insistent state to a sense of approaching conquest. A pessimist by instinct, Kravec thought this was way prema-ture. Still, he had to acknowledge that the attack on Gotti had taken great operational leaps forward over the past two months. First, in terms of sheer technological innovation, his Tech Squad had done the impossible. And they had done it time after time.

At the tail end of September, they had gone back into the rear room of the Ravenite. Kravec had hardwired the mike into the phone lines rather than into the electrical current, and the sound that now traveled from the club was pure. For the agents in the plant it was, quite literally, like listening in on an extension phone.

Next, in the middle of October, Kravec had returned to the building to have a go at spiking the hallway. This had loomed as a real nightmare. Tin ceiling, tile floor, and a metal door—"the hardest of hard rooms," he had moaned when Mouw gave him the assignment. But after kicking it around with his team, he had worked out an ingeniously simple plan of attack. He drilled a hole about half the size of a bottlecap into a corner of the baseboard adjacent to the back door of the Ravenite; wedged an ebony black mike into this cavity; and then—his stroke of inspiration—he ran the two hair-thin wires from the mike under the door and *back* into the club. That way the wires were not only easy to conceal, but also he was able to piggyback this mike, too, onto the phone lines. The transmissions from the hallway were remarkably clear.

And finally, in what many would later point to as the confirming proof of Kravec's genius, he, with the help of the Special Projects crew down at Quantico, was in the process of devising a scheme to monitor the walk-talks along Mulberry Street. Deep Street, they were calling it at the Special Projects lab. In fact, of all the targets Mouw had passed on to Kravec only one had proved to be a problem. It was an office C-16 was convinced Gotti used in a building on West 36th Street in the city's Garment District. Kravec and his team had snuck into the place on three separate nights in October, but each time Kravec decided to abort. The Scorpio Marketing Company was guarded by an armory of alarms, motion detectors, and even surveillance cameras. It just wasn't worth the risk of being detected and then jeopardizing all the other bugs. Especially since they were already delivering.

That was the truly encouraging part, the one that was helping to build the hopeful mood in the Bureau; as Mouw, the old salt, told his agents, land after such a perilous time at sea was finally in sight. So far there was only a small stack of transcripts, but it was rich with clues. Each day the C-16 agents typed out summaries of what they had overheard the night before, and even in those brief reports they could hardly restrain their excitement.

SDNY-1988
RAVENITE HALLWAY

October 27, 1989
Time: 6:48 PM

283

JOHN GOTTI and JOHN GAMBINO discuss a murder apparently involving TOMMY PATERA, a BONANNO LCN Soldier. It also appears that GOTTI and GAMBINO are discussing *bid rigging* on a job in Long Island.

November 1, 1989
Time: Approx. 6:28 PM

JOHN GOTTI and VINNIE ALOI (COLOMBO LCN Family—Capo) appear to split up money that belongs to both LCN families. GOTTI mentions CARMINE is supposed to hit (kill) someone named VANUZZI (ph) who may be a federal or state witness who is currently in jail. ALOI indicates TONY killed someone and GOTTI appears to know about the killing. Indicating it will ruin the state's case against someone.

November 7, 1989
Time: Approx. 7:24 PM

GOTTI states, *These tapes, the fuckin tapes, they're gonna get everybody and anybody. The fuckin rat cops and prosecutors.* GOTTI appears concerned that tapes of electronic surveillance of him and others will put them in jail.

And there was more, a confirming promise of larger revelations. Scattered throughout these reels of tapes were small hints that, each time Mouw and his team carefully and repeatedly dissected them, reinforced the speculative theory that the Cirelli apartment was vital; it loomed as the one last atom that somehow Kravec had to split. "Let's go upstairs, Lou," Gotti was heard whispering to Big Lou Vallario in the hallway, and this brief suggestion was replayed so many times in the C-16 squad room that it might as well have been an incantation. Or Gotti barked one evening, "Give me about five minutes upstairs," and heads nodded knowingly. Even the sound of Gotti's footsteps drumming on the stairs as he descended to the hallway was duly noted and underlined on each transcript. The team was convinced he had to be coming from apartment 10.

None of this was lost on Kravec. He understood the importance of getting C-16 up inside the apartment. In spite of all his previous ingenuity, in spite of all the risks he had so far taken, he realized that all of it might amount to only small moments if he was unable to capture the conversations in Gotti's most secret hideout. To his invariably objective way of looking at things, he was "going into the ninth inning with a no-hitter going. But, let the bad guys get one single, and it's 'Who's Kravec?'" That was why, although he certainly did not need any more pressure, he appreciated and could almost excuse Mouw's concerned plea for his success.

However, there was something else weighing heavily on Mouw. Tormenting him, even. Kravec had not picked up on it. The C-16 transcribers had also missed its significance. But to Mouw, although it was only the quickest of asides and spoken on just a single tape, it was a glittering nugget. On the evening of November 1, Gotti, with both concern and solicitude in his voice, had asked George Helbig for some help. The Don himself was appealing to Helbig—he wasn't even a made man!—to "try and find out" about an impending "pinch." Mouw heard the request and in that instant he was convinced he understood what was at stake: Gotti was ordering Helbig to reach out to the mole. It did not take his active mind long to make another leap: His private quest to find this traitor would only come to an end if Kravec could penetrate apartment 10.

It was just as well that Mouw decided not to share this secret with Kravec. By midnight on November 21, as he prepared to walk across Mulberry Street, his black bag flung rakishly over his shoulder, there was enough to keep him worried. His chief concern was Mrs. Cirelli. They had chosen this night for the break-in because the old woman had left that afternoon to spend the Thanksgiving holiday with her sister on Staten Island. At least that was what the Looker had told C-16. But the observation post had not spotted her leaving. Perhaps she had headed off earlier in the day than planned, before the watchers were settled in. That was a possibility. The pen register C-16 had placed on her phone line offered some confirmation of that thesis: She hadn't made a call all day. But then again, she rarely did. And when Mouw at around seven that evening ordered the Twins to drop whatever they were doing and rush to the sister's house on Staten Island on the off chance that they might spot a familiar profile in the window, the results were inconclusive. It could be her, Frankie Spero radioed in. Someone's talking to the sister in the living room. But, he also warned, we stay out here much longer and we're bound to get made. Mouw had no choice but to call them in. And Kravec had no choice but to proceed without any real proof that Mrs. Cirelli wasn't upstairs sleeping in her bed.

Tonight there were no elaborate ruses to get to the front door of the tenement. Things, Kravec had learned from experience, were usually pretty quiet on Mulberry Street after midnight. There was no need to sit in a refrigerator box, a target for every stray dog in the neighborhood. The plan was to walk up to the tenement as if he was coming home; the best cover, went the Bureau wisdom, was always the simplest. It should only take him a matter of moments to pick the lock; by now he had developed a real touch for the familiar mechanism. He had been inside the building so many times in the past month that this phase of the operation no longer concerned him. Still, he reminded himself as he approached the door, you never know what can go wrong.

When Kravec shined his Mini-Mag flashlight on the keyhole, it didn't take him long to find out. Someone had changed the lock.

Why?

Reasons flashed through his mind. A tenant had spotted him last time he was in the building. C-16's TE had given them up. The hallway mike had been discovered. And just as quickly, fear giving his thoughts a skittish momentum, he knew what would happen next. Gotti was onto him. A trap had been set. An army of tough guys was waiting by the stairwell. He was a dead man.

He took a deep breath, and that seemed to calm him. Or, he now told himself, someone in the building might have lost his key. That was reason enough to change the lock. It could be that simple. Still, he had a difficult time accepting that explanation. But what choice did he have? He could walk back across the street, get in a car, and in fifteen minutes be safe in his office at 26 Federal Plaza. Except then he would never know what might have happened if he had tried.

He decided to have a go at the new lock.

It was not that different from the one it had replaced. Kravec defeated it after only a brief battle. He removed the nine-millimeter from his ankle holster and placed it in his jacket pocket; the gun was now easier to reach. Then he opened the door.

The hallway was quiet. Quickly, his two wiremen joined him. It did not take the trio long to climb the flights of stairs to the third floor. And there it was—apartment 10.

He did not have to pick this lock. Kravec had a key. It was the key the Looker used when she went shopping for Mrs. Cirelli. "Just let yourself in, dear," the old lady had told the Looker. "I take a nap in the afternoon." Kravec, however, did not know this; he could only wonder how George Gabriel had managed to get a key that would open the door to John Gotti's most secret meeting place.

He put the key in the lock. If the old lady was in her bed, turning the key could wake her up, he thought. For that matter, if Gabriel was mistaken and the door was wired, it could wake up the whole building. Hell, his thoughts raced on with increasing fatalism, if this was a setup, there could be enough firepower on the other side of the door to wake up the whole neighborhood.

He turned the key. The lock clicked. He looked at the two wiremen. He gave them each a nod, and it struck him that he might just as well have been saying good-bye. Then he turned the doorknob, and walked into a blessed silence.

There were only two rooms, with a small, makeshift kitchen separating them. The bedroom was to the left, and

Kravec swung the beam of his flashlight into the room. It illuminated a brass bed with a floral-patterned spread and a lace dust ruffle. The bed was made. The room was empty. For the first time that night, Kravec's confidence started to return.

When he walked into the living room, Kravec immediately decided that this was where Gotti held his meetings. After all, he really couldn't see the Don and Frankie Loc and Sammy Bull holding a sitdown on a brass bed. There was an overhead light; the glass shade was imitation Tiffany, and he considered turning it on. But then he noticed that the two windows at the end of the small room faced Mulberry Street. That was all he needed, some busybody in the building across the street wondering why the old woman's light was on at one in the morning—especially when she was supposed to be at her sister's. Instead, he played his flashlight around the room.

He took his time, studying it all with a good deal of concentration. It was a small room, but a lot of care and a bit of taste had gone into its decoration. There was a cocoa brown moon-shaped couch against one wall. Across from it on either side of a narrow fireplace were two Deco-ish arm chairs covered in a complementary tan and white cross-hatched fabric. A cherrywood dining table surrounded by a set of bamboo-style chairs crowded the entrance to the room; its centerpiece was a vase full of plastic flowers. At the other end of the room, near the windows, was a television set on a metal trolley; on the top shelf was a cable box, on the bottom a VCR. And all the while as his flashlight hunted over the room, Kravec's wireman's mind was sorting through the possibilities. He was searching for the best spot to plant a mike.

Days ago, when this mission was still in the planning stages, Kravec had made up his mind to go strictly hardwire. It wasn't only that the sound quality of RF was too problematic. He realized he couldn't count on the widow's leaving the apartment often enough to allow him to replace the batteries. He had also already decided, since this job was lace-curtain all the way, to jump his mike onto Mrs. Cirelli's phone line. That would be the easy part. He didn't even have to risk going to the tenement's basement and poking around for the terminal box. A buddy in New York Telephone security, after having studied the court-ordered authorization, had told him the location of the pole where the line from apartment 10 made its "appearance," to use the wireman's phrase. He could do all his trick wiring from there, blocks away from the tenement. But first he had to get his mike up and running in the apartment.

There were a lot of possibilities in the living room, and not much time. Standing in the pitch-dark apartment, he sorted through them rapidly. The Tiffany shade above the dining table was a candidate, but he ruled that out because it was too close to the refrigerator; why risk the constant electrical humming? He considered the air conditioner in the window, but decided the mike would be bound to pick up a lot of street noise too. The TV and the cable box were both perfect—as long as nobody turned them on to catch a ballgame, and what guarantee was there of that? So, by process of elimination, he decided on the VCR. Sure, he reasoned, if Gotti popped in a cassette, the sound quality would be a little dicey. But Kravec was willing to take the gamble that Gotti and his guys didn't come up from the club to watch old movies.

It did not take him long to remove one of the screws that held the black metal frame of the VCR together, insert his mike in its place, and then splice the two wires that ran out of the mike into the electrical cord that was plugged into the wall socket.

Apartment 10 was now wired for sound.

But Kravec was not yet ready to leave. He had a point to make. In a vain moment, he had told both Mouw and Gabriel that it wouldn't be too hard to get a TV camera up in the apartment. "It'll be just like ABSCAM," he had promised them, referring to the sting operation the Bureau had run against Congress, and to the incriminating videotapes that had been shot of congressmen making deals in a hotel room. "I'll get you videos out of the apartment," Kravec had boasted.

He had brought a video camera with a very fast quarter-inch lens in his black bag, and now all he needed was a plan. There was an alleyway outside the kitchen window. This was a real possibility. He could hide the camera in a light fixture and run some RG11 coaxial cable out the window and up the side of the building to a transmitter on the roof. But this would take a lot of plastering and camouflaging. Hours of work, he estimated.

By now it was nearly four and Kravec was getting desperate. He played the light once more around the room. The beam settled on the fireplace, and in an instant he knew it was perfect. He would lower the camera down through the chimney on the roof until it came to rest on the top of the flue. There would be no wires to hide. It would all be nice and neat. The only tricky part would be cutting a hole through the flue for the camera's quarter-inch lens and then making sure its field of vision included the couch and chairs, but he was sure he could handle it.

Suddenly his concentration was interrupted. It was his walkie-talkie: A light had just gone on in another apartment. It could be, he knew, someone going to the john. Then again, it could be that someone had heard something and was calling the police to report a burglar. Or someone might even be ringing up DuPont, telling him he had better come over and see what was going on.

For the second time during the course of that long night, Kravec had to make a difficult decision. He could stay and try to get the camera up. And risk everything. Or he could settle for spiking the room. And run. He wanted to see Mouw's face when videotapes started coming in of the Godfather cutting his deals. But he also wanted to make sure they got Gotti.

"Time to pack up," he told his men. He put the video camera back into his bag.

Sometimes it seemed to Kravec that he spent half his life climbing telephone poles. It was daylight now, only hours after he had hurried from Mrs. Cirelli's apartment, and he was dressed in a telephone repairman's uniform, working high above the street. The pole was near a firehouse a few blocks west of the tenement on Mulberry Street. He opened the cover on the terminal box. There were at least three hundred terminal pairs inside, and each linked a telephone with the Central Office, but his friend in NY-Tel security had given him the coded number of the cables that serviced the Cirelli phone. He found those red and green wires, and next to them the yellow and black wires that wiremen call the spare pair. Normally, the spare pair is used by the phone company if a customer wants to put in an extension phone or another line. The FBI had leased the spare pair running into the Cirelli apartment from the telephone company.

Kravec first connected the yellow and black wires to the red and green ones. Then he hooked a tiny device called an infinity transmitter to the spare pair. All anyone in the plant had to do was call up the telephone number of the spare pair, and he would be silently connected with the microphone broadcasting from the VCR. It was, basically, the same technology used in the audio burglar alarms that allow anxious suburbanites to dial their homes when they are on vacation and listen in for strange sounds.

Before Kravec climbed down from the pole, he made one call. Mouw had been in his office waiting, and he picked up the phone on the first ring.

"I blew it," Kravec announced with genuine disappointment. "There was no time to get a camera up."

Mouw, hearing Kravec's disconsolate tone, understood at that moment that the whole operation was in ruins. He could not even bring himself to ask what had gone wrong. He was about to hang up when Kravec, still very low-key, gave him the rest of his report:

"Other than that, it went like a dream. You should be able to hear anything and everything that's said in apartment 10."

# 36

THE MIKE IN APARTMENT 10 WENT "UP" FOR THE FIRST TIME AT 4:35 that afternoon. Nearly four and a half hours later, at about nine, the observation post called the plant on the red phone to report, "Number One is out." That was the word-code to announce Gotti had left the Ravenite for the night. The apartment mike was immediately shut off.

Carol Kaczmarek was the plant manager that night. She was a heavyset, dark-haired woman who had been an agent for twenty-five years. Like everyone on the C-16 team, she understood what was at stake: *The apartment,* Mouw had promised, *will hold the key.* Yet she might as well have spent the night leafing through a magazine. The summary report she left in the black combination safe in Mouw's office read:

SDNY-2005
APARTMENT 10

*November 22, 1989*

No principals at location.
No pertinent conversations.

Mouw took it in stride. "You can't expect Gotti to use the apartment every night," he told Gabriel. "We've waited this long. We can wait a little longer." And, he pointed out with reassuring logic, "This was only the first night."

*November 23, 1989*

No monitoring.
Thanksgiving.

*November 24, 1989*

Club closed.
No principals at location.
No pertinent conversations.

*November 25, 1989*

No monitoring.

*November 26, 1989*

No monitoring.

*November 27, 1989*

JOHN GOTTI not at club.
No principals in location.
No pertinent conversations.

As these terse summary reports began to pile up, both Mouw and Gabriel grew increasingly on edge. They might have been waiting for a surgeon to call with the biopsy results; it was that difficult, that vital. Gabriel, slipping into despair, even found himself returning to a secret fear: They were in the wrong place. The Cirelli apartment was Gotti's cover, his bit of word-code for the hideaway where his meetings *really* took place. That was why it had all been so easy, why there hadn't been any alarms on the door. How could they have been naive enough ever to believe the Don conducted his Family business in an unprotected tenement apartment above the Ravenite? It was too reckless, and John Gotti was a very careful man.

Gabriel, however, did not dare share his concern with Mouw. He wasn't sure what he would do if Mouw agreed.

### November 28, 1989

No principals in location.
No pertinent conversations.

### November 29, 1989

No principals in location.
No pertinent conversations.

Yet all the while, adding to the growing sense of frustration and doubt, the two other mikes—the one in the Ravenite back room and the one in the tenement hallway—continued to transmit. And on the morning of November 30, as Mouw reviewed the tapes from the night before, he found himself riveted. For another listener, even for the agents in the plant, the words he heard on the tapes were merely cryptic. But for an exhilarated Mouw they were further pieces in a puzzle he had been working on for years.

It was a conversation between John Gotti, Joe Butch Corrao, and—the catalyst for all Mouw's attention—hulking George Helbig. Mouw heard the hallway door swing open and the three men talk for nearly five minutes, their voices a soft pattern of whispers.

Sitting at his desk, his headphones tight on his head, Mouw strained to hear each word. He played with the volume frantically. But it was useless. He could not decipher a word. Still, it almost did not matter. Helbig's presence was statement enough. Mouw knew Helbig had come to bring, as Gotti had requested weeks before, information about the "upcoming pinch." He was certain Helbig was delivering the report from the mole.

As Mouw continued to listen raptly, his important deduction was, he felt, quickly substantiated. For no sooner had the Don finished conferring with Helbig and Corrao than he summoned one of his attorneys, Gerald Shargel, into the hallway. Now the voices boomed authoritatively into the microphone.

"I was just talking," began Gotti with a very stagey offhandedness, "and I think of something. Say the state wanted to go after . . ."

For a moment Gotti's voice trailed away from the microphone, and Mouw's stomach dipped. Then, just as suddenly, it was back on track.

". . . for murder. But the Feds won't allow it. Be the same thing. Does that make sense that they would do it at the same time? Do the same charge, two different places?"

Shargel's response was immediate: "They've done it. They did. They've done it, sure."

Shargel went on to detail the specific statute. It was a very impressive performance; in other circumstances Mouw might have grudgingly applauded Shargel's knowledge of criminal law. But all he could concentrate on now was the growing tension in Gotti's voice as he began to question the lawyer. There was a little self-pity, a little humor, and even a little bravado in the exchange. As he listened, Mouw, who prided himself on knowing his adversary, could imagine what was rushing through Gotti's mind. The Don, he felt, was weighing his own predicament. First, Helbig had shared his report from the mole: Both the state and the Feds were planning to go after him for the murder of Castellano. Moments later Shargel, without any hesitation, had confirmed that two separate indictments for the same charge were indeed possible. Gotti had to be feeling the pressure.

Mouw was certain Gotti would try to learn more about the cases looming against him. That was the way he operated. He always tried to get the upper hand, to be one step ahead of the good guys. The Don would have to contact all his sources.

We're close, Mouw decided, when he finished listening to the tapes. Yet his emotions were all over the place, an unstable mixture of elation and anxiety. He tried to persuade himself that the next time, there would be no whispering in a hallway. Gotti would go where he could speak freely.

He needed to believe that very much.

Carol Kaczmarek was a devout Catholic. For over a quarter of a century her commitments to her church and to the Bureau had coexisted comfortably, with an almost equal and very often complementary intensity. But now, for the first time in her career, she found the work getting to her. She was having a hard time reconciling her job as plant manager with her sense of how a Catholic life should be lived. She was willing to put up with all the tedious hours in the windowless room on the twenty-sixth floor of Federal Plaza headquarters. She would not even think of complaining about how the headphones, no matter how carefully she tried to position them, always played havoc with her bobbed hair. But although she did not want to appear prissy, she found listening to the conversations at the Ravenite to be a distasteful, often embarrassing experience. The constant and gratuitous cursing was a sin against not only her notion of simple propriety, but also her religious sensibilities. She felt dirty, she would complain, just listening.

She began the evening of November 30, 1989, preoccupied with this growing uneasiness about her job. It was a busy night at the Ravenite and the conversations flowed freely and unexpurgated. Her discomfort was intensifying. And then quite suddenly and remarkably, a transmission began at precisely 7:38 that completely brought her around. She wouldn't have traded places with any agent in the Bureau.

"Carol," one of the monitoring agents called to her at that moment from across the room, "we might have something here." His voice was tentative; or, as another agent would later put it, "bordering on disbelief."

Still, all the small talk in the room ceased. The silence was abrupt and wary, like a swift intake of breath. Kaczmarek hurried down to the far cubicle where the agent sat and immediately put on a pair of headphones so she could listen too.

She heard the sound of a door slowly wheezing open. Next, a drumroll of footsteps. And then a booming and familiar voice coming in loud and wonderfully clear.

"She ain't home yet," said John Gotti.

"Yeah, she is," corrected Sammy Bull.

"She is home?" Gotti said with some surprise. "Oh, good; don't, don't forget to ask me for the money to give it to her."

Kaczmarek listened intently as the head of the Gambino Family and his *consigliere* made arrangements to pay the woman whose apartment they were borrowing for their meeting—Mike Cirelli's widow.

There was the distinctive sound of a bottle being uncorked. Wine, Kaczmarek realized. And she thought: Perfect. Get comfortable. Settle in for a nice, long chat.

Then the door opened again, and Gotti's voice offered a soft and curiously mournful greeting: "Mike."

"Yeah, John," Mike said sadly.

The agents in the plant had no further clue to Mike's identity, or why he was so downbeat. Ring up the OP *now*, Kaczmarek ordered. Get them to check tonight's attendance list. They'll be able to ID Mike.

The mournful conversation continued without pause. "First, you know we're sorry," Gotti said.

"Thank you."

"I don't have to tell you how sorry we are," Gotti emphasized.

The Observation Post was back on the line. "Mike," they were certain, was Michael Coiro, an attorney. And he had good reason to be upset. That afternoon he had been convicted in a federal court in Brooklyn of RICO charges tied to the Gambino Family's heroin-trafficking operations. He was facing a decade or more in jail.

And the first thing he did after his conviction, even before going home to his family, was to report for a meeting with John Gotti.

Carol Kaczmarek took off the headphones and punched a

button on the speed-dial phone. Bruce Mouw picked up the receiver in his cottage near Oyster Bay.

"It's the apartment. We're up!" Kaczmarek announced with unrestrained excitement. "Loud and clear. And Gotti has a guest—Mike Coiro."

"I'm on my way in," Mouw said very matter-of-factly. But, he would remember, when he hung up the phone and dashed to his car, his heart was pounding.

The November 30 conversation—"Apartment 10 Tape #1," as it came to be known in the case files—was a treasure trove. The Don, in addition to Coiro, was surrounded by the rest of his Administration: his acting underboss, the slow-talking and deferential white-haired Frank Locascio; and his *consigliere,* the calculatingly shrewd Iceman, Sammy Bull Gravano. Their meeting was wide-ranging, and went on for over an hour. The listeners at the plant had to put on a new reel of tape at one point, and that caused some commotion. But it was a problem that was quickly solved. After a few frantic moments it was once more as if they too were sitting around the Cirelli living room sipping a glass of Chianti. With their headphones on, they were drawn into Gotti's world. It was very seductive. They were wiseguys, hearing the tall tales, living the life. Sometimes they even had to laugh. The Don was, after all, a pretty good story-teller.

On that first night, they heard the Don launch into a complaint about how all the Family troubles had started after the FBI bugged Angelo Ruggiero's house. "You know how they invade your privacy," Gotti said with indignation. "Ya hear a baby crying, your wife crying. You say, 'It could be my house, my baby, my wife.' Where the fuck are we going? Maybe you wanna throw a fart in the bathroom, you hear it in open court. They hear you farting. Like that poor fuckin' 'Frank the Wop.' His phone was in the bathroom. He's taking a shit, and he's talking. That's a fuckin' shame . . . Then he goes, *Phphphhh! Bing!* He said, 'I feel better now. I couldn't move.' "

That cracked up Sammy Bull. And by now the team in the

plant, except for a stony Carol Kaczmarek, was laughing too.

"In open fuckin' courtroom," the Don went on, clapping his hands and guffawing uncontrollably. The Iceman couldn't seem to stop laughing either.

"Madonna!" Gotti managed to get out between his rumble of laughs. "You gotta get a heart attack."

Later in the evening, the Godfather once again turned to the intrusiveness of all the FBI's bugging operations. He lectured his *consigliere:* "You gotta relax in your fuckin' house. The way we're relaxing right here."

That didn't cause any laughter to break out in the plant. But the irony didn't escape anyone either.

After just a cursory listen to that first apartment tape, George Gabriel began sketching a preliminary indictment in his mind. At the very least, he was convinced they could make a RICO case against Gotti and his men for operating a criminal enterprise, and perhaps even for obstruction of justice in the Castellano murder investigation. This assessment, however, left him more stunned than elated. After all these years, he told himself with near disbelief, we're finally on the inside.

Mouw's focus on the conversation was more single-minded. Of course he looked for incriminating ammunition to use in the frontline war he was waging against Gotti. But he also relentlessly combed the transcripts for clues he could use in his long, solitary struggle. He continued his search for the mole.

With only the slightest of self-congratulatory nods, Mouw saw he had accurately anticipated Gotti's moves. Just a day after his talk with Helbig and Shargel, the Don was reaching out for more information about the forces lining up against him.

"Now the reason we got you up here," Mouw heard Gotti say to Coiro with a trace of embarrassment, "is we're getting a little selfish now. This is like you found out you got cancer. I tell you forget about your cancer. Let's talk about my headaches."

"I'm doing what I have to do, John," Coiro replied.

So Gotti, after a little more diplomacy, shared his problem with Coiro. "I've been told by a source, that, that a pinch is coming down. It's gonna be a joint pinch."

But he needed more details, Gotti explained. He wanted to know precisely who would be indicted and when. He wanted Coiro to "push all your heartaches aside." He was insistent, his voice building to a shout. "But what you gotta do is you gotta grab this guy. You gotta tell him, 'Listen, give us the motherfuckin' names.'"

The Don went on, only now more conciliatory. "Mike, we've been good to him in the past. We'll be good to him in the future. Give us the names." But when he concluded, it sounded more like an order than a request. "Can you see this guy pronto?"

"Tomorrow," Coiro said.

"Okay," the Don said, finally appeased.

Was Gotti sending Coiro on a mission to contact the mole, Mouw wondered? Or, he began to consider as he listened to the tape from that first evening for the tenth (or was it the twentieth?) time, perhaps not. Maybe Coiro had his own hook. Someone tied into law enforcement, but not the mole. A minor player. Someone like Mildred Russo, the elderly clerk in the U.S. Attorney's office that Joe Butch had used.

The more Mouw played with this theory, the more he came to believe it. It helped to explain why Gotti had reached out to Helbig first. Coiro was only a backup player. Further proof: After Coiro left the apartment and Sammy Bull, rather wishfully, suggested to his Boss that there wasn't anything to be concerned about, Gotti quickly turned on him.

"Oh, you forgot what the fuckin' bum told us," the Don snapped at his *consigliere*. "I wanted to strangle him last night, you know? He laughs when he brings us bad news, this fuckin' Georgie."

Gotti was talking about George Helbig, Mouw was convinced. The runner who serviced the mole.

And each time Mouw played through the tape, he re-

GANGLAND

turned as if pulled by an irresistible force to a brief exchange between Gotti and Gravano. A confident Gotti was predicting victory in his battles with the government.

"We'll break their ass, Sam. We got this little bit of an edge, you know . . . Fuck them."

Then Gotti's voice dipped to a whisper and he hissed, "Listen: *We know everything.*"

# 37

BUT ONCE AGAIN, THE DON TOOK MOUW BY SURPRISE. HE DID not return to the Cirelli apartment. Mouw told himself that Gotti might be preoccupied with his upcoming state assault trial. It could be that simple. But he also understood that in this investigation there were no such things as coincidences.

Mouw's concerns escalated as each day passed. Did Gotti suspect something? Or did Gotti *know?* Had the mole learned of the mike in apartment 10 and warned his master? Was the entire operation in jeopardy?

Mouw did not have any answers. All he could do was wait.

SDNY-2005
APARTMENT 10

*December 4, 1989*

No principals in location.
No pertinent conversations.

*December 5, 1989*

No principals in location.
No pertinent conversations.

*December 6, 1989*

No principals in location.
No pertinent conversations.

*December 7, 1989*

No principals in location.
No pertinent conversations.

Could that November 30 meeting have been a fluke? A one-time thing? Mouw did not know what to think. If he hadn't heard the tape with his own ears, if he hadn't read and then reread the transcripts so many times, he might have believed the sit-down in apartment 10 was just one more informant's report—full of promise, yet ultimately unfounded. In the past when he needed to steady himself, he had remembered that this, too, was how it was in the *Lapon*. A game of chase beneath the ocean, and then the waiting, the endless, silent waiting, until you heard the order to open fire. Or you heard the enemy's torpedoes coming straight at your boat.

Now that memory was small consolation. Torpedoes can only kill you. This wait was impossible.

*December 8, 1989, through December 11, 1989*

No principals in target location or no monitoring.
No pertinent conversations.

Finally, Gotti did return. At 7:13 on the evening of December 12, the Don sat down with his acting underboss, Frankie Locascio, in the living room of apartment 10 and the mike in the VCR picked up every word.

Gotti was in a tense, irritable state that evening. And the longer he sat in the apartment, the closer Frankie Loc's stolid, infuriating passivity brought him to a boil. His usual careful reticence was overwhelmed. Undone by his own anger, he spoke without thinking.

It was Sammy Bull who had initially sparked the God-father's irritation. The Iceman, Gotti was coming around to realize, had "green eyes." All he saw was money. His *consigliere*'s greed was so ruthless and obsessive that Gotti feared it could split the Family into warring factions. Yet there was something else, an even more disturbing vision pushing his anger. By the time Gravano was done, there wouldn't be anything much left over for the Godfather.

"Where the fuck are we going here?" Gotti ranted plaintively to Frankie Loc about the Bull's growing business empire. "Where are we going here? Every fucking time I turn around there's a new company popping up. Building, consulting, concrete. And every time we got a partner that don't agree with us, we kill him. You go to the Boss, and your Boss kills him. He kills 'em. He okays it. Says it's all right, good. Where are we going here, Frankie? Who the fuck are we? What do I get out of this here?"

Locascio's conciliatory reply was terse and nearly inaudible. But it didn't matter what the underboss said. Gotti was steaming.

". . . Sammy, slow it down. Slow it down. You come up with fifteen companies. For Christ sakes you got . . . concrete pouring. You got tiled floor now. You got construction. You got drywall. You got asbestos. You got rugs. What the fuck next? The other day . . . Sammy says, 'And I got the paint, and I got—' "

Gotti mimicked his own incredulous reaction: " 'You got a paint company?' I told him.

"He said, 'Well, six weeks ago we started a paint company. Don't you remember I told you?'

" 'I don't fuckin' remember you told me. What am I, fuckin' nuts? Now you got me thinking that I'm fuckin' nuts! When did you tell me you got a paint company? When I was looking over there?' "

Gotti sighed and then, without the least bit of irony,

complained bitterly, "Four fuckin' years. *I* got no companies!"

Yet to Gotti's fierce way of looking at things, what made Gravano's greed so intolerable and his own victimization so complete was the Bull's ingratitude. Especially since he had played such an essential role in the building of Gravano's empire. Gotti had killed anyone who got in the Iceman's way.

His fury overriding his usual concern about self-incrimination, Gotti said, "When Di B got whacked they told me a story. I was in jail when I whacked him. I knew why it was being done. I done it, anyway."

He had done it, Gotti continued with genuine indignation, for the same reason he'd been persuaded by Gravano to murder Louie Milito: "You told me the guy talked behind my back. Di B, did he ever talk subversive to you?" he asked Locascio.

"Never."

". . . I took Sammy's word that he talked about me behind my back. Louie—did he ever talk to any of you guys?"

Locascio's response was immediate: "No."

"I took Sammy's word," Gotti said with another put-upon sigh.

He now understood he was being played for a fool. He had had Robert DiBernardo and Louie Milito murdered simply because Sammy Bull complained about their disrespectful behavior. And now both Di B's lucrative construction company and Milito's Gem Steel were controlled by the Iceman.

Still, Gotti did not want his underboss to get the impression he was completely subservient to Gravano's machinations. He was planning to kill the Bull's old nemesis, Louie DiBono, not simply because the man was a business partner of Gravano's. Gotti's grudge was more immediate. "You know why he's dying? He's going to die because he refused to come in when I called. He didn't do nothing else wrong."

As he wound down, Gotti's rage left him drained. He was

in a melancholy mood, woeful and self-effacing. "I don't want nothing," he said. "I would be a billionaire if I was looking to be a selfish Boss . . . All I want is a good sandwich. You see this sandwich here? This tuna sandwich? That's all I want—a good sandwich.

"You know what I want you to do, Frank?" he asked, his sad voice full of the knowledge that one day even he would be forced to confront the limits of his own power. "We gotta both buy chemotherapy with the money I got."

The entire night's conversation had been a spontaneous performance. Gotti had revealed the self-assured and arrogant morality of a man whose way of thinking about the world was out of scale, out of proportion. And in his tirade he had destroyed himself.

C-16's official summary of the sit-down made its way quickly to Washington, and in the halls of Justice it could not have been greeted with more delight than if it had been Gotti's head itself; which, in a sense, it was. It began:

"This lengthy conversation intercepted between GOTTI and LOCASCIO lasted for approximately one hour. During which GOTTI and LOCASCIO discussed a variety of topics, to include the structure of the GAMBINO Family; chain of command and protocol within the ranks; murder and murder conspiracy; labor racketeering in the construction industry; interaction between LCN families; control of labor unions; and control of the carting industry."

When U.S. Attorney Andrew Maloney listened to this tape, he decided with a good deal of satisfaction that it was as incriminating as any confession. The Don, he would say, was "brought down by his own words."

Still, when Mouw recalled the pivotal Apartment Tape #2, he preferred to focus on Gotti's mournful, ruminative complaint to Locascio as the conversation was drawing to an end. He had been locked in his battle with Gotti for so long that his adversary had been transformed into a symbol—a monument of evil. But, Mouw was glad to be reminded, Gotti was just a man.

* * *

George Gabriel was ready to celebrate. The day he heard the tape, he went out and bought a bottle of champagne. His wife, Maureen, was resentful of all the time he had been devoting to the case. "We miss you," she had been complaining, speaking for herself and the two girls; and each time the words had stung. Now he was elated that he finally had reason to bring her such a stylish peace offering. He walked into the kitchen of their split-level ranch and waved the bottle in the air as if it were a trophy.

"The end is near," he announced. "We've got him." He was ready to pop the cork.

Maureen was more cautious; she, too, had lived through all the starts and stops of the Gotti investigation. "Let's wait until the case is over," she suggested. "We'll keep it on ice until then."

"Fine," said Gabriel. "It won't be long." And he added playfully, "I'll be all yours."

He was convinced that it would only be a month, perhaps two at the most before Gotti was arrested.

Bruce Mouw thought that was a real possibility too. And it troubled him. On the same evening that Gabriel was putting the champagne on ice, Mouw's mood was slipping. He realized there were many in the Bureau and the Justice Department who would insist the time had now come to arrest John Gotti. The Don was this generation's Al Capone; careers had been built on lesser conquests.

Mouw, however, understood that an arrest, an indictment even, was not a conviction. Gotti had vividly proved that. He was the master of escape. Mouw had too many reasons to fear that even with this new, unimpeachable evidence— Gotti admitting to murder!—the Don would once again beat the rap. He remembered all the fortuitous "coincidences" that had reinforced the Don's long-running streak of luck. He knew Gotti would win again. Unless he caught the mole.

And Mouw still did not have a clue to the traitor's identity.

Later that week Mouw reported to Jim Fox's office to

discuss "the status of the Gotti investigation." Jules Bonavolonta was also there, and as Mouw sat across from his two bosses, he could not help thinking that it was all over. In his mind he knew the reasons to end the operation. To keep it going would be a needless expense of time and money. The three wires at 247 Mulberry were costing a fortune in manpower, and the telephone bills for the "spare pair" lines that carried the transmissions were already in the six figures. Why squander resources when there was already enough to bring in an indictment?

Yet, he presented his case. "It's the chance of a lifetime," he argued with passion. "Who knows what we'll pick up. What kind of cases we'll be able to make." He shrewdly reminded his superiors that John Gotti was not the Bureau's only target. The mike in apartment 10 offered an opportunity to bring down the entire Gambino Family. "We're in the right spot," he said. "We have everything to gain and nothing to lose if we keep it going."

He did not mention the mole. That remained his secret.

When he was finished, there was a moment of silence. He waited. He saw Fox give a small nod to Bonavolonta, and he realized that their decision had been reached even before he had spoken. He felt foolish, and doomed. And then Bonavolonta, with not even a trace of a smile, told him, "It's your show, Bruce. We're behind you one hundred percent."

"Tickling the wire" was a common and often effective strategy in Bureau audio surveillance cases. The guiding principle had its roots in ancient blood sports: A little red meat was dangled to coax an animal to rush incautiously into a trap. In this technological variant, however, the goal was to provoke the hunted to *speak* with reckless—yet equally fatal—abandon.

Following his successful meeting at 26 Federal Plaza, Mouw began to think it might be necessary to use a bit of "tickle" to draw out Gotti. With the inventiveness of a screenwriter, he conceived a half-dozen or so elaborate yet feasible scenarios that he thought might provoke Gotti, in the privacy of apartment 10, to reveal his mole. But in the end, Mouw was his own harshest critic. He rejected them all. No matter how subtle his plot, he decided, it wasn't worth the risk that a shrewd Gotti would detect the calculating offstage hand pulling the strings.

As things worked out, Mouw need not have bothered. The trap was already being baited by politics. And no matter how farfetched or steeped in intrigue these convoluted machinations were, Gotti would never think to suspect anything out of the ordinary. Just city politics as usual.

On January 1, 1990—less than three weeks after the second apartment tape—Elizabeth Holtzman would step down from her position as Brooklyn District Attorney to become City Comptroller. Her successor was Joe Hynes, a man she disliked. She hadn't forgotten his past criticisms of her; and the dour Holtzman, who even on her best days looked taut enough to explode, was further put off by his convivial, backslapping ways. With the vindictiveness of a dowager cutting off an unworthy heir, she decided not to allow Hynes to inherit one of her office's crown jewels—the five ongoing mikes her wiremen had planted in Sammy "the Bull" Gravano's offices on Stillwell Avenue in Brooklyn and in Tali's. In one of her last acts as D.A., at ten minutes after eleven on the morning of December 30, she had a Brooklyn Supreme Court justice transfer the bugging operations to the State Organized Crime Task Force.

The judge's order was sealed, but it did not go unnoticed. *"Listen,"* John Gotti had boasted, *"we know everything."*

# 38

"I WANT GUYS THAT DONE MORE THAN KILLING," JOHN GOTTI grumbled, falling into the low, assertive voice he used when he was speaking as the Don.

Sammy Gravano, who had worked with too many triggermen not to know their limitations, concurred. He felt the Family needed earners, men who were capable, as he would put it, "of going out, putting things together." Of course, loyalty was important too. "He's down when he gets the call"——that was how a made guy should act.

"That's what you want. You don't want nothing else but that," Frankie Locascio interrupted. He spoke earnestly; he had been made when he was twenty-three, nearly four decades ago, and he felt he had come to understand what was important.

"I agree," Gotti said. That settled it.

The selection of new members was only one of the tasks on John Gotti's list when he convened the sit-down in the living room of apartment 10 on the evening of January 4. His assault trial was going to begin in less than a week, and he was determined to get his Family in order before he got caught up in, as he told Gravano, "all the heat."

It wasn't the outcome of the trial that concerned him. He knew the state had recorded him in the Bergin ordering Fat Ange (who had beaten the rap by dying of cancer) to "put a rocket" in John O'Connor's pocket. And, another potential problem, James McElroy, a Westie who was doing heavy time for a federal racketeering conviction, was going to take the stand to rat him out. Still, Gotti felt in control. He would walk out at the end of this trial, the same as he had after the other two. He had a plan.

What was weighing on him, however, was the possibility that the judge could decide to keep him in custody while the trial dragged on. Or just as likely, if Helbig's information was accurate, they might indict him for the Castellano murder and deny him bail in that case. The government had done that during his last federal trial, and he had wound up spending nearly a year trying to run things from a cell in the Metropolitan Correctional Center. It had been a rocky time. It affected business. And it left the Family unsettled. Some people even began to get big ideas. He didn't need that.

So, that was why he thought it was important to "put a little list together." Inducting new members into the Family would, Gotti hoped, send a message: It was business as usual. Even if the head of the Family was in jail being held without bail.

Sitting in the apartment, he tried to explain why this was necessary to Locascio. "Frank," he began slowly, and he continued in this measured, almost patronizing way, as if he felt it necessary to translate his words into an elemental, pidgin English for the older man. "I just didn't want to make it look like we're nuts. All the heat, going on trial— that we don't give a fuck. Hey, we just got the list out. You know what I'm trying to say?"

But even if he could grasp his strategy, Gotti wasn't at all persuaded the guileless white-haired Locascio could handle things if the Boss went to jail. It was one thing to have

Locascio, a man who looked as if he spent his Sundays in white wingtips playing golf, as the Family's acting underboss when Gotti sat at the head of the table. It was another if the Don was in jail. Gotti understood that he needed to take care of this, too, before his trial began.

He deposed Frankie Loc without apology. He was swift and brutal and, as always, calculating. He chose, instead, Sammy Gravano. All his previous complaints about Sammy's "green eyes," all his wild anger over how Sammy had manipulated him, were if not forgotten, at least temporarily restrained.

That night, sitting across from Gravano in the living room, he made the surprise announcement. He tried to give his words the solemn resonance of a royal decree. That was, he felt, La Cosa Nostra way. He said, "This is my wishes that if I'm in the fuckin' can, this Family is going to be run by Sammy. I'm still the Boss. If I get fifty years, I know what I got to do. But when I'm in the can, Sammy's in charge."

Gravano was the Family's underboss. Gotti would send the word tomorrow to all the Family's skippers. As for Locascio, he would become the Family's acting *consigliere*. It, too, was an important job, and Gotti's subdued voice when he announced the appointment seemed to imply that it was more than the old man deserved.

But Gotti had few doubts about putting Gravano, a man he was just coming to know, in the number two position. Perhaps it wouldn't be a permanent appointment; there would be time once all his legal problems were resolved, Gotti realized, to confront his repressed misgivings about Sammy. For the time being, Gravano was the perfect underboss. The way things were shaping up, with the possibility of his being remanded without bail, he needed someone who could keep all the ambitious factions of the Family in line. He needed an Iceman.

"Just the fact that you're out there," he said to his new underboss with a conspiratorial candor, "that you could sneak out in the middle of the night and hit a guy in the fuckin' head with a hatchet. You follow? Understand, Sammy?"

He did, of course.

And so did Mouw. He listened to the tape early the next morning, January 5; and then he drew a big *X* through an overly zealous summary report that tried to make something legally incriminating out of Gotti's offhanded comment. The Don was talking, Mouw told the circle of agents who were gathered in his office, metaphorically.

"Metaphorically?" Andy Kurins asked as if he had never heard the word before.

Mouw patiently explained that Gotti wasn't specifically ordering Sammy Bull to go out and scalp someone with a hatchet. It was just a figure of speech, Gotti's way of telling his new underboss that his reputation would intimidate anyone who considered going against the Boss.

"Oh," said Kurins. "I get it. He's not telling Sammy to use a hatchet . . ."

Precisely, Mouw said.

". . . For all Johnny Boy cares, Sammy can use a gun. Or a rope. Or even an ice pick."

The agents got a laugh out of that, but Mouw, usually Kurins' obedient straight man, didn't feel like playing games that morning. Apartment Tape #3 had left him very disappointed. It suggested that Gotti, for the short term at least, was winding down. As a last preparatory act, he had spent that night taking care of some Family housekeeping before he became immersed in his trial. If the Don was temporarily withdrawing, Mouw realized he would have no choice but to do the same. It was as if he and Gotti were living in parallel universes, their lives had become so intertwined. Gotti had only to be heard coughing on a tape before Mouw could almost feel the tickle in his own throat. And when the Don retreated, so did C-16. "No principals at location" would, Mouw anticipated, become the watchers' refrain for the next month at least.

He would make sure, however, that the monitoring team did not let down its guard. It would be kept at full pitch throughout the expected days of waiting. In fact, a fourth audio surveillance operation had just been launched—Deep Street. Kravec had pulled one more improbable rabbit out of his hat. He had produced a fleet of wired cars to monitor the Family's walk-talks along Mulberry Street. Deep Street's operational potential would not be tested, Mouw assumed, until the spring when the wiseguys returned to the streets. In the midst of an icy New York winter, it would most likely remain an unused contingency. Still, Mouw was not a gambler; a "belt-and-suspenders man," Frankie Spero had been known to call him. In a world full of imponderables, Mouw believed that every fallback plan was money in the operational bank. He would gladly hoard all he could get.

So as Gotti went to ground, C-16 remained poised for any contingency, no matter how remote. The agents were at battle stations, but they did not expect to see any action. In the navy, the commanders of nuclear submarines referred to this level of constant preparedness as a state of "violent peace." Mouw, the boomer veteran, would later say it was an accurate description of the state of his team activities as their target went off to trial. Some of the agents who worked with him would point out that it also came close to describing their supervisor's unhappy and ambivalent state. The fact was, Mouw just didn't expect anything much to happen until the trial was over.

But Mouw had not anticipated the gangland intrigues that Elizabeth Holtzman's antagonism toward her successor would set in motion.

On the evening of January 17, as John Gotti's trial moved into its second week and Mouw found himself settling into a period of limbo, he was pulled from this lull by, first, a call from the Observation Post: A walk-talk was in progress. In the freezing cold.

Heading down Mulberry Street, he was informed, were Sammy Bull Gravano and Joe Butch Corrao. And tagging right along, his hands stuck so deep into the pockets of his satin varsity jacket that he appeared to be nearly bent in half, was the lumbering figure of George Helbig. They were heading straight toward the mikes of Deep Street.

Mouw was certain Helbig, the legman, was delivering the latest report from the mole.

He also knew his certitude was not proof. He needed to hear them say it. He needed to learn the traitor's name. *Come out of the shadows,* his mind desperately begged. But Deep Street, for that night at least, was a failure. The microphones could not pick up a word. The mole had escaped.

Just when Mouw had given up all hope, a call came later that night from the plant. Gotti, still free on bail, and his Administration had met in apartment 10. And they had company—Joe Butch Corrao and George Helbig.

The tape that Mouw played the next morning for his inner circle left no doubts. Helbig, "the Grim Reaper" as Gotti bitterly called him, had taken a seat in the living room of apartment 10 and then in a whispery voice that only served to draw more attention to his words, he made his report: Sammy Bull's construction office and club were bugged. The Brooklyn D.A. had put the mikes in last year, but as of January 1, the State Organized Crime Task Force was running the show.

Gotti sighed like a wounded animal. He had spent a long day in court. He knew that both the state and the Feds were trying to indict him for the Castellano murder. And now the Grim Reaper was telling him that his underboss was a target too. For once the pressures of all the forces lining up against him seemed to overwhelm the Don. "This I can't believe. The state? Jesus motherfucking Christ!"

And for once, as Mouw had anticipated all along, Gotti's immense need to have an edge, to manipulate events, betrayed him. The Don, besieged, nearly in a panic, parted the final curtain. He ordered Helbig to get more intelligence from the mole.

"Tell him, Georgie, you could do me a favor . . . Tell him give me some—a little specifics . . . Even if he gotta get a few dollars, we give him a few . . . He could tell you the hour that, if he's that much in the investigation. He could tell you the hour, Georgie."

Gotti, so often abrupt and dismissive, was careful to be polite to Helbig. He was a man outnumbered and fighting for his life. He would do whatever was required to get back his advantage. "I'm just telling you," he said, "it's important to us right now, you know what I mean? Fuckin', this is our life! . . . Believe me, nobody's being a wiseguy. Nobody's feeling sorry for themselves. But right now we're in a hard time. So we will appreciate it."

And in case Helbig missed the point, Gotti went on, "No, what I'm saying is, as far as payments, *minchia!* . . . He broke the lottery."

"I send a message tonight," Helbig said, before leaving the apartment.

The next morning after Mouw played the entire tape—the conversation in apartment 10 went on for another twenty minutes after Helbig had gone off on his mission—an uncomfortable silence seemed to immobilize the men in Mouw's office. They were not merely stunned; they were daunted by their enemy's secret resources. A traitor was in their midst. How much of their work, their very lives for so many years, had been betrayed, blown and squandered, by one of their own?

Then Mouw spoke. His words were an order, and a challenge: "We're going to find that traitor. And once we do, we're going to nail both him *and* Gotti to the wall. *For good.*"

# 39

THERE WERE TWO CHECKS. ONE WAS FROM THE INSURANCE COMPANY of the driver of the van that had smashed into him that rainy afternoon on the Manhattan Bridge. It was for $145,000. The other was from the City of New York and its insurance company, Aetna Casualty & Surety Company. It was for $1,600,000.

William Peist received the checks in February 1990. It had been more than five years since the accident that left him, after three separate operations, with his left leg amputated up to his thigh. He had had to sue the driver for recklessness and the city for negligence, but in the end he had prevailed. After he paid his two lawyers their contingency fees, he had $1,345,000. He put $845,000 in the bank. The remainder was invested in an annuity.

It was, he would tell friends, hardly compensation enough for the pain he still suffered each day. For the leg he had lost. But it was more than the Police Department had done for him. The department had turned on him. The pension board had rejected his claim for a tax-free line-of-duty pension. He had been off-duty that day, taking his wife and mother-in-law to church, they ruled.

As soon as he was able to walk with a prosthesis, the department, however, allowed him to return. He was a gold-shield detective assigned to the Intelligence Unit. His expertise was in organized crime, and he was, as they say in intelligence circles, "cleared for the world." He was aware of nearly all of law enforcement's ongoing operations against the Mob. He worked with prosecutors, the State Task Force, and the FBI.

The week he received the two checks that made him a millionaire, he was working special duty. He was assigned to a wood-paneled courtroom in lower Manhattan. The Manhattan D.A. was trying a case involving an assault against a union official. Detective Peist's job was to protect the jurors from the associates of the man standing trial. The defendant was John Gotti.

# IV

## Nailing Them
## to the Wall

# 40

ALONG MULBERRY STREET THEY WERE CROWDING THE SIDEWALK and clinging to lampposts. There were fathers who stood in doorways holding small children on their shoulders, and old women who stuck their heads out of tenement windows and waved American flags. When the black Cadillac with Gotti in the backseat finally made its way up the block, the noise rose up in a sustained cheer. Some applauded. Others called out, "Way to go, John." Or, "You showed them." Or just a defiant, "All *riiight!*"

The big car stopped in front of the Ravenite and the Don got out. He was smiling broadly, beaming, and he gave a wide careless wave. It lasted only an instant, like someone taking a swipe at the blackboard with an eraser, and then with his cool, slouching jog he hurried into the club.

The cheering crowd, though, was reluctant to leave. John Gotti had done the impossible. The District Attorney had called Gotti a "bully." He had said the Don "could not let an affront to his authority go unpunished." He had argued that Gotti had hired "a bunch of brutal, vicious killers from

321

Hell's Kitchen to shoot" a union official. And he had played a tape in the Manhattan courtroom of the angry Don himself ordering his men, "Bust him up! Put a rocket in his pocket!"

But Gotti had thrown it right back in the government's face. For the third time straight! His third courtroom victory in a row! That afternoon when the jury foreman, after three days of deliberation, had read the not guilty verdict, he might as well have been announcing that the Teflon Don was beyond the law. No one could touch him. Gotti was having the last laugh, and now the crowd wanted to share it.

By nightfall on February 9, 1990, the crowd had dispersed but the victory party inside the Ravenite had picked up momentum. The Family had come to celebrate, and it was a fun-loving group. When Gotti was told that there were reporters outside, he said to bring them in.

"Congratulations, Mr. Gotti," one reporter enthusiastically greeted the Don.

"You showed them," a man from a television station added.

"Why do you think the government is out to get you?" asked the woman from Channel 7. "Is it a vendetta?"

"Hey," the Boss of Bosses told them, "you all were great during the trial. Without your helping, setting the record straight and all, who knows what they would've done to me."

Which was precisely what the C-16 squad was thinking. The mike in the heating duct was up throughout the party, and they heard every word. When the call had come from the Observation Post saying there were all these people on the street cheering the Don, everyone carrying on as if Gotti had hit a game seven grand slam to win the Series, it was very dispiriting. Matty Tricorico, who prided himself on being an agent out of the old J. Edgar Hoover crewcut, tie, and jacket school, told the guys it was just like during the Vietnam War: us on one side and them on the other. But if any of the agents were still reluctant to see things that harshly, they were brought around after listening to the secretly recorded tapes of Gotti's exchange with the press. "You heard them sucking up to this murderer," Andy Kurins said, "and you had to figure there was a goddamn fifth column on his side."

As well as a traitor.

It was this discovery even more than Gotti's latest acquittal that was now dominating the squad's sense of things. After the Grim Reaper tape, they had begun to understand how completely their final charge on Gotti would have to be a solitary attack. They had no allies—only potential enemies. There was no one they could trust. Goaded on by this knowledge, as well as by Mouw's single-mindedness, the team cut itself off completely from any lingering alliances. Decisions were made by Mouw, and supported by his superiors, that tacitly dissolved every one of the team's fraternal allegiances.

So, the Bureau kept the existence of a high-level traitor a secret from all other law enforcement agencies.

The Bureau also refused to pass on even a hint to the Organized Crime Task Force that its audio surveillance of Sammy Bull had been blown. The hours that would be wasted recording and transcribing tapes, the taxpayers' monies that would be squandered on a doomed operation amounted, it was decided with rigid detachment, to a small price.

And the Bureau, despite the assurances to Manhattan District Attorney Robert Morgenthau that it would alert his office to any evidence of possible jury tampering during the Gotti trial, had decided this commitment too was no longer binding. C-16 had the proof the D.A. wanted but they had refused to share it. On the January 17 apartment tape, the same tape that confirmed Mouw's suspicions about the mole, there was another revelation. Gotti was heard saying, "We got one guy who's on [the jury], his name's Hoyle or something. Irish, I guess. Boyle or something. He's a lineman. He lives here in Gramercy. Works, like, the lower West Side . . . Maybe we can reach him . . ." If Gotti had won this case by bribing a juror just as he had done in his federal case, if the state trial, too, had been played out as an elaborate predetermined farce, an extravagant waste of the prosecutors' energies and the public's funds, that was also of little consequence. This secret would be kept as tightly as the team had protected its knowledge of the bribe to the jury foreman three years earlier.

For the only logic that mattered, the only call to duty or even honor that had to be obeyed was the hunt for the mole. From the moment the C-16 team heard the Grim Reaper whisper his secrets, all other considerations had been peremptorily swept away. Nothing else was of operational importance. They were at long last entering the end-game in their grudge match against John Gotti. But until they could strip the Don of his tremendous advantage, they knew a final victory would be impossible. Gotti would always be beyond the law.

The cheering crowds and the fawning press that celebrated Gotti's courtroom victory served to reinforce—and sustain—the stern tactical decisions that had already been made. In fact, these events pushed the team toward an even more complete isolation. They grew to feel betrayed both in the field *and* on the home front. It was now the final stage of the final battle; and it was, as Tricorico had suggested, us versus them.

Jules Bonavolonta on the day of Gotti's acquittal would publicly disavow all previous support the Bureau had given to other law enforcement agencies and to other prosecutors. Instead he promised, "*We* have not yet brought a case against John Gotti. When *we* do, he can take all the bets he wants, but he's going to prison."

As for Bruce Mouw, it was as if the confirmation of his long-held suspicion was a liberating discovery. He would have no regrets, no squeamish misgivings over what had to be done. He was now prepared to be as ruthless as his enemy.

The week after his trial, Gotti, accompanied by Jack D'Amico, Jack Giordano, and Joe Watts, drove down to

Miami. They sat in the sun, played some cards, went fishing for marlin. After what he had been through, Gotti needed a rest. Still, he was feeling pretty upbeat about how it had all worked out. He told one of his lawyers before he left, "Fifty times we can beat them. And you know, like, let's call it the way it is. If I'm sitting there, we, we get the big edge."

# 41

As the group of sullen agents had filed out of his office after hearing the January 17 tape for the first time, Mouw motioned for Andy Kurins to stay. "You got the ticket," he said. There were no further instructions because none were necessary. Both men knew what was at stake.

"I'll find the bastard," Kurins pledged.

Kurins spent the next four days in the squad's audio room trying to put together a coherent transcript from the forty-eight-minute tape. There had been five voices talking in the living room of apartment 10 that night. They spoke, both deliberately and out of unconscious habit, in whispers and oblique, unfinished sentences; in the life, you learned to keeps things obscure. It was demanding, focused work for Kurins, and yet he found himself addicted to it.

One night sometime after midnight, headphones on, he shut his eyes as if that would help him to clear his way through a web of ums and ahs and half-phrases, and suddenly he fell asleep. The tape was still running, but in his dream he was in a basement. It was, he realized even while he was caught up in the dream, very familiar. Then he knew:

It was the mobster's basement where so many years ago they had found the handwritten draft of the warrant authorizing the Ruggiero bug. He had been there, part of the backup team, while the case agent had dismantled the asbestos-covered heating duct and reached inside. Only in his dream, he was the agent who was carefully unwrapping the yards of tape that held the duct together.

Mouw was also there now, in a crisp navy officer's uniform, smoking a pipe, and studiously observing his every move. And so was Sharon, his wife. She was wearing an apron, and she looked beautiful. When he returned to unwinding the tape, the Twins, Frankie Spero and Matty Tricorico, had come to help him. The three of them worked together to unwrap the tape, but it was Kurins who reached inside the duct. Slowly, very slowly, he began to extract something. He kept on pulling until he saw a shoe, and then one leg, and then a whole body was coming out of the heating duct. It was John Gotti. He was dressed entirely in black. And he was wearing handcuffs.

Kurins awoke with a start. He took off his headphones and poured another cup of black coffee. In those quiet, late night moments, he played with the dream, thinking it through. He realized as if for the first time how his entire life—his family, his work, his friendships—had been subtly betrayed by the mole's manipulations. And how everyone whose love and respect he valued was counting on him to put an end to the years of intrigue and deceit.

Yet he was still impossibly weary; he decided he had better call it a night. But the next morning he was in at seven and returned to the task with renewed vigor and concentration. When he finally finished, he had compiled a 114-page transcript. And for the next few days, he attacked these pages. He read, and then reread, and reread again. At last, he took a fresh copy of the transcript and using a red pen and ruler underlined the few telltale times when the men in the apartment let slip, however indirectly, a clue to the traitor's identity. There were no identifiable names: only at best, and a vague best at that, hints. He knew he might have it entirely wrong. But it was all he had.

He shared his findings with Mouw. There were four clues, and he ticked them off on the fingers of his right hand. "Golfer, lawyer, cop, and cousin," he said. He gave his words the cadence of a children's rhyme, but he was also quite deliberately casting his challenge as a Le Carré puzzle.

"Not even a handful," Mouw joked, trying to make light of what lay ahead.

But they both knew how tentative, almost arbitrary, was their evidence. And that they might very well have to sort through not 4, but 40 or even 400 names of living, breathing, scheming suspects before they were done. Until they eliminated all but one name.

*"It'll help to buy a set of golf clubs, or something."*

That night in apartment 10, Gotti had urged Helbig to reach out to the traitor "right away." "You won't sleep on it," he insisted. In return, the Don would be generous. With a confiding, conspiratorial rumble to his words, Gotti said, ". . . You tell him . . . be here. It'll help to buy a set of golf clubs, or something."

". . . He'll thank you," Helbig agreed.

From the moment Kurins pointed out this brief exchange, Mouw became convinced it held the key. His initial reaction was instinctive, and that spurred his mind to work deductively. He quickly found the evidence in his files to reinforce, if not completely affirm, his thesis. In rapid succession, he triumphantly put into place the two incriminating pieces that he believed completed the picture he already saw so clearly.

First: There was a stack of surveillance reports documenting Gotti's trips to suburban Westchester County. For a few years now, Gotti's black Mercedes had been occasionally tailed as it headed out of the city and up the Saw Mill River Parkway to the shaved lawns of Westchester. Time after time, Gotti's drivers had managed to lose the tail, and that only added to the mystery. Once, however, the watchers stuck with him and saw him enter Maxime's, a French restaurant in Granite Springs, New York. Later they went back and interviewed the waiter. It had been a party of six, three men and three women, and Mr. Gotti, a true gentleman, had paid in cash and left a $150 tip. After that, Mouw had decided the Don's trips to the countryside were romantic. Perhaps Gotti had a squeeze who liked to play when her husband was away. But now Mouw realized he had dangerously underestimated his enemy. Gotti's trips to Westchester were to visit a golf-playing suburbanite—the mole.

And second: A few months back, a Bureau accountant assigned to burrow through the tax returns of Gravano's network of companies had sent Mouw an exhaustively detailed 302. Mouw had read it dutifully, and not a numbers man, had stuck it just as dutifully in the file. But now he recalled something and hurried back to find it. And there it was: Sammy Bull's construction company had done the $2.7 million renovation of a country club in Westchester.

Mouw immediately assigned an agent to go up to Westchester and get a copy of the club's membership list. There was a small scene when the agent, caught up in the importance of his mission, theatrically presented his badge and demanded the list; and the stuffy club manager looked down his nose and told him to get a subpoena. After a number of heated threats on both sides, the incident was finally resolved when the club's lawyer was called at his office in Manhattan and summoned from a meeting. To his credit, he barked at the manager that, damn it, the membership roll was not an atomic secret. Besides, he added with deliberate cruelty as the agent listened in embarrassment, there was a pile of lists in the lobby just for the taking.

After all that, it was particularly disappointing when no familiar name leaped out from the pages. But Mouw remained certain the mole was a member. Or he played golf on the club's course with a member. Or, a long shot but still possible, he tagged along as a friend of a member's friend.

That was it, Mouw said obstinately. It was their most promising clue.

Kurins, however, wasn't so sure.

*"He's a legitimate lawyer."*
The Don, as the conversation in apartment 10 that night

took another turn, was suddenly flat out begging, "If he's that much in the investigation, he could tell you the hour, Georgie." Helbig's cryptic answer seemed to divert Gotti. He followed a meandering thought. Then Gotti said, "Every cop he knows there. But that's good. You know why? He's a legitimate lawyer . . . So it's beautiful."

That, Kurins decided, could mean Gotti had a prosecutor on his payroll. He was also ready to concede the passage was open to many other interpretations. But considering the nature of the leaks, the existence of a corrupt prosecutor was a logical thesis. Even Mouw had to agree it was worth pursuing. Gotti might very well have someone in the Brooklyn D.A.'s office. It would explain how the mole had learned about the transfer of the Gravano bugs to the state. Or Gotti could just as well have his hooks into a federal prosecutor, someone close to the Castellano murder case. That might be the reason he kept pressing for information about when an indictment in that investigation was scheduled.

However, the more they mulled it over, the more both Kurins and Mouw grew convinced the mole wasn't based in the Brooklyn D.A.'s office. If he were, the mikes would have been blown long ago. A corrupt federal prosecutor, someone who was involved in a variety of cases against the Gambino Family, seemed more likely.

And once they started thinking seriously about that possibility, they both independently came up with a name. The same name.

It was the name of an Eastern District federal prosecutor, and it was scattered throughout the apartment tapes. Gotti mentioned him. Shargel mentioned him. So did Sammy Bull. When the squad had first reviewed the transcripts, they found nothing particularly unsettling in this; after the years of running battles, both sides had become acquainted, even familiar, with their adversaries. But now these seemingly offhand references took on a more provocative significance.

Kurins, with Mouw's knowledge and consent, began an in-depth background investigation of the prosecutor. He hinted broadly to those he interviewed that the attorney was a candidate for a major government job. Everyone was glad to cooperate and readily agreed to keep the agent's inquiry a secret; they did not want to do anything to jeopardize a well-deserved promotion. When he was done, Kurins had uncovered nothing out of the ordinary. Except for one thing, perhaps. The prosecutor had worked his way through law school as a bartender at Studio 54. The club, which had been on Fifty-fourth Street until it closed just a few years back, had been a Gambino Family hangout. Jackie Nose D'Amico, Handsome Jack Giordano, Joe Butch Corrao—a lot of the guys were always stopping in.

Kurins, with not the least bit of supporting evidence, puffed those tantalizing facts into an elaborate theory. He imagined it might have happened like this: The prosecutor had been recruited while he was still in law school. He was a working-class kid with a big tuition bill and every night he was surrounded by guys flashing wads of cash. So he asked one of them for a loan; or they made the offer. Either way, a deal was done. Maybe they continued to help him out after he finished school. Maybe they even suggested he could get very rich working for the government. It would have been a shrewd investment for the Family. They would have their own man in the U.S. Attorney's office. Possibly he would even run for office someday.

It was a scenario, both Mouw and Kurins felt, that could not be flatly dismissed.

*"They all got a motherfuckin' cop that's a first cousin, or an uncle, or a fuckin' nephew."*

The Don was in a foul temper after Helbig and Joe Butch had left the apartment that night. He started complaining to Frankie Loc and Sammy Bull about both the Grim Reaper and the capo. He didn't like them, and he didn't like their friends, or even their relatives. "You know the fuckin' amazing thing about it," Gotti nearly whined in exasperation as he continued his tirade, "they all got a motherfuckin' cop that's a first cousin, or an uncle, or a fuckin' nephew."

Was Gotti referring to the mole? Kurins wondered. It made sense. It could be a cop. Still, not many city cops had access to such high-level organized crime intelligence as the mole seemed to possess. Unless, he suddenly realized, in Gotti's shorthand a "cop" was anyone who carried a badge.

Now that he was looking at the problem from a wider angle, two possibilities came quickly into focus. The first was a highly decorated police detective who had worked OC until putting in his papers not too long ago. He had retired to become an investigator for the State Organized Crime Task Force. When Kurins checked, he learned the ex-cop had started working for the Task Force only a week before the Gravano bugs were transferred to the state. And he had been assigned to the monitoring detail. These were just the sort of coincidences that kept Kurins up at night. There was also something else; it was what had brought the former detective originally to mind. His name, too, had come up in the apartment conversations. Both Gotti and Sammy Bull seemed to have a lot of animosity toward the detective. For all Kurins knew, it could be genuine. Or it could be a cover.

Now he had to consider both his and Mouw's greatest fear—they were looking for an FBI agent. It was impossible, and yet he also knew it wasn't. Kurins' mind jumped between those alternatives, depending upon his mood and his desperation. When his search seemed particularly futile, he found himself returning to a report on a conversation that had occurred less than a month before the Grim Reaper tape.

*Ravenite Social Club*
*December 22, 1989*

*Time*             *Participants*
7:02     JOHN GOTTI, BRUCE CUTLER, (Attorney)

. . . CUTLER then reports to GOTTI about a meeting with ex-FBI agent RICHARD TAUS. (TAUS was fired by the FBI when it became known, through a complaint and subsequent investigation, that TAUS had molested several young boys. TAUS is currently under indictment for these charges. Prior to this, TAUS had been used as a monitoring agent during court-authorized electronic surveillance of GAMBINO soldier ANGELO RUGGIERO.)

It was a report full of just the sort of coincidences that fueled Kurins' imagination. And his suspicions.

*"That's his first cousin."*

As soon as Helbig and Joe Butch left the apartment that night, Sammy Bull had told his boss, "See, I know this guy you're talking about. Pete."

"Yeah?" asked Gotti. "That's his first cousin."

This exchange confused Kurins no matter how many times he replayed it. Was Gotti saying the mole was the first cousin? And if so, whose?

Was he Helbig's cousin?

Or perhaps Pete's?

But then, who was Pete?

All Kurins knew for sure was that before George Helbig left apartment 10 on January 17, he had promised his boss, "I'll send a message." Kurins decided he might as well start finding out all he could about Big George. Who knew where that would lead? He could only hope it would bring him closer to learning who had received Big George's "message."

Golfer. Lawyer. Cop. Or cousin.

# 42

KURINS CAME UP WITH HIS PLAN AFTER READING THE BUREAU'S file on George Helbig. What struck him was how busy the Grim Reaper was. The man had his hooks in all over the place. Helbig had a German father so he wasn't made and never would be, yet he certainly got around.

He had money out on the street, part of Joe Butch's loan-sharking operation. At the same time he was also tied into a handful of businesses, some legitimate and some that might come out a bit impugned after the Bureau accountants went through their books. There was a disco in New Jersey, Cloud Nine, that had already attracted the IRS's attention. Another club out on Long Island, Plaza Disco. Something called J & G Realty. As well as Tri-State Petroleum, a Brooklyn fuel company that was a genuine money-maker and legit to boot. And Helbig also controlled several food concessions near the boardwalk in Coney Island.

Nevertheless, despite the demands of his varied businesses, all Joe Butch Corrao had to do was send word and Helbig would come running. If the Gambino capo needed to

be driven somewhere, Big George would be at the wheel.
Which meant he was a truly devoted friend. Or, the busi-
nesses were actually Joe Butch's—and the Family's—and
Helbig was the front man. Either way, the whole setup was,
Kurins told Mouw, "about as kosher as a ham sandwich."

Kurins decided to put the string of companies under close
scrutiny. There was always the chance the mole worked with
Helbig, or was a silent partner. Besides, since both Helbig
and the mole would immediately run for deep cover if they
knew why the FBI was showing so much interest, the
corporate attack was the perfect smoke screen. The feds on
the trail of funny money in gangland was, for both sides,
simply business as usual. And this battle plan had an
additional advantage: Kurins wouldn't have to get too close
to Helbig. By all accounts the Grim Reaper, a lumbering,
slow-talking colossus, had the social graces of a caged
animal. "Definitely not the sort of guy you want to screw
around with." And that was what his lawyer had to say
about him.

Kurins' first step was to apply pressure to Helbig's business partners. He would, as he told Mouw, "fugazy them to
death"—it was more Bureau-speak: a genteel euphemism
for mindfucking—with questions about money laundering
and unreported income. He would subpoena them to come
into federal court and give handwriting exemplars. He
would knock on their front doors, and with their neighbors
and wives watching, flash his badge and talk tough. He
would pull the records of their toll calls for the last six
months. And perhaps in their panic, or carelessness, or
ignorance they would reveal a name.

Golfer. Lawyer. Cop. Or cousin.

As he was driving along Shore Parkway in the early
morning, Kurins' small Chevy was rocked by the heavy
March winds coming off the Atlantic. He had to concentrate
to keep the car in its lane. Still, he could not help but notice
the day's strong first light shining on the white-chopped
water and illuminating the graceful curving lines of the

Verrazano Bridge in the distance. On his right, and already partially shaded by a rapidly moving cloud, was the Statue of Liberty. He was on his way to Brooklyn to serve a subpoena to a former cop.

The house was in Bay Ridge, a rather modest red brick building, and protected by a knee-high wrought-iron fence. A couple of cement steps led to the front door and Kurins had his badge out before he knocked. He also made sure his coat was unbuttoned and his revolver was within reach. He planned to keep the whole encounter very low-key, but he really didn't know what to expect.

Steve Iken answered the door himself, and as soon as he saw the badge and heard the word "subpoena," he seemed to Kurins' eyes to go pale. "Mind if we talk outside?" he asked. "No point getting my wife upset."

"No problem," Kurins agreed.

Iken immediately closed the door and began to lead Kurins down the steps and away from the house. Kurins watched him carefully, trying to determine what was going through Iken's mind. He was clearly anxious, that much was certain.

And why shouldn't he be? Kurins thought. He knew that Iken had been a cop for four years, working undercover narcotics, but had decided to resign. Now he was working as a private investigator, mostly digging up dirt for Mob lawyers. He also was a friend of Joe Butch Corrao. It was the capo who had allegedly brought him along to play poker with John Gotti; on the apartment tapes the Don had complained that Joe Butch should have told him that Iken, "that fuckin' bum jerk," was an ex-cop. No doubt, Kurins imagined, Iken was trying to guess what kind of trouble he was in now. For his part, Kurins was eager to let the tension build.

"I hear you're a friend of John Gotti," he began, deliberately oblique.

"No . . . not really."

"No?"

"I never met him. Not in this life or in any other," he said adamantly. "I'm doing some stuff for one of his lawyers. For Barry Slotnick. P.I. work. It's no big deal. I'm just trying to make a living."

"I see," said Kurins. The truth was, he didn't see a damn thing. Or have any idea how much longer he could string this out.

"Look, I want to cooperate."

"Good," Kurins said flatly. And he waited. He was in no rush.

"So tell me how I can help. I mean, what's this all about?"

Kurins tried to look very grim. "It's about Cloud Nine," he said at last.

"Hey," Iken said somewhat indignantly, "I lost money in that. It was a business deal. Nothing wrong with that. Right?" As he spoke, he seemed to be regaining some confidence. Iken was a short, compact man, and now that he was more at ease, he displayed an eager smile.

So Kurins, having quickly run out of maneuvers, played his second—and final—card. He said that his interest was actually not so much in the discotheque, but in money that apparently had been funneled from Cloud Nine into J & G Realty. The purpose of the subpoena was to get a sample of Iken's handwriting. The Bureau wanted to compare it to the handwriting on checks issued or endorsed by the real estate concern.

Iken was incredulous. "You're jamming me up over J & G?"

"Look," Kurins said, nearly apologizing as he handed Iken the subpoena, "it's no big deal. No one's saying you did anything illegal."

"Good. 'Cause I didn't."

"But you want to help, right?"

"Sure, but I'm telling you I know squat about J & G."

"You're certain?" Kurins said, hoping he didn't sound too desperate.

"Look," Iken said after some thought, "I got nothing to do with J & G. I got involved in Cloud Nine because of Georgie and Pete."

Kurins kept silent. And prayed Iken would continue.

In a moment he did. "They're friends from the old neighborhood. We grew up together. I've known George Helbig and Pete Mavis since we was kids."

"Like I said, it's no big deal," Kurins reassured Iken. He was suddenly in a hurry to leave.

As soon as he was in his car, Kurins turned to a new page in his notebook and wrote in big block letters at the top: "PETE MAVIS." Below that he wrote: "Pete???" He paused for a moment, and then on a third line he wrote: "Pete's cousin???"

Kurins looked across the street, once more compared the street sign to the address he had written down, and tried to rein in his anger. One of the records clerks at 26 Federal Plaza, he decided, had made an annoying mistake. After his interview with Iken, he had called headquarters and asked them to check through the state incorporation files for the location of J & G Realty. A day passed before someone got back to him with the address: 20 East Brandis Avenue, on Staten Island. Except now that he was parked in front of the building, he was certain someone had screwed up. This was a residential neighborhood. Number 20 was a brick two-family walk-up, one in a long row of similar houses. But, he told himself, as long as he had driven all the way out to Staten Island he might as well ring the bell.

There was no name on the door, and it took a moment before a woman answered. She had dark hair piled high on her head and she was wearing a bathrobe.

Kurins showed his badge and explained that he was investigating J & G Realty.

"Oh," the woman replied breezily, "we just get their mail. We're doing somebody a favor."

Kurins, very politely, trying to be offhanded, asked if she would mind telling him who the somebody was.

She weighed that for a moment. She offered a consoling smile, but she said firmly, "You'd better talk to my husband Pete about that."

"Fine." And doing his best to hold on to his easy, steady tone, Kurins tried, "So you're Mrs. Mavis?"

"Ann Mavis," she said with another smile.

"Well," Kurins said as he handed her his card, "if you could have Mr. Mavis give me a call, I'd appreciate that."

Pete Mavis never telephoned. But now that Kurins had an address to go with the name, he subpoenaed the phone company's records for the last six months so he could learn whom Pete called.

The toll records from the phone at 20 Brandis Avenue were added to a tall pile. Kurins had already obtained the lists of calls that had been made from Helbig's home in New Jersey, and from Tri-State Petroleum. He was hoping that if he discovered a series of common telephone numbers lurking in the long columns printed in a painfully tiny agate type, he would be able to trace one of them to a familiar name. Then, in a triumphant flash of recognition, he would be able to identify: Golfer. Lawyer. Cop. Or cousin.

There were nearly two hundred pages of phone numbers to sort through; perhaps five thousand different calls had been made. It took weeks. And it got Kurins nowhere. The mole's telephone number might very well be somewhere in these records. Or it might not. Kurins was stymied. He had whittled down the list to about two dozen possible names and numbers and, at first glance, none of them seemed even vaguely promising. Still, each was a lead that he would have to pursue.

But even more frustrating was the problem of beeper traffic. There were ten separate beepers leased by Tri-State Petroleum, and collectively those beepers had received thousands of calls each month. Kurins had spent enough time around wiseguys to know their fondness for beepers. He could imagine the mole beeping Helbig whenever he wanted him to get in touch. Another possibility—and one Kurins latched onto as fiercely as Mouw had to his golfer— was that the traitor used a beeper that Helbig had provided, a device leased and paid for by Tri-State. Yet, all his theories

and speculation about beeper traffic amounted only to an
agonizing riddle: He had no way of knowing who used a
specific beeper. The toll records provided numbers, not
names. Helbig's personal beeper could be any one of the ten.
Perhaps Mavis had a beeper too. And Iken. And the mole.
The secret was locked away in the office records of Tri-State
Petroleum.

# 43

"I CLOCKED FOUR LINCOLN CONNIES AND THREE BIG CADS," THE agent told Kurins. "Same as yesterday. Fancy cars coming and going all day." For the past four days, he had been recording the license plate numbers of the cars that pulled into Tri-State Petroleum's garage.

"You know the drill," Kurins said to the agent. "Run it through DMV and see what we got."

The fuel company's office, a long, low warehouse, was in Red Hook, a rundown corner of Brooklyn. There were metal grates on the windows and nearby was an elevated stretch of noisy highway. The littered street beneath the highway was obscured by thick, dark shadows, and it was there, adjacent to a pillar covered in graffiti, that the agent had parked. His name was John Meadows. A month earlier he had been a Bureau accountant assigned to 26 Federal Plaza. Then Kurins had drafted him to help give his corporate fugazying some bite. This was his first OC case, and his first surveillance assignment.

Meadows, a genial man with a down-home Southern way

about him, threw himself into the challenge. After all the years stuck behind a desk in headquarters looking for clues with a calculator, he was feeling positively rejuvenated. "I'm telling you, Andy, this is really something," he said enthusiastically. "We got the wiseguys worrying about one thing, and we're out attacking from a different angle altogether. I love it." It did not take an amused Kurins long before he started calling his earnest new partner "John Boy." Yet it was John Boy the accountant who stumbled onto "the angry divorcee."

He made his discovery later that afternoon. He was punching the names the Department of Motor Vehicles had come up with into the Bureau's computer. For a fuel company, Tri-State seemed to attract a lot of "Known Gamblers"; two of the shiny Lincolns belonged to men with records as KGs. But it was the name of the owner of a battered Dodge he had seen earlier in the day pulling into Tri-State's garage that kept running through Meadows' mind. As soon as DMV had turned up the information—a woman's name and a Queens address—it struck him as familiar. According to the Bureau computer, she was clean: no convictions, no arrests, not even a speeding ticket. Still, there was something about her name. He tried it on Kurins. Hurrying from the office on some mysterious mission, Kurins shrugged. "Never heard of her, John Boy."

But Meadows was sure he had. Or at least pretty sure.

He was in his car on the way home when it came to him: The J & G Realty file. At the next exit, he got off the highway. It was rush hour, and it took him almost a half hour to make his way back to the squad room. But when he searched the file, there it was. Nearly a dozen J & G checks, for about five hundred dollars each, had been made out to her name and then mailed to her address in Queens. Where does this fit in? he wondered. He called Kurins at home, but his wife said he was out and not expected for hours. "You know Andris," she told him with a small sigh. Meadows knew him well enough to realize Kurins would be furious if he did anything on his own. And with reason; Meadows was an accountant, not a fieldman. It made operational sense to wait until the morning when he could work out a plan with Kurins.

But it also was a tantalizing lead. Meadows drove out to her home in Queens that same night. She was a heavy woman, almost as wide as the doorway, and as soon as she saw his badge she asked him in. They sat in the living room for nearly two hours and the woman did most of the talking. She was full of anger. Meadows, out of politeness more than any strategic instinct, let her have her say. All the time she was railing on, her seven-year-old daughter lay on the floor across the room directly in front of the TV. The child, Meadows noticed, didn't look up from the set the entire time he was there.

The woman's rage was directed against her ex-husband. He was the one who had been sending her the $512 J & G checks each month. It was alimony and child support. She insisted she didn't have any idea why the checks were drawn on the real estate company account, although Meadows would not have been surprised if this was just a topic she didn't feel like getting into with an FBI agent. When he asked if her husband worked at J & G, she laughed. "Work? Those guys don't work. They're too busy to work."

The checks, she continued without pausing to take a breath or adjust her booming volume, had come like clockwork until about six months ago. That was when her ex-husband had vanished. "Probably shacked up in Florida with some bimbo," she suggested. And at that moment Meadows was thinking: I don't blame him one bit.

If it weren't for her job answering the phones at Tri-State, she insisted, they would have starved. While once again Meadows enjoyed a private thought: Fat chance.

When Meadows asked her how she had happened to find work at the fuel company, the woman suddenly became distracted. Let me get you some coffee, she suggested, and he realized it might be wiser not to press this question too.

Returning to the living room with the coffee and a box of powdered doughnuts, the woman went on bitterly for at least another half hour. She seemed determined to list every indignity she and her daughter had suffered at the hands of her ex-husband. After each sorrowful revelation, she bellowed, "That rat bastard bum." She said it so often that in his mind Meadows was soon joining in when she came to her refrain, a one-man Greek chorus. But his face showed only concern.

At last, after she'd finished the remaining doughnut in the box, the woman put her coffee cup down and looked straight into Meadows' eyes. "Can you help me?" she asked. "Can the FBI track down my husband? Can you make him pay? He owes us, that rat bastard bum."

Meadows returned her frank look. He tried not to stare at the white-powdered mustache that had formed above her upper lip. He spoke sweetly and with his best smile. "Well, ma'am," he said, "if you're willing to give the Bureau a little help on a small matter, I'm sure we can work something out."

Three days later John Boy handed Kurins a single photocopied sheet of paper. At the top of the page was the Tri-State Petroleum letterhead. Running down the left side of the page in a double-spaced column was a list of ten names. And opposite each name was the telephone number of a beeper.

The phone booth was just off Cropsey Avenue in Brooklyn. A small vacant lot was a few yards away; a car's bucket seat was balanced like a throne on a pile of ripped, gray mattresses in the center of the littered plot. Across the street, down the block toward the highway, was a bodega. In the opposite direction, along Cropsey Avenue, the neighborhood seemed to improve. The street was lined with squat, red brick apartment houses, the sort of buildings with shady, narrow terraces that developers had thrown up all around the city in the early 1960s.

Kurins stood in front of the phone booth and tried to figure out what to do next. According to the toll records, Helbig's personal beeper had been called dozens of times from a number in Brooklyn. When the trace came back indicating that it was a pay phone, Kurins grew excited. In his mind, he imagined the mole reaching out to his legman from work. Or from a bar. Or maybe Mouw was right—a golf club. But not a vacant lot. Only now that he was standing by the booth, that was all that was there. I'm smack in the middle of nowhere, Kurins groaned to himself.

Unless, he started thinking, perhaps whoever was calling Helbig's beeper lived in the neighborhood, parked here, where it was easy to find a space, used the phone, then walked to one of the apartment buildings along Cropsey Avenue. It was worth a try, he decided. He started up the block to the nearest building.

The glass doors in the lobby were locked, but there was an intercom with four rows of names and apartment numbers. Kurins searched the list. It was a long shot; he realized, in fact, he didn't even know what name he was looking for. When he was done, he buzzed the superintendent.

The super was Hispanic, and impressed by Kurins' credentials. "I met cops before, sure. But never an Eff-Bee-Eye agent. You guys are the best, right?"

Kurins nodded.

"Well, Mister Eff-Bee-Eye, how can I help?"

Kurins explained that he was looking for a man, except he didn't know his name. Or for that matter, what he looked like. All at once he was feeling very foolish.

"You're not shitting me?" the super asked, now cautious. "You really from the Eff-Bee-Eye or what?"

So, more to preserve his dignity than anything else, Kurins tried another tack. He showed the super a photograph of George Helbig. "Ever see this man around here?" he asked.

The super studied the photo. "It's a big building, you know," he finally decided.

But he hadn't said no, so Kurins showed him a shot of Peter Mavis. "What about him?"

The super's face lit up. "Five-C. Now I get it—you checking out the parties, right?"

According to the super, nobody really lived in the apartment. It was just a party pad. "You should see the *señoritas* coming in and out of that place," he said. "My wife tells me not to poke my nose where I don't belong, so I don't. But I see things."

When Kurins checked with the rental agents, he was told the apartment was rented by the J & G Realty corporation. They claimed they couldn't recall the name of the individual who had signed the lease, but Kurins didn't believe that. He considered subpoenaing their records, and then decided not to. It might frighten the mole. Meanwhile, he also found out there was a phone in apartment 5C. It was registered to Peter Mavis. He immediately pulled the call records. The most frequently dialed number was registered to George Helbig in New Jersey. But there were also a lot of calls to a number registered to a Constance Peist. The name meant nothing to Kurins. Probably one of the bimbos, he guessed.

Mouw, meanwhile, was losing his patience. His war was being fought on many fronts, his troops spread out across the city. He had agents monitoring the Cirelli apartment, in the Observation Post, questioning informants, and hunting for the mole. He knew that if he was to win, if he was going to bring down the Don, his victory would have to be total. And the strategic cornerstone, the one operation that had to succeed before there would even be the possibility of success on any other front, was to find the mole. "What's taking so long, Andy?" he prodded. He constantly demanded to know how the investigation was going, what Kurins had uncovered. And at the end of each session in his office, he always offered the same bit of advice. "It's the golfer, I'm telling you, Andy," Mouw insisted. "That's the key."

Kurins was not so sure, but he had to admit his response was just as much a hunch as Mouw's. Over the last two months, he had uncovered lots of stray pieces in the puzzle. He just didn't know how they fit together. Or if they did. All he could do, he told both Mouw and himself, was to keep on fugazying around and see what else turned up.

Part of this indirect attack was to keep up the pressure on J & G Realty. "Everywhere we look," he told Meadows,

"J & G seems to pop up. Listen to me, John Boy. This is one clue we play to the end. We follow J & G to wherever it takes us."

On a cold morning at the tail end of winter, it took the two agents to the Staten Island home of Peter Mavis's in-laws. Kurins, pursuing one more long shot, had decided to interview the couple because they held the mortgage on 20 Brandis Place—their daughter and son-in-law's home, and the mailing address of J & G Realty.

It didn't take Kurins long to decide this was another dead end. Why am I bothering these people? he asked himself. He was sitting with Meadows in their living room, drinking their coffee, nibbling on their Danish, and feeling very guilty. They were both retired city employees, living on a pension, and all they had done was to try to make life a little easier for their daughter. He didn't want to intimidate them. They had another daughter, the husband offered, who wanted to be an FBI agent. When Kurins heard that, he felt even worse. These were nice people. I should get out of here, and out of their lives.

"C'mon, John," he told Meadows. "Let's get back to the office." He thanked the people for their time, and before he left, helped the woman bring the coffee cups and the Danish plates into the kitchen. He felt it was the least he could do. He was trading small talk with the woman when something occurred to him. "You wouldn't happen to know a Constance Peist, would you?" he asked.

"Oh, yes," the woman said. "That's Pete's cousin."

Perhaps it was the look Kurins gave her that made her continue: "Maybe you know her husband? Billy."

"Billy Peist? Sounds familiar," Kurins lied.

"I knew you would," she said as she put the dishes in the sink. "He's a detective."

"Right," Kurins said. "Works out here on Staten Island . . ."

"No," she corrected. "I'm talking about the Billy Peist who lost his leg."

"Oh, *that* Billy Peist."

"That's right," she went on helpfully, "the one who works downtown. In Intelligence."

Mouw was sitting at his desk, smoking his pipe and talking on the phone, when Kurins walked in.

"Hang up," Kurins told his boss.

Mouw shot him a killing look, but he said into the phone, "Something just came up. Got to run." He placed the receiver in its cradle.

Kurins handed Mouw a three-by-five index card. As soon as Kurins left the house in Staten Island, he had taken the blank card from his coat pocket and written a name across it—"Det. William Peist." Now he asked Mouw, "You know this guy?"

Mouw studied the card for a moment. "Sure," he said. "He works OC for the Intell squad. Always calling me up. Asking things."

"Well," Kurins said, "I hope you didn't tell him anything . . ."

Mouw looked warily at Kurins. He did not like where this was going at all.

". . . because he's the mole, Bruce. I'm sure of it."

# 44

*PETE'S COUSIN.*

Now that he had a name to go with Gotti's shorthand description, Kurins set out to learn all he could about William Peist. Yet it was, by necessity, a low-key investigation. There was a real danger that as soon as Peist's friends and co-workers were asked even the most casual of questions, it would alert him. Peist was a detective and, if Kurins' deduction was correct, a spy: a man whose training and instincts prepared him to be suspicious. Kurins realized he would have to use the most soft-footed of covers as he went about the city asking about Peist. However, he knew it was a risk he had to take. All his evidence was, at best, circumstantial. He still had to prove Peist was the mole. And there was another factor pushing him along. It was the same reason Mouw monitored Kurins' every move with such interest. They both wanted to understand what made a man betray his sworn allegiances, turn on his friends, and side with the enemy.

* * *

Kurins' first stop was the red brick Police Headquarters tower in lower Manhattan, but as soon as he got a look at Detective Peist's file, he immediately began wondering if he had made a colossal mistake. Peist couldn't be the mole. It wasn't just that he was a one-legged detective. He was also a millionaire. He had collected, the way Kurins figured it, about $1.4 million from the two lawsuits settling his negligence claims for the accident on the bridge that had left him with only a right leg. Why would he need to sell information to Gotti? Was he that greedy?

Maybe he wasn't even Pete Mavis's cousin, Kurins thought. Could he have the wrong man? As those questions and doubts challenged him, he decided he might as well go talk to Steve Arniotes, the lawyer who was listed in the file as having represented Peist in the negligence cases. Maybe he would have some answers. And Kurins quickly worked out another bit of fugazying. He would pitch the lawyer a story about how he was doing a routine background check, standard procedure on all city cops who worked regularly with the FBI. He would soft-pedal all the way and see what happened.

The lawyer's office was on the second floor, above a busy commercial avenue in Bay Ridge, Brooklyn. A narrow, dimly lit flight of stairs led to the door. Kurins was greeted by Arniotes' secretary. Arniotes was in court that afternoon but the secretary, once she saw Kurins' badge and cheerful smile, was eager to help. There was a file, a scrapbook actually, she corrected herself, on Billy Peist. She had helped her boss put it together when it looked as if he might have to try the negligence claim against the city in court. The plan had been to give the jury the opportunity to thumb through a short history of Peist's life, to show them what kind of man he was and what he had overcome. Juries like that sort of thing, she confided. Feel free to take a look if you want, she suggested to Kurins.

Minutes later, Kurins was sitting in a closet-sized room crammed with filing cabinets, turning the pages of the leather-bound scrapbook. The initial entries were straight-forward.

Born and raised in Brooklyn, William Peist had graduated from Food and Maritime High School in 1965 and entered the Waldorf-Astoria's two-year training course for apprentice chefs. "Each year only a few young men can be selected from the many who apply," the hotel's general manager was quoted as saying in a yellowed news article about the program that filled a page in the scrapbook. On the pages that followed were Peist's cooking ribbons: Best Pastry Student, First Prize for a galantine, a blue ribbon for Classical Cooking. The Waldorf offered him a position as a banquet chef after graduation and Peist took it.

Kurins turned more pages, scanning entries that told about Peist's marriage to a Bay Ridge girl in a Greek Orthodox church and the birth of their first son a year later. Then in September 1974, Peist had decided to become a cop. Kurins could only speculate about the reasons. Perhaps it had been a boyhood ambition. Perhaps he had had enough of being a chef. But if he was looking for job security, he had made a mistake. He was laid off nine months later, a victim of a city budget crisis. An article in the scrapbook from the *New York Times,* dated December 26, 1977, revealed that he had found work instead as a chef for the Corrections Department. It reported that a Christmas dinner at Riker's Island for the prisoners and Mayor-elect Ed Koch "was cooked under the supervision of William Peist, a 30-year-old former chef at the Waldorf-Astoria."

But it was a news article on the following page in the scrapbook that convinced Kurins he was, after all, on the right path. It was a story that ran in the Brooklyn edition of the New York *Daily News,* and it was headlined "Laid-Off Cop Helps Nab Arson Suspects." The story reported that a twenty-eight-year-old former policeman and his cousin were leaving a Bay Ridge restaurant at about 3:30 in the morning when they spotted two men torching a mound of garbage piled against the door of an apartment house. The flames were preparing to ignite the building. The two cousins beat out the flames and then, after a brief struggle, subdued the arsonists. "You don't forget six months of training all that quickly," the laid-off cop, William Peist, had bragged to the reporter. His cousin was identified as Peter Mavis.

By 1979, the entries turned upbeat. Peist was rehired by the Police Department. Living in a small two-family house in Bay Ridge, he was now the father of four, a Little League coach, and an Exalted Ruler of the Elks. He continued to work some nights and many weekends at the Waldorf as a banquet chef. By 1983, after two years in the Public Morals Division, he was awarded his detective's shield.

Then abruptly the entries took a tragic turn. News articles about the December 3, 1984, accident on the rain-slicked Manhattan Bridge, the loss of his left leg, and his $75-million-dollar lawsuits against the city filled the pages. Kurins also read that Peist's petition for a tax-free line of duty pension had been denied by the Police Department. The detective had returned to the job, now assigned to the Intelligence Division. Peist's speciality: organized crime.

The final entry in the scrapbook was an article from a local newspaper, the *Brooklyn Spectator,* which reported the $1.4 million settlement that had been awarded to Peist just months ago. It concluded: "Arniotes said the money will enable his client to 'live comfortably despite his injuries.'"

Not if I can help it, Kurins though when he closed the scrapbook. He was once again certain he was chasing the mole.

Over the next few weeks, inventing a new cover story for each new situation he found himself in, Kurins went around trying to learn more about William Peist. A chef at the Waldorf remembered how Peist talked with such enthusiasm about his activities as a detective. "He really made police work seem exciting. He made it seem like he was a really important cop, a supersleuth," the chef said. "He'd always be telling us about the stakeouts."

A retired fellow officer also recalled one of the stakeouts: "It was the worst, the longest night of my life. It wasn't that it was so cold, or so dangerous, or anything like that. Actually, it was pretty routine stuff. We were waiting for a pimp who had threatened one of his girls to show up. But what made the whole night so rough was Billy Peist talking nonstop about his cakes. I mean, he started describing this chocolate layer cake extravaganza he had baked up over the weekend and my mouth started watering. Suddenly I was starving. I was stuck in that car for the whole night and all the time I was tasting his chocolate cake in my mind. It was torture."

The officers working with Peist, Kurins learned, called him "the Baker." One of them, a blunt, whippet-thin, sallow-faced tough guy, became nearly rapturous when he described the creations Peist had brought into the squad room. "Whenever a guy won his gold shield," the detective said, "Billy Peist would whip up a cake shaped like a badge and covered in yellow icing. It was pretty bush stuff, but, hell, they were the best cakes I ever had. You know, somehow he got it so the cake was really fluffy and the icing was creamy like melted butter."

But Kurins dug deeper. After a few beers with some of Peist's buddies and a look through confidential department files, he discovered that while Peist enjoyed parading the incongruous aspects of his life before his different audiences, playing "the Baker" to his fellow cops and supersleuth to his fellow chefs, he was secretly playing other roles too.

In violation of Police Department regulations, he had begun to collect guns. According to the eyewitness stories Kurins heard, hidden in Peist's basement were stacks of rifles, revolvers in a variety of sizes and calibers, and a few machine guns.

And he spied on his buddies. Unknown to the members of his squad, Peist was working covertly as one of the department's field associates. He had volunteered to monitor his fellow officers' activities for incidents of corruption. One year, after Peist attended a raucous Christmas party in the back room of a bar near Police Headquarters, a sergeant and his police officer girlfriend, both good friends of Peist, were immediately transferred to different precincts. No explanation was given, but Billy Peist knew.

After the accident on the Manhattan Bridge cost him not

only his leg but also the life he had previously lived, Peist, according to everyone Kurins spoke to, conscientiously tried to make the best of things. By all reports, he put in long hours working for the Intelligence Division. With a stoic resolve that brought nods of admiration from his fellow officers, he managed to limp his way to wiretap plants throughout the city. He was constantly telephoning around, reaching out to detectives, FBI agents, State Task Force investigators, as he tried to keep up with the latest battle plans in the war against the Mafia. He even bought his own airplane ticket and spent his vacation days at a national organized crime law enforcement conference in Las Vegas so he could get to know officials from all over the country. He was, it was agreed by the cops he worked with at the Intelligence squad offices on Hudson Street, very gung ho.

Yet Kurins was not fooled. He had lived enough covers, done so much elaborate fugazying in his time, that he knew the technique exactly. He knew what Peist was up to. And when he uncovered two more pieces of evidence—although not the sort of unambiguous, conclusive proof any prosecutor would find sufficient for an indictment—he was convinced beyond a doubt that Peist was the mole.

First, there was page 155 of the Intelligence squad's movement log. On January 17, 1990, Detective William Peist had signed out to go to the Brooklyn D.A.'s office. That night at the Ravenite it was whispered to Gotti that Gravano's trailer and club had been bugged by wiremen working for the Brooklyn D.A.

Also on that evening, Helbig had promised Gotti, "I'll send a message tonight." According to the phone records Kurins had subpoenaed, at 8:10 P.M. on January 17, 1990, Peter Mavis had called 718-375-0897. The number was registered to William Peist.

With the advantage of his newfound knowledge of all the players—Peist, his cousin Pete Mavis, and George Helbig—Kurins once more returned to the apartment tape and now it was easier to decipher. All the stray bits of conversation suddenly fell into place; for Kurins, the feeling of triumph was as soaring as if he had decoded the Rosetta Stone. And as he put the pieces together, he saw that the conspiracy must have unfolded almost by accident. It was Peist's cousin Mavis, Kurins decided, who had been the scheme's instigator.

A small-timer, Mavis, Kurins now understood as he replayed the tape, had two big-time problems. First, he had lost a street fortune gambling with Helbig. And second, he had borrowed money from Sammy Bull's loan-sharking operation to cover part of his debt to Helbig. That left him owing money to both men, and without any prospects for paying either one. It was, Mavis must have felt, a very dangerous situation. Perhaps even life-threatening. In his desperation, he came up with a resourceful scheme: He would market confidential information he obtained from his well-connected cousin, a detective in the Intelligence Division, to the Gambino Family.

The rest fell into place easily, Kurins could see. Billy Peist would meet with his cousin, Pete Mavis; Mavis would pass on the latest scoop to Helbig; and then the Grim Reaper and Joe Butch Corrao would rush to Gotti himself to announce the news. It was a chain of communication designed to protect each of the links. And it worked brilliantly. Peist was the perfect spy.

Why did Peist do it? That was Mouw's first question after Kurins had made his report. The tense, closed-door meeting was in Mouw's office and Gabriel was the only other agent in the room.

Kurins had been giving that very question a great deal of thought over the past few weeks. Part of the answer, he suggested to Mouw, was revenge. Peist was resentful because the department had rejected his petition for a tax-free line-of-duty pension following his accident. He was bitter because his $75 million lawsuit charging that the city's negligence had contributed to the unsafe conditions on the rain-slicked bridge was facing years of depositions and other legal delays. But whether Peist was simply striking back against the system or against fate itself was, Kurins had to add, anybody's guess.

Greed, too, no doubt had a role in Peist's decision. He had no way of knowing that his lawsuit would eventually be settled and he would become a millionaire. Working for Gotti gave him the money to move to a bigger house on a corner plot with an aboveground pool in the backyard for the kids. And, Kurins was convinced, Peist saw his relationship with the Mob as a lucrative long-term partnership. Even after he retired from the Police Department, Kurins suspected he planned to work as a private investigator specializing in Mafia cases.

Then, opportunity was also a real motivator. It was just so easy for Peist. All he had to do was go about his routine business. There was no need to steal documents, pilfer files, ask suspicious questions. He worked Intelligence; it was his job to know everything. It was such an ingenious scheme, one that insulated him so completely from any direct contact with the Gambino Family, that Peist had to believe he would never be caught, or even suspected.

Peist must be laughing at the ease with which he was outsmarting the FBI. He no doubt enjoyed every important moment of his secret life. The hapless Baker was suddenly significant. And this too, the desire to be at center stage, Kurins believed, had been a factor in Peist's decision to become the mole. The one-legged, overweight detective reduced to guarding the jurors in the Gotti case was, in reality, the man who made the Teflon Don invincible.

When Kurins had finished his report, Mouw considered all the evidence, all the theories. He had lived with this mystery for so long; it had tormented him, goaded him, and now, at last, he had discovered his formidable adversary—a one-legged cop called "the Baker." If it weren't so tragic, if the damage Peist had done weren't so irreparable, he might have laughed. Now that the traitor had a face, and a history, Mouw found himself caught in conflicted emotions: a sense of triumph, and of farce.

His first reaction to his men was to play it lightly. There was still one unresolved mystery, he said sternly. "What good's a set of golf clubs going to do for Peist?"

"Well," said Kurins, going along, "you've seen people ski with one leg."

"That's right," Gabriel joined in. "Maybe he has someone else swing the club for him."

The time for laughter was quickly over. "We've found our mole," Mouw told his men. "Now we have to make a case." He came up with a plan that owed much to the scheme the team had used to trap Mildred Russo, the court clerk who had been passing confidential information to the Family. This time a piece of "vital" FBI intelligence, perhaps word of an arrest in the Castellano murder, would be shared with the police's Intelligence Division. C-16 would monitor Peist's office and home phones, even the pay phones on the corner near his office on Hudson Street, waiting for him to reach out to Mavis. They would catch him in the act. It would be impossible for the mole to escape.

But he did. Just days later, while the team was preparing the warrants to tap Peist's phones, Kurins came into Mouw's office with the bad news. "He's onto us," Kurins announced. He explained that he had received two calls from contacts in the Police Department: Peist was wondering why the FBI was asking questions about him. "What do we do now, Bruce?" Kurins wanted to know.

Mouw considered the options. He could go ahead and try to catch Peist in the act. The "news" of the Castellano case arrests was certainly provocative enough, just the sort of secret for which Gotti would pay a fortune. Perhaps Peist would be greedy and reckless. Perhaps he still would reach out to Mavis with his scoop. But the more Mouw considered that possibility, the more he doubted it. Peist would be cautious. He was a millionaire with a wife and family. He had a lot to lose. That, Mouw now realized, should be his angle of attack. Bring Peist in, scare the hell out of him— and he'll turn on his co-conspirators. At the very least, Mouw told himself, we will have neutralized Gotti's spy. Peist will be out of business.

"Let's bring him in, Andy," Mouw told Kurins. "Maybe he'll flip."

They picked up Peist as he was leaving work. It was just after five on an April evening in 1990 and he was walking along Hudson Street on the way to his car. Kurins was there, but it was Captain John Haggerty of the police's Internal Affairs Division who handled things. He had a rigid, military demeanor, and he talked in clipped and authoritative sentences.

"I'll have your gun, please," the captain said.

Peist handed over his revolver without a word of protest. The blood seemed to drain instantly from his round face. He was surrounded by officers and led to the captain's car. He was put in the backseat with the captain. Kurins and an IAD lieutenant sat up front. Peist was told he was being detained for "departmental questioning."

The IAD headquarters was in downtown Brooklyn, in an ancient, gloomy building with bars on the windows. They led Peist to an interrogation room on the second floor. "You're being placed on restricted duty," the captain began.

Yet Peist seemed to gather a certain resolve as the hours of interrogation passed. He denied ever discussing confidential Police Department business with his cousin, Peter Mavis. He said he had never heard of a George Helbig. And he insisted he had never met or spoken to John Gotti. He would not confess.

Neither would Mavis, the FBI learned the next day. They picked him up for questioning ostensibly about his investment in the Cloud Nine disco, and from the start Mavis was reluctant to cooperate. When the interrogation turned to his cousin William Peist, he shut up completely. And the FBI could not force him to continue. They had no proof of any crime. They had no choice but to let him go.

And when George Helbig was indicted weeks later for getting a fraudulent mortgage, charges stemming from an investigation into J & G Realty, he told the Bureau, "Take your best shot. I got nothing to say."

There was no further pressure the FBI could put on any of

them. Not unless they were willing to reveal the existence of the microphone in apartment 10.

Bruce Mouw refused. Gotti would now realize the FBI was onto his mole, but he would not be able to deduce this knowledge was initially the product of a conversation in Mrs. Cirelli's apartment that the Feds had overheard. Mouw would not even inform the police of the existence of the January 17 tape. Not while John Gotti was still having sit-downs in the apartment. He trusted no one to keep his squad's secrets.

There was an unsteady moment later that month when Peist put in his papers to retire. Unless he was formally charged, the detective would be entitled to receive a $24,000 annual pension. Some members of the squad reminded Mouw of his promise to "nail the traitor to the wall." You can't just allow him to get away with it, they argued.

Mouw listened. The thought of Peist receiving $24,000 from the taxpayers each year for the rest of his life sickened him. He wanted to do something about it now. Instead, he went for a long jog. When he returned, he told Kurins, "We've done the most important thing. We've neutralized the mole. He can't help Gotti anymore."

After a pensive moment, he added, "Anyway, it's not over yet. We'll still get our chance to nail him to the wall. Someone will roll."

Kurins, however, wasn't so sure any of the three conspirators would testify against one another. "Peist is still laughing at us, Bruce," he said, his voice full of anger and frustration, "and there's not a damn thing we can do about it."

# 45

WHAT WAS HE WAITING FOR? THAT WAS THE QUESTION MOUW now began to ask himself. Certainly, there were ample reasons to move the operation to its next—and final—stage. The mole could no longer do any damage. The mikes had not recorded an incriminating conversation for months. The Cirelli bug, in fact, had dried up completely. Gotti had not entered apartment 10 since January 24. *Four months ago.* Mouw, who had already gone prematurely gray from a life whose every corner was jammed with unresolved worries, now had to make room for another: Gotti suspected the old woman's living room was wired. That alone was a powerful justification for finally rolling things up. Perhaps the time had come to present the evidence C-16 had gathered to a grand jury. Perhaps, he seriously considered, the time had come to arrest John Gotti.

Yet, he held back. Part of his rationale was as instinctive as any gambler's urge to keeping on playing until he wins just one more big hand. What if Gotti returned to apartment 10? What if for one jackpot evening the Don was accompanied by the heads of the four other Families? To break the bank, Mouw knew he had to stay in the game. There was also an operational imperative: Deep Street. Now that it was a warm New York spring, the sidewalks of Little Italy would be crowded with walk-talks. Mouw could send the fleet of wired cars into the action; slyly sneaking up on the Family one more time where and when they least expected it, would be, he liked to think, just the final touch the case needed.

And according to the men who worked with Mouw, there was another restraint, largely unspoken although no less significant, tugging not just at their boss but also filling all of them with second thoughts: They did not look forward to the end. They wanted to win, of course; but they didn't want to give up the thrill of the chase. A sullen John Gotti had been staring down from the top of the pyramid of photographs on the wall in Mouw's office for the past five years. Mouw focused on it each day while he sat at his desk; for all anyone knew, he gave it a good night before he turned off the lights. Kurins and the Twins had been following Gotti's violent trail since his days as a flashy, punk capo barking orders at the Bergin. It was back in 1986, during a lull in the first federal trial, that Gabriel had had his initial combative run-in with the new Don; and it was six long months since his wife had put the victory champagne on ice. It wasn't so much that these men needed to summon the resolve, or the courage, to go on to the final battle. It was the view from the distant sidelines once it was over that concerned them. "We land the white whale—then what?" Tricorico, who after all had been an English teacher, had wondered. And no one had an answer.

But on June 22, 1990, after more than five hundred hours of tapes had been recorded in the Ravenite and the hallway outside the club, after six remarkable conversations in apartment 10, after Deep Street had been fully operational for one productive month, Mouw decided the time had come to shut down all the audio surveillances. Another consideration: The open phone lines running from the

Ravenite to the plant had cost the Bureau more than
$1 million. "Enough is enough," he announced to his squad.
"Let's make our case."

It was Mouw's hope that the Justice Department would
authorize him to arrest Gotti within the next two weeks. It
was a short-notice schedule, and he had been around long
enough to know that the old wisdom about the laborious
pace of the wheels of justice applied with equal validity to
its namesake federal bureaucracy, but he could still dream.
The arrest and indictment of the Don and his Administration on murder and RICO charges would certainly put a
crimp in the annual Fourth of July 4 celebration outside the
Bergin. Anyway, he consoled himself, it would all be over by
the end of the summer.

Mouw was wrong. The days stretched on endlessly, each
one followed, he would soon say, by "sleepless nights."

"You know why they can't win, Sammy?" Gotti began.
The Don and Gravano were sitting in the living room of
Mrs. Cirelli's apartment while Gotti, fat with confidence,
held forth. "They got no fuckin' cohesion," he declared,
casually dismissing the threat from the combine of law
enforcement agencies arrayed against him. "They got no
unity."

As the summer of 1990 dragged on, Mouw found himself
turning more and more often to this passage in the January
4, 1990, transcript; and after each reading, he was coming to
believe Gotti's assessment was not just insightful, but
prophetic. For no sooner had he delivered his carefully
prepared bundle of evidence to the Justice Department than
he was nearly trampled by the rush of competing prosecutors charging in to claim it. Everyone wanted a piece of The
Gotti Case. With growing unease, Mouw could see a sweep-
ing, multifaceted indictment—all his team's work on so
many fronts—beginning to unravel as a flock of self-
promoting jurisdictions pulled at it. He felt that if the
Justice Department, placating and Solomonic, allowed the
case to be divided in half—or in thirds!—and presented in
separate jurisdictions, it would be a disaster. If a prosecutor

in Manhattan, say, indicted Gotti for murdering Castellano, while another in Brooklyn tried the DiBernardo homicide, there was a real possibility two separate juries would not find the parts as substantial or incriminating as the whole. The image of Gotti and his entourage of lawyers strutting victoriously from courtrooms all over the city filled Mouw's thoughts. He felt at a complete loss. "It was," he would say, "an ugly, ugly scene as politics took over." In a case history filled with so many low and discouraging valleys, the summer of 1990, he decided, "was the absolute worst." He knew there would be no second chances for him or his team if Gotti managed to beat them this time.

While Mouw watched, impotent and appalled, the prosecutors came out fighting. Round One, as Andy Maloney, the U.S. Attorney for the Eastern District and a former West Point middleweight boxing champ cheerfully called it, pitted him against Ron Goldstock, the head of the State Organized Crime Task Force and a much more cerebral sort. It was no contest at all. Maloney was a man with a grudge. He was still driven by the memory of the press conference after Gotti's first federal trial when he had announced, "The jury has spoken," holding back his secret knowledge that the jury's foreman had been bribed. There was also something else going for Maloney, and this was the knockout punch: The Bureau refused to share its wires with Goldstock. The FBI felt the state would immediately pull its bug on Gravano's construction office if it learned the operation had been compromised, and Mouw was adamant that nothing be done to alert Sammy Bull. The safest course, it was decided, was to deny the state access to its Title III surveillance evidence.

Nevertheless, Maloney, whose office had helped C-16 prepare the warrants to spike the Ravenite and the apartment, offered Goldstock what, to his mind at least, was a generous compromise. He would try the Gotti case, but one of Goldstock's assistants could sit with the prosecution and, it was implied, smile officiously at the press. Goldstock, a gregarious man whose instinct and training had taught him to speak in ruminative, lawyerly sentences, became, in Maloney's words, "teed off." He started shouting that he would make a deal with the Queens District Attorney to try the Gotti case in that jurisdiction. Their meeting ended when, full of fury, he stomped out of Maloney's office, slamming the door behind him.

Maloney was not concerned. He knew the Justice Department would never allow the Gotti case to be tried in Queens—not with that office's history of leaks. Goldstock would not be his problem.

Round Two. It was the week after Mouw had pulled the apartment bug, and the setting was the lower Manhattan office of Otto Obermaier, the new U.S. Attorney for the Southern District. Seated around the long, sun-lit room were Manhattan D.A. Bob Morgenthau and his assistant, Michael Cherkasky; Walter Mack, the former head of the Manhattan strike force who had recently gone to work for the Manhattan U.S. Attorney's office; Maloney and his chief criminal assistant, John Gleeson; and the man they were all intent on persuading, Paul Coffey, deputy chief of the Justice Department's Organized Crime and Racketeering Section.

For the first part of the meeting, Maloney sat back— "resting on the ropes," he called it—while the other prosecutors swung away. Mack was a large man and when he spoke, his orator's voice seemed to boom out from the depths of his diaphragm. For the past thirty-six months, he argued, he had been presenting evidence on the Castellano homicide to a Manhattan grand jury. Over two thousand witnesses had been interviewed. He made a passing reference to "sweat equity," but perhaps because he realized fairness would have little to do with the ultimate decision, his main argument hinged on his ability to win. "I've got witnesses who'll put Gotti at the scene. I can get a conviction," he insisted.

Morgenthau's argument was primarily territorial. Castellano had been murdered in Manhattan. The Ravenite was in Manhattan. The case, therefore, should be tried in his jurisdiction. While he lectured in his low-key, scholarly way, Mike Cherkasky was silently urging him on. Trying Gotti meant a lot to him too. He wanted another shot to avenge the loss in the assault case.

Finally, it was Maloney's turn. He had neither Mack's stentorian presence nor Morgenthau's erudition, yet that afternoon, despite his stammer, despite a tendency to stumble over his own thoughts, he threw himself into the fray with a passion that seemed to fill him with a newfound articulateness. He also—no small advantage—knew something no one else in the room knew: precisely what was on the FBI's tapes.

"God bless you," he offered, gesturing toward Mack. "I don't want the Castellano homicide. It's the weakest part of the case." But, he went on to argue, if the government decided to split the case, it would compromise not just the murder conviction, but the RICO case as well. He shrewdly ended his presentation not so much with an argument about why the Eastern District should try Gotti, but instead with a plea for a single, unified prosecution.

Two weeks later, Robert S. Mueller III, the Assistant Attorney General for Criminal Justice, called up each of the prosecutors and informed them that Attorney General Dick Thornburgh had reached a decision: There would be only one case presented against John Gotti. Who would try the case, however, had not yet been decided. A decision, he promised somewhat vaguely, would be made shortly.

Andy Maloney didn't celebrate, and he didn't wait. He instructed Gleeson to "go full steam ahead" and begin presenting evidence from the C-16 wires to the grand jury. His plan was "to be so far down the road, they'd have to give me the case."

While the prosecutors schemed and argued that summer, John Gotti remained a free man. When Sammy Gravano came to him with a beef about Eddie Garafolo, one of the guys in his crew, the Don listened. Sammy didn't like how Garafolo had been sentenced to only a light three months, or how he was given two furloughs while doing the time. The guy has to be ratting somebody out to get a deal like that, Sammy said. He asked his don for permission to kill Garafolo.

You got it, Gotti agreed. He had no problem making decisions.

A team of gunmen from the Bull's crew ambushed Garafolo on August 8, 1990, and shot him dead. One of the bullets hit him in the eye, close to the center of his pupil. Another in the mouth. The gunmen wanted people to see what happens to rats.

It was six weeks since Mouw had closed his investigation, and he was still waiting for the Justice Department to choose a prosecutor.

By October, as the wait dragged on, things grew increasingly vitriolic between the different contenders hoping to take on John Gotti. Then, when they began to hear whispered hints of what was on the apartment tapes—and what Maloney and the FBI had kept from them—it got worse. "Overnight," said Maloney, who, if nothing else, was consistent in his devotion to pugilistic metaphors, "it went from a boxing match to a street fight."

So, when Mack asked to hear any tapes pertaining to the Castellano homicide, Mouw refused. Mack exploded. According to a friend, he went "red-faced, furious." He felt betrayed by the FBI. But Maloney called him "paranoid," and Mouw, unwavering under all the pressure, still refused. He did not want to do anything that could be used to persuade the Justice Department to reverse its decision to present a single, unified case against Gotti. Mack, bitter yet realizing he was beaten, announced his resignation.

Next it was Goldstock's turn to be enraged. It seemed incomprehensible to him that the Bureau would not have disclosed that his Gravano bugs had been blown. "How could they not trust me?" he demanded. He did not realize it was not personal: Mouw trusted no one.

But it was Morgenthau whose anger seemed to run the deepest. When he learned the FBI had failed to keep its promise and inform him of any possible jury tampering in the Gotti assault case, he was genuinely shocked. "They think they're a government unto themselves," he complained about the FBI. Cherkasky, who had tried the case, kept his anger to more pragmatic concerns: "By keeping information from us, the Bureau acted in a way that significantly affected the outcome of the case." But Morgenthau, with his old-world manners and old school ties, could not help feeling the betrayal was, at its core, ungentlemanly. "The FBI lied to me," he said as if that was indictment enough. Yet unlike Mack, he was determined not to surrender. Now he wanted to prosecute the next Gotti case more than ever.

And the longer the government waited, the more time Gotti had to take care of business. On the December 12 tape, Mouw had heard the Don promising to take care of Louie DiBono. "You know why he's dying," Gotti had confided to Frankie Locascio. "He's going to die because he refused to come in when I called."

It took Gotti a while to catch up with DiBono. First, Patsy Conte was given the contract, but DiBono didn't surface. Then they got lucky. Sammy Bull heard that Jelly Belly, as the guys were now calling DiBono since he was pretty much a dead man, was working at the World Trade Center. Gotti sent a new team out, and they snuck up on Jelly Belly on October 4, 1990. He was in the garage below the World Trade Center, walking to his Lincoln, when he felt the barrel of a gun pressed hard against the back of his head.

When Jelly Belly's body was found in the trunk of the car a couple of days later, Mouw, his agents noticed, fell into a deep, seemingly inconsolable depression. It was, they said, as if he felt somehow responsible.

Round Three was the final round, and it was fought in Washington on a cool November day two weeks before Thanksgiving. Bob Mueller sat at the head of the long conference table in a wood-paneled Justice Department conference room. Flanking him were nearly a half-dozen grim-faced Justice officials. Down the table, fittingly close to

the door, were the petitioners: an edgy Morgenthau and a
dour Cherkasky; Maloney, full of red-cheeked hail-fellow
cheer yet ready for the fight of his life, and seconded by a
gaunt and deathly pale Gleeson; and Obermaier, who affected a detached, unconcerned inscrutability.

The battle was largely between Morgenthau and Maloney,
and this time Maloney traded blow for blow, counterpunching with a vengeance. Morgenthau, too, was exhaus-
tive. He raised the old territorial arguments, and a few
new ones. He insisted that the judges in Manhattan were
superior and the jury pool was more sophisticated. Then, as
if that wasn't reason enough, he said the Brooklyn courts
were more susceptible to jury tampering.

That was too much for Maloney. "The distance between
the Manhattan courthouse and Brooklyn is the length of the
Brooklyn Bridge," he pointed out dryly. "I think that if the
bad guys can find their way to Brooklyn, they can find it to
Manhattan too."

When the laughter subsided, Morgenthau shot back:
"There's only one reason Brooklyn is in this—the tap water
that runs through the faucets in New York County runs
through theirs too." He pointed out that Castellano had
been murdered in Manhattan, and that the tapes were
recorded in Manhattan just a mile from his office.

"You've really got chutzpah," countered Maloney angrily.
He launched into a long and proudly detailed lecture about
the role his office had played in cooperating with the Bureau
to prepare surveillance warrants, and then to obtain renew-
als. But while he was talking, a thought struck him:
Obermaier and Morgenthau had already struck a deal. That
was why Obermaier was holding his peace. That was why
Morgenthau was so confidently laughing up his sleeve.

By the time the meeting was over, Maloney was convinced he didn't have a chance. As he was walking out, one
of the participants sidled up to him and in a whisper seemed
to confirm his worst fears. "You'll never be as good as Bob is
at these meetings," Maloney remembers being told. "He's
unencumbered by the truth."

* * *

The call came at seven in the morning a week later. Maloney picked up the phone in the bedroom of his Westchester home on the first ring. He didn't want the call to wake his wife. "You've got the case," he heard Bob Mueller announce without preamble. When Maloney hung up, it was his own unrestrained shout that awakened his wife.

The order was sent later that day to Bruce Mouw to get ready to make his arrests as soon as the Eastern District grand jury voted its indictments. It was high time, Mouw thought. More than six months had passed since he ended his operation. Gotti had murdered two more men, and hints about the tapes were appearing in the newspapers. It was no wonder he was having a hard time sleeping at night. "Let's get this done quick," he told Gabriel, who agreed. Only now, as he was trying to track down each of his targets in preparation for a mass arrest, the Twins came into his office with some news.

"It's Sammy Bull," Frankie Spero said. "He's vanished."

# 46

MOUW'S PLAN HAD BEEN TO LULL THE FAMILY INTO A NICE, EASY calm. Still, he knew he shouldn't back off completely. There was always the chance that if things got too quiet Gotti would take that as a sign: the stillness before the final storm. There was no telling what the Don or his guys would pull if they thought the big bust was coming. So, taking his lead from Kurins, the master at fugazying, he decided to get handwriting exemplar subpoenas served on his targets. That way he would be able to check whether the Administration was in town, available to be rounded up once the indictments were voted. He would show Gotti that the Bureau was still on his case, and at the same time send a deceptive message, something to broaden the smirk on the Don's face: The Feds got nothing better than handwriting exemplars to throw at you.

During the last week in November, C-16 fanned out across the city and served the subpoenas on Gotti; his *consigliere*, Frankie Locascio; and Tommy Gambino, the multimillionaire capo who directed the Family's interests in the Garment District. The only target they couldn't find was the underboss, Sammy Gravano. By December the indictments had been voted, but Sammy Bull was still nowhere to be found. Frankie Spero and Matty Tricorico had tried his home, his office, Tali's, even the Brooklyn gym where he boxed. The Observation Post hadn't clocked him entering the Ravenite at all in the past few weeks. According to one TE, Sammy Bull was off in Pennsylvania doing a piece of business. Another TE was pretty sure he was down in Miami soaking up the sun. His lawyer, Gerry Shargel, insisted he had no idea where his client was.

But what gnawed at Mouw was not so much where Sammy Bull had gone, but why. Mouw's always fertile imagination seemed, now that he was within sight of the finish line, to race ahead uncontrollably. Sammy was on the lam because he knew about the bust, he decided. And if Sammy knew, so did Gotti. A new insight: They were setting up his team. He was the one who was being lulled. Gotti was pulling all the strings. It was a trap.

But then another long, sleepless night became another morning, and Mouw realized he might have it all wrong. Once again he was Chairman Mouw (as Kurins called him) and he could look at things operationally. There were, he decided, just two choices. He could charge ahead and make the arrests; Sammy would be apprehended sometime in the future: the next day, perhaps the next year. Or, he could wait until Sammy returned and make a clean sweep of the entire Gambino Family Administration.

After a decade chasing the Family, he told himself, what's a few more days' wait? Or so he hoped.

It was nine on a Sunday morning and Mouw was putting on his sneakers and a Navy sweatshirt, getting ready for a jog, when the phone rang. It was Gerry Shargel.

Mouw's first angry thought was, How the hell did he get my home number? But his anger dissipated when the attorney explained why he was calling. His client Salvatore Gravano had returned from a business trip and was willing to accept service of the subpoena for a handwriting sample. Would it be convenient to serve it Thursday morning at his office?

That would be December 13, Mouw pointed out. He liked to keep things precise when he was dealing with lawyers.

Correct, Shargel said. But, he added brightly, his client wasn't superstitious.

Maybe he should be, Mouw felt like saying. Instead, he thanked Shargel for the call.

As soon as Mouw finished his conversation with the attorney, he called Gabriel. "Sammy's back," he announced.

When Mouw finally got around to taking off on his jog that morning, he was feeling looser than he had in months. It was as if he could run for miles and miles.

By three-thirty the next afternoon, most of the squad had gathered in Mouw's office. There had been no formal announcement, but word of Shargel's call had spread. Now they were waiting to learn if the lawyer's information had been accurate. And to see what Mouw would do if it were.

The call did not come until six that night. That was when the agent in the Observation Post punched in the number of the phone in Mouw's office. For some reason Mouw let the black phone ring a few times. The agents watched him, but he was in no hurry. He finally picked up the receiver and listened silently. His face betrayed nothing. He hung up, and when he spoke, his voice was soft, yet taut. "Sammy just entered the Ravenite," he said.

No one in the room said a word. They waited. Mouw seemed to be lost in the glow of the Alexander's sign in the distance. Kurins, however, caught his boss's eyes drifting to the pyramid of photographs on the wall across the room, and toward the face at the top. It was an interlude that might have lasted only a minute, but for those in the room it stretched on like a journey across a desert.

At last Mouw spoke. "Wear your suits tomorrow, guys. We're taking them down." He was smiling.

\* \* \*

Mouw was counting on surprise. While he was putting together the operational orders, he thought about asking Bonavolonta for more men, more firepower. Maybe even a SWAT team. He had no doubt the Ravenite would be packed with bad guys. If one of them got feisty, or Gotti gave a signal, anything might happen. It could be a real firefight. But in the end, he decided to stick with just his squad. His men had taken the case this far. They deserved to be the only ones at the finish. Besides, ten agents should be able to take on thirty or so hoods. Especially if the bad guys didn't know they were coming.

He shared his plan with his men that morning, Tuesday, December 11, 1990. There were no frills, he told them matter-of-factly. It would all depend on timing. C-16 would assemble at headquarters in lower Manhattan at 3:30. By 4:00 they would be in a half-dozen unmarked cars cruising around Little Italy. As soon as the Observation Post announced that Gotti, Gravano, and Locascio were in the Ravenite, they would charge in and arrest them. They would go quietly. Or not. "It's anybody's guess," he conceded.

As he dismissed the squad, he yelled one last thought at his men: "Wear your bullet-proof vests."

At 3:30 that afternoon, George Gabriel was still in downtown Brooklyn. He had told Maureen to watch the television news that night. Maybe she would see him. And maybe they would have a reason to open that bottle of champagne he had precipitously bought almost a year ago to the day. Now he was convinced he had once again misjudged things. Mouw had sent him and Mark Roberts to pick up search warrants; as long as C-16 was hitting the Ravenite, they might as well try to grab an address book or maybe a list of beeper numbers. Only things were dragging on. He was still in the Brooklyn courthouse. Gleeson, for some reason, was having a hard time tracking down an amenable judge. The way things were going, Gabriel realized, he could miss the arrest.

* * *

By 4:00, Mouw was in his car cruising along Houston Street when the Observation Post came in loud and clear over the walkie-talkie: "Number two is in." That meant Frankie Loc had entered the club. "Read you," Mouw reported back. Then he announced over the encrypted frequency: "Nobody goes in until I give the order to take 'em."

Five o'clock and Gabriel and Roberts were still pacing around the Brooklyn courthouse. Gleeson had found a judge. "It shouldn't be much longer," he had promised. "I don't have much longer, John," Gabriel had barked back.

At 6:00, the Observation Post reported, "Number three is in." That was word-code for Gravano. Two for two, Mouw thought. Everything was looking good. Once again he spoke into the walkie-talkie: "Remember, nobody goes in until I give the order."

It must have been 6:30 when Gabriel finally had the warrants in his hand and along with Roberts was running to their car. If they hit the siren, Gabriel tried to convince himself, they should be able to get across to Manhattan in time. Unless the traffic on the bridge was bumper-to-bumper. Or the squad had already gone in through the front door.

At 6:40, Mouw and the team were still in their cars, and for the first time that day he was starting to think he might have to call things off. Where was Gotti? The Don usually arrived at the club by 6:00. He was a half hour late. Where the hell was he?

He could be on his way, tied up in traffic.

He could be home in bed with the flu.

Or he could be winging his way to South America. The Teflon Don.

Where the hell was he?

\* \* \*

Twisting in and out of traffic like an ambulance driver, Gabriel made it across the bridge in minutes. He was driving along Mulberry Street, siren off, when at 6:52 the Observation Post reported, "Number one is here."

As soon as he heard that, Gabriel stepped on the gas. "Perfect timing," he told Roberts. He sped down the block, pulled the car up on the curb, and burst into the Ravenite with his gun drawn. Roberts followed.

"FBI," Gabriel announced to the roomful of hoods. They stared at him and his partner, not moving. Gabriel stared back and told himself: The cavalry is on the way. Just tough it out, Georgie. Tough it out.

It never occurred to him that the rest of the squad was in their cars, scattered throughout the streets of lower Manhattan, still waiting for Mouw's command to "take 'em."

"Everyone just stay calm," Gabriel announced, making sure to stand tall. "We're here to arrest certain people."

No one had moved or said a word. And it was still two men against thirty.

"Get up against the wall," Gabriel ordered.

No one moved.

Gabriel went up to Gotti. "John," he said, "you can tell the men to cooperate, or we can do it the hard way."

"How you doing, Agent Gabriel?" Gotti said.

Gabriel thought he heard someone moving behind him, but when he turned abruptly, swinging his gun in front of him, everyone was still in place. Or had returned. "Don't fuck with me, John. We're taking you and Frankie Loc and Sammy in."

"We?" Gotti asked.

At that moment the rest of the C-16 team burst through the door. Gotti looked at the shotgun-carrying agents, and then at his men. "It's no big deal," he ordered. "Just do what they tell you."

The agents led the hoods into the street. The plan was to isolate Gotti, Locascio, and Gravano in different corners of the club until the drive to headquarters for booking. Gotti, however, returned to his seat. "Hey," he asked, "I got time to finish my coffee, right?"

Mouw walked up to him. "Things go the way I figure," he said, "that's about all you'll be doing for the rest of your life."

"You don't have to act like a tough guy around these people," Frank Spero would later explain. "They've been brought up around tough guys all their life. You show them respect and they respect that."

So when he and partner Matty Tricorico drove Sammy Bull that evening from the club to 26 Federal Plaza for booking and fingerprinting, they didn't come on like two hard cases. Besides, Sammy was from Staten Island. He had known the Twins from way back. What was the point of rubbing things in? "You want us to call Debbie for you?" one of the agents asked, referring to Sammy's wife. "We can call her for you." They also asked, "Want us to grab you a sandwich? A cup of coffee? It could take forever up there."

And just before they led him out of the car, while they were still in the garage beneath headquarters, Spero turned to Gravano and, not making too big a deal out of it, said, "Sammy, hey, you ever want to talk . . . you ever feel like sitting down with us—you know how to reach us."

"You plant a seed," Frankie would later tell people. "You never know."

Jim Fox, the head of the New York office, was at the Bureau Christmas party when he was pulled from a conversation and guided into a secluded corner by one of his aides. "Everyone's in pocket," he was told. "There were no incidents and they're all en route."

A moment later Fox was standing in front of a microphone and asking the partygoers for quiet. "Ladies and gentlemen," he announced, "I've got a Christmas present for all of us. John Gotti was arrested tonight by agents of the Federal Bureau of Investigation."

Cheers filled the room, and then applause. The applause kept building and building. It was like nothing Fox had ever heard before in his life.

Later that night, Fox was on the twenty-eighth floor of

headquarters where the three leaders of the Gambino Family were being booked. Mouw thought Fox should have the chance to see with his own eyes the men the Bureau had been pursuing for so many years; he might have been a hunter displaying his hard-won trophies to his patron. He led Fox into the room where Gotti was being held.

"Shame on you," snarled the handcuffed Boss of Bosses to the director of the FBI's New York office.

Frank Locascio was in a room farther down the hall. The *consigliere* turned his back on Fox when he walked in.

Sammy Bull was sitting with the Twins in a cubicle near the elevator. "Sammy," said Mouw, "this is James Fox. He runs this place."

"Mr. Fox," said Sammy as he extended his cuffed hands, "nice to meet you."

# 47

THREE DAYS LATER, THE LEADERS OF THE GAMBINO FAMILY SAT IN a fourth-floor Brooklyn courtroom listening as a series of tape recordings was broadcast from two huge speakers. The U.S. Attorney hoped to convince Judge I. Leo Glasser that the men should be kept in jail without bail, and he played excerpts from the conversations recorded in Mrs. Cirelli's apartment to support his motion. As the Administration heard their own voices booming around the high-ceilinged room, they realized for the first time just what the FBI had done, and the problems they were facing.

The December 12 tape, Gotti's angry and reckless complaints to Locascio, was the centerpiece of the government's argument. And now Gravano also learned what his two friends were saying about him behind his back. "I mean, where are we going here?" Gotti demanded to know. His words were loud and indignant, and they filled the courtroom. Gravano remained slouched in his seat at the defense table, his hooded eyes fixed on the speakers. He was drumming his fingers along the table edge.

"Where, where's my piece of the companies?" Gotti

thundered. "Let me tell you, Frankie, there's creating and creating. Now look, Frankie. You want to put your head with fuckin' Sammy. You're too bright for that."

By now Gravano was gripping the table. His knuckles were white. And he was looking straight at Gotti. The Don seemed to be studying his cuff links.

And all the time the raging, disembodied voice continued to swell: "It doesn't even bother me if he had six, seven companies, companies himself . . . I'll tell him, 'Let me know when you feel you going to choke.' . . . But you're not doing that! You're creating a fuckin' army inside an army. You know what I'm saying, Frankie?"

A new voice cut in; it was Locascio's, higher-pitched and begging for approval. "End up creating another faction."

"That's right!"

"You're, you're saying it mildly."

The Don had the final word: "And you're not going to do that! I'm not going to allow that."

Gotti turned for a moment to look at Sammy Bull and offered a lazy, apologetic shrug. Gravano fixed his dull eyes on his boss, and he let go of the table. Slowly, like a man feeling his way out of a deep sleep, he squeezed his right hand into a fist. Then his left hand. He put both fists in front of him, and turned away from Gotti to stare across the room.

The judge ordered that all three men be detained in the Metropolitan Correctional Center until the conclusion of their trial on murder, RICO, loan-sharking, gambling, obstruction of justice, and tax evasion charges.

They were being led out of the courtroom when Gravano made his move. He was walking ahead of Gotti when he suddenly turned and backed the Don into the wall. Gravano's hands were at his sides, but he was on his toes, stretching to get right in Gotti's face.

"How the fuck could you say those things about me?" he bellowed. He sounded like a man in pain.

"It was just talk, Sammy," Gotti said. "Don't mean shit."

"Yeah, talk," Gravano repeated as a marshal grabbed his arm and pulled him away. "Some fuckin' talk."

When Gabriel told Mouw about Sammy's bracing the Don, Mouw had to agree that things were going exactly as he had planned.

It wasn't easy time being locked in the MCC and knowing that all you had to look forward to was a trial. Or that if you were found guilty, you were facing life without the possibility of parole. The government would send you to Marion, the federal penitentiary in Illinois where they shipped all the hard cases. Gravano and Gotti had talked about that after their arrest. It would be twenty-three hours a day in solitary, and one shower a week. And the only way you got out was in a box. But after the detention hearing, the two men didn't talk much. In fact, the Don sent word to his underboss that he was not to meet with a lawyer unless Gotti was there. Which was the same as telling Gravano he didn't trust him.

But Gotti was in the north wing of the prison, and Gravano was "down south," as the inmates called it. It made it all a little easier. For a while, Gravano even thought about escaping. He came up with a couple of schemes. In one, the guys from his crew smuggled him out at the end of visiting hours. In another, a helicopter landed on the roof in the middle of the exercise period and swooped him off. But even Gravano realized the plans were pretty half-baked, and he never took them too seriously. It was just something to dream about, to help pass the time. Or to whisper about with some of the other prisoners, guys he saw every day like Billy Bright or Frankie Smith. It was a way of letting them know that Sammy Bull was always thinking. That he was too tough a guy to go down without a fight.

Sammy also kept up with business. He had a million and a half out on the streets and he was afraid some of his customers might think they could get away without covering their weekly vig since he was in jail. He wanted to make sure nobody got that idea. That was why he sent a message to Vinnie "Oil" Rizzuto. One of his men went up to Vinnie Oil and put a gun right to his head. You got a choice, Vinnie was told. Either you keep on paying the five hundred each week, or you get a bullet. Vinnie kept on paying, and so did all the others. Sammy was in jail, but the collections continued regular as clockwork.

By August, however, after eight months in jail spent waiting for the trial to begin, after days spent going over the transcripts of the apartment tapes and coming to grips with the power of the government's case, Gravano sent word to some of his best customers. He was willing to give them a break. He would accept a knockdown payment, a lump sum to settle their account. The way things were shaping up, he decided, it might be better business to take all the money he could, while he still had the chance.

His future, Gravano began to realize now more than ever, was bleak. It was in August that the government outmaneuvered the Family once again. The U.S. Attorney, using the Ravenite tapes as evidence, succeeded in getting the Administration's three lawyers—Bruce Cutler, Gerald Shargel, and John Pollok—disqualified. Judge Glasser ruled that the lawyers, particularly Cutler and Shargel, had acted as "house counsel" for the Family, and, as could be heard on the tapes, were "witnesses to a variety of significant events" that were intrinsic to the prosecution's case.

As soon as this ruling was announced, Gravano felt as if he had been shoved into a corner and there was no way out. Without the prospects of Cutler's Brucifying the jury or Shargel, whom he trusted, watching out for him, he was doomed. It didn't help his spirits much when at the meetings with his new attorney, Ben Brafman, Gotti kept on talking about "my" case. This is *our* case, Gravano felt like screaming. But he decided there was no percentage in making a scene. Still, he was convinced he knew where the Family's strategy was heading: John was going to beat the rap on Castellano—leaving him to take the heat for the murders of Louie Milito, Robert DiBernardo, and Louie DiBono.

And all the time he was in the MCC, Gravano kept on making a list. It was a list of the people he would have to kill if he ever got out. After hearing the December 12 tape, he knew he would have to whack Gotti. It wasn't so much a matter of honor as of survival. He had no doubts, after what the Don had said to Locascio about someday taking him down. Gravano realized if he hit Gotti, then he would also have to take care of the Don's brother Pete. And John, Jr.; the kid was now a capo and would surely come gunning for him. For that matter, he would have to off Frankie Loc, too, just to be sure. By the time Gravano finished counting up all the people he would have to kill, he had twelve names on his hit list. Hell of a life that would be, he told himself. I'd be busy hunting down guys. Or being hunted down.

That was the best he could hope for. And that was only if he somehow managed to convince a jury he wasn't guilty. If he didn't beat the rap, he would wind up in Marion. The only way out of there was in a box.

He was forty-four years old. He had a wife, a nineteen-year-old son, and a sixteen-year-old daughter. He was a millionaire. And he was about to lose it all.

It was the first week in October when, after ten months in jail, Gravano told his wife Debra he wanted her to make a call.

Frankie Spero was sitting at his desk in the Bureau's Staten Island office when the call came. "This is Debbie Gravano," she said. "Can we talk?"

Spero did not ask what was on her mind. He just wanted to make sure he didn't lose her. "How soon?" he answered. And he gestured madly for Tricorico to pick up the extension.

She said that she was ready whenever he was. Tricorico, now listening in, pumped his fist in the air as if he had just kicked a field goal.

Spero suggested they meet at her house in fifteen minutes.

"I'm sure you know the address," she said dryly, and then she hung up.

Before the Twins left the office, they called Mouw. "What do you think this is about?" Mouw asked.

Could be a lot of things, they told him. But they all were hoping.

* * *

First, she served the two agents coffee. Then, when they were all seated in the living room, Spero and Tricorico on a floral-covered sofa and Debra in a wing chair across from them, she began. "I have a message from Sammy," she said. "He wants to talk with you." She said she didn't know what he wanted to speak about. He just had one request, she insisted. "He wants to meet in private."

"We'll handle it," Tricorico told her. And both agents' hearts were racing.

They drove from Gravano's house straight to Mouw's office on Queens Boulevard. Their boss was at his desk, smoking his pipe and waiting for them.

"Take the pipe out of your mouth," Spero teased. "Don't want you to go biting your tongue off when you hear this."

Tricorico, meanwhile, had closed the office door and walked right up to Mouw's desk. "Sammy wants to talk in private," he said.

Mouw sat there as if stunned. At last he said, "He's reaching out."

The Twins nodded.

And Mouw asked, "Is it for real?"

If it wasn't for real, then it was a trap. The Family, running out of options, had come up with the perfect plan: Sammy Bull would be their new mole. He would spy on the prosecution for them. He would feed the government lies, or half-truths. He would lead them on, help them shape their case, and then when he took the stand, he would suddenly be struck with amnesia. Gee, I don't remember saying that, he would mumble. Gotti would break out in a big smirk. And the jury would be left to wonder what sort of underhanded scheme the government was now attempting against the Teflon Don.

But if it was for real, then it was, as Mouw would say, "the coup of a lifetime." Gravano was the number-two man in the Family. He, even more than Gotti, was in charge of its daily operations. He could help bring down not just the Don, but the entire Gambino Family. He knew enough to damage the other four Families too. It would be the most significant defection in the history of organized crime.

If it was for real.

Bonavolonta was against it from the start. He argued that the Bureau had made its case, why take any chances? Fox seemed to agree. Gabriel, too, was uncertain. "Just to think about it, left my stomach in knots," he later said. Mouw's convictions seemed to flutter drastically between two extremes. One moment he was sure it was "a trap, a Trojan horse." The next, he told himself it was "pure gold." He also found himself thinking a great deal about the chance to resolve one lingering, unsettled score. He would have a witness against Peist.

Only the Twins were sure it wasn't a trick. We know Sammy, they insisted. This fits. He's spent a lifetime playing all the angles, and now he's playing the only one he's got left.

There was one other concern. No one had any doubts that Gravano was a killer. Was it too repugnant to make a deal with a murderer? They all thought about this and, further testimony to the intensity with which this entire case had been fought, no one had any qualms. A deal with any devil was justifiable to get Gotti. If it was for real.

In the end, the Bureau decided it was just too tempting a possibility to ignore. Mouw, outwardly confident, agreed. Let's see what he has to offer, he announced to his team, and then go from there. "Either way, it's a gamble," he admitted. And he might have added: Just like any of a thousand other impossible gambles throughout this case.

"This shouldn't take long," Ben Brafman, Gravano's new attorney, reassuringly told his client as they sat in the Brooklyn courtroom on the morning of October 27, 1991. Handwriting exemplars, he explained, were routine. "I got nothing better to do," Gravano shrugged.

Brafman watched as a blank sheet of paper was placed in front of Gravano and the underboss began to write his name. The *S* was large and flowing, and the eight letters that followed were also distinct. But the *G* was not much more than a semicircle, and the rest of the letters were a stylized scribble. Gravano repeated his signature nine more times. After the papers were collected, Brafman rose with his client and said good-bye. He watched the marshals lead Gravano toward a door by the judge's bench. His duty done, he hurried to the car he had waiting downstairs and to his next appointment.

But that morning Gravano was not led back to the detention cells, but to a jury room. Waiting inside were Gabriel, the Twins, and John Gleeson, the assistant U.S. Attorney who would be trying the Gotti case. When Gravano entered, all conversation in the room stopped. For a moment, they stared at Gravano. He returned their looks. His eyes focused on one man, and then moved on to another. He was sizing them up.

Gleeson broke the silence. "Well," he began, "we think we all know why we're here."

Gravano nodded. He had prepared a speech and this was his moment to deliver it. "I'm concerned a lot about certain things. I'm an important figure. I have a lot to offer. I'm thinking maybe we can make a deal."

It was Gabriel who asked what kind of deal Gravano was looking for.

"If I talk, I walk," Gravano said. It came out so quickly that everyone realized he had sat in his cell preparing the line.

Gleeson said that would be impossible. Gravano would have to do time.

How much? Gravano asked. And, it was noted by the agents, he had already stepped away from his initial demand.

Twenty years, Gleeson said. It was the sentence Maloney had told him to offer.

Gravano didn't say yes. And he didn't say no. It was at that moment that everyone in the room realized a deal could be negotiated.

So Gabriel asked Gravano what kind of information he had to offer.

Gravano had prepared for this too. He led them through a minute-by-minute account of the murder of Paul Castellano. By the time he had finished describing how he had looked out at the bodies lying on Forty-sixth Street and then, satisfied, told Gotti to drive off, everyone in the room wanted to make the deal.

A plea bargain would have to be approved at the highest levels, Gleeson told Gravano as the meeting wound down. We'll get back to you as soon as possible.

"Just don't fuck around," Gravano warned.

Jim Moody, the chief of the Bureau's Organized Crime Section, met with Judge William Sessions, the FBI director, the next day.

Also that same day Bob Mueller, the Assistant Attorney General for Organized Crime, met with the United States Attorney General, William Barr.

Later in the week, Judge Sessions walked across Pennsylvania Avenue for a meeting in the Attorney General's office.

Bob Mueller called Andy Maloney with the decision: Gravano would have to agree to be fully debriefed by the FBI. He would be required to testify in trials for the next two years. He would have to plead guilty to a charge carrying a maximum imprisonment of twenty years, sentencing to be done at the end of two years. If Gravano accepted those terms, a deal could be made.

"It was just too good an opportunity to let slip by," Moody later explained.

Prisoners were routinely transferred from the Metropolitan Correctional Center in lower Manhattan to Otisville Prison in upstate New York at midnight. The scheduling was a matter of convenience, as well as security. It was easier for a bus full of prisoners to move through the late-night nearly empty downtown streets, and it was also easier to see if the bus was being followed.

A few minutes after midnight on November 8, 1991, a cold, wet night, Bruce Mouw and George Gabriel showed their badges to a sleepy guard and walked into the MCC. Gabriel handed the guard the transfer-of-custody papers. The guard was used to this procedure. He did it at least two, often three times every week. Still, when he glanced at the papers, he let out a whistle. The custody warrant was headed,

UNITED STATES OF AMERICA
—against—
JOHN GOTTI, *et al.,*
Defendants.

Further down the page was the name of the prisoner to be transferred: Salvatore Gravano.

"So you're here to pick up the big guy," the guard said.

"Yeah," Gabriel repeated absently, "the big guy."

The guard walked off and the two agents waited. It was a tense, strained wait.

And then the guard led in John Gotti.

"What the fuck is going on?" Gabriel bellowed.

"No! No!" Mouw yelled. "You got the wrong one."

Gotti all at once understood. "Jesus! That fuckin' rat." He was still screaming uncontrollably as the guard took him back to his cell. His raging shouts carried through the prison.

Gravano heard them as he was led downstairs. "Fuck him," he told Mouw and Gabriel as they led him to the prison door.

Gabriel went ahead, the point man. Mouw kept pace with Gravano, walking next to him in the rain to the waiting car. He noticed that Sammy Bull was on his toes, trying to seem taller.

"You're from Iowa, right?" Gravano asked.

"That's right." He wondered where Gravano had heard that.

"Never met anyone from Iowa before," Gravano said. The two men continued walking side by side in the rain toward the car. An agent held the back door open. "I guess,"

Gravano said after a moment, "if I'm going to trust any-body, might as well be someone from Iowa." And then he climbed into the backseat of the car.

An hour later they were in a motel room out on Long Island, and Gravano's mood seemed less certain. "After that fuck-up at MCC, how can I trust you guys with my life?" he moaned.

Frankie Spero told him the hall was protected by a SWAT team. "The Third Division couldn't get into this room without our say-so."

Gravano, however, seemed unimpressed. And he started complaining that the coffee was cold.

That was when Gabriel exploded. "You're here, pal. That's all the fuck that matters. Now do you want to go back, or you want to play ball?"

Gabriel's anger seemed to bring Gravano around. "Where do we begin?" he asked.

"Tell me about the cop," Mouw ordered. "Peist."

So Gravano did. He told the story plainly but precisely. He wasn't trying to impress Mouw. His only concern now that he had made up his mind to cooperate seemed to be to get the facts out in a straight-forward manner. As he outlined it, the scheme worked just as Kurins had figured. Peist passed the information on to his cousin Mavis, who then delivered the news to Helbig, and Helbig and Joe Butch Corrao delivered it to the Don. For his services, Peist earned five hundred dollars a week. But whenever he came up with a big piece of news, Gotti sent ten thousand to the cop.

When Gravano finished, Mouw knew he finally had enough to indict them all—Peist, Mavis, Helbig, and Corrao. I knew someone would roll, he felt like shouting. He had just never expected it to be Sammy Bull. It had taken one traitor to catch another. But now, at last, he could close his file. He had trapped the mole.

That morning an FBI agent delivered a letter to Ben Brafman's office near the Battery in lower Manhattan. "I have decided to retain new counsel," it began. It was signed by Salvatore Gravano and in its lower lefthand corner it was noted that copies had been sent to Hon. I. Leo Glasser and Andrew J. Maloney, Esq.

Brafman immediately telephoned Maloney.

"I have a letter here that purportedly comes from Salvatore Gravano—"

"It ain't purportedly, Ben," Maloney interrupted gleefully.

## 48

THE STAKES WERE IMPOSSIBLY HIGH. IT WAS AS IF $75 MILLION
dollars—the Justice Department's "ballpark estimate" of
what it had cost to make the Gotti case and bring it to
trial—were riding on this one roll of the dice. That was how
Mouw and his team felt as they waited in the Brooklyn
courtroom on Monday, March 2, 1992, for Salvatore
Gravano to take the stand and testify against John Gotti.

The four months since Gravano had agreed to cooperate
had been difficult. They had kept him in Virginia in a
building on the Quantico base that had once been used as a
safe house for KGB defectors. He played handball. He ran
four and a half miles a day. Jim Fox came down to play
chess. He sparred with some of the agents from the Academy team, and he proved to be a very tenacious, and often
cruel body puncher. A few of the agents wound up with
bruised ribs. When Maloney heard about that, the West
Point boxing champ who had won his medals forty years
before offered to go into the ring and teach Sammy a lesson.
Instead, the Bureau flew in an Indian agent from Illinois
who slammed Gravano around so forcefully that Gabriel

worried he "might get amnesia." Mouw worried about that too, but for other reasons.

After a sweep of phone lines of the Gravanos' Staten Island home, Kravec discovered two separate bugs. When Mouw heard this, his stomach dipped wildly and he ordered the low-key watch on Debra and the two children to be immediately reinforced.

Then on January 22, there was another rush of concern. An FBI microphone in Boston overheard a meeting between two Genovese tough guys and James Martorano, a capo in the New England Patriarca Family. They were discussing ways to kill Sammy Bull's wife and two kids.

Gravano, meanwhile, was becoming alarmingly mercurial. One moment he would be talking rosily about the imagined life he would someday lead, reunited with his family and running a drywall concern in Arizona. The next, thinking about the drawing of a rat with his face that had run in the *Daily News* and that had been foolishly faxed to Quantico, he would slip into a total depressive state. He wouldn't talk for hours, and he wouldn't eat. Or he would tell the Twins, who were his nearly constant companions, "I did it for my family," and that would be the signal he was heading off into another gloomy spell. As for Mouw, his mood and confidence seemed to rise and fall with his prisoner's. Also, now that Gravano had been fully debriefed the team had a chance to add up the number of murders the Iceman had committed: nineteen. Mouw came to realize the entire case was in no small way riding on the sworn testimony of a man who was about as upstanding as a serial killer.

Of course, there were also the tapes, the fruits of Mouw's decision to "go electronic" and Kravec's skill as a wireman. They had been introduced in the first weeks of the trial and they had made headlines.

"Your task will be quite simple," Maloney had told the jurors in his opening statement. "It will not be that complex because these defendants in their own words will tell you what it is all about . . . we will let John Gotti's own words

. . . tell you the story of the crimes set forth in the indictment." And when the jurors put on their headsets and
listened to the tapes recorded in Mrs. Cirelli's apartment—
"five extraordinary conversations," Maloney called them—
they did seem mesmerized, concentrating on every incriminating word. It was possible to believe, Mouw hoped, that
Gotti was, as Maloney had said, "a man trapped by his own
words."

Gotti, however, seemed untroubled by the tapes. He
refused to wear the headphones when a tape was being
played, or even to follow the typed transcripts the government had prepared. Instead, he would wait until Gleeson
rose from the defense table to explain the significance of a
certain sentence and then, with one flick of the back of his
hand, dismiss the entire tape. His attorney, Albert Krieger,
the ripples of skin on the crown of his shaved head gleaming
under the courtroom lights, told the jury, "We are not afraid
of the tapes. You will hear on these tapes that Mr. Gotti has
been through two trials where similar tapes were played and
the jury rejected them as not supportive of the case
charged."

When Mouw thought about that, he realized once again
how much was riding on Sammy Bull.


Still, on the morning of March 2, no one knew what to
expect from Gravano. There was perhaps one clue, however.
After Gravano had been flown in by helicopter from Camp
Smith in upstate Poughkeepsie, New York, where he was
staying during the trial, he met Jim Fox for breakfast at the
courthouse. The two men had become friends. Fox, who had
a gracious, reassuringly avuncular way, would talk to
Gravano about his two grown daughters, and Gravano
would, in turn, trade stories about his own two children. As
the breakfast, just a bagel and coffee, was ending, Fox asked
Gravano if he realized how important his testimony would
be.

"It will be the beginning of the end of organized crime,"
Gravano said proudly.

An hour later, John Gleeson announced, "Our next witness is Salvatore Gravano."

It took four minutes for Gravano to make his way to the witness stand from the room near the judge's chambers where he was being kept under guard. This morning the first two rows of the spectator section of the courtroom were filled with fifteen huge FBI agents, members of the SWAT team. They left their suit jackets open as if to display the revolvers in their shoulder holsters. Behind them, their view nearly blocked by this wall of flesh, were Gotti's supporters —his brother Pete, Jackie Nose D'Amico, and Joe DeCicco. In the back of the courtroom, silently watching it all, the moments to come so large that he was almost overwhelmed by a sense of anticipation, was Bruce Mouw.

Gravano seemed very small as he took his seat in the witness stand. His eyes were nearly closed and he was biting down on his lip. He was wearing a gray double-breasted suit and a red tie.

"Look," Gotti cheerfully taunted, "he's all dressed up." But in a moment, Gleeson asked his first question and Gravano, his voice soft and hoarse, answered: "John was the boss. I was the underboss."

As Gravano continued, Gotti focused on him. The Don's posture was erect, his shoulders back, his head high, and all the while his eyes continued to fix Gravano with a rock-hard stare. But Gravano could not be intimidated. He seemed impenetrable. It was as if he was saying to Gotti, I can take your best shot. In his soft, almost lazy voice, he told how Gotti had planned and participated in the murder of Paul Castellano. At the end of the first day of steady, unruffled testimony, Gotti had his hands clenched into tight fists as he was led out of the courtroom. And Fox went up to Mouw and predicted, "We've won."

Gravano was on the stand for six more days. He testified about how Gotti was elected Boss, the five murders the new Don ordered, about the money that poured into the Family, and about Gotti's mole, William Peist. By the third day, Gotti's rigid, challenging defiance seemed to crumble. He struck a new, more philosophical pose. He slouched in his chair as if he was above the fray, unassailable by the confessions of a rat. The life he lived, his own sense of honor, seemed to fill him with a power and a satisfaction that was beyond Gravano's incriminating words.

Only on the final day, after the cross-examination by his own lawyers failed to unsettle Gravano, did Gotti begin to show some realization of his predicament. As the lawyers met for a sidebar discussion with the judge and Gravano remained seated in the witness stand, Gotti turned to the rows of reporters covering the trial and, pointing to Gravano, mouthed the word "junk." Then, his gestures exaggerated, almost manic, he repeatedly stuck an imaginary syringe into his arm. Gotti was still playing for laughs later that afternoon when, his testimony finally completed, Gravano left the stand. With two federal marshals leading the way, Gravano exited through the jury room, while Gotti, a smirk on his face, made a sign of the cross. The door closed, and the Don turned toward the reporters. He wanted them to see him wipe the false tear from his eye.

When the summations came, it was almost an anticlimax. Gleeson spoke first, his tone grave and deliberate. He was talking to the jurors about the strength of the government's case, but he might just as well have been congratulating Bruce Mouw and his men. "I submit to you, ladies and gentlemen, when you have this type of criminal committing this type of crime, there are only two ways to prove it . . . One, catch them talking about their crimes. Figure out a way to find those secret meetings and record them. There's one other way. Get one of them to come in and tell you about the crimes. We did both."

All Krieger could do was attack the deal that had been made with Gravano. "Nineteen murders . . . Where are we? Is that where our system of justice has dropped to? Award a sick, demented serial killer his freedom, in exchange for what?" Then he pointed to his client. John Gotti smiled at the jury. His silver hair was perfect. His shiny blue double-

GANGLAND

breasted suit was carefully pressed. He was the Boss of
Bosses. "In exchange for that man's head!"

The end came on April 2. After deliberating for just a day
and a half, the jury returned to the courtroom with their
verdict.

The clerk, Louise Schaillat, read from the verdict sheet.
Her voice was loud and precise: "Count one, RICO. Con-
spiracy to murder Paul Castellano and murder of Paul
Castellano. How do you find, proven or not proven?"

"Proven," said the forewoman.

Gotti's head pulled back as if he had been shot. In a
moment, he seemed to recover. He stared ahead blankly as
the voices droned on.

"Count one, RICO," the clerk continued. "Murder of
Thomas Bilotti. How do you find, proven or unproven?"

"Proven," said the forewoman.

"Count one, RICO. Conspiracy to murder Robert
DiBernardo, murder of Robert DiBernardo. How do you
find, proven or not proven?"

"Proven," said the forewoman.

John Gotti was found guilty of all fourteen counts in the
indictment. Frank Locascio succeeded in beating one minor
charge of illegal gambling; other than that, he was convicted
on all counts.

When Fox heard the news, he got into his car and drove to
the Brooklyn courthouse. He told the press, "The Teflon is
gone. The Don is covered with Velcro." When the press
conference was over, he went looking for a phone. There
was a call he had promised to make as soon as a verdict was
reached. "Sammy," he said into the receiver, "we did it."

George Gabriel was also at the press conference. When it
ended, he too found a phone. "Maureen," he told his wife,
"tonight we finally open the champagne."

Bruce Mouw had been standing next to Gabriel throughout the session with the press. His head was nearly bowed.
He didn't want to speak to anyone. He wasn't sure he could
keep a steady voice; so many emotions were rushing through
him. He had succeeded in bringing down the most powerful

Mafia don in the country. But it was a private victory: his and his team's. He did not want to stand under the glare of television lights or answer questions into the dozens of microphones that were bunched on the podium. Where had all these people been when he and his men were spending nights outside the Ravenite, meeting with informants, tracking down the mole? This was their victory, the spoils of the C-16 team's own private war, and he did not want to share it with anyone else. He could not wait to leave.

Later that afternoon at Gabriel's persistent urging, he went to the retirement party for Don Storey, one of the assistant directors of the New York office. The racket, as those farewell shindigs are called, was in the Downtown Athletic Club and it had been planned months ago. Agents had flown in from all around the country to say good-bye to Storey. When Mouw walked in, the room fell into silence. Then one agent rose and started applauding. Then another. Then everyone was on his feet, applauding Bruce Mouw. The noise broke out around him, and he tried to stand stiffly in the center of it all until it passed. But it lasted a while.

Later, after a beer or two, he found himself sitting next to his old friend from the Sun Luck Club, Jim Moody. "Well," Moody asked, "what's next?"

Mouw took a puff on his pipe and considered the question. The entire case, all he had done over the last seven years, seemed to race through his mind in an instant. He thought about Willie Boy Johnson and Louie DiBono, deaths that could have been avoided. He thought about sacrifices. The Looker. Easter. And how he had demanded so much of them, and others. He thought about the endless hours of surveillance. About the ingenuity and bravery of Kravec and his men, and how they had done the impossible: planted a mike in the most secret of the Don's meeting places. He thought about betrayal. Peist's and Gravano's. He thought about a ruthlessness and greed and violence that had become commonplace. Of a treachery that had succeeded in bribing juries and a police officer. He thought about the many times when the case had fallen apart, only to be put back together again through the cunning and commitment of his men. And by luck. He thought about victory.

"Well," he said at last, "there are still twenty-one capos . . ."

John Gotti was sentenced to life imprisonment without the possibility of parole. On June 24, 1992, he was delivered to the federal penitentiary in Marion, Illinois. His son, John, Jr., a Gambino capo, visits him twice a month. The two men sit separated by a thick Plexiglas partition and talk over a phone. There are no slots to pass notes. Nevertheless, Gotti hopes he can use his son as his emissary. He is determined to continue to rule his Family.

Salvatore Gravano has testified in four additional trials as a government witness. Most of his days, however, have been spent alone in special federal detention centers known as "rat units." He will be formally sentenced in November, 1993. His wife and children still live in the house on Staten Island. Once a month, Pete Gotti comes to visit, to tell them they are not to blame for what Sammy did.

William Peist pled guilty to charges involving the sale of confidential information to John Gotti on February 26, 1993, just two days before his trial was to begin. He lost his $24,000-a-year Police Department pension and he could be sentenced to twenty years in jail.

Bruce Mouw was awarded the Attorney General's Distinguished Service Award in a ceremony at the Department of Justice on December 13, 1992. The next day he returned to his office on Queens Boulevard, and to the C-16 squad.

# A Note on Sources

On the first day of testimony at John Gotti's federal trial in Brooklyn before Judge I. Leo Glasser, the government called FBI agent George Gabriel as its initial witness. Gabriel, somber as an executioner, took the stand and his eyes immediately began to dart around the courtroom. It seemed as if he was caught up in a fierce struggle between his combative instinct to engage Gotti's derisive stare head-on and his pre-trial instructions to focus intently on the jury. But fortunately for the prosecution, in a matter of minutes Gabriel settled down and even started to smile. And as he did, the prosecutor launched into a series of formal questions that, I realized from my seat in the rear of the crowded courtroom, suddenly hinted at the secret heart of the case against John Gotti.

"How long has the investigation, this investigation, been under way?" asked John Gleeson, the dour young assistant U.S. Attorney. "Since March 1987," Gabriel answered matter-of-factly. Gleeson paused to review his notes, and then took a step forward, moving closer to his witness. In the back, I did some quick arithmetic: since March 1987!

Today was February 13, 1992. That meant the Bureau had spent at least five years constructing its case against John Gotti.

Meanwhile, Gleeson had moved into his next question: "Can you describe for the jury, briefly, the types of investigative techniques that are used by you and your fellow agents?" "Yes," said Gabriel. "We deal with cooperating witnesses, confidential sources. We utilize bugs. We do surveillances, that type of thing."

As the questioning continued, and Gabriel in his stolid way provided the jury with textbook definitions of such terms as "confidential sources," "bugs," and "physical surveillance," my reporter's mind was excitedly focusing on what Gabriel had just, however obliquely, acknowledged. There was, it seemed, an aspect of the case against John Gotti that had yet to be revealed. I began to consider how, as Gabriel had guardedly put it, the FBI had managed to pull off "that type of thing."

I had been attending the trial sporadically on assignment from *The New York Times Magazine* as part of the research I was doing for a piece that would be published under the title "The Cop They Called the Mob's Mole." But after mulling over Gabriel's terse yet tantalizing testimony, and then following up on this provocative angle with a flurry of interviews with law enforcement officials—many old contacts from my former tour of duty as a *Times* reporter—I began to discover there was indeed a larger, still unreported story to tell about how the FBI made its case against John Gotti. And one that complemented and reinforced the tale I was already pursuing about the FBI's hunt for a traitor in law enforcement. It was the story that would become *Gangland*.

Of course, I realized from the start that to tell such a tale effectively would depend on the cooperation of the FBI. And I also realized that obtaining this cooperation would be a challenge almost as daunting as the one that faced Bruce Mouw and his team when they set out to get the Don himself. The frustrating fact was that the Bureau didn't like to talk about how it did things. It wasn't just that the agents were shy or even antagonistic to the press; rather, they sincerely felt it would jeopardize future operations if they were too forthcoming. For a long time, it seemed a very real and distressing possibility that Gabriel's careful testimony would be my only insight into the inner workings of the C-16 team.

Then, after months of beseeching phone calls and trips to Washington to plead my case before officials both in the Bureau and in the Justice Department, I received a letter from Inspector Thomas F. Jones, the head of the FBI's Public Affairs Office, approving my request to speak with the C-16 agents. Such formal permissions to interview field agents, I realized with gratitude, were rare—if not unprecedented.

Inspector Jones's letter immediately opened many doors. A bit. At first, several of the agents would talk to me only with a member of the public affairs staff present. This restrictive condition was abandoned in time. Other agents, however, even after the Bureau's permission had been granted, would talk only if I promised not to reveal their identities—and they also insisted that these interviews be held far from the team's Queens Boulevard squad room and the presence of their fellow agents. A few other members of the team, again even with the Bureau's approval, politely yet adamantly refused to speak either on or off the record. They disagreed, they explained with some passion, with "Washington's decision to share secrets with the press." (But one of these reluctant agents, rightfully proud of his contribution to the operation, in the course of a nearly two-hour telephone conversation explaining why he chose not to be interviewed, gave me—inadvertently?—enough background detail to fill an entire legal pad with my hastily scribbled notes.) Finally, a few other agents, as the news of the film Jon Peters and Columbia Pictures were planning to make based on my still in-progress book appeared in the press, began to search me out, eager to suggest why Tom Cruise, perhaps, would be the perfect choice to play them.

Or to mention that if the production needed technical expertise, well, they had been right in the thick of things and would be glad to share their knowledge.

In the end, I wound up conducting nineteen interviews with FBI agents and supervisory officials involved in the Gotti case. Some of these were quite lengthy; one mostly off-the-record interview filled eight legal pads over the course of six months. On another occasion, an agent went to the trouble of typing a detailed (and fascinating) summary of his role in the investigation. Other interviews were more terse. Yet, even the most forthcoming of agents were adamant about not giving me information that would allow their confidential informants to be identified. Therefore, while Easter is the official code-name of an informant who played a key role in the case, her biography and her description have been altered at the suggestion of certain agents to protect her identity. Similar caution has been taken to protect the true identities of such pivotal characters in this drama as "the Looker," and "Frankie," and "the angry divorcée."

A final thought about my interviews with the FBI—the specific, on-the-record sources are acknowledged chapter-by-chapter at the conclusion of this note—concerns my relationship with these men and women. I must admit that as a product of a Liberal (the capital is deliberate) education, I first approached these agents with a good deal of apprehension and even testy misgivings; I had gone to college and graduate school at a time when, with some reason, the FBI was often seen as the enemy. The agents of the C-16 team turned my preconceptions around completely. To my mind, Bruce Mouw and his team are true American heroes, patriots who serve their country with dedication, honor, and skill—and at great risk.

And yet, *Gangland* is not an authorized FBI account of how the Bureau broke the mob. No doubt there are characterizations in my reporting that specific agents will dispute, incidents that the Bureau will prefer had gone unreported, and descriptions of technical operations that some officials might feel will jeopardize future operations. So be it. My primary concern—and ultimate responsibility—was to tell the story as accurately as possible. The only times I agreed to withhold previously unreported information or—as in the description of informants—knowingly went along with the Bureau's somewhat edited version of reality were when lives would be jeopardized by the publication of these facts.

Therefore, in addition to my conversations with the FBI, I also conducted eighty-nine supplemental interviews. These ranged from talks, many of them once again off the record, with police officers who served with Detective William Peist, the mob's mole, to interviews with past and present government prosecutors, defense attorneys, expert wiremen, members of the Gambino Family, and even a fascinating telephone conversation with Sammy "the Bull" Gravano from one of his government hideouts. The specific, relevant on-the-record interviews are also detailed at the conclusion of this note. However, with the hope of giving the reader a greater understanding of how this book was reported, the obstacles I faced (and the fun I had) obtaining several of these interviews are worth noting here.

There was a long-martini-fueled lunch I had with a member of the U.S. Attorney's staff just days following the guilty verdict. It was my third interview with this source—our second lunch—and previously he hadn't been very forthcoming. His attitude was generally winkingly coy, his judicious remarks punctuated with the infuriating refrain of "I wish I could tell you more, but Judge Glasser would have my head." Perhaps it was the intoxicating, still fresh thrill of victory. Or maybe it was just the stiff martinis served at Gage & Tollner. But whatever it was, that afternoon the prosecutor had a story to tell. He talked in detail about the turning of Sammy Bull Gravano (Chapter 47) and he spoke candidly of the bitter fight among the various jurisdictions for the assignment to prosecute Gotti (Chapter 45).

As his stories poured out, I tried to keep up with him, scribbling away on the legal pad I had opened on the table.

When the long meal was finally done, his intriguing tales exhausted (and perhaps the prosecutor, too), I paid the bill and hurried with my legal pad to the subway. As I was about to descend, I felt a tap on my shoulder. I turned and there was the prosecutor, looking decidedly sheepish. "You're not going to use any of that," he said with as much challenge and indignation as he could muster. "Of course I am. You saw me taking notes." "Well," he tried, "I shouldn't really have told you all that." "I know," I agreed, and with a commiserating wave headed down to the subway.

But it wasn't just the good guys who had second thoughts about their having spoken to me. Thanks to an attorney who was involved in the case, I was able to spend some time with a wiseguy who hung out at the Ravenite. He was clearly envious of Gotti and since his own career on the periphery of the Family was going nowhere, he also had an axe to grind. He was, therefore, the perfect source—as long as you took his words with more than a grain of skepticism. I used his mean-spirited gripes as a catalyst to help pull information about Gotti's active social life (Chapters 3, 14, 27) from the FBI agents who, after keeping the Don under such intense surveillance for all those years, were familiar with his every move. Yet my relationship with this source came to an abrupt end when he called me up one afternoon with genuine fear in his voice. He said he had mentioned to one of the guys that he was thinking about talking to me; after all, there was a book and movie coming out and why should the Feds get all the glory? He was told, "You talk to some fuckin' reporter and you'll wind up dead." And now he was telling me, "You use my name and I'll tear your heart out." Maybe he didn't mean it literally, but his name is not mentioned anywhere in this account.

I also had an opportunity to talk to Sammy Gravano. Through his two weeks of trial testimony and the debriefing reports the FBI had, by law, provided to the defense attorneys, I already had a good feel for the man and his contribution to the case. Our conversation lasted perhaps fifteen minutes and was off the record; nothing of substance to the case was discussed. Nevertheless, I did get, I believe, a further appreciation of Gravano's surprising articulateness, his calculating intelligence, and his genuine sense of mission as the one individual who will in time dismantle the entire Gambino Family. One small remark he made, however, is worth repeating, for it gives both a sense of the past he was trying to escape and the new world he was now inhabiting. "After reading what you reporters write about me," he said with a small laugh, "I got to tell you that a lot of you guys are worse than anything I used to be." Before becoming a government witness, Gravano had been a murderer—a man who, he now admits, killed nineteen people.

In addition to the 108 interviews I conducted to help tell this story, I also relied on large stacks of government documents and trial transcripts. One defense lawyer told me that his photocopy fees alone were in excess of $70,000; after perusing all the tens of thousands of pages, I can easily understand why. I made my way through a wall-high pile of transcripts from Gotti's three trials and also found valuable insights in supporting prosecutorial documents submitted in the final federal case: The Government's Memorandum in Support of Its Motion for Pretrial Detention of Certain Defendants, its Memorandum in Support of Its Motion for an Order Disqualifying Counsel, its Memorandum in Support of Its Motion for an Anonymous and Sequestered Jury, as well as the original and superseding indictments.

Then there were the tapes. In addition to the transcripts of the tapes the C-16 team recorded in the Ravenite, the hallway outside the club, and in Mrs. Cirelli's apartment 10 (nearly 600 hours of recordings), I also relied on the State Organized Crime Task Force tapes recorded in the Bergin Hunt and Fish Club and at the room next door to the club, the premises adjacent to the Nice N EZ Auto School. And throughout my telling of this story, I used as source documents the government's affidavit requesting electronic surveillance prepared by Agent Gabriel, FBI 302 reports, and official progress reports submitted by the FBI to the judges who authorized the C-16 oral intercept orders (Chapters 35, 36, 37).

Further, in telling the background of the Gambino Family as well as Gotti's rise to power, I was helped by several informative books, notably *Mob Star,* by Gene Mustain and Jerry Capeci; *Goombata,* by John Cummings and Ernest Volkman; *Mafia Dynasty* by John H. Davis; and *Boss of Bosses* by Joseph F. O'Brien & Andris Kurins. I was also able to benefit from coverage of the case and the trial in the press. The daily trial reports in *The New York Times* by Arnold Lubash (who was also kind enough to answer my many questions during the trial) were a model of concise yet exciting reporting. The dispatches by Gene Mustain and Jerry Capeci in the *Daily News* often broke news in the case. Similarly, Mike McAlary in the *New York Post* consistently beat his colleagues to scoops, always managing to write entertainingly. In *Newsday,* Peter Bowles's accounts were both vigorous and accurate.

I further benefited from a well-researched piece written in the aftermath of Gotti's conviction by Ralph Blumenthal of *The New York Times* ("How Tapes and a Turncoat Helped Win the War Against Gotti") and a provocative piece about the battles between the various Gotti prosecutors and the Bureau in the January 1992 *Vanity Fair* by Frederic Dannen. My knowledge of the technical aspects of electronic surveillance was supplemented by *How to Get Anything on Anybody,* by Lee Lapin and a revealing article in the May 1992 *Police Magazine* ("The Art and Mystery of the Wireman's Craft") that was faxed to me by an FBI wireman. In addition, I gathered insights into Mouw's background and his life in Orange City, Iowa, through articles written by George Clifford III that appeared in *The Des Moines Register* and through subsequent reporting and interviewing he did for me.

The specific sources for each chapter are listed below. The more frequently cited sources are indicated by the following abbreviations.

# A NOTE ON SOURCES

*Author interviews:*

Barry Agulnick (BA)
Steve Arniotes (SA)
Scott Behar (SB)
Jules Bonavolonta (JB)
Michael Cherkasky (MC)
Paul Coffey (PC)
James DiPietro (JD)
James Fox (JF)
George Gabriel (GG)
Ronald Goldstock (RG)
Douglas Grover (DG)
Jim Kallstrom (JK)
John S. Kravec (JSK)

Andy Kurins (AK)
Doug LeVien (DLV)
Andrew Maloney (AM)
Ed McDonald (EMD)
Leonard Michaels (LM)
Jim E. Moody (JEM)
Robert Morgenthau (RM)
Bruce Mouw (BM)
Jan Mouw (JM)
Joe O'Brien (JOB)
Gerald Shargel (GS)
John Sullivan (JS)

*Transcripts, Documents, Books and Articles:*

Transcript of testimony at John Gotti's federal trial before Judge I. Leo Glassner (Gotti III).

Biographical scrapbook of Detective William Peist prepared by Steve Arniotes (PS).

*Boss of Bosses* (BB); *How to Get Anything on Anybody* (HOW); *Goombata* (G); *Mafia Dynasty* (MD); *Mob Star* (MS); Dannen article in 1/92 *Vanity Fair* (VF); "The Art and Mystery of the Wireman's Craft," *Police Magazine*, May 1992 (PM).

## Chapter 1

Author interviews: SB; BM; GG; JK; JSK; agents who requested anonymity.

Documents, transcripts, and articles: FBI surveillance video; Gotti III; accounts in *NY Times* of state assault trial.

## Chapter 2

Author interviews: JK; JSK; BM; agents who requested anonymity.

# A NOTE ON SOURCES

*Chapter 3*

Author interviews: AK; BM; GG; agents who requested anonymity.

Documents, tapes and transcripts: Gotti III; Apartment 10 tape; Gravano 302 report.

*Chapter 4*

Author interviews: JEM; JB; JK.

*Chapter 5*

Author interviews: BM; JM, Norman Bastmeyer, Happy Millen.

Articles: George Clifford III, *The Des Moines Register* (4/6/92).

*Chapter 6*

Author interviews: BM; AK; agents who requested anonymity.

Books: BB.

*Chapter 7*

Author interviews: AK; GG; BM; agents who requested anonymity.

Books: BB.

*Chapter 8*

Author interviews: BM; GG; AK.

Books: G; MS; MD.

*Chapter 9*

Author interviews: JOB; BM; agents who requested anonymity.

Books: G; MS.

*Chapter 10*

Author interviews: JB; BM; agents who requested anonymity.

Transcripts and books: Ruggiero bugs; G; MS.

# A NOTE ON SOURCES

## Chapter 11

Author interviews: EMD; AK; BM; agents who requested anonymity.
Books: MS; G.

## Chapter 12

Author interviews: BM; Aaron Rosenthal; SA.
Transcripts, books, and documents: Ruggiero tapes; MS; G; PS.

## Chapter 13

Author interviews: AK; JOB; EMD; MC.
Books and articles: MD; G; MS; VF.

## Chapter 14

Author interviews: AK; GG; agents who requested anonymity; organized crime sources.
Documents and books: Johnson bail hearing; Ruggiero tapes; MS; G.

## Chapter 15

Author interviews: JEM; BM; agents who requested anonymity.
Transcripts: State Organized Crime Task Bergin tapes.

## Chapter 16

Author interviews: organized crime sources.
Transcripts and documents: Gotti III; Gravano 302s.

## Chapter 17

Author interviews: organized crime sources.
Transcripts and documents: Gotti III; Gravano 302s.

## Chapter 18

Author interviews: Stillwell Avenue residents; organized crime sources; agents who requested anonymity.
Transcripts and documents: Gotti III; Gravano 302s.

# A NOTE ON SOURCES

## Chapter 19

Author interviews: AK; BM; James LaRossa; agents who requested anonymity.

Transcripts, documents, and books: Gotti III; Gravano 302s; New York Police DD-5 reports; BB.

## Chapter 20

Author interviews: AK; BM; agents who requested anonymity.

## Chapter 21

Author interviews: organized crime sources; agents who requested anonymity.

Transcripts and documents: Gotti III; Gravano 302s.

## Chapter 22

Author interviews: Len Buder; BM; agents who requested anonymity.

Transcripts and books: Bergin tapes; G; MS; MD.

## Chapter 23

Transcripts, documents, books, and articles: Gotti III; Gravano 302s; G; MS; MD; *NY Times* coverage of federal trial before Judge Nickerson.

## Chapter 24

Author interviews: agents who requested anonymity.
Transcripts: Gotti III.

## Chapter 25

Author interviews: GG; AM; MC; BM; AK.
Transcripts, articles, and books: Nickerson trial; VF; G; MS.

# A NOTE ON SOURCES

### Chapter 26

Author interviews: SA; JS; police internal affairs officials; BM.
Documents: NY Police Internal Affairs report; Arniotes scrapbook.

### Chapter 27

Author interviews: AK; GG; agents who requested anonymity.
Transcripts and books: Gotti III; Bergin tapes; G; MS.

### Chapter 28

Author interviews: BM; EMD; MC; JB; JEM; police officials; AK.
Books: BB.

### Chapter 29

Author interviews: AK; BM; LM; DG; GG; agents who requested anonymity.
Transcripts and books: Gotti III; G; MS.

### Chapter 30

Author interviews: BM; agents who requested anonymity; organized crime sources.
Transcripts and documents: Gotti III; Gravano 302s; FBI informant information filed along with wiretap applications.

### Chapter 31

Author interviews: JSK; JK; agents who requested anonymity.
Books and articles: HOW; PM.

### Chapter 32

Author interviews: BM; JSK; JK; JB; GG; DG; agents who requested anonymity.

Transcripts and documents: Gotti III; FBI wiretap summary progress reports.

## Chapter 33

Author interviews: Organized crime sources; GG; JEM; JB; JF; JSK; BM.
Transcripts and documents Gotti III; Gravano 302s.

## Chapter 34

Author interviews: RM; MC; JF; BM; JSK; GG; agents who requested anonymity.
Transcripts, documents, books and articles: Gotti III; oral interception authorization request papers; G; MS; MD; VF.

## Chapter 35

Author interviews: JSK; JK; BM; GG; agents who requested anonymity.
Transcripts, documents, books and articles: FBI summary wiretap progress reports; Ravenite tapes; Gotti III; HOW; PM.

## Chapter 36

Author interviews: BM; AK; GG; GS; agents who requested anonymity.
Transcripts and documents: Gotti III; summary progress reports; Government's memorandum to disqualify counsel; Ravenite, hallway, and apartment tapes.

## Chapter 37

Author interviews: BM; GG; JF; JB; DLV; RG; agents who requested anonymity.
Transcripts, documents, and articles: summary progress reports; apartment tapes; Gotti III; VF; Mike McAlary, *NY Post*, 12/18/90; Murray Weiss, *NY Post*, 12/17/90.

*Chapter 38*

Author interviews: AK; BM; agents who requested anonymity.
Transcripts and documents; apartment tapes; Gotti III; FBI
videotapes.

*Chapter 39*

Author interviews: SA; BA; MC; police officials.
Transcripts and documents: Peist indictment; Gotti III
exhibits.

*Chapter 40*

Author interviews: AK; JB; JM; JF; BM; agents who requested anonymity.
Transcripts; documents, books and articles: apartment
tapes; Gotti III; summary progress reports; G; MS; MD;
VF.

*Chapter 41*

Author interviews: AK; BM; GG; agents who requested
anonymity.
Transcripts and documents: apartment tapes; Gotti III;
summary progress reports.

*Chapter 42*

Author interviews: AK; JD; organized crime sources; Steve
Iken; agents who requested anonymity.
Transcripts and documents: apartment tapes; Gotti III;
Gotti III exhibits; Peist indictment and pre-trial papers.

*Chapter 43*

Author interviews: AK; BM; agents who requested anonymity; organized crime sources.

*Chapter 44*

Author interviews: AK; SA; JS; RG; MC; police officials,
Waldorf-Astoria chefs; agents who requested anonymity.
Documents: PS; Gotti III exhibits.

# A NOTE ON SOURCES

*Chapter 45*

Author interviews: BM; AM; RG; PC; MC; RM; agents who requested anonymity.
Transcripts, documents, and articles: Gotti III; apartment tapes; Gravano 302s; VF.

*Chapter 46*

Author interviews: BM; GG; GS; AK; JF; agents who requested anonymity.

*Chapter 47*

Author interviews: BM; GG; AM; JF; JEM; Ben Brafman; prosecutors; agents who requested anonymity.
Transcripts and documents: Gotti III; apartment tapes.

*Chapter 48*

Author interviews: JF; GG; BM; JEM; agents who requested anonymity.
Transcripts, books and articles: Gotti III; MD; *NY Times* on Peist plea, 2/27/93.

# Acknowledgments

Between the idea and the hardbound reality of this finished book, a lot of people were working in the shadows, generously helping me out along the way. I owe a lot of thanks. An appropriate place to start, though, would be with my publisher, Simon & Schuster. At the top of the list is my editor, Fred Hills. He's wise, he's critical, and he's my friend—what more could an author ask for? Burton Beals, too, was deft with his magic green pen as well as being a buddy whose advice (and criticism) I rely on—and sometimes even followed. Laureen Connelly, the newest member of the Hills team, put up with all my calls, demands, and nudging—and never lost her smile.

I also received a lot of support and encouragement for this project from Carolyn Reidy and Dick Snyder; I'm grateful. In fact, this is my third book at S&S and by now I feel that I'm working with many old friends. Marie Florio, Marcella Berger, Felice Javit, Leslie Jones, Leslie Ellen, Nina Olmsted, Michael Selleck, Wendy Nicholson, Victoria Meyer, Frank Metz—all of them have contributed to the birth of this book and I appreciate their efforts.

I've also been helped, guided, coddled, cajoled, and lectured by my agent Lynn Nesbit. I value her support and her friendship. And I've been assisted by her energetic staff—Eric Simonoff and Cullen Stanley, both of whom have pulled off publishing coups for which I owe them big time. On the West Coast, Irene Webb, witty and warm and indefatigable, made sure the book would become a movie. And many people associated with the film gave me a lot of support: Jon Peters' wonderful enthusiasm was a constant source of encouragement; Adam Fields read the book chapter by chapter and offered impressively perceptive comments; Sid Ganis was a valued cheerleader; and Steve Klain was inventive and tireless in his efforts.

*Gangland,* as I've mentioned, originally started as an assignment for *The New York Times Magazine* and the truth is that without the initial encouragement of Warren Hoge at the *Times,* my friend since he was my boss on the city desk, there probably wouldn't have been a book. Warren, a true gentleman, was an intelligent editor and a generous friend. Catherine Bouton also played a big role in whipping that magazine piece into shape.

And, as always, Dan Wolf was friend, advisor, confidant and editor; truth is, I count on him in so many ways. Phil Werber, too, kept me going and laughing. Of course, my sister Marcy and my brother-in-law Peter, generous and supportive with their kindness, always kept things interesting. And my mother could always be counted on to provide whatever the moment or the emergency needed. The gang at the Orchard—Cathy and Wayne, Bob, Mike, Judy, Gilda, and Dale—were also willing to help me out and sometimes even laugh at my strained jokes. Their kindness and friendship is a real pleasure. But above all, there is Jenny, our son, Harold Anthony, and our daughter, Anna McKee: They make it all worthwhile.

FOR NEARLY FIFTY YEARS THE GOVERNMENT HAS
BEEN HIDING WHAT IT KNOWS ABOUT UFOs.
NOW, FIND OUT WHAT IS REALLY...

# OUT THERE

## HOWARD BLUM

**Bestselling author of *Wanted!* and *Gangland***

"Mr. Blum authoritatively uncovers...decades of
government duplicity...**OUT THERE** is a pleasure."
—*The New York Times Book Review*

**Out There**
**0-671-66261-9/$5.99**

POCKET
B O O K S

**Simon & Schuster Mail Order**
**200 Old Tappan Rd., Old Tappan, N.J. 07675**
Please send me the books I have checked above. I am enclosing $_____ (please add $0.75 to cover the postage
and handling for each order. Please add appropriate sales tax). Send check or money order–no cash or C.O.D.'s
please. Allow up to six weeks for delivery. For purchase over $10.00 you may use VISA: card number, expiration
date and customer signature must be included.

Name _____

Address _____

City _____ State/Zip _____

VISA Card # _____ Exp.Date _____

Signature _____1113

# Read about the
# SHOCKING and
# BIZARRE
## Crimes of our Times from Pocket Books

TED BUNDY:THE DELIBERATE STRANGER
Richard Larson ..................72866-0/$5.50

DEAD BY SUNSET
Ann Rule ..................00113-2/$6.99

A FEVER IN THE HEART
Ann Rule ..................79355-1/$6.99

THE DIARY OF JACK THE RIPPER
Shirley Harrison ..................52099-7/$5.99

DEVIANT: THE SHOCKING TRUE STORY OF
ORIGINAL "PSYCHO"
Harold Schechter ..................73915-8/$5.99

DERANGED
Harold Schechter ..................67875-2/$5.50

COP TALK
E. W. Count ..................78341-6/$5.99

UNABOMBER: ON THE TRAIL OF AMERI-
CA'S MOST WANTED SERIAL KILLER
John Douglas and Mark Olshaker
..................00411-5/$6.50

IF YOU REALLY LOVED ME
Ann Rule ..................76920-0/$6.99

A ROSE FOR HER GRAVE
Ann Rule ..................79353-5/$6.99

IN THE NAME OF LOVE
Ann rule ..................79356-X/$6.99

EVERYTHING SHE EVER WANTED
Ann Rule ..................69071-X/$6.99

YOU BELONG TO ME
Ann Rule ..................79354-3/$6.99

THE RIVERMAN: TED BUNDY AND I HUNT FOR
THE GREEN RIVER KILLER  Robert B. Keppel,
Ph..D, with William J. Birnes
..................86763-6/$6.99

UNFINISHED MURDER: THE CAPTURE OF A
SERIAL RAPIST
James Neff ..................73186-6/$5.99

SIGNATURE KILLERS: INTERPRETING THE
CALLING CARDS OF THE SERIAL MURDERER
Robert D. Keppel with William J. Burnes
..................00130-2/$6.99

THE A - Z GUIDE TO SERIAL KILLERS
Harold Schechter and David Everitt
..................53791-1/$14.00

MINDHUNTER: INSIDE THE FBI'S ELITE SERIAL
CRIME UNIT  John Douglas and Mark Olshaker
..................52890-4/$6.99

WASTELAND: THE SAVAGE ODYSSEY OF
CHARLES STARKWEATHER AND CARIL ANN
FUGATE
Michael Newtown ..................00198-1/$6.99

DELLA'S WEB
Aphrodite Jones ..................01379-3/$3.99

POCKET
BOOKS

## Simon & Schuster Mail Order
200 Old Tappan Rd., Old Tappan, N.J. 07675

Please send me the books I have checked above. I am enclosing $_____ (please add $0.75 to cover the postage
and handling for each order. Please add appropriate sales tax). Send check or money order--no cash or C.O.D.'s
please. Allow up to six weeks for delivery. For purchase over $10.00 you may use VISA: card number, expiration
date and customer signature must be included.

Name _____

Address _____

City _____ State/Zip _____

VISA Card # _____ Exp.Date _____

Signature _____

944-16

The #1 <u>New York Times</u> Bestselling Author

# ANN RULE

<u>Uncovers The True Stories Behind True Crimes</u>

☐ **EVERYTHING SHE EVER WANTED**
69071-X/$6.99

☐ **IF YOU REALLY LOVED ME**
76920-0/$6.99

☐ **A ROSE FOR HER GRAVE**
and Other True Cases  Ann Rule's Crime Files Vol. 1
79353-5/$6.99

☐ **YOU BELONG TO ME**
and Other True Cases  Ann Rules's Crime Files Vol. 2
79354-3/$6.99

☐ **DEAD BY SUNSET**
00113-2/$6.99

☐ **A FEVER IN THE HEART**
and Other True Cases  Ann Rules's Crime Files Vol. 3
79355-1/$6.99

☐ **POSSESSION** (A Novel)
52788-6/$5.99

☐ **IN THE NAME OF LOVE**
and Other True Cases Ann Rule's Crime Files Vol. 4
79356-X/$6.99

------------------------------------------------------------

**Simon & Schuster Mail Order**
**200 Old Tappan Rd., Old Tappan, N.J. 07675**
Please send me the books I have checked above. I am enclosing $_____(please add
$0.75 to cover the postage and handling for each order. Please add appropriate sales
tax). Send check or money order–no cash or C.O.D.'s please. Allow up to six weeks
for delivery.  For purchase over $10.00 you may use VISA: card number, expiration
date and customer signature must be included.

POCKET
B O O K S

Name _____

Address _____

City _____ State/Zip _____

VISA Card # _____ Exp.Date _____

Signature _____ 1042-06